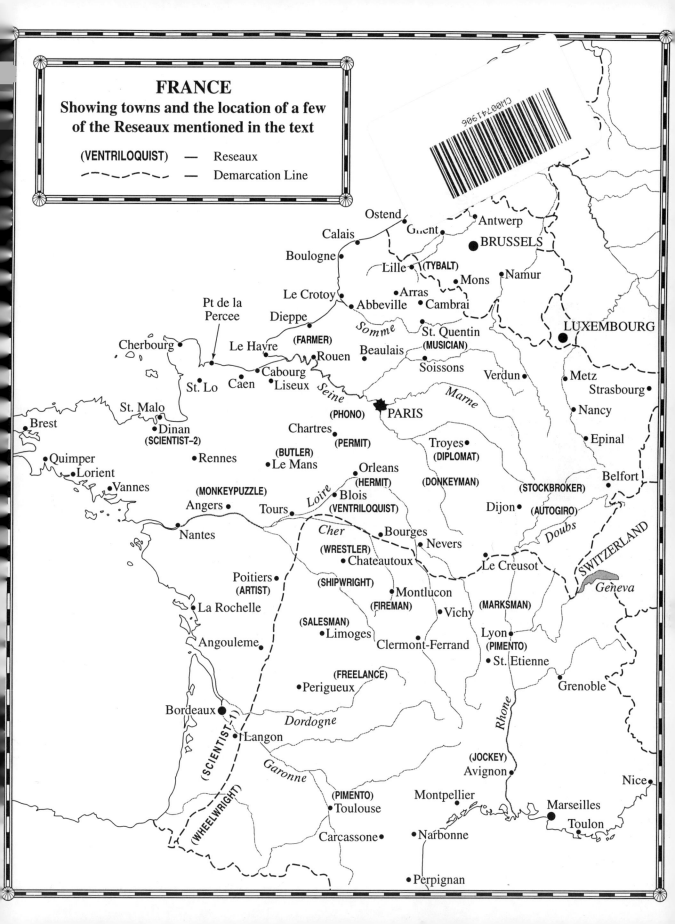

FRANCE

Showing towns and the location of a few of the Reseaux mentioned in the text

(VENTRILOQUIST) — Reseaux

– – – — Demarcation Line

AGENTS BY MOONLIGHT

Other titles by the author

PETER FIVE

AGENTS BY MOONLIGHT

The Secret History of RAF Tempsford During World War II

Freddie Clark

TEMPUS

First published 1999

PUBLISHED IN THE UNITED KINGDOM BY:

Tempus Publishing Ltd
The Mill, Brimscombe Port
Stroud, Gloucestershire GL5 2QG

PUBLISHED IN THE UNITED STATES OF AMERICA BY:

Tempus Publishing Inc.
2A Cumberland Street
Charleston, SC 29401

Tempus books are available in France, Germany and Belgium from the following addresses:

Tempus Publishing Group	Tempus Publishing Group	Tempus Publishing Group
21 Avenue de la République	Gustav-Adolf-Straße 3	Place de L'Alma 4/5
37300 Joué-lès-Tours	99084 Erfurt	1200 Brussels
FRANCE	GERMANY	BELGIUM

British Library Cataloguing in Publication Data.
A catalogue record for this book is available from the British Library.

ISBN 0 7524 1691 X

Typesetting and origination by Ace Filmsetting Ltd, Frome.
Printed and bound in Great Britain.

This book is dedicated to all those aircrew and their SOE/SIS passengers who flew from RAF Tempsford and to the groundcrew who by their skilful toil put and kept them in the air. Not forgetting those who waited for us in the field.

The plaque on the wall of the barn at former RAF Tempsford. (Author)

The restored barn that houses the plaque – all that remains of Gibraltar Farm at Tempsford Airfield. (Author)

Gibraltar Farm prior to demolition. It was here that the agents were taken and made ready for their flight. The existing barn is on the left of the picture next to the square roofless building. (John Burton)

Contents

Preface

By Air Chief Marshal Sir Lewis Hodges KCB, CBE, DSO*, DFC*, DL, Grand Officer de la Legion d'Honneur, Croix de Guerre.

In the early months of the Second World War, following the German attack on Poland, Hitler's armies advanced rapidly across North West Europe and one country after another – Norway, Denmark, the Low Countries and France – succumbed to German occupation. By the summer of 1940 Britain stood alone, facing the threat of German invasion, cut off from our Allies across the channel.

It quickly became apparent that we urgently needed to rebuild our contacts and intelligence networks on the Continent, and to give as much support as possible to the Resistance groups which were beginning to spring up in the occupied countries. The most rapid and effect-ive way to achieve this was by using air transport, and from very early beginnings two Special Duties squadrons were formed charged with the tasks of parachuting agents and weapons into the occupied countries and carrying out secret landings in small fields in France to transport agents and Resistance leaders.

This book, which has been meticulously researched, describes the work of these Special Duties squadrons (138 and 161), from the early beginnings in 1940 up to the time of the Normandy landings and the liberation of Continental Europe. Although other books have been written describing these operations, it is only recently that more detailed information has become available and this has made it possible to give a fuller account of the work of 138 and 161 squadrons in support of Secret Intelligence Service and Special Operations Executive.

The author, who was himself a member of 138 squadron, is to be congratulated on his painstaking research. The story which unfolds highlights the dangers endured by the aircrews who night after night, during the moonlight periods, flew long distances over enemy territory, often in adverse weather conditions and with the ever present threat from enemy night fighters and anti-aircraft fire.

Furthermore, tribute must be paid to the many agents and Resistance fighters both men and women, who showed such outstanding courage and bravery in the face of very great dangers to their lives, parachuting into the occupied countries to carry on the fight, and who made such an important contribution to the eventual victory.

L.M.H
1998.

Acknowledgements

I first met Mark Seaman in the company of my son Paul who was researching the wartime 'SOE Toyshop' housed at The Natural History Museum where he worked. Mark is the Historian of the Research and Information Office at the Imperial War Museum and was responsible for the assembly of that excellent 'Secret War' exhibition now to be seen there. He had a wealth of information on SOE parachute operations in particular the part that Group Captain R C Hockey, DSO, DFC, played in them. Among these papers was a list of all the Public Records Office files that dealt with SOE matters. With the encouragement of Mark I decided I would research these files with a view to writing another book. He, in the meantime, up dated the biography of W/Cdr Yeo-Thomas, GC, MC, with his book entitled *Bravest of the Brave.*

I wrote to Ken Merrick and told him what I intended to do. Ken is the author of a number of books one in particular *Flights of the Forgotten, Special Duties Operations in World War Two* is a brilliant treatise on the subject. He replied 'Delighted to hear from you and to read that you are back in the writing game. Infectious is it not?' Such was his generosity he gave me carte blanche to use anything and everything from his book. There is no doubt that our narrative will intermingle, that cannot be avoided, but I am hoping that between us we will have completed a study of these unique air operations from the UK that otherwise would have remained uncompleted. Moreover he airmailed me from Australia a package containing all the photographs he had used in his book. I will use some of these in an endeavour to connect the crew with the operations in which they were involved.

Bill Chorley author of that excellent series *Royal Air Force Bomber Command Losses of the Second World War* was kind enough to grant me permission to use the information for 138 and 161 Squadron losses up to 1943. From there onward I was able make a very small contribution to his forthcoming 1944 and 1945 volumes.

Ben Chamberlain a semi-retired house master, recorded a list of casualties for both Tempsford Squadrons, a tremendous task, from which a book of remembrance for those who died was compiled and is now displayed in the church at Tempsford Village. There were 431 deaths from No.138 Squadron and 192 from No.161 Squadron. He was generous enough to prepare copies of these lists for me and furnish me with other relevant information. Ben's interest in Tempsford was motivated by his neighbour a former Commanding Officer of No.138 Squadron, the late Group Captain Ken Batchelor, CBE, DFC. His knowledge and interest in SOE operations and his willingness to share this information with me was of inestimable value. He was also responsible for compiling a list of PRO SOE files (without which my task would have been almost impossible) which was photocopied for me by Mark Seaman. Alan Thomas of the Air Historical Branch also assisted greatly in answering my casualty and other questions. A special thanks should also be made to my editor, Colin West, for his help and guidance.

John Reid who had researched the Short Stirling and sent to me no end of information and photographs concerning the Stirling crews of 138 & 161 Squadrons. Also notes and photocopies of Stirling operation reports compiled by the late Jim Breeze, formerly a Sergeant Flight Engineer who flew in the last 138 Squadron Stirling to be shot down. These proved invaluable as did the various other items of interest John sent to me.

Tempsford Airfield Farm is now in the safe keeping of John Button, a Tempsford enthusiast proven by the small museum in his office. I thank him for allowing me to scratch around the airfield with my grandsons and his desk where I found some interesting photographs.

The Public Record Office was my main source of information where I was able to delve into the pilots' operation reports and write what they said occurred. Two PRO publications by Louise Atherton *SOE Operations In Scandinavia* and *SOE in Eastern Europe* sometimes told me why. Also in the PRO records I found three RAF foolscap exercise books in which were recorded a rough diary of operations and included such information as dates, pilots, targets, operations completed or not completed, loads, SOE or SIS targets and other remarks – a veritable mine of information. From these I was able to keep my narrative in chronological order and select from them operational reports.

Professor M R D Foot kindly permitted me to refer to his HMSO publication *SOE in France*. This made it possible for me tie into the flight information some of the agents dropped in France.

Inside SOE written by E H Cookridge, published by Arthur Baker Ltd in 1966, supplied me with information of agents dropped in Holland and Scandinavia. Regrettably I was unable to trace him.

One other book I must refer to and that is *We Landed by Moonlight* written by Group Capt Hugh Verity, DSO*, DFC, the revised edition published by Air Data. This is a brilliant story of those pilots who landed their Lysanders and Hudsons in France. Although these operations are briefly touched in my narrative, I thank Group Captain Verity for allowing me to do so.

I would also like to thank those who unselfishly lent me photographs.

Another book, the *Code Postal* obtained from a bemused Normandy postmaster on the payment of ten Francs, told me my whereabouts in France.

I have allowed myself one anomaly, my heights are in feet and my continental distances are in kilometres. I could not visualise myself flying at metric heights. For the purists dividing feet by three will give an approximation in metres.

To convert kilometres to miles:

10km=6.21 miles, 20=12.43, 30=18.64, 40=24.85, 50=31.07.

I never was any good at arithmetic!

Lastly I must give my sincere thanks to my wife Dorothy for her support and encouragement. Support in that she rarely complained when I said I was too busy to comply with her wishes. Support in that she waded through the early micro filmed Tempsford and Squadron ORBs, deciphering bad hand writing and making copious notes. (Simon, my eldest grandson, helped with this too). Also editing my original work. Encouragement speaks for itself, but for that I would have flung my word processor out of the window many times! On second thoughts perhaps this would have been the better idea.

Foreword

By Mark Seaman
Historian
Research and Information Department
Imperial War Museum, London

The history of the Royal Air Force's Special Duty squadrons during the Second World War reveals British airmen at their most dogged, skilled and valiant. But, throughout the war, clandestine operations were largely considered an unusual and peripheral aspect of the RAF's work. Support from senior RAF commanders was, at best, only grudgingly furnished and they generally resented this distraction from mainstream wartime operations. The subsequent hostile environment in which the squadrons had to work, while at the same time having quickly and often painfully to learn specialised aviation techniques, makes their achievement all the more commendable.

There were some precedents for this type of military flying but examination of them largely serves to show that the Tempsford squadrons virtually had to start from scratch. The use of aircraft to exfiltrate secret agents from behind enemy lines had been undertaken by the Italians as early as the Italo-Turkish war of 1911-12. However, the Royal Flying Corps took a little longer to embark upon such clandestine operations and it was not until November 1914, shortly after the outbreak of the First World War, that a secret flight into enemy territory was attempted. Sadly the pilot and agent were killed when the aircraft crashed. However, other operations were subsequently undertaken and the increase in clandestine activity, not to say the static nature of the front, increased the need for such specialist flights and, in April 1917, a special duty flight was formed in France. A second flight was created in 1918 to carry out similar tasks in Italy.

The end of the First World War also marked the cessation of the RAF's special duty work. An RAF Staff College paper produced in 1924 examining 'The use of Aircraft in Connection with Espionage' at least indicated that someone was continuing to consider the potential of clandestine operations but no further development appears to have taken place. The worsening world crisis in the late 1930s does not seem to have brought about any renewal of RAF interest and, when the

Secret Intelligence Service (SIS or, as it was also known, MI6) needed to mount rapid operations to rescue key personnel from danger, it chose to employ foreign aircraft and crew. In March 1939, on the eve of the German invasion of Czechoslovakia, SIS organised the escape from Prague of the leading members of the Czech Military Intelligence service together with a substantial number of their files. The aircraft was chartered from the Dutch airline, KLM, and, as intended, aroused less attention than a British aeroplane. A similar means of transport was employed later that year when SIS needed to rescue its compromised German agent, Wolfgang zu Putlitz, from the clutches of his fellow countrymen.

Such *ad hoc* arrangements were sufficient during the years of peace and the Phoney War period but the German invasions of 1940 and the subsequent Nazi domination of Western Europe changed everything. Britain was alone, faced by an implacable enemy that ruled its new conquests with powerful and terrifying forces of repression. Consequently the prospects of acquiring intelligence from occupied Europe were bleak. The pre-war SIS networks had been overrun and the chances of inserting new agents on closely guarded coasts or through the strict border checks with neutral states was slim. Similarly, hopes of locating, encouraging and co-ordinating resistance against the Nazi oppressor were blighted by a shortage of information about prevailing conditions in the occupied countries. The Special Operations Executive (SOE), the secret British organisation formed to aid the resistance movements of Europe, would prove to be stillborn unless it could find the means of regular and reliable transportation of men and supplies into enemy territory. It was evident that aircraft offered the best means of establishing clandestine links with Europe. Therefore, in the Summer of 1940, SIS approached the Air Ministry with a suggestion that experiments might be undertaken to investigate the feasibility of landing aircraft and parachuting agents into enemy territory. The Special Duty squadrons had been born.

Freddie Clark's analysis is based primarily upon the squadrons' records in the Public Record Office, coupled with his own insight as a wartime Special Duty pilot with No. 138 Squadron. It offers a fascinating exposition of the development of a unique type of military aviation and reflects the immense difficulties and dangers encountered in these secret wartime operations. Nowhere is this better illustrated than in his account of the tragic *Englandspiel* during which the German counter-intelligence services devastated British and Dutch clandestine operations in the Netherlands. The Allied networks were penetrated and their wireless traffic controlled so that Dutch agents were regularly delivered to dropping zones in German hands. The ghastly fate of most of the agents has been the subject of several books but here we are made graphically aware of the additional cost in airmen's lives. Freddie Clark's researches reveal a dreadful litany of the RAF losses on these compromised operations. The files disclose the shooting down of aircraft en route to their objectives or on the way back to base, their fate constituting a macabre bonus to the German successes on the dropping zones.

Anyone lucky enough to have met the men of the Tempsford squadrons will have noticed amongst them a common trait of modesty and diffidence regarding their wartime activities. They deflect any praise of themselves by constantly emphasising the bravery of the agents they dropped and the resistance fighters they supplied. They aver that aircrew had the reassurance of a hot breakfast and a warm bed awaiting their return to base while their passengers faced a dangerous and uncertain future. Freddie Clark has left us in no uncertain knowledge that these élite squadrons were more than the mere 'taxi drivers' that they self-deprecatingly describe themselves. Their own future was often as uncertain as their passengers. This book helps to confirm that aircrew, agents and resistance fighters were linked by the common bond of a unique form of bravery and dedication. Freddie Clark is to be congratulated for making this valuable contribution to the study of an enduringly fascinating and significant aspect of the RAF's history.

MSM
London 1998

Introduction

The 21st Tempsford reunion took place at Williamson's Tavern in London on the 8th November 1968, the toast 'Tempsford and the Squadrons' was proposed by Major-General Sir Colin Gubbins, KCMG, DSO, MC. The reply was given by a good friend of mine Squadron Leader Greg Holdcroft who was the SADO (Senior Administration Officer) at Tempsford and an RFC first world war observer. 'The Queen' was proposed by Air Marshal Sir Lewis Hodges, KCB, CBE, DSO*, DFC*. His RAF career at that time was still to advance.

Regrettably I do not remember what was said which is a pity because I am sure what was spoken was worthy of note, I can only guess that three words used by one of the proposers were 'Gentlemen, The Queen'. I am flattered to see I was in such distinguished company.

During my post war correspondence with Greg Holdcroft at Bowerham he told me how proud he was to have served at Tempsford. I also discovered how deeply he felt each Squadron casualty. He said he could have written a book on Tempsford, he didn't, the loss was ours. He died soon after the 21st reunion. I hardly knew anyone else and did not attend another re-union until the 47th in 1994.

The 47th re-union sparked off a desire in me to return to Tempsford after 50 years. I hoped that my visit would not cause me distress, Tempsford held some very sad memories for me.

I was surprised to see how little of the airfield had survived. All but one of the runways had been broken up and the remaining 600 yards of No.2 runway was covered with loose stones and a pile of pallets stacked to one side. A small wood now straddled its path, and beyond, a row of tall high tension pylons marched at right angles to it and parallel to the railway, which had now been electrified. It too had its pylons and cable – fortunately these two hazards were not there when the airfield was operational!!

The airfield is now arable land covered with the greenery of a winter crop. What remained of the taxy tracks were pitted with potholes and deep ruts. A few concrete bases remained where buildings once stood. It was impossible to even guess where the hut in which I slept was located. Neither could I find the base of that warm, friendly mess, where the recordings of Glenn Miller, the Ink Spots and the Andrew Sisters entertained us and where mulled beer flowed when flying was cancelled. It was January 1944 when I first arrived there, an easterly wind swept over the airfield bringing with it snow direct, it seemed, from Siberia.

A small cluster of buildings remained at the entrance to the airfield, probably the old operations block and base headquarters. These are now used as the farm manager's offices, and houses a small museum.

This was Tempsford, September 1994.

Glossary

AFC	Air Force Cross
AG	Air Gunner
ASI	Airspeed Indicator
ATF	Air Transport Form
Capt	Captain
DCAS	Deputy Chief of Air Staff
CVO	Commander Royal Victorian Order
DFC	Distinguished Flying Cross
DFM	Distinguished Flying Medal
DR	Dead Reckoning
DSO	Distinguished Service Order
DZ	Dropping Zone
Eureka	Portable radar beacon on which aircraft may home
FANY	First Aid Nursing Yeomanry
FFI	*Forces Francais de l'Interieure*
F/E	Flight Engineer
F/O	Flying Officer
F/Sgt	Flight Sergeant
Form 28	Operation instructions for despatch of personnel by air
F/Lt	Flight Lieutenant
G/Capt	Group Captain
Grp	Group
HCU	Heavy Conversion Unit
IFF	Identification Friend or Foe
IWM	Imperial War Museum
Lt	Lieutenant
MBE	Member British Empire
MU	Maintenance Unit
MVO	Member Royal Victorian Order
NICKELS	Leaflets
NID	Naval Intelligence Directorate
NKVD	Soviet Secret Service
PAF	Polish Air Force
P/O	Pilot Officer
OBE	Officer of the British Empire
ORB	Operational Record Book

OSS	Office of Strategic Services (USA)
OTU	Operational Training Unit
Pinpoint	The exact position on a map
PoW	Prisoner of War
PRO	Public Record Office
QDM	Compass Bearing (Q code)
RAAF	Royal Australian Air Force
Rebecca	Aircraft radar receiver used in conjunction with Eureka
Reseau	Network
RNoAF	Royal Norwegian Air Force
RNZAF	Royal New Zealand Air Force
SAS	Special Air Service
SAAF	South African Air Force
SD	Special Duties
Sgt	Sergeant
S/Ldr	Squadron Leader
SIS	Secret Intelligence Service (MI6)
SOE	Special Operations Executive
Sqn	Squadron
TA	Territorial Army
u/s	Unserviceable.
USAAC	United States Army Air Corps
USAAF	United States Army Air Force
WAAF	Women's Auxiliary Air Force.
W/Cdr	Wing Commander.
WOp/AG	Wireless Operator /Air Gunner.
WO	Warrant Officer.
WO2	Warrant Officer Second Class (RCAF).

CHAPTER ONE

Tempsford

Doth the moon shine that night we play our play?
A calendar, a calendar! Look in the almanack; find out moonshine;
find out moonshine!
Yes it doth shine that night.
A MIDSUMMER NIGHT'S DREAM, Act III, Scene 1

Tempsford was one of the many airfields spread like confetti over the Central Midlands and East Anglia. It was situated nine miles east of Bedford and built on marsh land previously owned by the Astell Estate. The nearby village of Tempsford on the Great North Road (A1) and the local manor house being known as Tempsford Hall, gave rise to its name. The close proximity of Sandy Station on the main London line, some three miles away and King's Cross some 45 miles from here made this desolate spot a little more amenable to those airman who were posted there.

Work by John Laing & Son Ltd began late 1940 and the three concrete runways were completed by the late summer of 1941. The main runway, No.1, was 2,000 yards long by 50 yards wide, its QDM 250. In this direction it headed straight for a railway embankment carrying the LNER (The London & North Eastern Railway) mainline service from King's Cross to Edinburgh. Runway No.2, the shortest, was 1,383 yards long, QDM 310, also headed straight towards the railway embankment. Runway No.3, 1,600 yards long, QDM 010, ran almost parallel with the railway. Bearing 175 degrees north and about 3½ miles away at Great Barford was the cooling tower of a small power station. If you hooked your take-off this came into play otherwise the only use it had was a turning point for the Luftwaffe for their raids on London. Twice during the winter of 1944 I remember seeing this tower illuminated by Luftwaffe flares for their Me 210/410 low level bombing attacks to the south on London. Fleeting shadows of attacking aircraft could be seen below drifting flares that lit the surrounding countryside as if it were day.

Behind the control tower, which faced the main runway were clustered six T2 type hangars. (One of which was dismantled after the war and reassembled at Duxford). A B2 type hangar sited close to the railway to the west of the airfield, where it still stands today, was used by No.161 Squadron.

All that remains today of the main runway. (Author)

In the shadow of the T2 hangars were the technical, administration, and living quarters. A mixture of steel, asbestos, wooden and brick construction. There were also two bulk petrol installations each storing 72,000 gallons of aviation petrol, enough to refuel 65 empty Halifaxes. And, as one would expect on a bomber base, on the north side of the field there was a bomb dump. The aircraft were dispersed around the field on 47 hard standings. The majority of concrete, but some were of perforated steel decking.

This was a typical, widely dispersed, war time bomber base which the company of John Laing & Son Ltd built for the RAF. They also built airfields for other RAF Commands and for the USAAF. In fact they had been in the business of building airfields for a long time.

Oddly enough there were still some 300 of their Irish workmen living and working within the confines of this secret base during 1944.

On the 16th December 1941 Tempsford received its first unit – No.11 OTU, providing Wellington crews for No.3 Group. They had come temporarily to Tempsford while at Bassingbourn, their home base, concrete runways were being built.

On the 19th January 1942 a No.3 Group Squadron, No.109, had its Headquarters and wireless development flight join No.11 OTU at Tempsford. It was a Wireless Intelligence Development Unit. Largely experimental, its task was twofold, developing wireless and radar navigation aids for Bomber Command, identifying German radio beams and methods for jamming them. They too, like the OTU, were equipped with the Wellington Ic. They also operated for a short time two Wellington Mk VI. These Merlin powered Wellingtons had a pressurised cabin and were intended as high altitude bombers with an estimated ceiling of over 40,000 feet. It looked like a standard geodectic constructed Wellington with a thermos flask attached to it to house the crew of four. It was being used to test their suitability to carry 'Oboe', a system of radio beams transmitted from the ground to an aircraft receiver. At the intersection of these beams the aircraft dropped its target markers. Eventually using Mosquitoes it had an accuracy of 120 yards. The fact that the Mk VI was only used for two weeks shows how suitable it was! On the 1st of March 1942 No.1418 Flight joined 109 squadron with four Wellington III's, with which they conducted trials of 'Gee'.

All three units left Tempsford in April 1942. No.11 OTU returning to Bassingbourn and the flight from No.109 Squadron to Stradishall. Here a reunited squadron developed 'Oboe' and later in August went to Wyton where it flew the first 'Oboe' equipped DH Mosquitoes. It became fully operational with Pathfinder Force in January 1943. No.1418 Flight went to Gransden Lodge here it became the station's first unit and in July 1942 was absorbed in the formation of Bombing Development Unit.

Tempsford as it can be seen already had the foundations of a security conscious base laid before the arrival of No.138 Squadron in March 1942.

No.138 Squadron was originally formed on 1st May 1918, an intended bomber squadron. Disbanded on the 4th July and yet reformed in September it was equipped with Bristol Fighter F2b's. The 1st February 1919 saw it finally disbanded at Chingford in Essex.

The tiny seed of its resuscitation was sown on the 21st August 1940 by the formation, at North Weald, of No.419 Flight under the control of No.11 Group, Fighter Command. It was without a hangar but had a small hut on the far side of the airfield. Its initial equipment, arriving on the 10th August, was two Lysanders and two in reserve. F/Lt W R Farley was the officer in command. Two brand new Whitley's were shortly added to the flight but lacked radio and guns. F/O A J Oettle was posted in to fly them. The first Whitley operation took place on the evening of its arrival at North Weald. The agent was taken on board at Tangmere and flown to France to be parachuted into a field near Paris. A second parachute operation took place on the night of 28/29th August 1940 when a Dutch naval officer, Lado van Hamel was dropped into Holland 'blind'. That is to say without any assistance from the ground. Regrettably Lieutenant van Hamel was soon arrested by the Germans and executed in June 1941.

On the 3rd September after three attacks had been made by the Luftwaffe on North Weald it was decided to move the unit to Stapleford Tawney a satellite some five miles to the south, an airfield with two grass runways. Here they lived in bell tents until they were bombed out and moved into a nearby farm house. In the meantime F/Lt Farley, an experienced Hurricane pilot, filled in his spare time flying in the Battle of Britain with Nos 46 & 151 Squadrons who shared the airfield.

As a boy I knew the airfields at North Weald and Stapleford Tawney well, cycling ten miles or so from home to watch the flying there. The only memory I have of North Weald was the tall radio masts standing close to the aerodrome. Stapleford Tawney was then a small private grass airfield with a single hangar, close to the road at the top of a rise. The landing area sloped gently downhill from north to south.

At North Weald a Whitley had 1,600 yards of take off run, at Stapleford Tawney they had 1,133 yards. I flew a Whitley for over 100 hours out of a grass airfield at Forres in Morrayshire. We never stopped complaining about the narrow margins we had on take-off, although I see we had 1,700 yards in which to do it.

Two Whitley operational sorties were flown from Stapleford and another intended Whitley pilot, F/Lt F J Keast, was posted in. He came from No.24 Communications Squadron, Hendon, and had 3,500 hours flying experience.

October 9th 1940 saw 419 Flight moved to Stradishall, control passing from No.11 Group Fighter Command to No.3 Group Bomber Command. That same evening F/O Oettle and his crew flew to Abingdon, picked up Phillip Schneidau, flew him to France, and parachuted him into the Fontainbleau area. A previous attempt to complete this SIS operation had been foiled by bad weather.

*   *   *

The move to Stradishall, a permanent base in Suffolk built in February 1938, must have been a welcome change for the Flight after conditions at Stapleford. However, the flight's arrival was punctuated by a spectacular crash on the edge of the airfield of Whitley P5025 flown by P/O Greenhill, just posted in as a Lysander pilot, his Whitley flying experience was nil. No lives were lost, the only casualty seemed to be Greenhill whom, it would appear, was smartly posted out again. It took almost a month for a replacement Whitley to arrive.

The first Lysander pick-up flight of the war, operation FELIX I, had been arranged to bring back Phillip Schneidau on the night of the 19th/20th October. In the meantime Farley's Lysander was modified by removing its rear canopy and fitting a short ladder to the side of the aircraft to make it easier for Schneidau to climb on board. Farley flew to Tangmere on the 19th but bad weather delayed his departure until the following day. Taking off late the following evening in appalling weather, his radio was soon immobilised by the downpour through the open rear cockpit. The weather improved over France and aided by moonlight he was able to map read his way to the inverted 'L' shaped flare path prepared for him by Schneidau and landed in a field near Montigny-sur-Loing some 7km south of Fontainbleau. Shortly after take off a single German rifle bullet reputedly fired from the nearby village of Marlotte (1km north) came up through Farley's knees taking away his compass. He was fortunate not to have had a more painful and embarrassing encounter with that bullet.

On the return flight the weather front, coming from the south west, had intensified to gale force and must have been lying across Northern France, the Channel and the east of England. Unable to get underneath Farley chose to climb to 16,000 feet in an effort to fly over it. (The Lysander has two 750 litre oxygen bottles provided for the pilot and passenger but there is no mention of them using it). Without a radio, a compass or a sight of the ground he flew a rough course to Tangmere. They flew on until 06.50 hours when the fuel ran out and he was forced to land. The landing completely wrecked the Lysander but fortunately without injury to Farley or his passenger. They had landed in Scotland, Oban was the nearest RAF Station. Had the 150 gallon long range tank been fitted to his Lysander he would have probably finished up in the Western Isles or worse still in the Atlantic Ocean.

The planning of this first Lysander pick up operation, it is said by Hugh Verity, took place at Oddenino's restaurant in London, where on a table cloth Farley and Schneidau conceived the flare path to be used. This layout, with very little modification, was eventually used on all pick up fields and parachute dropping zones. It consisted of three to four white lights approximately 50 metres apart in the shape of an inverted 'L' with a red light flashing the site code beside the first white.

I have never sat in the cockpit of a Lysander to get the feel of it. It looks a big aeroplane. Thumbing through the Pilot's Notes and examining photographs of the cockpit layout I am convinced that the pilot of it, in its original role of Army co-operation, must have assimilated the multi-skills of all aircrew categories. Doubtless many of the activities essential for Army co-operation became superfluous when the aeroplane was used for SOE/SIS work. However, in this role he still had to fly accurately by moonlight, map read, navigate, operate the radio and land on a map reference in France.

The Pilot's notes say take-off safety speed was 80 mph. Steep climb at 70 mph or even down to 60 mph. Approach and landing speeds; gliding 85 mph; engine assisted 80 mph; the creeper 65-70 mph, opening up engine on the last stages of approach. The fuel capacity was 95 gallons enough to give a range of approximately 600 miles. The first 150 gallon auxiliary fuel tank was not fitted to the Lysander until March 1942.

I had a letter from an old friend of mine, Master Pilot, Ian 'Jock' Craig, AFC, who wrote:

On the 2nd August (1944) I went to Ballah to get a Lysander and take it to Cairo West. Ballah was a dried up salt lake and had been a gunnery school using the Lysanders, which had been parked at dispersal awaiting disposal for about a year. We were told the aircraft were to be taken to an MU at Brindisi in Italy where they would be refurbished and used for delivery and recovery of agents in Yugoslavia.

We had one pilot who had flown Lysanders in the desert when they were used for army co-operation and he told us of the tricks of the trade in flying this 'Pterodactyl'. It had a Mercury engine which I had experienced with the Master II and a two speed propeller. It had leading edge slats which were connected to the wing flaps. As the nose was raised and the speed reduced, the slats came out and operated the flaps; combined with the use of the engine a very slow landing speed could be achieved. Nobody had invented the term STOL in those days! The elevator trim which was gradually wound back during the approach and landing, was at fully nose up position at touch down. It was controlled by a nine inch metal wheel on the port side of the cockpit. One of the vital actions after landing was to set that wheel in the neutral position. Any attempted take off with the trim fully back resulted in a loop off the runway and usually a fatal crash. The flying controls were unbalanced but the aircraft was not difficult to fly, just a bit different!

He went on to say that on his flight to Brindisi, he lost both the wheel spats and a belly panel due to salt corrosion, which was also rife in the cockpit, 'everything was crumbling'. For the record the aircraft was T1679, he flew V9585 on the same trip two weeks later.

In December Farley briefed F/O R C Hockey a new Whitley pilot also from Hendon and No.24 Squadron. Farley told him that after completing a number of long range trips he may be given the opportunity of flying the Lysanders as a rest!! Farley then went on leave and during a visit to North Weald borrowed a Hurricane and flew it during a German raid, was shot down and broke his leg. F/Lt Keast then took command of No.419 flight.

The posting of F/O Hockey to No.419 flight was fortuitous (if not inspirational!). Volunteer Reserve trained at Fairoaks in 1938, he was a skilled, experienced pilot who knew Europe well having flown VIP's from Hendon with No.24 Communication Squadron. During the fall of France in May 1940 he carried out many daylight transport flights, 19 of which are logged as operational. His log book records being attacked by Ju87's at le Bourget on May 21st and on the 3rd June 'bombed on the ground' at Villacoublay with Air Marshal Sholto-Douglas and Admiral Blake as passengers on board a DH Flamingo R2765. A flight in an Anson on the 26th June to Jersey via Portsmouth is recorded as 'To Destroy Fuel Stocks'. Among the VIP passengers neatly recorded in his log book include: General de Gaulle, Marshal of the Royal Air Force Sir John Salmon, Air Marshal Joubert le Ferte, Air Chief Marshal Bowhill, Marshal of the Royal Air Force Lord Trenchard and Air Marshal Billy Bishop, VC.

Bringing this experience with him he joined No.419 Flight on the 26th November 1940. He flew with F/O Oettle as second pilot on December 4th for 30 minutes to air test Whitley T4264. Then exhaustion resulting from overwork with his previous Squadron put him in hospital for two months to recover. He returned to flying on the 13th March 1941.

Tentando Superabimus (by striving we shall overcome) was Hockey's school motto (Hele's School, Exeter.) appropriate words in view of the opposition these early Special Duty Operations were receiving. His contribution to Nos 419 and 1419 Flights and later 138 Squadron had much to do with the confidence in and the development of these operations.

In the final months of 1940 political wrangling finally identified the purpose of SOE operations as being, industrial sabotage and the raising and supplying of secret armies. SIS (MI6) operations, simply explained, were for the purpose of collecting intelligence information.

At the end of 1940 No.419 Flight in its short and difficult career, had so far completed ten Whitley operational flights – four to France, four to Belgium and two to Holland, dropping at least one agent on each occasion. In addition one successful Lysander operation had been completed. The establishment of the flight was then three pilots (Farley, Oettle, Keast) 30 airmen, three Lysanders and two Whitleys. One Whitley had been lost and, not surprisingly under the circumstances, one Lysander. Whitley operations in these early days carried a pilot and co-pilot, so far all of the Whitley operations had been carried out with Oettle as the pilot and Keast as the co-pilot. These were the pioneers, the pathfinders, the men who, to 'coin a phrase', correct in this instance, 'got SIS/SOE air operations off the ground'!

It is remarkable to see so soon after the fall of France, Belgium and Holland we were already preparing for our return.

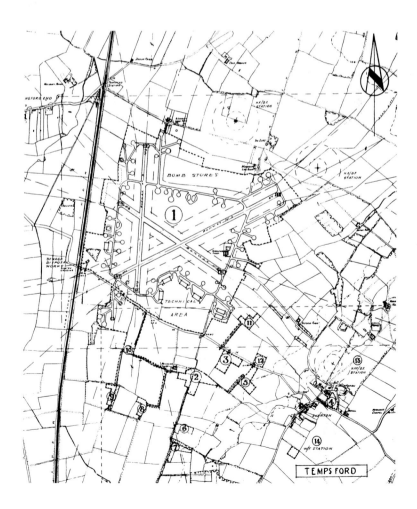

Plan of RAF Tempsford.
(RAF Museum)

CHAPTER TWO

January–August 1941

On the 4/5th January 1941 F/O Oettle and S/Ldr Keast attempted an operation to France, it was aborted because of bad weather. On the 9/10th they flew to Brussels, bad weather over England forced them to divert to Honington. On the following night they attempted the longest Whitley flight so far, an SIS operation to the south of France, a flight of over nine hours, bad weather again forcing them to divert, this time to Digby. Two French operations were flown on the nights of 16/17th and 18/19th January, another on the 13/14th of February this time with Keast as Captain.

The very next night S/Ldr Keast flew to Poland. A round trip of 1,800 miles and 11 hours 20 minutes flying time. Extra fuel tanks were put in the bomb bays and inside the fuselage. Their destination was in the Cracow region. They parachuted three Polish agents S Krzymowski, C Raczkowski and J Zabieski inside Germany some 95km from the Polish border, their supply containers were lost. It took the three of them sometime to reach their destination and reported it had been an extremely hazardous flight. The weather must have been appalling.

The Whitley V was a docile enough aircraft to fly providing the Merlin X's, developing 1,145 hp, kept going, their reliability was certainly questionable. It would lumber off the ground at 95 mph and climb away at 115 mph. It carried a normal crew of five, however, in these early SD days a co-pilot was carried and a volunteer from the ground trades who sat freezing in the rear fuselage with the agent to see he parachuted safely from the aircraft together with his packages. Later this crew member was given the rank of Sergeant and was called the despatcher. With the arrival of the Halifax without a mid-upper turret the surplus gunner performed this duty.

Physical contact between the crew in the front of the aircraft and anyone in the rear was made difficult by the centre section of the wing, a box like structure, through which there was a tunnel making it necessary to crawl through on one's belly. Not easy when wearing a parachute harness and a Mae West.

The normal fuel load for a Whitley was 705 gallons, an extra 132 gallons could be carried in two auxiliary fuel tanks in the bomb bay and in the fuselage a maximum of four tanks with 66 gallons in each, making a grand total of 1,101 gallons. The fuel cock settings in this configuration appear to be very complicated.

The wreck of Whitley T4264 photographed by the Belgian Resistance. Note the early type roundels and fin markings. It would appear that No. 416 Flight did not have aircraft code letters. This was the first Special Duty aircraft to crash in enemy held Europe. S/Ldr F J B Keast (inset) was the pilot. (via K A Merrick)

The 17th February saw S/Ldr F J B Keast flying Whitley T4264, his third consecutive night's operation, this time taking an SIS agent to Namur in Belgium. After parachuting him, they were at a height of 200 feet when hit by flak in one engine. Shortly after the other engine failed, seizing up from a coolant leak. Too low to bale out they crashed into a wood fortunately with only minor injuries. Their interrogation by the Germans lasted five days and was said to have been physical.

It is interesting to note that Merrick reports Brigadier Gubbins had arranged an SOE flight to Czechoslovakia for the 17th February. A great deal of preparatory work had been made, including a reception committee at the destination. This had to be cancelled due to SIS demanding that their operation to Namur had the greater priority. The Czechs considered the cancellation of this flight resulted in a great loss of morale to their SOE forces.

This confliction of priorities between SIS and SOE resulted in the loss of S/Ldr Keast and his crew in Belgium. However it must be said since they were the only crew available at that time and of the two aircraft available, one as it has been seen, had a coolant problem. Taking also crew fatigue into account, S/Ldr Keast and his crew had a very thin chance of making it to Czechoslovakia and back. Keast had been Hockey's second pilot on No.24 Squadron.

Gubbins had organised a full SOE flying programme to take place during the month of March. Some sixteen sorties in ten days of full moon. With S/Ldr Keast's aircraft a wreck in Belgium, F/O Oettle nursing a damaged aeroplane in the Orkney's, F/O Hockey still in hospital and SIS now having priority, it looked as if there weren't going to be many SOE sorties flown during the moon period this month.

Air Marshal A T Harris, then Deputy Chief of Air Staff (DCAS), was always difficult over the release of further aircraft from the bombing effort. Judging by the navigation problems then being encountered by Bomber Command, he did not believe it possible to find a torchlit target in a field, in the middle of nowhere. He therefore decided to release a modified Handley Page Harrow and crewed by No.271 Squadron instead of providing another Whitley. No wonder Hockey had *Tentando Superabimus* painted on his Halifax! However, another Whitley T4165 arrived in March from No.78 Squadron – it didn't last long.

Ken Merrick says that in May 1942 modifications to four new No.161 Squadron Lysanders were held up due to the lack of Handley Page Harrow 150 gallon fuel tanks used to extend their range.

However 10/11th March saw F/O Oettle and his crew again parachuting Schneidau near his home in the Forest of Fontainbleau. The following night the first double Whitley operation was to be flown. Oettle was to fly to Czechoslovakia but returned early when he realised he would not be able to complete under the cover of darkness. They had been in the air 6 hours 10 minutes when they landed. The second Whitley was flown by a new pilot S/Ldr E V Knowles, DFC.

F/O Oettle flew operation SAVANNA on the 14/15th March dropping blind east of Vannes (Morbihan) at midnight a French parachute company, Captain G R P Bergé, J Letac, A Forman and two others. They and their two containers of small arms landed some 8km from the intended pinpoint. SAVANNA's task was to disrupt the German bomber pathfinder squadrons based at Meucon by ambushing the leave bus to Vannes and killing the aircrews onboard. They found that the buses were no longer running and the operation failed!

March also saw the Flight renumbered to No.1419. The number 419 being allocated to a No.3 Group RCAF Bomber Squadron formed at Mildenhall on 15th December 1941.

About this time F/O Scotter a new Lysander pilot was posted in. He was an experienced Lysander pilot having served with No.2 (Army Co-operation) Squadron, a replacement for F/O Baker, a New Zealander, who is said to have been lost on a 'night navigation exercise over Europe'. It had become the practice that new Lysander pilots flew such an exercise over occupied territory before taking part in active operations. It would appear that Baker merely failed this test and was replaced since there is no record of any Lysander being lost over France at this time.

Hockey, now out of hospital, was given the task of evaluating a Martin Maryland AR718 for SD long range work, flying it for the first time on the 31st March. It was thought by using a comparatively fast aeroplane its speed would extend the range of operation during the short summer nights. Hockey was the only pilot put to this task (up to that time he had flown at least 20 different types of aircraft) and whilst he enjoyed flying it, surviving an engine failure, runaway propellers, and parachute static lines damaging the tailplane he decided after some 40 flights it was unsuitable for its intended task. The other idea that it could be used for long range pickups was also abandoned since when landing the long nose masked the view ahead and the instruments reflected on the windscreen. He further remarked that the Americans had obviously never flown a Maryland at night. Hockey returned it to Benson on the 23rd October. This particular Maryland was part of an order given by the French before capitulation. Although designed to meet specific requirements of the USAAC the Glenn Martin Company was unsuccessful in obtaining production orders from them.

Hockey flew his first operational sortie to Belgium on the 8/9th of April, acting as second pilot to F/Lt Jackson a South African and a newcomer to the flight. The route Whitley P5029 took was Base–Knocke–Lille–Bruges–Base, the flying time was said to have been 3.35 hours.

The following day, the 10th, F/O Hockey was over the airfield in a Whitley giving two French agents parachute practice. Regrettably one parachute failed to open and the agent was killed.

That night F/O Oettle was to lift six Polish saboteurs, their task was to destroy the Passac Power Station in the suburbs of Bordeaux. The aircraft he was flying was T4165 which had recently been received from No.78 Squadron. Over the Loire an electrical fault released the containers. As these were essential to the operation it was pointless to continue and he returned to Manston. Attempting to overshoot F/O A J Oettle stalled the heavily laden aircraft at 100 feet and the aircraft crashed and caught fire. The rear gunner and the observer were killed and four including F/O Oettle were injured. Fortunately the six Poles were only shaken. I wonder if the Flight had inherited from 78 Squadron an aircraft with an electrical fault?

This was probably the first of the ADJUDICATE operations, using the remains of the Polish Army left in France to undertake sabotage.

The same night, 11/12th April, F/O Scotter was to fly the Flight's second Lysander sortie, operation CART to a field near Châteauroux, the surface of which was bad and in addition to which he had to take-off in a hurry. His arrival at Tangmere was further complicated by the airfield being under attack. He finally landed safely and was awarded an immediate Distinguished Flying Cross (DFC) for this fine performance.

On the 16th April, (this is the date of the signing of the report and there is no record of the name of the operation) Jackson flew to Belgium. He had a rough flight. North east of Zeebrugge he met heavy flak and was coned at 2,000 feet by searchlights. The rear gunner put out one light by machine gun fire and destroyed the other.

*   *   *

May was to be a busy month for the flight. At the start of the moon period on the 5/6th Hockey as second pilot to Jackson went to Belgium (MARINE/ALBION) via Aldeburgh–Knocke–Ath–Liège–Ardennes. But they aborted due to icing before reaching their Ardennes objective. They met heavy flak at the coast and landed after being in the air 4.10 hours. Hockey and Jackson tried once more on the 6/7th to complete this Belgium operation but icing again caused them to abort. They finally succeeded on the 9th/10th.

Also on the 5/6th as part of a double Whitley operation the flight's new Commanding Officer, S/Ldr Knowles was flying operation BOMBPROOF dropping blind the very first French SOE agent, Georges Bégué, some 32km north of Châteauroux between Valençay and Vatan. Knowles reported that he parachuted him within a furlong of the pinpoint. Bégué, to his annoyance, claims he actually landed several kilometres beyond it and had to walk through the night carrying his radio transmitter in his suitcase with his clothes. The greatest of care was always taken by the aircrews to find the exact spot before parachuting agents blind, I wonder if Knowles was given the correct map co-ordinates for his pinpoint?

On the 10/11th April in reply to Bégué's wireless report to London on the 9th May, Knowles flew another operation to France AUTOGYRO D & E/JOULLY and parachuted two more agents: Pierre de Vomécourt (Lucas) and Baron Emanuel d'Astier de la Vigerie (Bernard) into the same area as Bégué was dropped. The safe drop of Pierre de Vomécourt was particularly important, as it has been said, but for him F section of the SOE would never have been founded. He was to form his first *reseau* in the Rhone area and was a true pioneer of SOE operations, 'a member of a proud French aristocratic family who through the generations had served France faithfully'.

On their return the rear gunner shot down an Me 110 north of le Mans, a five second burst exploded it.

S/Ldr Knowles completed another operation (CEZAREWICH) the next evening to Vielsham in Belgium and in spite of engine trouble completed this operation successfully.

Scotter took out the Lysander again on the 11th May (Operation FELIX II) to pick-up Schneidau, which he did without any problems.

The May moon period finished with two further sorties. Hockey and Jackson flying on the 11/12th May a newly allocated Whitley Z6727 on operation JOSEPHINE to Bordeaux. From Abingdon they went to Tangmere–Isle-de-Ré–Bassin-d'Arcachon (some 36km west of Bordeaux)–Target where they parachuted blind three Frenchmen, Captain A Forman, R P Cabard and Lt Varnier who were endeavouring to complete the destruction of Passac Power Station which had finished in disaster on the 10th April. This operation was abandoned when it was found the target was surrounded by a nine foot wall and a high-tension wire. However they returned in June, found their buried containers, climbed the wall, opened the main gate and set their charges. The subsequent explosion caused no end of trouble in the

Bordeaux area. Hockey recorded in his log book 9.35 hours flying time for the operation.

The next night they flew for 6.00 hours to Vannes, operation AUTOGYRO, their route being Abingdon–Tangmere–Vannes area–Abingdon this was their fifth operation within nine days. They returned to Stradishall from Abingdon the next day. This was probably the drop of Roger Cottin (Albert) which took place on this date.

Hockey spent the time before the next moon period flying the Lysander and testing the Maryland. About this time Hockey's log book was endorsed qualifying him as a Whitley 1st pilot, which sounds patronising.

The Flight moved to the racecourse at Newmarket on the 22nd May 1941, a grass field and at the time with the longest take-off run in the RAF of some 2,500 to 3,000 yards. Hockey was accommodated in a nearby hayloft, the Flight was camping out again. Two new pilots were posted in, F/Lt Nesbitt-Dufort, DSO, a former nightfighter pilot to fly the Lysanders and Sgt Austin a new Whitley pilot.

*   *   *

At this time talks at Bomber Command were apparently proceeding to give the Flight full Squadron status, its establishment raised accordingly. It transpired that the thinking was for the new Squadron to join the bomber force and to carry out SD duties as a secondary task.

Only six sorties were undertaken in June, on the night of the 11/12th two were flown. Knowles flew OUTHAULLE to France which must have failed since he flew the same operation on the 13/14th. Likewise on the 11/12th Austin flew AUTOGYRO to Mortain in Normandy which again must have failed since he flew it again on the 13/14th.

A third operation on the same night was flown by Hockey in a Whitley Z6727, his first sortie recorded as captain, operation FITZROY. With him flew F/Lt Jackson as his second pilot. Their route was Abingdon–Tangmere–le Havre–Tours where they were forced to abandon the operation due to bad weather.

The fourth and final sortie of this moon period operation ZEBRA, took place on the 12/13th, Austin going ten miles to the east of Limoges to deliver two containers, an attempt to complete an operation that had failed three times before. Having trouble with his delivery due to a fault in the aircraft's electrical system he finally dropped the second container an hour after he had dropped the first. The containers landed near the château of Phillipe de Vomécourt, (Pierre's brother) and were hidden in the shrubbery near the house. This was the first supply drop for an SOE circuit. Ken Merrick says 'nearly 60,000 would follow over the next three and a half years'.

On the 20th June Germany invaded Russia making necessary a complete reassessment of SOE requirements. Drops to Czechoslovakia and Poland were to be drastically reduced. France was now given priority. Belgium and Holland were also to be supplied.

Of the twelve operations attempted in July, ten were successful. Hockey and Jackson flew FITZROY again on the 4/5th in an endeavour to finally complete. They went via Tangmere–Isigny–Tours–le Blanc–Target, taking 6 hours 40 minutes for the flight. Austin that same night went to ARAMIS Holland. The following night, the 5/6th July, Hockey and Jackson also took, unofficially, F/Lt Romanoff on a sortie to Belgium (MARBLES) for operational experience. Romanoff was a cousin of the late Tsar and had previously flown with Hockey at Hendon. The route they flew for 4.45 hours was Nieuport–Charleroi–Namur–St-Hubert.

Also on the 5/6th Knowles flew to western Normandy and dropped blind a two man team, J L Cartigny and H Labit. Their task was to carry out a reconnaissance of the German air base at Carpiquet near Caen with a view to sabotaging it. Regrettably Cartigny was captured and eventually shot. This was a RF operation, i.e., SOE Gaullist section, aptly coded TORTURE. Labit, a twenty year old, evaded capture and proceeded to Toulouse to form his own circuit FABULOUS. He was to die by a self inflicted cyanide pill in April 1943.

On the 6/7th Austin went to Belgium via, Charleroi-Namur-Dinant. On the 7th July Hockey and Jackson took off for operation SHE in France in a new Whitley Z6727. After 4.15 hours in the air the sortie was abandoned because of engine trouble.

Austin re-flew MARBLES on the 7/8th obviously Hockey's efforts of the 5/6th had been unsuccessful. Knowles flew TRIPOD successfully to Limoges in France on the same night. He reported that an He 111 flew over the top of them on a reciprocal course. Both the front and rear gunner opened fire in turn but it continued on its course.

The 9/10th saw Hockey off again to France, operation ADJUDICATE, again unofficially with Romanoff as second pilot. From Tangmere they went to Ouistreham–Tours–Limoges, landing in fog at Abingdon on return. They had been in the air 7 hours 5 minutes and Hockey recorded flying on instruments for 6.50 hours.

On that same night Austin flew AUTOGYRO 'C' to France, dropping N F R Burdeyron and his wireless operator, a man who had been in jail for rape when the German occupation had released him a year before. A few days later he was recognised by a local policeman, arrested and put back into jail. This was an additional team to that dropped on the 5/6th July to complete the reconnaissance of Carpiquet airfield. It was a quick trip to Isigny then to St-Lô, south of Cherbourg. Unhappily this circuit wasn't very successful and collapsed in April 1942. Fundamentally, carelessness caused arrests by the Germans which resulted in its demise.

*   *   *

F/Lt Jackson who joined the Flight in April, although not cleared for first pilot, it is unbelievably said, completed his first solo sortie on the night of 10th/11th July when he went to France to complete ADJUDICATE which had obviously failed on the 9/10th. Austin during this period went to Belgium to complete sortie FELIX. Since two further trips were laid on for FELIX in August it can only be assumed that this one failed.

Hockey had another lucky escape on the 12th whilst taking off Whitley Z6473 on operations, an engine failed. He managed to land his Whitley, fully loaded, back at base.

Jackson also had a narrow escape on the 25th July when taking off Z6727 (that new aeroplane again) an engine failed. Unable to maintain height he hit a telegraph pole and crashed near Newmarket. There were no fatalities but the eight persons on board were injured, four of them 'non RAF'. They were on a test flight with 'secret equipment'. It is doubtful if the identity 'secret equipment' will ever be known but I will hazard a guess that it was a trial of a 'Rebecca/Eureka' set, a method of guiding an aircraft into a dropping zone with the aid of a special radar set. The aircraft was 'factory new' when it arrived on the unit three months before, on the 3rd May.

I have since found a letter on file from RAF Stradishall to a Major H Perkins dated 14th May 1941. In it is a suggestion that it would be more convenient that the experiment for the homing on to a field set be carried out just off the aerodrome at Newmarket. This to be held in daylight either on a Saturday or a Sunday. A night show to be held on Tuesday 20/5/41 when the wireless operator will try and home on the ground station and drop a container. Undoubtedly the beginning of 'Rebecca/Eureka'.

July 1941 had been a busy month for No.1419 Flight. Two pilots sharing the bulk of the work. There had been three engine failures to contend with, all of which could have had a more serious consequence. Nearly all, if not all of the successful drops were made blind. That is to say, without the aid of reception committees displaying ground lights to guide the aircraft into the dropping zone.

The loss of Whitley Z6727 was to be No.1419 Flight's last. At Newmarket on the 25th August 1941 the Flight became No.138 Squadron commanded by W/Cdr E V Knowles, DFC. The Whitleys of 'A' flight being commanded by a newly promoted S/Ldr Jackson and the Lysanders of 'B' flight by S/Ldr Nesbitt-Dufort. The aircraft establishment of No.138 Squadron at that time was six Whitleys and four Lysanders.

In the meantime August operations commenced on the 3rd with Hockey taking Nesbitt-Dufort as second pilot to Belgium for a 3.35 hour sortie operation PERIWIG. The route being Southwold–Nieuport–Ath–Mons–base. The same night Austin went to Chimay in Belgium for operation MILL. On the 5th Hockey took a newly arrived Canadian Whitley pilot Sgt Reimer to the south of Saumur for a seven hour sortie operation LUMOND. Why this sortie of comparatively short distance should have taken so long is not explained.

A further sortie to France was flown by Austin on the 6/7th, operation THEORIM/VALIENT, where in Vichy France he dropped two agents who became very active, G C G Turck and J V de Guélis.

Turck leaving the aircraft late, landed in a quarry, and was knocked unconscious.

On the 12/13th August Hockey again attempted to complete SHE, outstanding since the 7th July. His co-pilot was F/Lt Murphy, a former Cranwell cadet and a navigation expert who usually flew with Knowles. He later flew Lysanders. They went via Abingdon–Tangmere–Périgeaux–Bay of Biscay–St-Eval–Abingdon. What they were doing in the air for 10.15 hours is not quite clear but I imagine that they flew to a map reference in the Bay of Biscay area and then north to St-Eval so not to be caught over enemy territory when daylight came.

This same night, Austin was flying a double target PERIWIG & MILL that had failed on the 3/4th August. As these operations do not reappear later it must be presumed that he completed them successfully.

*   *   *

Reimer about this time flew an operation to France and Belgium coded LUMOND/ADJUDICATE/FABULOUS/CHICKEN Dropping a wireless operator and a package at FABULOUS to support Labit who had been dropped on the 5th July. It looks as if this operation involved four separate DZ's. Like Knowles, who is recorded as flying FELIX to Belgium twice, the actual date of these operations cannot be determined since they are omitted from the pilot's reports. The date these reports were signed are the 13/8/41 and 14/8/41 respectively, and were the last operations made during the August moon period.

A flight DOWNSTAIRS/LUMOND by Murphy on the 20th/21st August to France appears to have taken place without the aid of the moon. This was the third attempt at LUMOND.

The honour of flying the first 138 Squadron operational sortie fell to F/O Hockey who, with his close friend S/Ldr P C Pickard, DSO, DFC, as his second pilot, flew Whitley Z6473 on the 29/30th August for 7.45 hours on operation TROMBONE. They went via Abingdon–Tangmere–Grand Champ–Tours–Châteauroux–base, dropping near Châteauroux without the aid of a moon, R Lencement, an electrical engineer. He was arrested before the end of the year but was fortunate to survive both concentration camps Buchenwald and Dora.

Pickard at that time was based at Exning, RAF 3 Group Headquarters flying VIP's. Hockey says he took him along to practice map reading at night! He would take a more active part in SD operations when taking command of No.161 Squadron in October 1942.

On the last day of August a No.214 Squadron Wellington flew to Holland. Both the aircraft and its crew had been borrowed because of Whitley unservicabilty. Its load was six 250lb bombs and a load of (says Ken Merrick) 500,000 cigarettes. This flying tobacco warehouse was flown by F/Lt McGilivary the second pilot was S/Ldr P C Pickard. The cigarettes were for the Dutch, the bombs for the enemy!

It is interesting to note that at this time most of the French operations

Lysander Cockpit
Photo: Crown
Copyright.

were limited to Vichy France where there was only a partial blackout and most of the big towns could easily be identified at night.

CHAPTER THREE

September–October 1941

The rising moon at the beginning of September signalled another busy month for the Squadron. On the 4/5th S/Ldr Nesbitt-Dufort was to fly the first Lysander SOE sortie, LEVEE/FACADE, to France NE of Châteauroux (Indre). Due to the police carrying out an identity check there was a delay causing a sudden change in the location of the landing ground – hastily made ready and very small. A man named G Morel was landed without trouble but Nesbitt-Dufort on taking off fouled some telephone and high tension wires and finally the tree tops. He landed in the fog at Tangmere trailing a length of wire having dodged the attention of two night fighters on the way home. Morel had an equally hair-raising adventure, arrested six weeks later but eventually spirited back to the UK immediately after serious abdominal surgery.

On the 2/3rd September, F/Lt Jackson parachuted, in poor visibility, a Polish Count, T Dziergowski into France. This was the fourth attempt to complete operation ADJUDICATE and the Count had spent 28 hours in the air before this final successful blind drop – successful only that he was, at last, outside the aeroplane, he fell into some trees and was badly injured. Sgt Austin went to Belgium and aborted PORTER in poor weather, so poor he even brought his pigeons back! Austin was out again to Belgium, the following night, for operation CONJUGAL. Again bad weather forced him to abort and bring his pigeons back. This must be the original story of the weather being so bad that even the birds were walking. Obviously Austin thought in this case they were too far from home to walk back safely!

On the 6/7th Sgt Reimer parachuted, south of Châteauroux, six SOE agents the largest number for eighteen months. Operation DRAUGHTSMAN/AUTOGIRO/DOWNSTAIRS & VESTIGE combined with TROPICAL & UKELELE – an endeavour to clear up a number of outstanding operations. Reimer saw the reception committee signalling with torches through a gap in 10/10th cloud. The rear gunner reported that all the parachutes opened safely and later in the moonlight the agents, B H Cowburn, M A Trotobas, H V Gerson, G Langelaan, the Comte J P M du Puy and a wireless operator A G Bloch were seen standing on the ground.

F/Lt Murphy also flew to France on the same night to attempt two operations FELIX & DASTARD. Cloud at 1,000 feet was 10/10ths.

While circling some ground lights he damaged his tailwheel, he then aborted! Bad weather caused Jackson to abort the other unsuccessful sortie to France, STUDENT. The next night he reported heavy flak at Boulogne where six Wellingtons of Bomber Command were operating. In excellent visibility he dropped his agent from 500 feet.

The night of the 7/8th there were a further three sorties flown. Sgt Austin flew GLASSHOUSE to Holland. In the bright moonlight he saw a light shining from a dinghy in the North Sea. He circled and radioed its position. The weather was for a change 'fair and fine with good vis'. He dropped his agent at 23.37 hours. This must have been Johannes Ter Laak a former Dutch Army Officer – his radio transmitter was badly damaged on landing but was later repaired by the Germans after he was captured. He was executed at Mauthausen in September 1944. F/Lt Murphy again flew FELIX/DASTARD this time successfully dropping some 80km south-east of Paris a Parisian agent named Laverdet and his radio operator.

Taking off at 20.00 hours F/O Hockey with S/Ldr Nesbitt-Dufort as his second pilot flew operation FENGLER to France. His route was Base–Tangmere–Saumur–Toulouse–Carcassonne–Target (south of Carcassonne in the Pyrenees)–Arcachon–Ushant–St-Eval. At 07.00 hours they landed at St-Eval short of fuel.

One night later, the 9/10th September. Hockey and Nesbitt-Dufort, were together again flying operation ESMOND/COLUMBUS to Denmark to drop Lt T Sneum and his wireless operator Christofferson. Fog caused them to abort. Some 6km south of Ostende, at 14,000 feet they were coned by searchlights and a near flak miss put the Whitley into a vertical dive finally pulling out at 400 feet. (There is no report what the agents thought!) Newmarket, Stradishall and Waddington having refused them because of fog they landed at Leuchars after nine hours in the air. It took two hours to fly back to base the following day. Reimer completed this operation the following night parachuting them west of Copenhagen.

Thomas Sneum together with a friend, Kjeld Petersen, created a sensation on the night of 21st June 1941 by flying from Denmark to the UK in an aeroplane they largely rebuilt.

The night of the 10/11th saw F/Lt Jackson in the Toulouse area with SARDINE, visibility being poor he aborted. Fog and erroneous radio information made it difficult for him to find Newmarket. When he landed he had been airborne 10.30 hours.

Austin was luckier, managing to pinpoint Chinon in the fog and low cloud. At 03.00 hours he parachuted two BARTER agents in the Mimizan (Landes) area south of Bordeaux. The reception was lit by two fires and flashes from a torch. The objective of this party was to reconnoitre the airfield at Mérignac, prepare a detailed attack then radio back details for the assault party. However the transmitter was damaged on landing and they for the time being, disappeared.

Murphy went the same night to drop GIPSY/VERMILLION via Cabourg–Saumur–Châteauroux to St-Amand where they dropped the two agents. The fog was so bad when he returned, rockets were fired from Stradishall to help them find base.

The month finished on the 30th with Austin flying MUSTICK/ OUTCASTE/ BALACLAVA one of the two Belgium sorties that night. At Courtrai he was coned by searchlights and strong evasive action was needed. However one agent and his package were seen to drop safely. Hockey flew the other, LUCKYSHOT, with a new second pilot P/O Smith. Their route was Base–Abingdon–Tangmere –Berck–Charleroi–Ardennes–base. Cumulus cloud and heavy rain forced them down from 7,500 feet to 2,000 feet, low cloud over the target area forced them to abort. Murphy took TEAMAN to Holland, one agent was dropped.

In all the Squadron flew one Lysander and 19 Whitley sorties during the month of September.

*   *   *

Three operations took place on the 1st October. Two meeting with success. Austin to Belgium operation BINDER and Jackson to France operation BEAU GESTE.

The No.138 Squadron ORB is now recorded on film and that coupled with the scrawl of the Intelligence Officer compiling them has made them difficult to read. It would have helped if the place names had been written in capital letters.

S/Ldr Nesbitt-Dufort flew a successful SIS Lysander sortie FITZROY on the 1st/2nd October to a disused airfield in occupied France just west of Compiègne. The reception committee and the passenger Captain Roman Czerniawski of the Polish Air Force rested in the abandoned and unguarded hangars. Here in brilliant moonlight Nesbitt-Dufort landed, picked up his passenger and landed back at Tangmere in time for dinner. The sheer impudence of it all is breathtaking.

The 3/4th saw P/O Austin making a deep penetration into Belgium via Namur and Liège to Verviers. Here, within 25 miles of the German border, he completed the outstanding LUCKYSHOT operation that had eluded two previous attempts made by Hockey and Reimer, four containers and one package being dropped onto a reception committee. He then went to Lake de Gilepe (?) and dropped two agents RHUMBOLD & HIRELING. The pigeons weren't so lucky, the log says they were dropped seven miles from their pinpoint.

In a letter headed LUCKY SHOT – P/O AUSTIN, it said that a message had been received from the field saying:

> Operation has succeeded perfectly . . . Enthusiasm everywhere. Congratulate pilot for quickly finding the point and exact delivery. Long live England and Belgium.

W/Cdr Knowles on the 3/4th October near the French coast saw in the moonlight a flak ship shoot down a Hudson in flames, which was strange. This could have only been a Coastal Command reconnaissance flight. The Ventura did not appear until Summer 1942. Knowles flew on to Tours which was obscured by 10/10ths cloud and the DZ further south was illuminated by an unusually large number of lights, by mutual consent the agents (SABOT/SPEED) parachuted blind a further 15km to the east.

That same night the longest Whitley sortie so far was to be flown by F/O Hockey. Since there is an operational report available it is worthy, for the sake of posterity, to quote this in full. It will give some idea exactly what went on:

SECRET

From: F/O Hockey, 138 Squadron, Newmarket.
To: Officer Commanding, 138 Squadron, Newmarket.
Date: 9th October 1941
Ref.: 138/S.12/air
Subject: Report on Operation PERCENTAGE
3/4th October 1941

Crew: F/O Hockey	Captain
P/O Wilkin	2nd Pilot
S/Ldr Cousens	Air Observer
F/Sgt Judson, DFM	W/Op
Sgt Hughes	R/Gunner
Major Sustr	Czechoslovakian Army Despatcher

Sir,

I have the honour to report on the above operation carried out on the night of 3rd October with the above crew,

The aircraft took off from Newmarket at 14.16 hrs. and course set for Tangmere; during this flight the automatic pilot became unserviceable due to compressor failure. Tangmere was reached at 16.02 hours, where the aircraft was refuelled to 1,100 gallons, and bombed up with four 50 lb G.P. bombs and one hundred and twenty 4 lb incendiaries. Total weight for take off was 33,964 lbs; C.G. position 92.7' aft of datum point.

The take off from Tangmere was delayed 25 minutes owing to the late arrival of Percentage (Corporal Frantisek Pavelka) and luggage. The aircraft finally took off at 1910 hours. The English Channel was crossed at Hastings –le Crotoy in order to miss the prohibited area Dieppe–Newhaven.

Le Crotoy was reached at 20.20 hours flying at 6,000 feet over 7/10. Visibility was poor owing to 8/10 altocumulus cloud above obscuring the moon.

Course was set for the Rhine at Stockstadt (49° 48'N, 8° 28'E) (approximately 12km south west of Darmstadt) Both layers of cloud persisted, and no actual pinpoint check was obtained. Course was altered on DR Stockstadt (i.e., when the navigator had calculated that the aircraft was over this position) at 22.38 over cloud for south of Prague.

The amount of medium cloud above prevented normal astro-navigational methods, but full use was made of loop bearings.

A few breaks occurred in the low cloud on this leg, but lack of topographical features and poor visibility beneath, rendered pinpointing inaccurate.

The Southern suburbs of Prague were reached at 00.35, where the low cloud commenced to disperse, but leaving a thick ground haze. We were engaged by the ground defences, no searchlights were observed, but desultory and inaccurate flak.

A little later five or six searchlights wandered around and picked us up momentarily.

The Elbe was picked up near Kolin where we encountered more anti-aircraft fire and a few searchlights; the flak was more accurate than that at Prague.

We flew down the Elbe at 3,500 feet, visibility being poor, about 3–4000 yards It was impossible to see the ground at all looking into the moon and only with difficulty directly below, owing to the thick haze.

Pardubice was reached at 01.03 at 2,000 feet, and course was set south for target area. The lighting system of the reception committee could not be identified, probably owing to the bad visibility; after sometime reconnoitring the country it was decided, in view of the late start, to carry out the operation, which was completed at 01.12 hours in an open field adjoining a wood. Major Sustr, who carried out the despatching, claimed to recognise the area as being within 2–3 miles of the target, and both he and the wireless operator reported both parachutes landed successfully within twenty yards.

Course was now set for Kolin, but cloud had formed and it was not possible to identify the bombing target from 3,000 feet, owing to the layer of cloud beneath. It was decided, owing to previous delays, not to waste time attempting to distinguish the target, but to release the bombs on the return journey.

Course was then set for Stockstadt over cloud. A railway line was noticed though a gap, and bombs were dropped on tail fuse 11 seconds delay from 4,000 feet at 02.00. Results could not be determined with exactitude owing to patches of cloud, but the rear gunner and navigator reported bursts and fires.

At 03.12 DR position Rhine, course was set for le Crotoy at 6,500 feet between two layers of cloud. On this return leg some flak and searchlight opposition was encountered of some accuracy. Medium flak bursts were noticed on the port side at 50 yards range.

Over England the weather had deteriorated and rain had commenced. It was decided to land at Tangmere and we homed over the aerodrome, which was circled at 06.10 at 600 feet. It could be pinpointed by means of a searchlight shining beneath a 9/10ths cloud layer.

Height was lost in a southerly direction, and cloud was broken at 200 feet over the sea. The aerodrome was reached by flying back beneath the cloud layer just above the tree-tops, when the funnel lights on the west side of Tangmere were sighted through the rain.

A landing was effected at 06.30 hours.

The weather conditions at this time were: continuous moderate rain, visibility 2,000 yards, cloud 9/10, 150–200 feet.

Signed: R C Hockey, F/O

The aircraft they flew for 11 hours 25 minutes (8 hrs. 30 mins. on instruments!) was Whitley Z9158, taking five minutes longer than

A selection of containers on show at the SOE Demonstration room, Natural History Museum during May/August 1945. (Imperial War Museum)

Keast's flight to Poland in January. This was the longest flight made by a Whitley.

Hockey added in his notes of the flight that it was the first successful drop in Czechoslovakia and opened up, for the first time, communications between Czechoslovakia and the UK. The target being on the ridge between the Elbe and its tributary about 80 miles east of Prague. The agent Frantisek Pavelka was arrested in Prague three weeks later. The crew were awarded the Czech War Cross for their effort.

A week later the first Czech Crews were posted in and captained by P/O Anderle and F/Sgt Jedoenek.

Riemer flew down to the Loire on the night 10/11th October and in the Angers area on the first run in dropped packages on a reception committee manned DZ. He then flew on to the Berthegon (Vienne) area (on the railway halfway between Chinon & Poitiers) and dropped an agent blind about 5km north-west of the pin-point. Double operations, servicing two DZ's, were now becoming a regular feature in the Squadron's activities. This particular sortie was INTERALLEE/ SUZANNE.

On the same night Hockey flew PEAR to France via Tangmere–Cabourg–Tours–Vierzon–Target. Dropped an agent in the Neuvy-sur-Barangeon (Cher) area, some 16km NE Vierzon, meeting with heavy flak at le Havre on the way home and landing after 8.30 hours in the air. Austin was down in the Toulouse area flying MAINMAST where there was no reception.

On the 13/14th October, Murphy flew down to the Toulouse area again in an endeavour to complete MAINMAST He reports that Tours was well lit up and that the lights of Toulouse went out street by street! However he successfully dropped two agents, Lt A Forman and wireless operator, to aid Labit's circuit FABULOUS. (Unfortunately he was arrested later in the year). Murphy says only one parachute was seen to open because there was no moon and the parachutes were camouflaged. Incredibly this was Forman's third operational drop his previous two being on the 15th March and 11th May 1941. Murphy reports on the way back Toulouse was blacked out.

This was the last operation for this moon period. The ORB, dated 13th October 1941, reported that 'operations from September to October, weather throughout this period was bad'. In spite of this the programme was completed and, except for one sortie, 13 were carried out.

On the 28th October F/Lt H J Oettle, DFC, the unit's first Whitley pilot, returned from convalescence. The very next day on a local flight, he stalled Whitley Z9225 near the ground on the landing approach. An accident similar to that which hospitalised him in April. He and two of his crew were killed.

This was the main gate and guard room at Tempsford before the chickens took over. There are now detached houses behind the site of the old guard room. The airfield reverted to Care and Maintenance in June 1947. Photo: L Dibin via S Tomlin.

CHAPTER FOUR

November–December 1941

Flight Lieutenant Hockey was now in charge of the long-range work as two Handley Page Halifaxes, plus one in reserve, were added to the establishment. A further three Whitleys were also added and delivered. A Halifax BII L9613 (NF-V) was the first to be sent to Ringway to be modified.

A Halifax could carry 15 containers as against the Whitley's 12. It also brought Warsaw within range. You could move freely about the fuselage, providing you ducked your head at the right moment and took care not to injure yourself when clambering over the mainspar, which straddled the fuselage. There were only two other Squadrons operating Halifaxes at this time, No.35 and No.76 and they could only muster 17 serviceable aircraft between them.

The pilot's notes says the normal fuel load of a Halifax BII was 1,636 gallons carried in ten self sealing wing tanks. Provision could also be made for three, 230 gallon, self sealing long range tanks carried in the fuselage bomb bays. Later aircraft also had an extra tank with a capacity of 125 gallons and, much later, long range tanks were carried inside the fuselage leaving the fuselage bomb bays free to carry stores. At zero boost, 2,000 rpm and 10,000 feet in weak mixture, fuel would be used at 148 gallons an hour. It took off at 100 mph, climbed at 150 mph, cruised at 160 mph and landed, engine assisted, at 100 mph. I never flew a Halifax as high as 10,000 feet on 138 Squadron and plus four boost at 200 mph comes to mind.

The Halifax Mk V, which was in Squadron service when I joined them, was a BII with a Dowty undercarriage system. It had few vices and four superior Merlin XX to those Merlin X's of the Whitley. She swung gently to port when you opened up the engines for take off and providing you caught her quickly by leading with the port throttles it was easily controlled.

F/Lt Hockey flew L9613 for the first time on November 30th, one week later, on the 7th December, flew it for 10 hours on a fuel consumption test. He was leaving nothing to chance!

In the meantime Bomber Command wanted Newmarket for their Bomber Operations.

On the 29th October S/Ldr Jackson and P/O Austin were ordered to Luqa, Malta, to assist supply dropping operations in Yugoslavia. They landed their Whitleys at Portreath in a gale and were further

delayed by appalling weather conditions over France. They finally left at 08.30 hours for Gibraltar on the 1st November landing at 16.30. Refuelled they took off at 22.00 and arrived at Luqa the following morning at 05.00 during an air raid. It had been a long day involving some 15 hours flying. On the 7th November a submarine and a flying boat brought in the equipment and a passenger. A night drop was considered far too dangerous. Nevertheless on the 9th it would appear that Austin made a night drop, operation BULLSEYE, in the Mitrovica area, of two containers onto three or four bonfires in the mountains. Bad weather prevented any further Yugoslavian operations and they were recalled on the 15th – a long way to go for such a dangerous and unrewarding effort.

On the night 31/1st November F/Lt Murphy flew operation EMILE/LOUISE, heavy snow making map reading impossible. Following the Marne with difficulty he dropped his agent 12km south west of his pinpoint in the Châlons-sur-Marne area. This must have created a problem for the agent as he had to land in terrible weather conditions without the aid of a reception committee .

The 1/2nd saw F/Sgt Reimer flying CHILBLAIN (an appropriate code name, almost mocking the weather!) to Esbjerg in Denmark without success. The weather conditions, low cloud and icing, dooming the operation to failure.

On the 6/7th S/Ldr Nesbitt-Dufort took a Lysander to France but in spite of orbiting for an hour could not see the landing lights clearly through the falling rain. He completed the sortie BRICK the following night in better weather conditions, landing, it is thought, at the disused airfield west of Compiègne again. He disembarked his passengers safely

L9613 NF-V, 138 Squadron's first Halifax (Nov. 1941–Jan. 1943) seen here at Fayid, Egypt, when ferrying urgent supplies in December 1942. Among its many operations it carried the Heydrich assassination team to Czechoslovakia in December 1941. Note the protective tailwheel fairings. L9613 was the oldest flying Halifax when it was written off at No. 1662 HCU in April 1944. (H Levy via K A Merrick)

The wreck of 138 Squadron Halifax L9612 seen here at Tomelilla, Sweden. When returning home on the 7/8 November 1941, after a successful operation in Poland, shortage of fuel caused the pilot, F/O T Jasinski, PAF, to make a forced landing. The Polish crew were interned and later returned to England. (T Olausson via K A Merrick)

and brought back two SIS agents, one of whom was Claude Lamirault (FITZROY) who had originally been dropped by Hockey in July 1941.

The 6/7th also saw F/Lt Murphy busy flying FIREFLY in a Whitley to France. The lights of Périgueux were seen reflecting in the sky. Two minutes later he made a successful drop.

*   *   *

A Polish crew posted in from No.301 Squadron and led by F/O Jasinski (from No.300 Squadron) with his second pilot Sgt Sobkowiak finished their Halifax conversion at Linton-on-Ouse and came to pick up their aircraft from Newmarket. On the 1st/2nd November[1] they took off from Linton for a flight to Poland carrying three agents, named by Ken Merrick as Bidzinski, Segiera and Lt J Piwnik (PONURY), the latter became one of the greatest Polish field commanders but was sadly killed in action on the 15th June 1944.

Near the Polish border the hydraulic fluid froze and the undercarriage lowered. East of Poznan they found the reception committee waiting and parachuted onto it the three agents, six containers and two packages. The lowered undercarriage and flaps would not retract due to the hydraulic problems, this coupled with a strong headwind found them over Denmark at 04.15 hours left with only 1½ hours of fuel. Under

---

[1] Other 'sources' give the date as 7th November but recent research confirm the date quoted in the text.

these circumstances they decided to turn back and head for Sweden.

They made a successful crash-landing at Tomelilla near Ystad where they were interned at Falum and later repatriated to England. W/Cdr Rudowski, acting as despatcher, was in command of the operation and the first to be repatriated in January 1942. F/O Krol, the navigator, returned to No.138 Squadron, joined a new pilot, Stanislaw Klosowski, and together flew 120 operations. Jasinski returned to No.300 Squadron and flew another operational tour with them.

Also on the 7/8th November F/Lt Murphy flew what was to be the last Dutch sortie (CATARRH) of the year. Crossing the coast 15km north of Ijmuiden, (which is almost a suburb of Amsterdam) at a height of 100 feet he flew on to Ommen, within that area he dropped two SOE agents, Thijs Taconis and his wireless operator Hubertus Lauwers. Again crossing the coast at a height of 100 feet, he spotted a German convoy of 20 large ships, and took avoiding action, he was not attacked.

This operation was to result in the biggest single SOE disaster of the war. Unbelievably the two agents were dressed alike in every detail, their identity cards bore the royal arms of the Netherlands with the two supporting lions facing the same way. Their protests at Newmarket were ignored and they were assured that nobody would take any notice of details like that. However this wasn't to be the operation's undoing. Briefly, Lauwers worked in The Hague and Taconis working in Arnhiem had unknowingly employed an informer in his circuit.

On the 6th March 1942 Lauwers was arrested, unfortunately with three ciphered texts in his pocket that he was about to transmit giving the Germans a clue to the code he was using. Lauwers decided to send the messages as the Abwehr instructed leaving out his personal security checks warning London he had been compromised and assuming that this would be noticed, London chose to ignore this warning. Lauwers continued to transmit and London continued to ignore his warnings. As a result all future and past operations to Holland were put in jeopardy. It is difficult to believe this wasn't negligence on the part of London – he had radioed this warning too many times. Taconis was arrested three days after Lauwers. These events were the start of the deadly deception, '*Der Englandspiel*'.

However, historians are pleased to relate the effects this had on the SOE ignoring the effect it would have on the many aircrews that were to fly future Dutch operations. Already Holland was the gateway to Germany and heavily defended against air attack now, in addition, future DZ's were to be manned by the Abwehr. Later, in the vicinity of some Abwehr controlled DZs, light flak was installed ready and waiting to shoot down any unsuspecting aircraft, after their load had been parachuted down. There had been little future for aircrew flying at low altitude in moonlight over Holland at the best of times now the effort and sacrifice would be in vain.

*   *   *

F/Sgt Reimer was busy from 6/7th November flying to France CUTLASS & FABULOUS parachuting a young man, L Yvon Morandat (CUTLASS), in the area of Lyon. Morandat later became one of de Gaulle's finest political agents. His second target is reported found 15 minutes after leaving Toulouse at 23.30. He had taken off at 18.30 and landed at 05.05.

The moon period finished on the 8th/9th with Reimer flying ARBORETUM & IRRADICATE to France. A short trip, one hour from the coast he found the first pinpoint and dropped one agent, the parachute was seen to open. At the second pin-point he found a reception committee and dropped a second agent. There is no reference in his report where this happened.

The Squadron was stood down when Farley, now promoted Wing Commander, arrived on the 17th November to take command, S/Ldr Jackson and W/Cdr Knowles being posted out. Jackson probably for removing the telephone wires on the main road from Newmarket to London with the wheels of his Whitley whilst taking off. An accident causing considerable military embarrassment. Knowles went to Command Jurby on the Isle of Man. He borrowed a Whitley, that had landed in transit for Belfast, and took some friends with him. He crashed on take-off and all were killed, among them a civilian woman, a tragic end to an officer who had flown so many of the early SD operations.

During this period there were a number of other personnel movements. P/O's Dobromirski and Zygmuntowicz, two Polish pilots, and a complete Polish crew to replace those who had landed in Sweden were posted-in, and two new Halifaxes, L9618 and L9613 were added to the inventory.

F/Sgt Reimer started the new moon period operations with a flight on the 26/27th November to France coded PLAICE. Reimer known for his brevity, reports that a parachute opened over a triangle of lights (no location). In view of a reception committee being in attendance this operation was very probably the dropping of Norman Hinton, a 28 year old Australian art student, the 'lone wolf mission' dropped late November.

On the 28th November the Lysander flight suffered a loss when, flying in bad visibility, F/Lt A J de V Laurent flew into some trees and crashed at Hungry Hill, Farnham, Surrey, unhappily he and LAC J A M Harkness, ground crew, were killed. Laurent, a Frenchman, was born 18/2/1910, joining the French Navy via *L'Ecole Navale* in October 1930. He went to sea on the cruiser *Jeanne d'Arc* in 1934, became a naval pilot in 1937 and a fighter pilot in 1940. He came to the UK via Gibraltar. The aeroplane T1771 was the long-range prototype Lysander III developed for SD work by the A&AEE at Boscombe Down.

The 30th/1st December saw P/O Gibson flying operation IRRADICATE 3 to France. He went via Chimay thence to the aerodrome at Tournes-Belval (Ardennes) west of Charleville where he searched for the lights of the reception committee which were absent. He returned home landing at Abingdon.

On December the 6th the Japanese attacked Pearl Harbour while, in Europe, the weather remained foul.

* * *

Two Whitley pilots, F/Lt Lockhart and F/Lt Murphy, volunteered to join the Lysander flight with Murphy flying his first pick-up, an SOE operation STOAT, on the 8/9th December. He flew to the airfield at Neufchâteau in Belgium where he circled but, when the ground signal came, he was convinced that those to be picked up were being pursued. He made an attempt to land but when he switched his landing light on he saw a dip in the ground ahead. Quickly putting on more power he avoided the dip but overshot and landed on the other side of the airfield. His two passengers had now come under German fire as they fled. Murphy was sitting on the ground with his engine running when he too came under rifle fire. The aircraft received some 30 or more hits but he managed to take off safely but sustained a wound in his neck. Fortunately, and in true RFC tradition, he was flying with one of his wife's stockings around his neck for luck – which in this case it was. He tightened it, staunching the flow of blood, and flew the aeroplane, not without difficulty, back to Tangmere.

The two agents waiting to be picked up were Captain Jean Cassart of the Belgium Air Force and Henri Verhaegen his wireless operator. In spite of Henri Verhaegen being wounded and both closely pursued they scrambled away. Captain Cassart was captured a few days later and taken to Berlin for trial. He escaped and eventually returned to

Westland Lysander T1771 lost at Hungry Hill, Farnham, Surrey on 28 November 1941, killing the pilot F/Lt A J de V Laurent, a Frenchman, and LAC J A M Harkness. T1771 was the prototype Lysander developed by A & A E E for Special Duty work. The ladder for the easy access of passengers was fitted to the port side of the aircraft. (Imperial War Museum)

England. This was to be the one and only Lysander pickup sortie outside of France.

That same night P/O Gibson was flying to France on operation COOL, 2 km west of Ménétréol-sur-Sauldre, 35km north of Bourges (Cher), and although the reception committee did not appear to be in place he parachuted blind a French army Subaltern, J Thomé, and Corporal-Major J Piet, his wireless operator.

The 8th/9th also saw another sortie flown to France by F/Sgt

The headstone of F/Sgt A W Reimer, RCAF, at Haverhill. He died two weeks after being shot down on the 28 December 1941. (via K A Merrick)

Reimer, operations CLAUDIUS & BERYL. The locations are not recorded but he reports that he did not find the first DZ and proceeded to the second where a waiting reception committee signalled him and he dropped an agent. He then returned to the first pinpoint where a second agent was dropped, his parachute was seen to open.

On the 12/13th P/O Anderle, one the first Czech pilots to join the squadron, flew his first sortie as a Whitley captain in Z8125. Although the weather was bad due to snow and low cloud, he found the reception committee waiting for him near Vannes (Nievre), where he dropped his containers.

The moon had now waned and during this stand down period the Squadron was again moved, returning to Stradishall. A proposed move to Graveley having been postponed, it was said, until February. No.138 Squadron appear to be treated as a tribe of wandering gypsies. Doubtless to soften the blow of their inconvenience the Whitley establishment was increased from eight to twelve aircraft.

On Christmas Eve two sorties were mounted to Belgium. Sgt Jones flying PERIWIG having reached Southampton was recalled to Stradishall due to the rapidly deteriorating weather. He landed at Abingdon. F/Sgt Reimer having left a half an hour earlier continued through the bad weather and was unable to find either of his two DZs MUSTICK & PERIWIG, both obscured by unbroken low cloud.

Two days later on the 27/28 F/O Wodzicki, PAF, (navigator captain) took off in Halifax L9613 (NF-V) from Leconfield with six agents and containers to drop in Poland. It would appear that this operation was unsuccessful since he was to go again to Poland, with the same manifest, early in the new year.

There were two other Whitley's (Ken Merrick says three, I cannot find the third one) out that night. In bad weather on his return F/Sgt A W Reimer, RCAF, over the airfield was shot down by an Me 110, Reimer's Whitley (Z9385) immediately caught fire and crashed on the airfield. Two of the crew the WOp/AG and the Rear Gunner baled out, three of them died in the crash and F/Sgt Reimer died two weeks later. It was a sad loss of an experienced pilot and crew, having joined the Squadron in August (a Canadian Casualty list says the aircraft crashed during an air battle over Stradishall).

The second Whitley flown by Sgt Jones went to Denmark in an attempt to drop the first SOE team into that country. It was an endeavour to complete CHILBLAIN, an earlier operation flown by F/Sgt Reimer at the beginning of November, which failed due to the weather. Sgt Jones was seeking a DZ near the small town of Haslev in Southern Zealand. Weather deteriorated when the Danish coast was reached and low cloud which obscured the moon made map reading at a height below 2,000 feet difficult. To complicate matters Jones was carrying a small bomb load which was destined for the electrical works at Vordingborg. With the target identified Jones made the first bombing run at 1,000 feet but, not satisfied, he made a second run when the bombs landed 150 yards from the target! The DZ was found shortly

S/Ldr R C Hockey sitting in the cockpit of Halifax L9613 showing his badge with the motto Tentando Superabimus – 'By striving we shall overcome'.
(via K A Merrick)

afterwards the agents Dr Carl Johan Bruhn and Morgens Hammer his wireless operator plus their package were dropped blind from 500 feet at Torpeskov near Haslev 65km south of Copenhagen. Although the rear gunner reported seeing three parachutes the despatcher discovered one of the static lines was missing. The missing static line had been attached to Bruhn's parachute and sadly he had plunged to his death. The package containing the radio was also lost but recovered by the local police. Another Danish agent was able to examine it and remove the crystals.

Jones encountered low fog, on his return, which prevented map reading and radio contact with base could not be made as his WOp/AG had been given the wrong radio beacon list. The aeroplane had adopted a nose up attitude and, even with the elevator trim in the fully forward position, it became difficult for both pilots to handle. Jones drained the fuel from the fuselage tanks to those in the wing and moved all the crew forward to the front of the aircraft. Oakington was contacted on the 'emergency radio' and a flare path was laid with which a difficult and dangerous landing was made. He returned to Stradishall the following afternoon but his subsequent report does not mention what caused the problem.

It was to be nearly four months before an attempt to parachute other agents into Denmark was attempted. Hammer was the sole SOE officer in Denmark until the spring of 1942.

The 28/29th December saw the last operations for the year 1941. W/Cdr Farley taking off Whitley Z6728 only to lose his airspeed indicator and his radio transmitter shortly after becoming airborne. He turned back over the airfield and jettisoned his containers. As he touched down on the landing run the port engine failed followed by the starboard engine. Not surprisingly, under these circumstances, without power in the port engine the pneumatic pump failed and he ran out of brake pressure.

The end of 1941 brought one of the most spectacular long range SOE operations of No.138 Squadron into being. The Czech government-in-exile had made an urgent request for an assassination team to be parachuted in for the destruction of SS General Reinhard Heydrich, at that time the brutal deputy head of Himmler's SS and 'Protector' of Bohemia and Moravia, who was engaged in the penetration and the virtual destruction of the intelligence service in Czechoslovakia. F/Lt Hockey was assigned the task of flying this team to Czechoslovakia on the night of the 28/29th December.

Hockey relates that weather forecasts for target areas as distant as this were always very chancy coupled with heavy snow at this time of the year. All agents to Czechoslovakia were dropped blind it being the responsibility of the pilot to visually assess the terrain and determine the wind force in the chosen area before parachuting any one in. Czech sorties were particularly difficult, they could only be carried out in the longer nights of winter and usually during the worst weather conditions.

> The terrain was unsuitable for parachuting from 4–500 feet, since the country is saucer-like surrounded by high mountains. During the winter, the country was usually snow covered – so breaking cloud down to operating height was particularly hazardous. Navigational facilities were nil other than basic instrumentation and the heavens whilst above the cloud (i.e., accurate instrument flying, DR and astro-navigation). followed by map reading from some identified pinpoint if snow storms permitted. The fuel situation was tight and did not permit much search time. Also there was always the possibility of stirring up night fighters with only one target.

Of the code names ANTHROPOID was the assassination squad of Heydrich, SILVER A and SILVER B were communication and training squads.

It was the practice at this time for the pilot of any SD operation to report it in the form of a letter. A standardised operational report form was to follow much later. Like operation PERCENTAGE that took place three months earlier there is a detailed operational report dated 6th January 1942. It bears relating in full:

Subject: Reports on Operations ANTHROPOID, SILVER A,
             SILVER B
             28.12.41

             Aircraft: Halifax NF-V. L9613

Crew: F/Lt Hockey Captain
        F/O Wilkin 2nd Pilot
        Sgt Holden Navigator
        F/Sgt Burke W/Op
        Sgt Bramley Front Gunner
        Sgt Hughes R/Gunner
        Sgt Berwick Flight Engineer
        Sgt Walton Despatcher

Sir,

I have the honour to submit the following report on the above operations:-

The aircraft took off from Tangmere at 22.00 hours with the above crew, all up weight 59,800 lbs. The take off run was 1,300–1,400 yards into a 10–15 mph easterly wind. Course was set for the French coast which was crossed at le Crotoy. Course was set for Darmstadt, and shortly after an enemy fighter was sighted astern on the port quarter. Two flares were dropped by this aircraft but no attempt to attack us was made; owing to the heavy loading and consequent lack of manoeuvrability, we did not take any punitive action. After some twenty minutes contact was lost.

Visibility was good and several pinpoints were obtained despite the snow covered ground. The amount of snow increased rapidly with easterly longitude, and although there was little low cloud, the Rhine was not easily seen. Darmstadt was reached at 00.42 hours and at this time another aircraft was seen, but was lost sight of shortly after. Course was set for target ANTHROPOID, and eventually pinpointing became impossible owing to the heavy snow, which completely blotted out all roads, railways, rivers and small towns. Some low cloud was now encountered which eventually became 10/10ths. Height was lost gradually until at 02.12 flak was seen ahead, and identified to be from Pilsen. Course was altered to the south of the town and then for the target area. By this time the moon (which was hidden in low cloud) had set, and visibility beneath the clouds had deteriorated to 4,000 yards. Operation ANTHROPOID was completed at 02.24.

From this position course was set for SILVER A target; the cloud which had been 10/10ths at 2,500–3,000 feet became lower and visibility

deteriorated to 1,000–2,000 yards with frequent fog patches. A few minutes before ETA for SILVER A, the aircraft flew into cloud at 1,000–1,500 feet , and as there was rising ground ahead, it was considered unsafe to break cloud over snow covered ground in bad visibility at a low height at night. The aircraft therefore turned on the reciprocal and SILVER A operation was carried out, it is considered within ten miles of the target, from a height of 800 feet.

Course was then set for SILVER B target, but bad visibility, low cloud and occasional snow prevented accurate identification of the landscape. The operation was completed at 02.46 hours, considered to be within 12 miles (of target).

Both the two latter operations were completed under difficult conditions owing to their urgent nature and according to instructions received before take-off.

Course was set for Darmstadt and height gradually regained to 10,000 feet. Flak was again encountered at Pilsen, and no other pinpoint was recognised until more flak was encountered at Brussels at 05.40 where course was changed to westward. Heavy and accurate flak was seen at Lille and also a considerable number of flashing lights, similar to those flashes on an electric railway system. These were noticed at nearly every town near the coast, but it was not considered to be flak, as no bursts were noticed.

The French coast was crossed near Fecamp at 07.20 hours, and shortly after the cockpit hood blew up and jammed. The second pilot held the hood to prevent it being jettisoned and fouling the controls, speed being

Corporal Vilem Gerik, reputed to have been the youngest of them all. He surrendered.

Karel Curda an ex-customs officer who turned informer and was executed after the war.

Czech Operations
A further Czech SOE Operation Zinc/Steel/Outdistance was to be flown on the 27/28th March 1942 by a Polish crew captained by F/O Wodzicki. Among those dropped were:

Sergeant Arnost Miks who was killed on the 30th April 1942.

reduced to 140 mph.

The English coast was crossed at 08.07 hours near Selsey Bill, and a landing effected at Tangmere at 08.19 hours

Most of the flight, except while completing the operations was carried out at an average height of 10,000 feet — the temperature being − 27 degrees centigrade. Oxygen was used to assist the crew in maintaining warmth, all of whom complained of the cold, especially after seven to eight hours, particularly in the nose compartment i.e. front gunner, navigator and wireless operator.

Signed: R C Hockey F/Lt.

The ANTHROPOID team consisted of two men Sgt. Jan Kubis and Sgt. Josef Gabcik, they were both orphans and well aware what their fate would be after the assassination attempt. One package was dropped with them. They landed somewhat off their target of Borek aerodrome and nearer to Prague than anticipated. The SILVER A were a three man team, Josef Valcik, Jiri Potuceka and led by Alfred Bartos they were dropped with two packages. Their mission was to attempt to re-establish communications with an important intelligence contact of the Abwehr and to form a reception committee for future air operations. Regrettably they all were to die. SILVER B consisting of, Vladimir Skacha and Jan Zemek who also dropped with two packages. Their objective was to deliver a transmitter and to arrange supply drops. The mission was abandoned since the equipment was lost.

With the addition of Major Sustr the Czech liaison officer who flew with this crew, although not mentioned in the report, meant there were initially 16 persons onboard.

Kubis and Gabcik were to take part in sabotage operations for nearly six months before the assassination attempt on 27th May 1942. As it is known, Heydrich was mortally wounded from the splinters of a hand grenade thrown at him by Kubis and died on the 5th June. A reward of a million gold Reichsmarks (£100,000) offered by the Germans for information leading to their arrest led a man named Karel Curda to betray them. Kubis and Gabcik killed themselves in a crypt of a church after a gunbattle with the SS. Curda, a modern Judas, was hung for treason after the war.

The German reprisals destroyed a number of resistance organisations based in Prague in addition to the horror of the levelling and decimation of the population and the villages of Lidice and Lezaky.

It is a sobering thought that had it not been for the skill of Hockey and his crew these events may never have happened.

CHAPTER FIVE

January–February–13th March 1942

The new year began with a notable operation on the 1/2nd January, the dropping of Jean Moulin together with two other companions. Moulin was a confident of General de Gaulle and possibly the only challenge to his leadership, later, in 1943, he was to become the President of *Le Consiel National de la Resistance* the most important resistance body within France. This was the third attempt to complete MAINMAST. The previous two took place in October 1941 P/O Austin returning on the 10/11th there being no reception, and F/Lt Murphy dropping two agents on the 13/14th, both in the Toulouse area.

This particular MAINMAST operation was entrusted to Sgt Jones who took his Whitley off from Stradishall at 16.20 hours and flew to St-Eval to refuel, taking off again at 20.45 hours. One hour later at the French coast he encountered heavy and accurate flak. A fighter reported seen by the second pilot was unconfirmed. At 22.00 he altered course for Limoges and reduced height from 9,000 to 2,000 feet. They were now flying above thin stratus, the ground barely visible. At 23.25 hours the cloud cleared and intense light flak was again encountered. A pinpoint being unobtainable they set course from their DR position les Sables-d'Olonne (the heavy flak probably came from St-Nazaire). They pinpointed on the Rhône and set course due south for the coast. At 02.10 hours a mountain range appeared ahead; by flying alongside the highest peak it was decided it was Mount Canigeu. Fifteen minutes later they were on the coast of Golfe du Lion and altered course for their intended pin-point on the Rhône, from here they map read their way to the target. There were no reception lights so the three men and their package were parachuted blind; the rear gunner observing four parachutes opening safely. The return home appeared uneventful landing at St-Eval at 08.45. Although their flying time was 11.57 hours, they had been awake for over 24 hours.

Professor M R D Foot says that Jean Moulin should have been dropped during the November moon and received on a DZ organised by Forman (dropped during the same month). He also says that the pilot claimed 'exact pinpoint located without difficulty' (this did not appear in the pilot's report) but Moulin and his companions said they landed 16km (ten miles) from it, in a marsh east of Arles.

It was a pity that Jean Moulin, of all people, should have been so inconvenienced. It should be remembered that the drop was made blind, had the reception committee been in place it would have been accurate. There is a possibility that the navigator was given the wrong map co-ordinates. We shall never know the answer, Sgt Jones and his crew were to die before the month ended.

Ken Merrick credits this flight to Sgt James but I can assure him that it was Sgt E E Jones.

Another notable operation took place the following night, the 2/3rd, when P/O Smith, his first operation as a Whitley captain flew CHEESE/FASTING to Norway. The target was on the southernmost tip of Norway in the Flekkeford area. Smith encountered trouble with his port airscrew soon after leaving the English coast at Cromer. He decided to continue and crossed the Norwegian coast 16km south of Flekkenford where there was 2/10th cloud and patches of mist. However the target area was clear and they dropped two agents and a package successfully from 2,000 feet. Three parachutes were seen to open, two were camouflaged and one white.

Norwegian targets could only be reached during the long winter nights and were particularly hazardous because of the distance flown over water. A ditching crew would not survive long in the freezing waters of the North Sea. One has also to admire the bravery of the Norwegian agents parachuting in these extreme temperatures and the reception committees receiving them on the ground.

On the 3rd of January two Squadron Whitleys Z9295 and Z9140 were lost. Apparently these two aircraft had been detached to Malta for SD operations over the Balkans and were destroyed by the Luftwaffe during an afternoon air raid on Luqa. There is no reference to this detachment in the ORB.

The 5th of January saw the repositioning of two Whitleys together with their passengers at Wick for W/Cdr Farley and Sgt Jones to fly ANVIL/LARK to Norway. This airfield was one of the most northern on mainland Scotland, the north west tip, and used to shorten the flight to Norway. However, the weather became so bad that the operation was abandoned and they returned to Stradishall. Later Kinloss and Lossiemouth became the starting points for Norwegian operations.

F/Lt Hockey flew a Whitley sortie with Sgt Wilde as his co-pilot on the 6/7th. The route they took was Base–Tangmere–Cabourg–Saumur–Target–Cabourg–St Eval. They were in the air 6.30 hours. Although recorded in Hockey's flying log book there is no record of this flight in the Squadron ORB and the operation cannot be identified.

Another long range operation took place the same night, SHIRT/JACKET to Poland – the deepest penetration of this country so far. F/O Wodzicki took his Halifax (L9613) crew to Lakenheath to commence this operation. Here they took on fuel, containers and six passengers. When he took off at 19.55 hours the total aircraft weight was 61,198 lbs, which was 1,198 lbs over the maximum all-up weight. They set course for Esbjerg and here at 00.25 altered course for the island of Bornholm. A further two hours flying took them into the target area near Minsk Mazowiecki about 22km east of Warsaw reaching it by 02.10 hours. Bad visibility caused them to circle for 40 minutes in search of the reception committee. At 02.55 hours no lights had appeared, they decided to parachute the six agents and their containers blind. These dropped into a forest, some landing in trees, and were met by a German patrol, two Poles and four Germans were killed. This resulted in arrests and reprisals among the population.

Wodzicki, on his way home, saw Warsaw at 03.15 and at 04.46 they crossed the Polish coast and two hours later the Danish coast north of Esbjerg. Short of fuel and unable to get a satisfactory QDM they crossed the Norfolk coast in daylight at 08.35. They landed five minutes later at Attlebridge, (ORB says Attleborough!) about eight miles (12km) north-west of Norwich. When opening the bomb doors they found one container had 'hung up'. I imagine Hockey was pleased to see his favourite L9613 back safe and sound!

*   *   *

On the 7th January P/O Anderle took off a Whitley for France at 23.37 hours on operation MOUSE/VERMILLION. At 01.18 he encountered a heavy storm and his air speed indicator began to behave erratically. When switching over to reserve tanks both engines cut out five times! To cap it all the W/T transmitter burnt out a valve and went U/S. He then abandoned the operation and turned for home landing at Tangmere at 03.15.

The last operation of this moon period was completed by P/O Smith taking Whitley Z9287 to France on the night of 10/11th. He had a multi-target mission in DACE/HORNBEAM & TENTERHOOK/TRIPOD 2. He crossed the Normandy coast at Point de la Percée south-east of Cherbourg and at 2,000 feet set course for the target area. There was thick mist up to 3,000 feet and the forward visibility was down to 500 yards. He could not identify the first target and then set course for the Loire and HORNBEAM where he identified the DZ but there were no lights. He decided to abandon the operation.

The new moon having already risen, on the 25/26th P/O Anderle flew to France in an attempt to clear up two abandoned operations DACE/HORNBEAM and for good measure was given CYPRUS to complete. The ORB says that DACE dropped 4km south of Mulsanne (Sarthe) and HORNBEAM/CYPRUS dropped south west of Verneil-le-Chetif 8km north of Vaas (Sarthe). Four parachutes were seen to open, these were both blind drops. Mulsanne, south of le Mans, was in close proximity of the Luftwaffe's airfield at Arnage.

Bad weather started to hamper operations once more. On the night 25th/26th Sgt White, was forced to abandon OVERCLOUD 2 over

France. This was the second time weather had interfered with the completion of this operation. The following night F/O W Smith flew operation TURNIP to Holland. In spite of being over the target area the agents refused to jump blind because of snow. They were returned to base.

The night of the 28th/29th January was another unhappy one for the Squadron. Severe weather, icing and engine trouble caused P/O Austin to abandon his Belgium operation BALACLAVA/CANTICLE /DUNCAN dropping only leaflets over Lens. On return to the UK his Whitley was diverted to Newmarket. P/O Anderle could not find his Belgium LUCKY SHOT/WEASEL target. Sgt Peterson had to abandon his BREADROLL/BALDRIC French SIS operation owing to snow over the target — he was unable to recognise any ground detail.

The only operational success came to Sgt Wilde who flew his Whitley to Mons in Picardy (the scene of many bloody battles in 1914/18). Where, in this area, operation PERIWIG/MARMOSET/MANFRIDAY/ INTERSECTION was completed when he successfully dropped three agents. What they experienced when they landed in the snow is not said. At the French coast he met with 'slight enemy opposition from the ground'. P/O Smith flying MOUSE/VERMILLION & WHITSUN (SIS) to France was abandoned because of icing and electrical disturbances.

This same night Sgt E E Jones had been assigned a double operation MUSJIDE & MADAMUS/MAJOR DOMO in Belgium and was nursing his crippled Whitley Z6728, now on one engine, back to base. He ditched it some 20 miles from the coast. The bodies of P/O D O Weeks the rear gunner and Sgt F W Smith the despatcher were believed to have been washed ashore in a dinghy on the Kent coast on the 10th February, it is said near Hawkinge. The remaining names of Sgt Jones's crew appear on Runnymead Memorial. There was also a W/Cdr J E D Benham on board, in spite of intensive research, I have been unable to find out what he was doing there.

The 28/29th also saw the last 138 Squadron Lysander operation BERYL take place. But for the skill of the pilot, S/Ldr J Nesbitt-Dufort, DSO, it could have ended in complete disaster. He landed in a field near Issoudun picking up two passengers. Returning he met with the severe frontal conditions that had harassed all the other nights operations. He attempted to fly through it and round it without success. His engine iced up and with fuel running short he decided to return to the landing field near Issoudun. Unable to reach it he forced landed in a field traversed by a road and a deep ditch into which the aircraft dropped finishing up on its nose. No one was hurt and Lysander T1508 was virtually undamaged, they abandoned the wreck and disappeared into the surrounding countryside. The aircraft was hit by a train and completely destroyed on a railway crossing when an attempt was made to tow it away. The Squadron, that would bring Nesbitt-Dufort back, had yet to be formed!

On the 29th January 1941 F/Lt Hockey was promoted to Squadron Leader.

*   *   *

On the 31st January OVERCLOUD II & III were flown to France, both successfully, P/O Simmonds dropping four containers on 'III' and Sgt Peterson adding four more ten hours later on 'II'. Bad weather hampered their return. Simmonds had an additional SIS target NUTMEG which he could not find and diverted to Steeple Morden on his return. Peterson on the other hand, in spite of thick fog, managed to scrape into Stradishall.

On the 13th February P/O Simmonds flew the SIS operation NUTMEG to France again. For the second time he failed to find his pinpoint and returned to base.

The following day, the 14th February, plans for Bomber Command to use 'Gee', a new radio navigational aid, were formulated.

In the meantime on the 15th February a new Squadron, No.161, was to be formed at Newmarket. Like its sister Squadron No.138 it too made a brief appearance during the first World War. Forming on the 1st June 1918 as a day bomber squadron and disbanding one month later on the 4th July 1918.

Considerable outside pressure must have been brought to bear for the formation of another Squadron for conducting clandestine operations within Bomber Command. The non-bombing activities of No.138 Squadron within the Command was still resented. The rôle of No.161 Squadron was initially to be solely for SIS parachute operations and all pick up operations.

Remembering that SIS/MI6 operations were considered solely for gathering intelligence, it was argued that there would not be sufficient SIS parachute operations to warrant the formation of a new Squadron. It was therefore agreed that they should share the burden of No.138 Squadron's SOE operations.

Wing Commander E H Fielden, MVO, AFC, was given command of No.161 Squadron. His previous command had been the King's Flight at Benson. He and W/Cdr Easton surveyed both Tempsford and Graveley from the ground and air seeking a base to house his new Squadron. His preference fell on Graveley, then a satellite to Tempsford. A problem presented itself due to the length of the southerly runways which were considered too short for the operation of Halifaxes, their eventual equipment. Difficulties were also foreseen in operating two like Squadrons from two different airfields. It was then decided that they would both operate from Tempsford. It is interesting to note that in August 1942 No.35 Squadron began bombing operations from Graveley using Halifax II's!

Thus No.138 Squadron passed their Lysanders to No.161 Squadron, a Hudson from Benson was added to the establishment. 'A' Flight consisted of five Lysanders (a number of them arriving smartly from No.41 group having first said that none were available!). 'B' Flight consisted of five Whitleys and a Wellington. No.138 Squadron also passed over a number of airmen, on the credit side 138 received two more Halifaxes.

On the 22nd February Air Marshal Sir Arthur Harris succeeded Air

Chief Marshal Sir Richard E C Pierse as C-in-C Bomber command. Harris during his previous appointment as Deputy Chief of Air Staff, had not shown much sympathy to the air requirements of SOE/SIS having suggested they use modified Handley Page Harrows. This great commander now with his foresight firmly blinkered on winning the war through bombing alone considered the SD Squadrons were pilfering his resources, consequently he either harassed or ignored them. Already they had had to struggle for every facility granted to them so far, Harris would undoubtedly make it even more difficult for them to make them progress. It was fortunate that SD operations had by this time expanded thus far.

Two days after the appointment of Harris, the DCAS held a meeting to discuss who should control SD Operations. Briefly it was agreed that the aircraft would depart and land under Bomber Command procedures but when and where they went would remain unspecified. As far as possible the two Squadrons were to have exclusive use of the airfields they were allocated. HQ Bomber Command was to give 'sympathetic consideration to any particular proposals submitted to the Station Commander for ensuring adequate facilities regarding buildings and security, etc.' (Ken Merrick).

On the 25th February S/Ldr Hockey completed his 24th operational flight taking P/O Wilkin in Halifax L9613 to Norway on operation CLAIRVOYANT. His 27th log book says the target was Kjosnes. The operation failed, bad weather obliterating the target. He recorded 10/10th cloud and freezing and that he was nine hours in the air.

The same night two Whitley sorties to Holland failed because of bad weather F/Lt Davies, flying CATARRH, and P/O Smith, flying CARROT. Smith's route was via Southwold–Vleiland–Zwolle where land details over the target area were obscured by low cloud.

On the 27/28th February P/O Simmonds completed operation CARROT & CATARRH. He crossed the Dutch coast north of Alkmaar in 10/10ths cloud. However the cloud cleared over the target area and an 'agent dropped (blind) in the centre of a clearing in a wood, successfully'. The agent was a South African, George Dessing who landed, it is said, on the roof of a hut in the middle of an SS camp at Ermelo. He eventually realised where he was, folded up his parachute and walked out of the camp saluting the sentries with '*Heil Hitler*'. The salute was returned and Dessing went on his way! Simmonds was able to drop two containers onto his second target. It is also said that one of these was carried away in a high wind and lost. Ridderhof, a Dutch informer, working with the reception committee handed the other container over to the Germans. On March 6th the reception committee who had arranged this drop were arrested.

Also this night F/Lt Murphy carried out the first 161 Squadron Lysander SIS operation BACCARAT. He took off from Tangmere and with difficulty and in bad weather found the lights of the reception committee and landed at St-Saëns (Seine-Maritime) – some 25km south east of Dieppe.

Also on the 27th S/Ldr Hockey, with P/O Wilkin, flew operation

BOOT to Poland. He returned after 9.20 hours. Ice on the wings, control surfaces and the propellers of his Halifax (L9613) created a severe problem. He landed back at Stradishall in a snow storm, 'all taxy-tracks were covered in frozen snow. I had the misfortune to run over one of the ground crew who went out of sight under the Halifax nose'. His brake pressure was low by that time and it was doubtful if he could have prevented the accident as Cpl V F White rolled instinctively outwards and under the wheel and was killed. Hockey did not notice the accident due to the rough state of the taxy track.

Operation COLLAR to Poland had been attempted on the 25th by F/Sgt Pieniszek in Halifax (L9618). Cloud over the target and along the route caused him to abandon it. He met with heavy flak at Kiel and two other (unreadable!) locations on their return. On the 27th he made a further attempt taking off at 18.50 and reaching the Danish coast at 21.15 where engine trouble caused him to turn back. This operation was again flown in the same aircraft this time by F/Sgt Harrison on the 3/4th March. He reports that the sea was frozen in the Baltic and that he dropped his load at 900 feet over the pinpoint. He had been in the air 10.58 hours when he landed. Although Polish records say this took place over the 'proper reception point' strangely, Harrison is not mentioned in operational records again.

*   *   *

On the 1st March No.161 Squadron moved from Newmarket to Graveley, F/Lt Murphy being promoted to Squadron Leader and given command of the Lysander flight.

Fortunately the weather for the next moon period improved and a busy month began.

During the night of 1/2nd March two pick up flights were started from Tangmere and completed. F/O Lockhart flew CREME, an SOE operation, collecting two passengers on his first pick-up flight. The other, S/Ldr Murphy borrowed an Anson from No.10 OTU Abingdon and painted the yellow aeroplane black. From Tangmere they flew operation BERYL II & III/BRICK setting course for and landing at Issoudun, a disused airfield about 27km miles due east of Châteauroux (Indre), Here they picked up three agents and S/Ldr Nesbitt-Dufort. When they landed back at Tangmere their airborne time was 5.40 hours. It was the first twin engined pick-up and the only one ever using an Anson. It was a courageous effort but they did not have sufficient courage to face the OTU's wrath when they returned that black aeroplane, parking it and leaving hurriedly. With such audacity it could now be said that No.161 Squadron were operational!

The following Whitley sorties were made by 138 Squadron on the 1/2nd March. Sgt Wilde flying following French operations PERIWIG & MASTIFF/ IMCOMPARABLE/CANTICLE/DUNCAN. Taking off at 18.18 and crossing the French coast north of the River Somme at 8,000 feet pinpointing Douai to descend to 400 feet over the dropping zone for PERIWIG. Here he circled for fifty minutes. No reception was seen so he moved onto MASTIFF/INCOMPARABLE where he successfully parachuted in two agents. He also had to deliver some pigeons on the same DZ since he says, 'pigeons for CANTICLE/DUNCAN became detached and one was left in the aircraft.' (At least that bird had a lift home). He then dumped his leaflets over Douai and returned to base, with very little enemy opposition, landing at 01.50.

Sgt Thompson flew COLLIE/TIGER/TERRIER to France crossing the coast near Abbeville. He successfully dropped three agents 'with pigeons' and returned home. F/Sgt Peterson flew BALACLAVA (which had failed on the 28th January due to engine trouble) crossing the French coast south of Abbeville at 5,000 feet then down to 2,500 feet to Sedan (Ardennes), and here finding his pinpoint between some woods. After circling for an hour he says one light became visible, this being carried by a man wearing it! Containers he says were successfully dropped in one salvo. He says nothing about the two agents he also dropped. S/Ldr Davies flew BREADROLL/BALDRIC, an SIS operation which due to bad weather had also failed on the 28th January. He crossed the French coast west of Somme went halfway to Douai losing height to 800 feet over pinpoint which was clearly visible, dropping two passengers. He had an early night, landing at 00.22 hours.

Finally, W/Cdr Farley flew MOUSE/VERMILLION (another abandoned operation from January). Crossing the coast at Caen at 8,500 feet and eventually pinpointing on the River Loire 6km east of Blois. One agent, one package and pigeons (they were a long way from home) were dropped successfully at a height of 5–600 feet, 16km SSE of the actual pinpoint. He landed at Tangmere.

On the 3/4th March ADJUDICATE flown to France by P/O Smith, at a height of 1,500 feet they identified their pinpoint by a wood (the place is unidentifiable due to bad handwriting). They searched for one hour, eventually finding the reception lights 22km to the south of their proper pinpoint probably as a result of having been given the wrong reception co-ordinates. Here at 600 feet they dropped their package and returned home. ADJUDICATE operations, of which there were a number, were supporting members of the Polish Army in France to undertake sabotage and to maintain an evacuation line to England. The organisation collapsed in August 1942 when the leadership was arrested.

Holland and operation TURNIP was the task of P/O Rymills. The pinpoint was covered in snow and the agents refused to jump for the second time, the last being the same operation flown by F/O Smith on the 26th January. They were lucky, the pigeons did not have any option and were dropped. I doubt if any of them survived in the cold on the ground. P/O Rymills returned home with his passengers.

Pigeons were dropped in a small parachute container, their heads just visible through the top of it. In a Halifax we would put the flaps down and flying as slow as we reasonably could, the despatcher would bale out these containers through the flare chute at the back of the aircraft. Also inside the container was a questionnaire to be filled in by the finder and a request to put it into a small capsule, attached to the pigeon's leg, then release the bird to fly home. Some excellent intelligence was gathered this way, in particular from Normandy where information of the German defences was sent. Also sent by pigeon post were obscene messages from the Germans! In our jaundiced opinion most of them ended up on the dining table!

There is a bland report from P/O Anderle, the Czech pilot, flying Whitley Z9158 on operation RUM on the night of 3/4th March. He states:

> . . . crossed French coast at 2,000 feet climbed to 6,500 feet in central France to cross mountains and descended to 600 feet. Aircraft pinpointed Agde (Herault) on the Mediterranean to Lake Thau (this was Bassin de Thau) then North to pinpoint. Dropped three men and two packages, all five parachutes were seen to open. Returned to base. Landed 0536.

What he didn't know was that he was parachuting three Russian NKVD agents, of a party of five that had arrived in Scotland on the 12th February 1942 via a Soviet Ship the *Arcos*. They were given parachute training at Ringway. There is a letter on file concerning the three agents for this operation from Lt Col R M Barry to Capt Wooler, saying, 'Those directly concerned should not be told there is a girl in the party' and went on to instruct 'not to speak French to her in the presence of those who are not aware of the fact that she is a passenger'. Her name was Anna Frolova, aged 25, her pseudonym was 'Annette Fauberge' and she was the first women agent to be dropped by parachute into France. The other two agents were Grigory Rodionov, aged 40, who went under the name of 'Georges Ribigot', and Ivan Danilov, age 31, using 'Pierre Daudin'. Their mission was to set up wireless communication between Lyon and Moscow. They had asked to be set down east of the River Hérault, north of the railway line from Paulhan to Montpellier.

F/Lt Outram this same night flew the last of the eight successful operations during the past two days. His task was BERET/BRAVERY/BOQUET, & PERIWIG to France. He crossed the French coast at Pnte du Haut-Banc south of le Touquet (and very close to a German airfield at Berck) flying at 4,000 feet. From here he pinpointed on the Oise Canal then to target dropping his three passengers for BERET/BRAVERY/ BOQUET from 600 feet. He then set course for PERIWIG, a Belgian operation, when immediately a triangle of lights was picked up, he dropped his six containers thus completing Sgt Wilde's operation of the 1st March.

About this time Air Marshal Bottomley visited Stradishall to discuss the question of a Polish flight being formed within 138 Squadron. Not the least of the problems of the formation of such a flight was the discontinuation of Polish operations after the March moon period until the autumn since there were insufficient hours of darkness needed to complete these long distant flights. For obvious reasons the duplication of the meagre maintenance resources by forming a Polish maintenance section was impossible. However it was agreed that where possible complete Polish crews would be used on Polish operations thereafter they would carry out tasks over any country. Three complete Polish crews were to be established within 138 Squadron.

Sgt White flying FRENSHAM I to France on the 8/9th had climbed to 4,000 feet as he crossed the English coast when his altimeter failed. He returned landing at Tangmere fully laden. He had been airborne for two hours.

The waning of the moon on the 10th March resulted in a disaster. S/Ldr Boris Romanoff, newly posted in as 'B' Flight Commander, was carrying out his first flight as captain in Whitley Z9125 and he had an all Czech crew. His operation, FRENSHAM I, was the same that had failed on the previous night. Having wished him luck Hockey watched him take-off from the control tower. He saw the tail light disappear below the tree level and then heard the awful thump. Rushing down the stairs, to his van, he drove to within a half mile of the burning aircraft and then ran across the ploughed fields to be first on the scene. When level with the port wing tip the flames must have reached the containers in the bomb bays and the aircraft blew up. Hockey says he must have been blown over backwards some 30-40 yards, his heavy greatcoat absorbing most of the splinters. The fire crew had now arrived and they managed to get the rear gunner out of his turret who's name Hockey thought was Vanicek (actually it was Vaverka). In a letter to Ken Merrick he writes not only was he deaf for days but 'rather magnetic' with bits of metal coming out of him. Although a rather frantic night he was in the air again on the 14th but not operationally until the 25th. This must have been a great personal loss to Hockey as his friendship with Romanoff dated back to their days with No.24 Squadron.

CHAPTER SIX

Tempsford 14th March– 8th April 1942

During the 'dark period' that followed, and a delay of two days, No.138 Squadron moved from Stradishall to Tempsford on the 14th March 1942. It was to be their home for another three years. Tempsford was built on a swamp and was reputed to be the foggiest and the boggiest airfield in Bomber Command. If your wheels wandered off the taxy-track they sunk up to their axles in mud.

Later Group Captain Hockey said when they moved in:

> Only the runways were showing through the water and when I inspected the aircrew accommodation most of it was under water as well, Nissen huts and so forth. So the first job I had to do even before we unbogged one of the aircraft was to billet all the aircrew out, 80 of them anyway, in the local village that same night.

One cannot help thinking that the allocation of Tempsford to the Special duty Squadrons must have pleased the C in C Bomber Command. Due to the state of the airfield it is probable that the first Tempsford operations' started from Tangmere – they certainly finished there, the Tempsford ORB at that time does not mention the state of the airfield.

Behind the scenes problems were being encountered in obtaining delivery of the aircraft that had been allocated to the two squadrons and the facilities for the training of crews to fly them. Harris had to be reminded by the Secretary of State for Air and the Chief of Air Staff (CAS) that claims of the two Squadrons had to be met, it could not have pleased him.

The next moon period operations commenced on the 23/24th March and was disastrous. Of the 17 operations mounted only four were completed, five if the operation to Holland on which an aircraft and crew were lost after they had completed their drop. The Squadron's luck seemed to run out at their new base.

P/O Smith appears to have been the first crew to commence operations at Tempsford, taking off at 19.00 hours on the 23/24th March 1942 for Belgium and LUCKY SHOT/WEASEL. The target

area was 32km west of Givet (Ardennes). Here they searched for one hour forty minutes. Nothing seen they returned home to Tangmere. S/Ldr Davies flew the same operation the next night, and arriving at the target area saw a triangle of lights that were immediately extinguished. He circled for an hour, they never came on again so he set course for home and landed at Tangmere

P/O Russell took-off at 19.01 hours. His was operation MINK in Belgium. He crossed the French coast near le Touquet at 7,000 feet and pinpointed a large wood north of Abbeville (which can clearly be identified on a map), then making for Douai (taking them very close to the two German airfields of Nuncq and Vitry-en-Artois) Having pinpointed Douai they set course for the dropping zone where they circled for 40 minutes over the target area before dropping their passenger from 600 feet. They returned home to Abingdon.

Ken Merrick says many of the agents destined for Belgium were dropped in France close to the Belgium border, completing their journey overland. Belgium was a difficult country in which to drop parachutes because of the density of its population and its split factions, some of whom were sympathetic to the Germans.

P/O Miller is reported to have taken off for operation FUERTY in France when exactor trouble in his port engine caused him to jettison his containers and land smartly back at Tangmere. An exactor was an airscrew pitch control system hydraulically linked to the airscrew governor unit. If I remember correctly after starting up the engine one had to prime the hydraulic system by lowering and raising the pitch control lever a number of times. It was one of those systems regarded with suspicion as it had been known to freeze. Fortunately most of the

RAF Tempsford facing north and taken on 13 October 1942. There was much work to be done. The main line from King's Cross to Edinburgh can be seen to the left.
(RAF Museum)

Whitleys I flew the pitch levers had direct airscrew control through a screw cable within a small tube, a system called Teleflex.

The completion of FUERTY was attempted the following night by P/O Kingsford-Smith, nephew of the famous Australian airman, flying his first sortie as captain. Finding Tours he set course for Vass (Sarthe), some 40km NW Tours, pinpointed the target area and circled for half an hour before returning to Tours. He then returned to Vass where he spent an hour over the target area. As there were no lights to be seen he returned to Tangmere.

The 24/25th saw another 'first captain' flight to Belgium, Sgt Owen flying PERIWIG II his flight was similar to that of P/O Russell on the previous night. His pinpoint was also Douai although he crossed the coast at le Crotoy. Circling the target area at 700 feet an observed light went out and they too returned home to Tangmere.

The following night Sgt Thompson flew an SIS operation BURR/BOQUET to France. Half way across the English Channel his port engine began to give trouble but he continued and crossed the coast at le Crotoy at 7,000 feet here he set course for Cambrai. Ground haze made pinpointing impossible. They abandoned the operation and returned home via the north of Dieppe.

On the 25/26th three Halifaxes operated for the first time on the same night. L9618 and L9613 to Czechoslovakia and L9976 to Austria. F/O Zygmuntowicz, a Polish pilot, took off first at 20.00 hours, flying his first sortie as captain to Austria, operation WHISKEY, an endeavour to despatch the two remaining Russian NKVD agents, from the Soviet Ship *Arcos*. These were Sevolod Troussevitch (Johann Traun) and Peter Staritsky (Peter Schulmburg). Crossing the enemy coast at le Touquet at 21.27 hours the weather was good until they reached south of Mannheim, from here to the target area the ground was covered in mist. Over the target area they searched for one hour and being unable to identify their pinpoint, abandoned the operation and returned home, landing at Tangmere at 06.00 hours.

S/Ldr Hockey took off at 20.15 hours for a Czech operation BIVOUAC/ZINC. A communications mission intended to supplement SILVER A flown by Hockey in December 1941. He cleared the French coast at 9000 feet at le Crotoy. The ORB says his last definite pinpoint was Worms in the heart of Germany north of Mannheim. Haze and fog prevented the operation being completed and they returned to Tangmere after 10.50 hours in the air. Hockey complains in a letter to Ken Merrick that he has no details of this trip, since coming to Tempsford the security had been tightened. No target, code words, or load details in log books. No marks on maps which had to be surrendered after every trip with navigation logs.

A second Czech trip was flown by F/Sgt Pieniszek, operation STEEL/IRON taking off at 20.25. This was yet another sortie attempting to establish communications between London & Prague and to drop a 'Eureka' beacon for 'Rebecca' homing. He too crossed the coast at le Crotoy and set course for Metz, (some 50km west of

Saarbrucken) thence to Pilsen where haze prevented them from identifying the pinpoint. After 25 minutes they moved on to seek another pinpoint but the haze and visibility became worse. Unable to identify the valleys and rivers they were flying over they abandoned the operation and landed back at base at 05.45

P/O Smith that night flew ADJUDICATE 3 to France, crossing the coast at Pointe de la Percée and set course for Limoges, pinpointing on the Loire after which he says 'he lost his course and flew over mountainous country to the east of his intended course flying at 8,000 feet'. He found Cahors (Lot) but not the reception committee so he decided to come home. Denmark and operation TABLETOP was F/Lt Outram's target. He found his way to Horsens Fjord (south of Arhus), then to his pinpoint where he circled for half an hour. There being no reception he returned home.

*   *   *

The night of the 26/27th at last saw some successfully completed operations. Although Sgt Wilde failed to complete the second attempt of PERIWIG II, abandoning the operation, because of haze, in the Douai area. P/O Kingsford-Smith had little difficulty finding the target for BOQUET(SIS)/BURR/BREACH/BROCK. Crossing the French coast at Berck (Pas-de-Calais), encountering haze he reduced height from 7000 feet to 2100 and set course for Cambrai. In this area dropped his four passengers and pigeons successfully, moving on to Arras where he dropped his leaflets. He landed at Tangmere.

P/O Russell flew an SIS operation, SHAKESPEARE to France crossing the coast at Fécamp, then flying over Paris in a thick haze and very lucky that he was not spotted from the ground. He later pinpointed Mâcon which had its street lights on, only to see them extinguished as they circled the town. Following the Rhône, in good visibility, they went to Lyon, which also had its street lights alight. In this area they found a triangle of lights with one flashing 'K'. Here they dropped their package accurately and then made for home dropping their pigeons 24km from the coast.

ADJUDICATE II/HARRY, the latter an SIS Operation, was partially completed by F/Lt Lewis dropping a package in the Limoges area, afterwards setting course for Périgueux to complete the second part of the operation. They could see the street lighting of Périgueux eight miles away. Although searching for 35 minutes at a height of 500 feet they did not see any reception lights and returned to base.

F/O Lockhart, on the 27/28th, flew a successful 161 Squadron Lysander SIS sortie BACCARAT II to Saumur. He stuck in the mud on landing for 17 minutes. The same night saw P/O Miller making a third attempt in a Whitley to complete LUCKY SHOT/WEASEL in Belgium, icing forced him to return. While F/O Wodzicki and his crew also took off on the 27/28th to fly Halifax L9818 on an 11.35 hour operation to Czechoslovakia for the SOE, ZINC/STEEL/OUTDISTANCE.

ZINC/STEEL was a communications mission comprising of three agents, Oldrich Pechal, Arnost Miks who eventually were killed and Vilem Gerik who surrendered. The purpose of OUTDISTANCE was to establish a 'Rebecca' guidance beacon (Eureka) for the RAF to bomb the Skoda works at Pilsen. Two of the agents, Ivan Kolarik and Adolf Opalka subsequently died and the third, Karel Curda, surrendered and became a Gestapo informer betraying his fellow countrymen after the Heydrich assassination.

Crossing the French coast at 11,000 feet, over Northern France they experienced 10/10ths cloud and severe icing at Metz. Here bad report writing loses them until over the target area with mist in the valleys. 16 to 24km north of Pilsen they parachuted six agents and four parcels in open country near a wood. On the return journey they encountered flak south of Mannheim and at Calais, when flying at 5,000 feet, they met with intensive and accurate flak.

Sgt Wilde flew a Whitley to Belgium PERIWIG II. Entering 10/10ths cloud at 4,000 feet at the coast, he climbed to 8000 feet where he met with icing. Descending to 700 feet where the cloud was 3/10ths but with haze below, he saw the lights of two airfields (probably Arras and Douai). One hostile aircraft was also seen. He circled each airfield at about 300 feet, really asking for trouble. He then abandoned the operation and came home.

F/O Zygmuntowicz flew Halifax V9976 on operation BOOT to Poland. In good visibility they map read their way to the pinpoint, the reception was seen on their arrival. The operation was carried out successfully and they returned by the same route, landing at Leconfield. (There are no other details of what they did and where.)

This was the night (27/28th) Tempsford was to suffer its first loss. F/Sgt J Thompson (the flight operations book states that P/O S Widdup was the second pilot) crashed Whitley T4166 into the sea at Den Holder when returning from operation WATERCRESS/ CATARRH. Den Holder is just south of Texel, an island well known among RAF bomber crews for its lethal concentration of anti-aircraft guns. Watched from the ground by the Germans he dropped his agent Lt A A Baatsen near Steenwijk in the north of Holland, some 30km north of Zwolle. Baatsen was captured and handcuffed as soon as he landed. He suffered two and a half years of interrogation before being executed in Mauthausen concentration camp. The site of the DZ, in the moorlands north of Steenwijk, was suggested by the Germans and approved by London. Once again Lauwers tried to warn London in his W/T transmission but was ignored. Baatsen was the first SOE agent to fall into the trap

CATARRH, the second half of this mission, was a supply drop. An operation last flown by F/Lt Murphy in November 1941 where the severe consequences of the operation, previously reported on page 28, seriously marred all future Dutch SOE sorties. However this is the first example, of an agent arrested immediately, plus an aircraft with all the crew lost. Among those lost was Sgt W C Evans, a fabric worker, a volunteer acting as despatcher, there was not yet an official aircrew category for this job. The Germans sent a field report by wireless confirming that the mission had been successfully accomplished.

The following night the 28/29th three of the five sorties mounted went to Holland. S/Ldr Outram flying an SIS sortie NASH identified Leewarden on his port side, followed the railway line south to his pinpoint, there parachuting one passenger and a container and returned home. Strangely the Germans were unaware that the SIS and SOE in Holland were operating independently to each other.

P/O Russell flew TURNIP/LEEK, to Holland his Whitley leaving the English coast at Cromer and finding himself over Texel Island, he went down to the Zuiderzee, pinpointing Oosterdijk. Thence to Elberg and Deventer where they map read their way to the TURNIP dropping zone, where he dropped his passengers. He then proceeded due south to the dropping zone of LEEK, where the agent considered the neighbourhood of the DZ to be too populated and refused to jump. He was brought back, landing at 02.53 hours.

P/O Kingsford-Smith was the third flying to Holland that night flying operation LETTUCE, taking a similar route to Russell. He too found himself in the Deventer area and map read his way to the DZ. Kingsford-Smith landed at base at 02.04 hours.

Both these operations mention Deventer from where they map read to the target area. Holten is roughly 16km to the east. I believe TURNIP to be the drop reported in the Holten area of Hendrik Jordaan and Gerard Ras and LETTUCE to be the drop of L Andringa and Jan Molenaar. Molenaar was mortally wounded when he landed fracturing his skull on a concrete watering trough, Andringa administering a cyanide pill to him. The body of Molenaar was found in the Holden area by the German Field Police. Jordaan and Ras were said to have been the first team to land. Both teams had been received by a genuine Resistance group and the Germans were unaware of their existence. Russell took-off at 19.30 hours Kingsford-Smith at 20.28 hours.

Two operations to Norway were completed this same night. The Whitleys commencing their flights for the first time from Kinloss. F/Lt Davies took off first at 19.53 for operation CHAIN making landfall at Raege Fjord, following the coast round to Jumsfauland Island then to Lyr Fjord and target. (I am unable to locate any of these on a map) About 8km south east of the pinpoint they saw a stationary car parked off the road with its headlights on and a dim orange light in some bushes. While Davies circled, the driver of the car flashed a torch repeatedly and took the car out on to a track and turned it several times. When satisfied this was the DZ Davies dropped their four containers and headed for home. They had been in the air 10 hours when they landed.

P/O Smith flew operation GROUSE, taking off at 20.13 hours and making a landfall between Sole(?) and Stavanger then to Areks Fjord(?) and straight to the pinpoint. The agent refused to jump! He was finally induced to jump some 3-6km south west of pinpoint. ('in the icy waste, Hardanger Vidda' – reports Cookridge). They landed at Acklington after more than eight hours in the air.

GROUSE was the code name for operations connected with the destruction of the Norsk Hydro plant near Vemork producing 'heavy water' used in the research for atomic energy. The agent dropped was Einar Skinnarland an engineer who had worked on the building of the plant. He had been taken to Aberdeen by a highjacked steamer *Galtesund*, discussed plans for the destruction of the plant, had eleven days training including parachuting and was dropped by P/O Smith and his crew. He reported back to work in less than three weeks explaining his absence through illness!

The next night P/O Rymills made the 5th Attempt at LUCKY SHOT/WEASEL in Belgium. After identifying the pin-point there being no reception he came home and landed at Boscombe Down having jettisoned his containers. P/O Miller also in Belgium for operation PERIWIG 2 had a similar experience but wandered off course on the way home into the flak and searchlight zone of Termonde north of the River Schelde. He landed at Tangmere.

The night of the 30/31st saw two successful Halifax flights to Poland flown by F/O Zygmuntowicz (LEGGING) and F/Sgt Pieniszek (BELT) both were in the air 11.45 hours. Once again I have found it difficult to decipher the writing of the recording officer and am unable to locate the towns en route on my maps. Zygmuntowicz crossed the enemy coast at Manda(?) pinpointed Heriady(?) and map read his way to the target which he found without difficulty. Here he dropped six agents, four containers and two packages. He returned via Esbjerg (Denmark) and landed at Langham.

On the other hand Pieniszek flew via Denmark north of Esbjerg and crossed the German coast at Kolburg(?) arriving in the target area without any problems and dropped six agents from a height of 1200 feet above ground. He returned via Stettin.

*   *   *

The first No.161 Squadron Whitley operational sortie was a French SIS operation MACKEREL flown on the 1/2nd April by Sgt Peterson, a former 138 Squadron pilot. The ORB report is short and to the point. One agent dropped from 500 feet, two circuits one package and two more passengers dropped. The same night S/Ldr Murphy flew a Lysander SIS operation EASTER landing near to les Andelys (Eure) south of Rouen, then in occupied France.

There were two other French operations this night, flown by 138 Squadron. P/O Miller flying FUERTY to the area of Tours where he searched one hour for the lights of the reception committee, which he failed to find and came home. This was the second attempt to complete this operation first flown on the 23rd March. SYCAMORE & AJUDICATE 2 were the targets for S/Ldr Davies, the former he completed successfully, parachuting in Phillipe de Vomecourt (after a spell in the UK) south of Limoges. AJUDICATE 2 failed, cloud over the target area at Périgueux (Dordogne) being almost down to ground level.

P/O Russell flew to Belgium on the night of the 2/3rd April on Operation MADAMUS. Crossing the coast at Pointe du Haut-Banc (Berck) they flew to Soissons, following the River Aisne in an easterly direction, they failed to identify their landmark. They continued to search at a height of 1500 feet for sometime but failed to see a reception and finally set course for home making a landfall at the Needles.

Kingsford-Smith meantime was flying a supply drop for operation BALACLAVA to France. He too flew to Soissons but at a height of between 2,000 to 3,000 feet. He reports:

> Maps used to pinpoint all land features being visible especially the double head of the Meuse south of Mouzon (Ardennes) and the line of the forest edge and gaps in the forest near St-Léger (a village some 30km due west of Luxembourg).

They also reported seeing a train proceeding north (what a wonderful sight – a steam engine in the moonlight!). Without difficulty they found their DZ where a flashing light was extinguished when they dropped six containers.

The night of the 5th/6th saw four Whitleys off to Belgium. Kingsford-Smith was given the fifth attempt to complete LUCKY SHOT/WEASEL. Reporting visibility down to zero in target area P/O Smith endeavouring to complete MADAMUS reported map reading impossible owing to the intense darkness, searching without success for 10 hours. P/O Miller flying PERIWIG a fourth attempt to complete, reported visibility down to zero over target. P/O Russell flying MANFRIDAY reported, by radio to base, of trouble to his port engine when he was 8km south west of Arras. His rear gunner then sighting an enemy aircraft, which Russell attempted to evade by flying through the cloud tops. Unable to maintain height he was forced to jettisoned his containers, finally making a safe landing at Abingdon.

While this was going on F/Lt Outram was flying the second attempt to complete operation LEEK over Holland. Crossing the coast north of Alkmaar he pinpointed Enkhuizen; from there flying straight to Harderwijk which he recognised and circled at 700 feet for ten minutes to make sure of his pinpoint before parachuting his two passengers, Barend Kloos (LEEK) and Hendrik Sebes (HECK). Outram returned home via Callantsoog (south of Den Helder) on the Dutch coast. Kloos and Sebes were parachuted into safe hands but later betrayed to the Gestapo, the former on the 28th April the latter on the 9th May.

On the 8th April 1942 No.161 Squadron left Graveley, and moved to Tempsford, here it was to stay until Special Duties were no more.

*   *   *

The bonding of the two Squadrons with Tempsford came at a time when the corner stones of SOE/SIS operations had been firmly laid, and basic procedures had been established. The call alerting reception committees to receive a drop at their particular site was broadcast by the BBC's overseas programmes in the form of a 'personal message'. For example the personal message for Alec Rabinovitch (Arnaud) a wireless operator working with Peter Churchill and Odette was *Le carabe d'or fait sa toilette de printemps* (the golden beetle is performing its spring toilette!). This sentence repeated two or three times would alert the team concerned to go out into the curfewed night. Regardless of the weather they would lay out the reception lights in moonlit fields or glades and wait.

The arrival of an aeroplane spewing parachutes lowering to the ground either agents, containers or packages, meant chasing after them, recovering them, disposing and hiding them (and perhaps spiriting away an agent). Each container loaded with arms and ammunition needed four men to carry it (A Halifax carried 15, a Whitley 12 and a Stirling 18). Then finally clearing the site, disposing of the parachutes and debris, to make ready for the next drop, or perhaps the reception for a landing Lysander or Hudson. It was a tremendous task which had the admiration of all aircrew engaged in these activities.

The operational briefing of aircrews was unlike that for other Bomber Command units. There was a crowded room, I remember it well, but we were there only for weather and signals briefing. There was no dramatic unveiling of the target with the route marked out in red tape. A cuss or two about the weather perhaps, but no gut feeling about where you were going, no German city at the end of the tape. A rough idea how long you would be away from base could be obtained by taking a sneak look in the afternoon with your flight engineer at the night's fuel states chalked on a black board in the flight office. (not encouraged!)

Weather briefing over, the pilot, navigator, bomb aimer and wireless operator were taken to one side for the specific target briefing given by an intelligence officer. Map co-ordinates of the DZ and the identification letter of the red light that would flash in morse at the head of the white reception lights. Sometimes we were told if Bomber Command were operating in the vicinity of our DZ. (Once turning at Trappes, just SW Paris, and flying at 500 feet, Target Markers dropped beside us onto the railway yards. It was alarming and totally unexpected.)

The navigator, pilot and bomb aimer would then decide the route we would fly, using the benefit of previous experience and plotting our way carefully between known flak areas. We were left entirely to our own designs. The despatcher would depart to Gibraltar Farm for special instructions if an agent was carried. A crew bus would take us to our aircraft and we would take off at our allocated time.

A week before the beginning of the moon period the Lysander pilots and ground crews of 161 Squadron proceeded to Tangmere on detachment, where the pilots slept in a small cottage and dined in the officers mess. The ground crews were accommodated in the main camp. This must have developed a tremendous Squadron spirit and probably, the added benefit of discussing their operational experiences. In my time Halifax crews were not allowed, it was said for security reasons, to discuss operational details among themselves, which was a pity since I am sure we could have learnt a lot from each other.

*   *   *

Two nearby airfields played an important part in the activities of Tempsford. Henlow some 10 miles (16km) to the south in the then heart of the brick building industry. The tall brick chimneys of the London Brick Company dominated the area in those days looking like a petrified forest, (and causing a fatal accident in 1943 to a 138 Squadron Halifax). RAF Henlow dated from the First World War and was the home of No.13 Maintenance Unit responsible for parachute trials. Here, presumably under the cloak of parachute trials, we used it for training, dropping containers on lights as would be seen on operational DZs.

Somersham some 20 miles to the north east of Tempsford was a small grass airfield, at one time a 'Q' site for nearby RAF Wyton. This would be used by Lysanders and Hudsons to practise circuits and landings and as a landing field at the end of cross-country flights, using the flarepath layout the pilots would see in France. I wonder if anyone ever became bogged down on it?

Ken Merrick reports at length the struggle that was going on with Harris at this time. Harris stating, for example, that the number of operational hours flown each month by No.138 Squadron could easily be doubled with the amount of resources they had. Emphasising that there was no need for the formation of No.161 Squadron and he was going to write an official letter to propose that the two squadrons be disbanded and their work be carried out by ordinary bomber squadrons. Ken Merrick goes into this very comprehensively in his book. Regrettably I have over simplified what was actually written. I am surprised, with the arguments that Harris used, the disbanding of the two squadrons did not come about.

However, It is difficult to see how 138 Squadron could have doubled their operational hours. Likewise it is doubtful if any bomber squadron pilot flew six operational sorties in April 1942 as did three 138 Squadron pilots, (two flew five), more so bearing in mind the short period it takes for the moon to rise and to wane.

CHAPTER SEVEN

9th April–31st May 1942

With the moon on the wane the 8/9th April saw F/Sgt Pieniszek taking Halifax L9618 to Poland on operation CRAVAT. They crossed the Danish coast after 02.39 hours flying, at Malmo in Sweden a cone of six to seven searchlights looked for them without success. Setting course at 10,000 feet for Kolberg 10/10ths cloud prevented them from pinpointing their position over the German coast. Reducing height to 3,000 feet at the River Vistula a pinpoint at Plock was obtained (some 80km north west of Warsaw). They reported that a PoW camp was easily recognised as were the lights of the reception where they dropped six passengers from 1,000 feet. The lights were extinguished before the four containers could be released and were brought home. On the return flight at 02.55 hours they ran into heavy and accurate flak whilst flying at 12,000 feet at Stettin, engaging them, they said, for eight minutes. At 05.15 hours the west Danish coast was crossed. It must have been daylight when they landed at 07.47.

One hour twenty minutes after Pieniszek took off P/O Anderle got Halifax L9613 airborne for Austria in an attempt to complete operation WHISKEY, which had failed on the 25th of March. His instructions were to drop the two NKVD agents Troussevitch and Staritsky at a pinpoint 15° 52′ 30″E, 48° 06′ 00″N or alternatively, if the pinpoint was not located, in a valley between Linz and Vienna. Flying at 10,000 feet he encountered heavy cloud and icing. He recognised Mannheim in the north and near Karlsruhe met with two searchlights and flak. However icing and cloud prevented him from finding the pinpoint and he returned south of Mannheim, and unknowingly flew over Paris. Channel conditions were very bad before he landed at Tangmere at 04.40 hours. The Russian agents had now spent over 18 hours in the air!

There followed three Whitley sorties to Denmark on the 12/13th, 15/16th and the 16/17th April in an attempt to complete TABLETOP, first failing when F/Lt Outram flew it on the 25/26th March. On the 12/13th S/Ldr Davies encountered fog 30km into Denmark and returned. On the 15/16th Sgt Wilde's attempt ended with exactor trouble immediately after take-off, he landed within an hour.

However, on the 16/17th F/O Smith crossed the Danish coast north of Nissum and map read his way across country to the target area. He circled and observed some reception lights, although not in the expected position. He dropped his three passengers and two packages, the rear

P/O S Smith together with his ground and aircrew in front of Whitley Z9287 NF-K Fourth from the left; Sgt Owen (2nd pilot), P/O McFadden (Nav.), P/O S Smith, Sgt Oldham (WOp/AG), F/Sgt Brinton (A/G). On the 16/17 April 1942 this crew carried, in this aircraft, Rottboll Johannesen and Mikkeisen who parachuted into TABLETOP in Denmark. Sgt Owen was to lose his life with his own crew on 25/26 July 1942. (R Wilkin via K A Merrick)

gunner reporting all five parachutes were seen to open. They returned home via Horsens Fjord. Landing at base after 8.15 hours in the air.

They had parachuted into a field near Aggersvold, Lt Christian Rottbøll, who landed safely, but Paul Johannesen and Max Mikkelsen landed in some trees some 3km from the DZ and were injured. The reception committee were unable to find them, in spite of this, they got safely away to Copenhagen. In September Johannesen died by taking his cyanide pill and Rottbøll died from 12 gunshot wounds. It was thought they were betrayed.

The night of the 18/19th April saw F/O Zgmuntowicz flying a Halifax to Norway on operation RAVEN A/RAVEN B. They crossed the Norwegian coast at Stavanger map reading their way to the target area but were confused by the numerous lakes and could not identify the DZ. Returning home they recognised Lagne Fjord and map read their way back to the target area. When certain the aircraft was within the area limits allowed they dropped four passengers, six containers and six packages. They returned to Lossiemouth.

The same crew were out on the 20th/21st to fly operation WHISKEY to Austria, albeit so soon after their 8.40 hour flight to Norway. This was the third attempt after 18 flying hours to deliver the NKVD agents Troussevitch and Staritsky. S/Ldr Hockey had been briefed to fly this operation but delays had caused him to be absent on the day it was finally arranged. Hockey arrived back at camp just before the operation's departure to find W/Cdr W R Farley, DFC, had elected and insisted that he took Hockey's place. Halifax V9976 used on their previous operation to Norway, struck a hill in dense fog at Kreuth south of Tengernsee roughly 48km south of Munich. Map spot heights in this area vary between 942 to 1,863 metres. There were no survivors.

The use of RAF aircraft for parachuting NKVD agents, as in operations RUM and WHISKEY was the result of an agreement reached between the British and Russian governments.

This same night, the 20/21st April, three Whitleys of 138 Squadron were out dropping leaflets over France. Sgt Wilde abandoned his flight when near Bourges when the exactor control on one of his airscrews froze solid. He had a long and difficult flight back to Boscombe Down through 10/10th cloud. P/O Russell reached his target Toulouse and took 25 minutes flying around dropping his load. On the way home he was shot at by two 'friendly' trawlers, it was said, near Whitby, (this must be wrong Whitby is N Yorkshire!) fortunately they missed.

P/O I A Miller was less fortunate. Returning in Whitley Z9158 from the St-Étienne area he found Tangmere covered with a heavy mist. He was diverted to Boscombe Down, on the way struck high ground at the experimental ranges at Porton, Wiltshire. With the exception of the rear gunner all were killed.

*   *   *

It had been suggested at an Air Defence Committee meeting on the 18th March that Bomber Command leaflet operations which Harris so abhorred should be undertaken by the two SD squadrons unless they were otherwise engaged. Merrick reports that 170 packages of leaflets were delivered to Tempsford for dropping as soon as possible, to be distributed evenly over eleven towns in the south of France. In an attempt to appease Harris four men and an aircraft were lost.

Shortly after the loss of Farley, S/Ldr R C Hockey was promoted Wing Commander and given command of No.138 Squadron, at the same time Outram was promoted Squadron Leader and given command of the Halifax Flight.

There followed on the 23/24th two operations to France on ADJUDICATE targets '2' and '3'. S/Ldr Davies dropping three containers on the former and P/O Smith returning from the latter without success, there being no reception.

P/O Russell was to fly operation CATARRH 3 to Holland on the 24/25th. He crossed the English coast at Southwold and went north to Harlingen where crossing the Dutch coast he followed the coast down to Hindeloopen and the target area. He sighted a triangle of lights but being situated in a wood he was unable to keep them in view for his run up. It took him a further 45 minutes before he found them again and successfully dropped his six containers and six packages.

Unbeknown to him, Russell and his crew were the focal point of a bizarre and deadly experiment. *Oberstleutnant* H J Giskes (a brilliant officer of the 'old school') Chief of Abwehr III/F counter espionage in Holland and Belgium had guarded this German operated DZ with three mobile 3.7cm flak batteries borrowed from the Luftwaffe at Leeuwarden. Not sure of the success of the radio game Giskes had been playing with his captive Dutch radio operator Lauwers and London, the guns had instructions to open fire if the aircraft dropped bombs. As it was, Russell's parachuted supplies fell directly into German hands, his aircraft being tracked in the moonlight by the gunsights of the German 3.7's. Russell unharmed by the ambush returned home safely via Enkhuizen north of Alkmaar.

Merrick reports that later Giskes, in charge of these operations, allowed some of the dropping aircraft to be shot down after leaving the DZ. It will be interesting to see as we progress what losses in men and aeroplanes this involved.

The same night Sgt Wilde went to Belgium for the second time to complete operation PERIWIG II, first attempted on Christmas Eve 1941. It failed again. as it did when S/Ldr Davies made a further attempt on 25/26th. Although Davies said he was unable to pin-point there is little doubt there was no one to receive him. Sgt Owen also flew to Belgium on operation LAMB/MULE/SABLE/RETRIEVER bad visibility prevented him from finding his pinpoint. Likewise Outram flying DASTARD to France. Another failure the following night was P/O Smith making the seventh attempt to complete SPANIEL/WEASEL bad visibility prevented him from pinpointing.

It had now been three weeks since No.161 Squadron began operations. On the 24/25th April they flew three sorties. Peterson flying a French SOE operation NELSON but tells us little in his report other than he went south east of Ardentes (roughly 10km south west of Châteauroux) and that poor visibility prevented him from dropping his passenger and package. The same night S/Ldr Gunn flew an SIS operation WHITSUN & BRIMSTONE to France. He tells us in good visibility he dropped a package for BRIMSTONE (no location is mentioned) and then set course for la Roche-Guyon on the bend on the River Seine (some 15km east of Vernon, north west of Paris). He was picked up by searchlights two white one blue. There was no reception committee at WHITSUN so he came home.

F/Lt Lockhart also flew an SIS operation APOSTLE 3/GAZELLE in a Lysander on the 24/25th. Bad weather prevented him from completing it. The next night Lockhart flew JELLYFISH/GAZELLE. When landing near Châteauroux his engine caught fire but when switching it off the flames went out. Fortunately when he restarted the engine the flames remained out! He delivered two passengers and picked one up.

P/O Anderle started an interesting operation on the 25/26th taking Halifax L9613 to Czechoslovakia on operation BIVOUAC/BIOSCOPE. Airborne at 20.55 hours he crossed the French coast at Abbeville, his next recorded pinpoint was the Rhine. He was now over cloud and says he overshot Pilsen by ten minutes. After turning eastwards saw flak a few miles to the north at 01.40 hours. Low cloud made it impossible to drop either his stores or his passengers. He returned landing at 06.04 hours with all on board.

Russell flew again on the night 26/27th April, to CHEESE 1 in Norway flying a 9.30 hour flight. He crossed the English coast at

Cromer 50 minutes after take-off and was at 5,000 feet when he crossed the Norwegian coast pinpointing Ordne Lake. He then map read, in bright moonlight, his way to Ardel Fjord, following the river Ottenden to Lake Boro. At this point their ETA had expired but they continued on this course and picked up a lake just west of their DZ pinpoint identifying at the same time Berdal. Here they dropped six containers.

P/O Anderle was off the following night, the 27th/28th, at 20.57 hours to complete BIVOUAC/BIOSCOPE. This time he crossed the French coast at le Crotoy and setting course for Givet (15km south of Dinant) which he pinpointed at 23.10. From here to Karlsruhe, pinpointing Nuremberg at 00.03. North of Pilsen in Czechoslovakia they map read their way to the target area and successfully dropped seven passengers, two containers and one package. They landed at base at 05.57.

Operation BIVOUAC was a three man team (Frantisek Pospisil, Jindrich Coupek, Libor Zapletal) to sabotage the railway bridge and signals at Prerov and later the power station at Brno. It failed when the agents were arrested early in May. Operation BIOSCOPE was another three man team (Bohuslav Kouba, Josef Bablik, Jan Hruby) to sabotage railway communications between Germany and the eastern front, centred on a bridge at Hradnice and a transformer station at Vsetin. It failed, one of the agents being arrested almost immediately and the other two were killed in the Karel Boromejsky church in Prague along with ANTHROPOID team. The seventh agent dropped that night was Oldrich Dvorak STEEL A probably an attempt to link up with the operation dropped on March 27/26th. However, he was shot on the 30th June.

Among the five operations on the night of 27/28th April S/Ldr Murphy flew a Lysander to France, an SIS sortie BRIDGE, picking up Pierre Brossolette, having spent two dangerous years in the field.

The 28th/29th saw Russell out again this time to Belgium flying operation MANFRIDAY dropping four containers on the flashing lights of a reception. S/Ldr Davies took a Whitley to Norway, operation COCKEREL crossing the English coast at Wells-Next-The-Sea in Norfolk. Their landfall in Norway appears to have been in the Lyngdal area. He found the pinpoint they were looking for beside a lake. Davies says that they circled for a while to see if the reception committee was going to play. They didn't, so he dropped from 800 feet his two passengers, six containers and two packages on the east side of a hill by the lake and returned home.

The next night the 29/30th, F/Lt Outram flew CHEESE 2 to Norway and with little difficulty identified his target and dropped another six containers which they watched land. Sgt Owen at last completed LUCKYSHOT 2, in Belgium, dropping six containers, the seventh attempt. They map read to the Meuse and found their target in a wood west of Champlon and dropped. Two men were seen running towards them. F/O Rymills should have flown PERIWIG 2 in Whitley Z9159 to Belgium but had exactor trouble over the Channel and returned to base.

P/O Anderle was again flying a Halifax to Czechoslovakia his third sortie to that country within five days, another 8.30 hour flight. This operation was STEEL/INTRANSITIVE/IRON. There is very little said of this flight in the Squadron ORB. It says they crossed the French coast at 22.21. Set course for the Rhine between Mannheim and Karlsruhe; from there they went to Nuremberg whence they map read their way to the target. Here they circled once and dropped their five passengers, two containers and one package from 400 feet. On the way home they once again traversed Germany in bright moonlight to complete the operation!

INTRANSITIVE was a three agent team (Vaclav Kindl, Bohuslav Grabovsky, Vojtech Lukastik) dropped near Trebon to sabotage the oil refinery at Kolin. Their equipment was lost on landing. Although the RAF record the name of this operation as IRON it would appear that it's official name was TIN and was an assassination team comprising of Ludvik Cupal and Jaroslav Svarc. Their target was thought to be Emanuel Moravec, the Minister of Education and Propaganda. All of these brave men were either dead or arrested by March 1943

Four operations took place on the following night, the last in April, and apart from P/O Russell who could not identify BASS in France, S/Ldr Davies dropped three agents and four containers on a triangle of lights near Valenciennes, a Belgium operation LAMB/MULE/ SABLE/RETRIEVER. F/Sgt Pieniszek flew an SIS operation VEGA to Norway via Flamborough Head. Making the Norwegian coast he followed it down to Nareste then went inland to Bokkaa and after searching for 40 minutes found the reception lights near Vegars Lake. He then dropped three packages on a light flashing 'K', returning home via Langesund Fjord. Gibson in the meantime completed the outstanding Belgian operation PERIWIG 2.

The 30th April/1st May saw four 161 Squadron Whitleys flying SIS operations to France all of which were completed. Peterson flying BEVY/BOUGLE/BOON into occupied France where three passengers jumped safely from 1,200 feet. S/Ldr Gunn flying WHIRLWIND dropped a passenger and a parcel in the Dompierre area some 50km NE of Vichy, diverting to Boscombe Down.

S/Ldr Murphy (who normally flew Lysanders) flew with F/Lt Boxer acting as second pilot (so the RAF records say, strange since F/Lt Boxer was a very experienced Whitley captain) to fly operation BRANDY. This was a formidable team and BRANDY was previously associated with SOE/NKVD operations. However the passenger they dropped into a reception committee in the Tours area from an indicated altitude of 1,300 feet was not a NKVD agent.

Finally P/O Mott was flying operation WHITSUN taking-off from Tempsford at 00.15 hours for France. By the time he had reached Tangmere he was at a height of 2,500 feet, crossing the French coast at Cabourg at 7,000 feet. He says he set course for the target area keeping north of Évreaux (Eure) and Dreux, in clear visibility located the pinpoint, completed a circuit and dropped his agent from 1,500 feet. When on the ground the agent flashed a light indicating that all was well. Returning to Dreux he flew over the nearby German airfield and was met with a searchlight and light flak. A little later at Évreaux he again passed over a nearby German airfield, where 12 searchlights and light flak greeted him, the rear gunner opening fire at the searchlights. Tracing their progress on a map they appear to have gone a long way north of track. They were diverted to Boscombe Down for landing.

One could hardly call April a busy month for the Tempsford Squadrons with 54 sorties flown. Of these 138 Squadron flew 32 (completing only 19) and lost a Halifax and a Whitley – an unpromising 6.5%

On the 30th April the Whitleys of Bomber Command were replaced with four engined aircraft, only Coastal Command and SD Squadrons continued to use them. History was to repeat itself in early 1944 when Merlin powered Halifaxes were withdrawn from Bomber Command service.

*   *   *

With the coming of May operations to Poland, Czechoslovakia and Norway ceased, there being insufficient hours of darkness in which to complete them. Although F/O Gibson and P/O Rymills on the 3rd/4th May failed to complete operations WOODCOCK and CRANE to Norway due to bad weather. France, Holland and Belgium now received the main effort.

The 1st/2nd May saw two French targets completed, Sgt Owen dropping two containers and one package onto DASTARD 1 and P/O Rymills dropping an agent and a package onto CRANE. S/Ldr Davies the following night had a little more to do on his French operation, parachuting two agents and one package onto CAMELIA/ASPEN. The name Krol crops up this night as a captain of a Halifax flying CRAB/MINNOW/PERCH to France. It failed because of the weather. The PRO files do not have an operational report for this sortie. We left F/O Krol, a navigator, interned in Sweden having survived a crash landing in that country on the 7/8th November 1941. This was Krol's first operation since his return from internment and he was to fly another 120 operations with his pilot W/O Klosowski..

They flew ADJUDICATE 3 in a Halifax L9613 to France a few nights later on the 6/7th May crossing the French coast near Caen and setting course for their target. They pin-pointed Cahors (Lot) and identified Châteaux-de-Lagrézette ?? (quite unreadable!) but there were no red triangle of lights to be seen. There were however many other scattered lights including one flashing 'V'. They circled the target area at a height of 3,000 feet for 38 minutes and finally set course for Limoges where they dropped their leaflets. On the way back to Caen they reported that many lights were visible. What they were is a mystery they certainly weren't reception committees as they were the only SD sortie out that night.

161 Squadron flew two operations on the night of the 5th/6th May. F/Lt Boxer dropping an SOE agent in France, operation ELM. F/Sgt Peterson also went to France, an SIS operation PILCHARD & CHROME. He crossed the French coast at Cabourg flying at 4,000 feet and headed for Blois on the Loire but pinpointed the river at Amboise. He then turned towards Tours and followed the Cher down to Vierzon. Finding the pinpoint he considered it unsuitable, being scrub and bushes, but eventually found a suitable dropping point some 8km to the north east, near a road and on the edge of a wood. Here they dropped three agents and one container from 900 feet. They then set course for Melun, south of Paris, to complete CHROME, dropping their leaflets in the Orléans area. Here they report seeing to the NNW an aerodrome lit up (probably Bricy). With visibility worsening and being short of time Peterson decided to turn back. They landed at 05.50 having taken off at 21.53.

I have no record of any operations flown between 5/6th May and the 24/25th May (perhaps it was a moonless stand down period). But, after this period, 138 Squadron flew five operations. F/O Russell had trouble with his exactors on Whitley Z9159 bound for PERIWIG 3 in Belgium, abandoning his flight after ten minutes in the air. I looked up the last sortie where engine failure caused abandonment, it was F/O Rymills attempting to fly a PERIWIG target on the 29/30th April. He too experienced exactor failure with the same aircraft, Z9159! (I wonder what Russell said to the Flight Sergeant?).

138 Squadron officers, Summer 1942. From left (back row): Unknown, unknown, P/O F Pantowski (WOp) – killed 30/10/42, P/O R Wilkin (Pilot) – killed 20/9/43, P/O K Dobromirski (Pilot) – killed 17/12/42, P/O J Pieniazek (Pilot), P/O L Andrele (Pilot) – killed 10/12/42, P/O F E Rymills (Pilot), F/O K J Szrajer (Pilot), unknown, unknown, F/O Fosket, unknown, unknown, unknown, unknown. (Front row): F/O M Wodzicki (Nav.) – killed

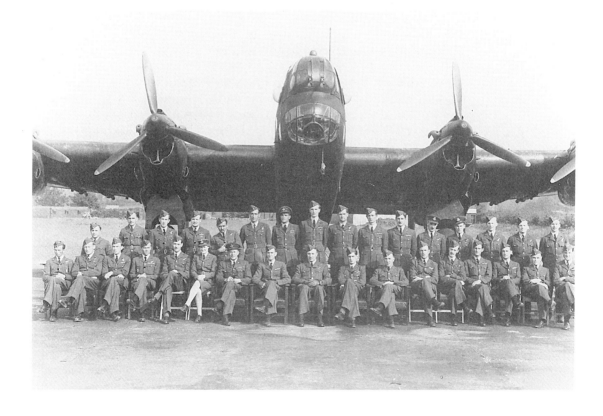

30/10/42, F/O R
Walzak (Nav.), F/Lt S
Krol (Nav.), F/O V
Krcha (Nav.) – killed
10/12/42, unknown,
unknown, unknown, F/O
H A Outram (pilot)
evaded 25/8/42,
W/Cdr R C Hockey
(CO), S/Ldr W T
Davies (Pilot) – killed
30/7/42, F/Lt Jaffe
(Adj.), P/O Smith
(Pilot), P/O McFadden
(Nav.), P/O P
Kingsford-Smith (Pilot) –
PoW 20/3/43,
unknown, F/O A Firth
(Tech.), F/Lt J C
Sutton (pilot)
(K J Szrajer)

F/O Rymills flew Halifax W1012 to France, operation GORSE. Crossing the French coast at Cabourg he set course for Tours. Afterwards pinpointing Châteauroux on the way to Montluçon and the River Sioule west of Vichy. Here after 20 minutes they picked up a triangle of lights and parachuted in from 600 feet one agent, three containers and a package. They still had 40 bundles of leaflets and 24 pigeons to dispose of. They landed after 7.20 hours in the air.

The remaining three sorties were successfully completed to France and Belgium. 161 Squadron this night, the 24/25th May, flew two Whitley SIS operations to France. Weather preventing F/Sgt Boothby from completing BOTTE/BRUCE and meeting on the way home light flak and searchlights north of le Havre, landing at Tangmere. S/Ldr Gunn was more successful parachuting two agents onto operation BATON/BRICE also meeting light flak on his way home.

BOTTE/BRUCE was completed by F/Lt Boxer on the 28/29th flying via Beachy Head and crossing the French coast south of Berck. From here to Valenciennes, where he flew above the railway track (this has to be in a northerly direction) and turned over a wood, the swamp on his map appeared, on the ground, more like a lake. Flying over the pinpoint his passengers requested he dropped them 20km due east of it. At a speed of 100 mph and at a height of 700 feet he parachuted two agents who in the bright moonlight floated down to earth into a gap in the woods. There remained six bundles of leaflets to dispose of. He reported that on the way home he saw industrial activity at Brebières (5km WSW of Douai) at the railway junction – a good target to bomb and easily picked out. I cannot help thinking this observation influenced Bomber Command on the immediate operational activities of No.161 Squadron, as it will be seen!

F/Sgt Peterson had little difficulty in dropping three agents, one container and two packages into a French SIS operation TENNIS/GOLDFISH. Two unsuccessful Lysander flights took place this same night. F/Lt Lockhart failing an SIS operation GEAN through lack of ground signals and P/O Mott flying an SOE operation TENATURE. We last heard of Mott flying a Whitley over two German airfields on operation WHITSUN. This time he was less fortunate, his Lysander V9595, having bogged down when landing near Issoudun at le Fay, a small airfield west of Ségry (Indre), was abandoned. It would not burn, and was displayed in a German museum of captured aircraft at Nanterre near Paris until destroyed during their retreat in 1944. P/O A J Mott was arrested by the Vichy police and jailed in Nice, he eventually escaped. This was the first 161 Squadron Lysander loss and Mott's first and only Lysander operation.

Operation PERIWIG must have caused 138 Squadron pilots to raise their eyebrows. On the 28/29th F/Sgt Owen flying operation PERIWIG 3 to Belgium had an engine failure, the third failure for this target within a month. The very next night flying operation MANDAMUS to Belgium Owen again returned a Whitley on one engine.

F/O Russell was again sent to Holland, his target LETTUCE. He eventually made his way to Harderwijk where landmarks were clearly visible but no reception lights. Just north of Putten they could see a stationary car on the road with its headlights on. When the aircraft arrived the car moved slowly north. They circled for half an hour and then made for home.

The night of the 29/30 saw seven completed operations. Among the five successful 138 Squadron sorties were P/O Sutton who finally completed PERIWIG 3 and Krol whose pilot flew a Halifax on operation ELDER to France.

Another, operation CATARRH 4 /BEETROOT was flown to Holland by S/Ldr Davies in Whitley Z9230. His load consisted of two SOE agents Herman Parlevliet (BEETROOT) and Anthony Steen (SWEDE) who were trained saboteurs, six containers, one package, ten packs of leaflets and twelve pigeons. In the containers were two radio sets. In the package was a 'Eureka' apparatus, carefully wrapped in sorbo-rubber and packed into two large boxes. It was to be dropped on a special parachute. Davies crossed the Dutch coast at Callantsoog and set course for the target area near Enkhuizen. He says he overshot the target slightly to the north then turned and pinpointed Enkhuizen resetting course following the railway down until the lights were picked up. After circling twice he dropped his cargo and passengers. Unhappily straight into the hands of the Germans.

Thus Giskes was provided with two more active radio links with London and what they deduced, correctly, a radio homing device. They were later able to demonstrate the value of this to the RAF when they arranged an operation during which it was used. They did not see the aircraft but six containers were to land within 100 metres of the 'Eureka' transmitter!

The remaining two operations for the night were completed by 161 Squadron. S/Ldr Murphy successfully flying an untroubled Lysander operation SHRIMP, and S/Ldr Gunn dropping an agent into OPAL, both in France.

The closing nights of May saw two successful Halifax sorties to France F/O Rymills dropping an agent into EEL and F/O Wodzicki two more into PRIVET/BLACKTHORN. This could only be the blind drop near le Mans of Chris Burney, a former commando subaltern, dropped to join the already dead circuit AUTOGYRO, an incredibly brave man, surviving Buchenwald and the war. His fellow parachutist was Charles Grover-Williams.

S/Ldr Outram completed MANDAMUS in Belgium, which F/Sgt Owen flying on one engine failed the previous night. He dropped eight containers which was two more than usual. The last two operations of the month were to Holland. F/O Russell to LETTUCE 1, making a landfall on the island of Vlieland off the Dutch coast and flying his Whitley at 400 feet down to the Zuiderzee and to the target area. He picked up the lights and dropped cargo (six containers) returning home via Oosterleek (east of Hoorn) and Callantsoog. The dropping area would seem to tie in with Davies's flight of the 29/30th.

The other sortie to Holland was flown by F/Sgt Owen on the 31st/1st June to CATARRH 6. He made tracks for the Zuiderzee dam but was unable to map read because of haze but they later identified the pier north west of Kampen. From that point they set course for the DZ but again had to turn back because of haze. They found Urk and from there went to Elberg and tried again. This time they flew right on to the reception lights and after two circuits dropped their cargo of six containers. They landed after being airborne 5.10 hours.

Tempsford Control Tower – Callsign "Brasstray".
(via K A Merrick)

CHAPTER EIGHT

June–Ending with 161 Squadron Operations, August 31st 1942

Summer operations began with 138 Squadron flying two Halifax sorties to France. F/O Wodzicki flying in two agents and two containers for operation PALM/SPRUCE and P/O Rymills flying without success operation CRAB/MINNOW/PERCH where there was no reception to receive him. W/Cdr Hockey making a now rare sortie on the 3/4th to complete it. S/Ldr Outram flying as his second pilot, probably for Halifax experience. (P/O Rymills appears to have converted to Halifaxes exactly one month before). However Hockey says little in his report (all reports are brief for this period). He crossed the French coast at Pointe de la Percée and set course for Tours where he flew to Montluçon seeing the marshalling yard floodlights. At Montluçon he followed the river to the pinpoint, where searching for half an hour he dropped three agents and a package. There remained 40 bundles of leaflets to dispose of. He landed after being airborne 7.20 hours.

P/O Anderle successfully flew SNAKE to France and F/Sgt Owen complained it was too dark to complete MANDAMUS 2 in Belgium which finished the moon period for 138 Squadron.

As for 161 Squadron the beginning of summer, the 1st June, saw a change in operations for them. All of their Whitley crews F/Lt Boxer, F/Sgt Boothby, Sgt Walls, F/Sgt Peterson and Sgt Wynn. appear to be flying 'Nickel' operations (dropping leaflets). The previous night Sgt Smith and Sgt Cresswell had already flown two nickel sorties. Each aircraft was loaded with between 55 and 60 bundles of nickels. The moon had just waned. Among the most recent 138 Squadron operations five aircraft were carrying 40 bundles of leaflets as well as a normal manifest (it really didn't matter what you were carrying the enemy still shot at you!).

And then! On the 2/3rd June 5 Whitleys of 161 Squadron were despatched to bomb the marshalling yard at Tours. They carried 4 x 500lb bombs plus 6 x 250 lbs. Sgt Cresswell turned back due to compass failure, W/Cdr Fielden, F/Lt Boxer, F/Sgt Peterson and Sgt Smith bombed as briefed.

On the night of the 7/8th, 8/9th, 9/10th, 138 Squadron joined in the distribution of 'Nickels'. P/O Turnham flying to Alençon, P/O

This is a photograph of a 138 Squadron Halifax at Tempsford 'bombed up' to take pert in the second 1,000 bomber raid on Essen 1/2 June 1942. (G/Capt R C Hockey)

Sutton to Chartres, F/O Gibson and S/Ldr Davies to Paris (Davies having exactor trouble on his starboard engine), F/Sgt Owen to Fécamp, P/O Anderle to St-Michel/Redon, P/O Sutton to Isigny/St-Malo. P/O Russell reported that he lost his trailing ariel, presumably, he said, by striking another aeroplane! From the 10/11th June to the 21/22nd June saw another 13 'Nickel' sorties, one by 138 and 12 by 161 Squadron, two of which failed through compass and ASI problems.

On the 21/22nd June Sgt W Smith taking off at 23.00 hours a 161 Squadron Whitley Z9224 crashed due to a faulty ASI. His mission was to have been 'nickelling'. There were no injuries but the aircraft was written off. Smith was commissioned one week later.

From the 1st June to the 21/22nd I calculate the contents of approximately 1,200 packs of leaflets were scattered. The size of a leaflet was roughly 8 inches by 10 and the packs were about a foot thick and heavy. In a statistic file (Air 20/8170) it was said that the number of leaflets dropped from Tempsford between 15/6/42 and 13/7/42 were 7,700,000.

I recall dropping leaflets in brilliant moonlight over Sully-sur-Loire (Loiret) when there was a roar of laughter from the rear gunner (F/O G H Ash, DFC, who sadly was to die in a Hudson in November) as he told us he saw the package plummet to the ground with the string still tied round it. I trust it did no hurt to those below.

LE COURRIER
DE L'AIR

APPORTE PAR LA R.A.F.   *LONDRES, MARS 1944*

Le général de Gaulle définit la politique générale du Comité National

La situation de la France en guerre, les causes qui l'y conduisirent, les conséquences à prévoir pour l'avenir, telles sont les données de fait servant de base à la politique par laquelle le gouvernement entend conduire le pays à son salut, sa libération et sa rénovation.

Je voudrais aujourd'hui exposer les conditions et les buts de cette politique aux points de vue de la guerre elle-même, de la libération du pays, de nos rapports extérieurs, enfin de l'orientation de l'avenir de la France.

Quand au milieu du tumulte de la guerre il s'agit de décider ce qu'il faut faire pour incliner la balance du conflit, les hommes qui portent la charge de diriger l'effort national doivent — considérer les froideurs et dures réalités sur lesquelles se bâtit l'action.

Une nation comme la nôtre joue sa vie, n'admet de la part de ses chefs ni faiblesses ni illusions. On se demande-nous ? Quelles sont nos forces actuelles et virtuelles ? Que voulons-nous faire pour tirer de la coalition dont nous faisons partie, la plus grande efficience possible ? Dans ce domaine terrible il n'y a pas d'autres questions.

Les moyens militaires dont la France dispose en dépit de la situation dans laquelle l'ont placée l'invasion et la trahison, sont de nouveau importants en nombre et en qualité. Sans doute, au cours d'une guerre où rien ne compte dans les batailles terrestres, aériennes et navales, sinon les unités pourvues d'un matériel moderne et dotées par conséquent de cadres bien instruits et de multiples spécialistes, le gouvernement ne peut-il actuellement songer à aligner des forces de campagne comparables à celles dont la France disposait naguère et à celles dont elle saurait disposer demain si par malheur les démocraties devaient une fois encore se disloquer dans la paix.

Cependant à l'heure qu'il est notre effort de mobilisation des éléments européens de l'Empire, effort qui atteint 14% de cette population, la bravoure et le dévouement de nos soldats nord africains et coloniaux, l'armement livré à notre armée, les navires fournis à notre marine par les gouvernements américain et britannique, les appareils mis à la disposition de notre armée de l'air par ces mêmes gouvernements et par celui de la Russie soviétique, enfin les aptitudes guerrières de notre race, aptitudes qui se révèlent intactes partout où nos troupes combattent, font que les forces françaises jouent en ce

moment même un rôle notable là ou on se bat à l'ouest et sont en mesure d'en jouer un qui peut être considérable dans la bataille décisive en France.

Il est considérable, et d'autant plus qu'à l'intérieur de multiples éléments de combat dont beaucoup sont déjà à l'œuvre dans les actions de détail, ne manqueront pas — nous en répondons — de participer au grand effort militaire des armées françaises et alliées en attaquant l'ennemi sur les arrières suivant les ordres que leur donnera le commandement français d'après le plan d'opération du commandement interallié.

Concours français

Il est évidemment impossible de prédire ce que sera au juste l'efficacité militaire de nos organisations combattantes de l'intérieur, efficacité militaire qui dépendra de leur armement, de la date plus ou moins proche de la grande offensive. Mais il est également impossible de contester que leur action, appuyée au moment voulu par l'insurrection nationale contre l'envahisseur, pèsera lourdement sur la décision stratégique.

Si chez les Nations Unies quelques organismes ont pu se montrer incertains quant à la puissance éventuelle de ce concours français, l'ennemi n'en doute aucunement, lui qui fait prendre par sa Gestapo et par ses collaborateurs, et continuera de faire prendre jusqu'au jour de sa déroute, les mesures préventives de la plus féroce répression. En vérité, malgré tous ses malheurs la France guerrière est debout avec tout ce qu'elle peut mettre en ligne. Je ne doute pas que dans une situation semblable d'autres nations en eussent fait autant. Mais je

dis que ce que la France a réalisé par delà son désastre et ce qu'elle est capable de réaliser demain pour la victoire commune, lui donne droit d'avoir à l'avantage général, voix délibérative dans la politique et la stratégie du camp de la liberté.

En ce qui concerne l'emploi de ces forces françaises le gouvernement s'efforce de faire en sorte qu'elles soient mises en œuvre sans réserve et au plus tôt, et qu'elles le soient en tous cas dans la bataille que la Nation appelle de tous ses vœux, je veux dire dans la Bataille de France.

Le peuple français n'ignore pas quel surcroît de douleur ce grand choc jettera sur sa terre et sa chair. Mais ces douleurs, d'avance, il les accepte comme toutes celles qu'il supporta, du moment que l'offensive concertée et résolue de la coalition vise à la victoire complète et rapide. Sans que je puisse entrer ici dans le secret des plans d'opérations, je dois dire à l'Assemblée — et je souhaite que m'entendent par delà cette enceinte tous nos soldats, marins, aviateurs et tous les combattants du maquis, des villes et des usines — que l'effort du gouvernement dans la coalition tend à amener, comme ils le veulent et l'espèrent, la rencontre tous ensemble le plus tôt qu'il le pourra pour chasser de notre sol l'envahisseur détesté.

J'ai dit : combattre tous ensemble. J'entends par cette expression non seulement la simultanéité de l'engagement de nos forces dans la suprême bataille, mais aussi l'union des esprits et des âmes de tous nos combattants. A ce point de vue qui fut délicat, mais qui s'il mérite encore de l'attention ne justifie pas de l'inquiétude, le gouvernement apporte toute sa sérénité. Après les épreuves morales indicibles que nos armées tra-

versèrent, il était inévitable que certaines tendances divergentes s'y fissent jour.

Mais quand on voit à l'œuvre nos magnifiques troupes d'Italie, quand on mesure les trésors d'ardeur que mettent nos unités qui se préparent pour les grandes batailles, quand on regarde les yeux, les sentiments et souvent les poumons de nos vaillants garçons qui, dans le maquis, sans uniformes et presque sans armes, mais armés de la plus pure flamme militaire, reprirent possession de notre âme et de la terre natale, on a le devoir de proclamer que nos armées n'ont qu'une âme, de même qu'elles n'ont qu'un drapeau, et que cette âme est maintenant comme aux plus grandes heures de notre histoire, noblement soumise aux volontés de la nation et humblement dévouée au service de la Patrie.

Quels que doivent être la date et le rythme de la libération du territoire métropolitain, les problèmes immédiats que le gouvernement devra alors résoudre revêtiront un caractère d'emploi et de difficulté que l'Assemblée mesure parfaitement bien.

Les problèmes de la libération

Ces problèmes, pour ne parler que des principaux, concernant la poursuite de la guerre aux côtés des Alliés, l'indispensable participation des Français à l'élaboration et à l'application des armistices européens, le maintien de l'ordre public, la mise en place de l'administration épurée, le fonctionnement de la justice, le ravitaillement, la monnaie, les salaires, le régime du travail, l'organisation de la production, des échanges extérieurs et des communications, la sauvegarde de la santé publique, le rétablissement des libertés essentielles : liberté individuelle, liberté syndicale, liberté de presse, le régime de l'information, le retour des prisonniers et déportés, les mouvements des réfugiés, enfin la préparation matérielle de la grande consultation nationale d'où sortira l'Assemblée Nationale Constituante qui instaurera le régime de la Quatrième République.

Il suffit que la Nation évoque ces problèmes, et elle le fait, nous le savons, dans la nuit de l'oppression, pour discerner à la fois leur importance vitale pour le pays et l'étendue de la responsabilité du gouvernement qui devra les résoudre avec le concours de l'Assemblée Consultative. Bien qu'il soit impossible de prévoir exactement les conditions physiques et psychiques dans lesquelles ces problèmes se poseront alors le peuple français, et qui dépendront des multiples épreuves qu'il aura en-

core à traverser avant de pouvoir se dresser au soleil de la liberté, nous avons pensé qu'en de telles matières la préparation des solutions d'ensemble devait être poussée à fond en dépit de tout ce qui nous manque ici en fait de moyens d'étude.

Votre Assemblée, Messieurs, est déjà saisie d'un certain nombre de ces questions. Elle sera saisie des autres. Il y a là un travail constructif, absolument nécessaire et urgent pour lequel vos conclusions sont de la plus haute importance. Sans vouloir préjuger des dispositions précises qui sont à adopter cependant au plus tôt, je dois faire connaître à quelles conditions le gouvernement juge indispensable qu'elles répondent aujourd'hui dans leur conception et demain dans leur application.

D'abord rien ne pourra être fait que dans l'ordre. C'est la loi de toutes les réalisations, mais combien impérieuse dans la situation où la bataille est sur son sol, où la retraite de l'ennemi, les destructions de toute nature, l'effondrement du système actuel d'oppression vont placer notre pays. Il ne saurait donc y avoir, je le déclare avec force, aucune autre autorité publique que celle procédant du pouvoir central responsable. Tout essai de maintien même partiel ou camouflé de l'organisme de Vichy, comme toute formation artificielle de pouvoir extérieur au gouvernement, serait intolérable et par avance condamné.

Localement, dès l'instant où se feront connaître les autorités désignées par le Comité Français de la Libération Nationale, les citoyens auront la stricte obligation de se conformer à leurs instructions, sans préjudice bien entendu du rôle à jouer auprès d'elles par les organismes consultatifs que leur fourniront certainement nos comités locaux de libération, en attendant que soient constituées les assemblées locales prévues. Malheur à qui attenterait à l'unité nationale !

Période initiale de rétablissement

En second lieu la vie même du pays dans les conditions économiques très difficiles où il se trouvera forcément plongé au cours de cette période initiale de son rétablissement excluera, il faut qu'on le sache, toute facilité subite en matière d'approvisionnement et par suite de distribution.

Certes il est possible de dire à la Nation qui aura si durement souffert que l'arrivée des forces françaises et alliées ne marquera pas le commencement automatique de l'euphorie. Mais le gouvernement a le devoir de le proclamer dès à présent comme il aura celui de prendre les mesures

Voir au verso

F.33

Nous publions dans ce supplément spécial le texte intégral du discours prononcé à Alger le 18 mars 1944 à l'Assemblée Consultative par le général de Gaulle

The 21/22nd June 161 Squadron despatched to two Whitleys piloted by S/Ldr Gunn and F/Sgt Peterson to bomb la Trait Shipyard on the Seine, west of Rouen. Gunn completely missed the target when taking evasive action from flak. His rear gunner F/Sgt Clayton engaging the flak battery was struck on the head from a shell splinter which pierced his turret and his helmet.

This night 138 Squadron despatched two operations. F/Lt Smith flying operation PERIWIG 4 to Belgium failing because of the weather and S/Ldr Davies to Holland. Davies was flying a PICKAXE operation, that is dropping a Soviet NKVD agent into Europe (not necessarily of Russian nationality). This operation was named BARSAC and had been scheduled for May. Davies crossed the Dutch coast at Callantsoog, flew down to Hoorn and thence to Harderwijk which he pinpointed. After searching for 16 minutes he parachuted his passenger, Nicolai Kravets, blind from 500 feet. Davies returned by the same route.

It was said that this mission was undermined by the SOE's failure to send the right baggage with him, and was the cause of extensive complaint by the Soviet Union. Looking at the cargo manifest for this flight there were no instructions for a container or a package to be dropped with him. It could have been that the Soviets did not ask for one. The dropping zone required by this document was '7km east of Harderwijk in a clearing in a wood'. There is no mention of a reception committee. Tracing Davies's flight on a 1/400,000 Michelin map of the Netherlands this was exactly where he was dropped. 5km to the south of Harderwijk was a German operated DZ at Ermelo. There is no record of an agent being captured by the Germans this night.

The following night F/O Gibson went to Belgium in an endeavour to complete PERIWIG 4 complaining that it was 'Too Dark', it failed!

F/O Russell again went to Holland, his fifth Dutch sortie to date, flying operation LETTUCE 3/SPINACH/PARSNIP. His route was much the same as before. Coast at Callantsoog then to Harderwijk from there straight to target. When the lights were picked up, two agents Lt Jan Jacob van Rietschoten (PARSNIP) and his radio operator Johannes Cornelius Buizer (SPINACH), were parachuted from 650 feet into a German operated DZ reported by Cookridge to be near Assen. If the DZ was at Assen then Russell would certainly not have flown from Harderwijk to the target area reported in the ORB. The exact location of the DZ according to the cargo manifest was 1km SSW Rijssen and 4km West of Enter (roughly 25km east of Deventer). The reception lights were then dowsed after the first drop and came on again allowing Russell to drop six containers. He still had 25 pigeons and six packs of leaflets to deal with.

The two young men dropped that night had escaped from Holland to England by rowing a 40 foot open boat for 64 hours across the North Sea. Their capture gave Giskes a fifth radio link with London.

The 23/24th June saw three 161 Squadron Whitleys out bombing Serqueux (Haute-Marne) marshalling yard. More astonishing so were

Opposite: *Photocopy of a leaflet taken from the author's crashed aircraft by the Resistance and given to him after the war.*

four Lysanders flown by P/O Vaughan-Fowler, P/O McIndoe, P/O Bridger, and F/Lt Lockhart. Each Lysander carried 2 x 250 lbs bombs. Because of bad visibility Lockhart preferred not to bomb in case he hit nearby houses.

At this time Lysanders were not easily obtainable. Four long awaited Lysanders were still waiting for their 150 gallon, Handley Page Harrow, fuel tanks needed for long-range operations and now in short supply. (This was the fuel tank carried under the fuselage). On June 1st six extra Mk.IIIAs had been allocated in reserve but this was probably only the paper work.

It would now appear that Harris was the one using the resources of the SD Squadrons and not as he complained, the SD Squadron using his. There is no mention of any of these bombing sorties in Martin Middlebrook and Chris Everitt's book *The Bomber Command War Diaries* and one wonders if they were mentioned in the original diaries. For 161 Squadron purposes they were recorded as 'navigational training flights'.

There is a paragraph from a lengthy letter to the Bomb Target Committee dated the 3rd July 1942. Probably written by G/Capt MacDonald the CO of Tempsford at that time. It recommended that Whitleys would attack targets 180 miles from the French western seaboard and Halifaxes 230 miles. The bomb load of a Halifax being 15 x 500 lbs. There is no mention of targets to be bombed by the Lysanders. Crews were to select their own routes to targets as on normal SD operations. It continued:

Three Lysander Mk IIIAs being modified for Special Duty work in the Flight Sheds at Yeovil. Possibly three of the four that were to be delivered to 161 Squadron. It is thought that the aircraft, second from the left, is V9287. (Westland Group plc)

In view of the amount of special training which has been given to the crews, it is most important that they should not be wasted or lost by sending them on to targets in which there is a risk of them being lost, since a replacement would take a very considerable time, and in the meantime there would be a limitation on the special operation which they carry out. For this reason, it is undesirable that they should be sent to any target which may be heavily defended.

On the same night, 23/24th June F/Lt Boxer was spared bombing to fly an SIS Operation BARRAT/BORIS/BRIAR to France, where in Occupied France he parachuted three passengers from 850 feet. The first two, he says, went possibly into a wood but this was unconfirmed as visibility was bad. He dropped his six pigeons between Lens and St-Pol.

138 Squadron in the meantime were flying normal parachute operations or perhaps one that wasn't quite so normal! There were four sorties to Belgium PERIWIG 4, an outstanding supply drop completed by S/Ldr Davies and F/Sgt Owen completing SPANIEL.

Weather prevented completion of a Belgium operation MANFRIDAY/KOALA flown by F/Lt Sutton. This was completed the following night by S/Ldr Outram when he parachuted one agent and six containers 2km north east of Blaugines. A memo on file, following a field report, asked that the pilot be reminded not to leave his trailing ariel out when dropping. It did not say whether the agent was struck by the wire or by the heavy weight that held it away from the aircraft but it must have given him a nasty shock.

F/Lt Smith flew a PICKAXE operation to Belgium coded BURGUNDY. In *SOE in Eastern Europe* (p28) it says:

> It was a plan for the despatch of one PICKAXE Von Krunin to Belgium. The mission did not appear to have taken place due to the dispatch of his equipment with the BARSAC agent to Holland (see 21/22nd June) and the unsuitability of the agent himself.

Smith reports he took-off Whitley Z9287 at 23.07 and reached the French coast at le Crotoy 1 hour 10 minutes later. Setting course for Givet (south of Dinant) and from there to the target area. where 'low cloud made accurate map reading impossible but dropped passenger from 600 feet about 10km north or west of pinpoint'. A package was also dropped. Smith landed at 05.20 hours.

The cargo manifest instructions dated May 1942 said one person to be dropped 10km NNE. Marche (-en-Famenne? in Belgium), 1km NE of Melreux. The alternative being at a suitable spot same neighbourhood, if possible as near as is safe to a station on the Marche-Durby (Durbuy?) railway line.

Bombing sorties continued for 161 Squadron from the 25/26th to 26/27th June, five Whitley and eight Lysander sorties bombing Oissel Chemical Works at Rouen. Two Whitley sorties were unable to find the target. The moon period and operations for the month of June finished on the 29/39th with four Whitleys and four Lysanders bombing the power station at Aure. Three Whitleys did not complete, the 161 Squadron commander, W/Cdr Fielden, returning early with engine trouble. W/O Boothby flew the only successful Whitley sortie.

*   *   *

During the same period 138 Squadron flew seven sorties. F/O Wodzicki flying in a Halifax was unable to complete ROACH/MACKEREL in France the reception lights being dowsed as he approached the target. F/Sgt Owen and Sgt Freeland completed operations in Belgium. The former had a supply drop and the latter dropped three agents successfully for operation LUCKYSHOT 4. P/O Anderle flew SYRINGA to France but returned home as, in spite of circling the pinpointed target area for over half an hour, he could see no sign of any reception lights.

There were two operations to Holland when F/O Russell, flying supply drop TURNIP 1, had little trouble finding his target as the lights came up immediately he approached the DZ and he was able to drop six containers. Regrettably, his report was brief and I was unable to trace his progress. However, on the way home he reported seeing fires at Norwich from 60 miles out at sea.

F/O Gibson flew operation CATARRH 6/MARROW on the 26/27th June and pinpointed himself on the Zuider Zee dam flying down to Elberg. In the target area they picked up the reception lights immediately and from 600 feet he parachuted into the hands of the Germans, George Louis Jambroes and his radio operator Lt Joseph Bukkens together with six containers and one package. London suggested that the 'Eureka' apparatus dropped on the 30th May might be used to pinpoint the DZ which was in the vicinity of Apeldoorn (The exact location according to the cargo manifest was 3km SW Hatton, SW of Zwolle). Jambroes and Bukkens were met by a deputation of Dutch traitors who handcuffed them and took them to the Gestapo office at Binnedorf. Jambroes was to have been the leader of the Dutch resistance. Giskes now had a seventh radio link with London. Gibson flew home via Oosterleek (SW of Enkhuizen) and Callantsoog.

The 27/28th June saw S/Ldr Davies making his way to France to complete the outstanding operation MONKEYPUZZLE, parachuting his passenger Raymond Flower blind in the Tours area. Flower's task was to start a circuit in the name of the operation but it never really got going.

138 Squadron concluded the month of June by flying four successful Halifax sorties to France. P/O Rymills dropping three agents and a package onto operation ILEX/ALMOND/GREENHEART and S/Ldr Outram flying a Whitley to Holland finding the reception committee failed to turn up for operation LETTUCE 4/LEEK A. Giskes was playing his cards with finesse! S/Ldr Outram returned to Abingdon with his passenger.

The moon period for 138 Squadron closed on the 5th July, five sorties being flown between the end of June and this date. Three were by Halifax to France and two others by Whitley to Holland. F/O Walczak flew a Halifax sortie on the 1st/2nd July a French operation PIMENTO. He was to drop blind Anthony Brooks the youngest SOE ever to be sent into the field, an Englishman born in 1922. He was 20 years old when he made his jump. The area in which he was dropped was near to Phillip de Vomecourt's chateaux in the Limousin.

In an article published in the Autumn of 1988 told that on the night of his operation he was driven past some huts and parked aircraft to a small clutch of farm buildings (Gibraltar Farm). Here he was asked to check his cover story and his documents, (he had already changed out of his uniform and into his French clothing). Naturally he felt a little apprehensive but his confidence returned when a RAF Flight Sergeant helped him into an 'outsized boiler suit' which covered his civilian clothes. He was then introduced to the equipment he was to take with him, two field dressings, jack knife to sever the parachute rigging if in trouble, folding shovel (to be used as a splint if a leg was broken), emergency rations and a hip flask full of rum. He refused to take either his automatic pistol, benzedrine tablets (to keep him awake) or his 'L' suicide tablets. He was then fitted with a parachute harness, driven out to his Halifax aircraft where he met his pilot F/O Walczak, a Polish airman, and the despatcher.

Once airborne the despatcher produced a sleeping bag and suggested he might like to sleep, which he did. He was woken with coffee and sandwiches and was informed shortly afterwards that they were approaching the target and that he should make himself ready. The despatcher showed him that the safety pins holding the static lines to the aircraft and to his parachute were in position. His suitcase was pointed out to him as being in position directly over the hole. The despatcher then opened up the hole and motioned him forward. Brooks says he watched in amazement the chequerboard of fields of France 800 feet below.

A red light came on and the despatcher motioned him to swing out his legs into the hole. A little later a green light came on, the despatcher tapped him on the shoulder and out he went. He saw the aircraft climbing away into the darkness and as he drifted down he could see the ground quite clearly in the moonlight. He could see he was near a village and heard voices from below shouting '*Le voila!*'. As he had dropped blind he found this less reassuring than had he dropped on a reception committee. He started to swing violently one minute looking at the moon the next, the ground – an eternity!

The next thing he knew he had crashed violently through the branches of a tree and hit the ground with a 'hell of a thump' injuring his knee and his back. It was obvious that he would not be able to retrieve his parachute and use his shovel to bury it as he had been trained. He crawled into the nearest ditch. A friendly voice told a young lad to remove the parachute and hide in a barn while he searched for the parachutist who was probably injured. Brooks made himself known

and was carried like a child in the arms of his rescuer into a small stone
farmhouse. Here his damaged foot was manipulated into place with a
thump! His work in the field was to earn him a Distinguished Service
Order and a Military Cross.

F/O Gibson's Dutch sortie in Whitley Z9288 was unable to complete
a cargo drop, TURNIP 2, because of the weather. F/Sgt Freeland, on
the other hand flying Whitley Z9286, dropped six containers onto
CATARRH 7 but on his way home his aircraft was hit by accurate flak
and was badly damaged although not that damaged as to be written off.
He landed at base after five hours in the air. One wonders if Giskes
had released his hounds after the quarry. On the 5/6th July F/O
Wodzicki's crew failed at his second attempt to complete operation
ROACH/MACKEREL left over from 25/26th June, again the weather
defeated him.

Both squadrons record their next operations on the night of the
23/24th July. It had been a long stand down period. 161 Squadron
began the new moon period with five Whitleys and a Halifax of 138
Squadron briefed to bomb Folligny marshalling yard (some 14km east
of Granville (Manche). Two Whitleys and the Halifax bombed the
primary target. Two aircraft bombed railway lines as the secondary
target. One attacking the railway between Avranches and Folligny from
a height of 1,200 feet and the other between St-Lô and Bayeux.
Wg/Cdr Fielden having failed to identify the target jettisoned his bombs
into the sea.

The following night the 25/26th five Whitleys of 161 Squadron were
joined by four from 138 Squadron and detailed to bomb a power
station at Cholet which is approximately 50km south east of Nantes.
Tempsford ORB reports only four aircraft attacked the primary target,
two attacked railway bridges. W/O Lord of 161 Squadron bombed a
railway bridge across the Loire 17km south west of Angers. Sgt Walls
also of 161 Squadron bombed the railway line north east of Loudun.
His starboard engine caught fire and flew home on his port engine
landing at Tangmere. F/Sgt J Owen and his crew from 138 Squadron
flying Whitley Z9282 crashed at Vire about 50km west of Cacn, only
one of the crew survived.

These bombing sorties could hardly be called successful, and more
important, what G/Capt MacDonald feared most had become a reality.

138 Squadron began their new moon period on the 23/24th July by
flying three operations to Holland. P/O Wilkin completing the
outstanding TURNIP sortie by dropping from his Whitley Z9428 four
containers into TURNIP 3. P/O Newport-Tinley flying Whitley Z9146
dropped six containers into LEEK 1. S/Ldr Davies was to complete
operation LETTUCE 4/LEEK A left outstanding by S/Ldr Outram
three weeks before. He dropped one agent, Lt Gerard John Hemert
into the hands of the Gestapo. He carried a message to a man named
Taconis, who had been in captivity for five months, ordering the
destruction of the German Naval radio station at Kootwijk. Packed
inside one of the six containers dropped was his wireless transmitter,

giving Giskes a sixth link with Baker Street.

Halifaxes flew all five parachute sorties for the next two nights, the Squadron's available Whitley force being engaged in bombing operations. P/O Rymills French sortie dropped three agents on the 24/25th into CRAYFISH/BRILL. F/O Wodzicki's crew the following night finally completed ROACH/MACKEREL after his third attempt, dropping three agents and two containers.

S/Ldr Davis flew a lone parachute sortie to Denmark TABLETALK/ TABLELEG on the 26/27th but there was no reception committee to greet him. The Squadron's remaining aircraft, seven Halifaxes took themselves off in brilliant moonlight to bomb a tank farm at Gien (Loiret). (A town on the Loire approximately 55km south east of Orleans). Crews taking part, mainly Polish, appear to have been by invitation of F/O Krol seemingly the instigator of the operation! It was decided that P/O Dobromirski would lead the attack from 2,000 feet. Bombing instructions were given over the R/T in clear language and every one followed flying a left hand circuit. P/O Rymills and his crew were the only Englishmen involved and held off when the Poles decided to shoot up the German airfield at Châteaudun. The bombing was said to be extremely accurate.

There are a number of unidentified photographs on file taken by a PRU aircraft of a target consisting of a large number of bombed buildings. I wonder if these are the photographs to which Merrick refers that led to questions being raised in Parliament accusing Bomber Command of misleading the public by using the SD Squadrons primarily as bombers. However, the end of August saw the cessation of bombing sorties for both squadrons. Perhaps this was the reason for raising the Parliamentary questions in the first place!

The aircraft establishment for 138 Squadron was altered in July to an equal number of Halifax Mk.II's and Whitley Mk.V's – five of the former and five of the latter, the number of Whitleys having been reduced by three.

The last two days of the month saw 138 Squadron mounting nine sorties, four by Halifax and five by Whitley (one to France, four to Holland and one to Denmark). Of the Halifax sorties one was operation SCIENTIST/AUTHOR flown by P/O Anderle to the south of France in the Nîmes area. Here he parachuted blind two agents, Claud de Baissac and his wireless operator H L T A Peuleve. Baissac broke his ankle and Peuleve had a multiple fracture of his leg. Fortunately de Baissac was soon up and about but Peuleve wasn't so lucky, his accident was said to have been caused by being dropped too low. P/O Anderle was at the time one of the most experienced pilots of 138 Squadron and it was a blind drop. Unhappily the full operations report is missing, it would have been interesting to find out what the weather (the windspeed and visibility in particular) at ground level had been at that time.

None of the Squadron aircraft were fitted with radio altimeters, which would have given the exact height of the aircraft above the ground. A parachute landing on a rough, uneven or stony surface, perhaps aided by a strong wind would cause this type of injury. It is surprising that this did not happen more often. P/O Anderle and his crew were airborne for just over 11.00 hours. Unhappily they were to lose their lives before the year ended,

F/Sgt Freeland was flying Whitley Z9288 on the sole sortie to Denmark in an attempt to complete operation TABLETALK/TABLELEG, left outstanding by S/Ldr Davies from the 26/27 July. He parachuted three agents to a reception committee (prepared by Rottbøll whom we have met before) waiting in a field near Farso in Jutland (some 40km SW of Aalborg). They were Hans F Hansen, Peter Nielsen and Knud E Petersen. Two containers were also dropped, but landed some way away near Ranum and fell into the hands of the German Field Gendarmerie.

Three of the four sorties flown on the 29/30th July to Holland were supply drops flown by F/O Russell into TURNIP 4, P/O Turnham into CATARRH 8 and P/O Newport-Tinley into LEEK 2. They did not appear to have met with any problems. However, S/Ldr W T Davies, DFC, flying LETTUCE 5 from Tempsford, his fifth sortie to Holland, was attacked, while running up to the pin-point and was shot down by a night fighter piloted by Lt August Geiger, III./NJG1. They crashed in the vicinity of a wooded area known as the Haarlerberg some 7 km WNW of Rijssen. There were no survivors. Giskes, no doubt, having informed a nearby Luftwaffe base of the Whitley's impending arrival – this was the first aircraft and crew to have been destroyed as a result of the 'radio game' played by Giskes with Baker street.

F/Lt Boxer was promoted Squadron Leader as the replacement for S/Ldr Davies.

S/Ldr W T Davies with his ground and aircrew in front of Whitley Z9282 NF-M Standing (left to right) S/Ldr W T Davies, DFC, F/Sgt L S Franklin, Sgt E H Kerry, Sgt T M Grey, Sgt P T Wright, Sgt Hill, F/Sgt Herd (i/c 'B' Flight ground crews). With the exception of Sgt Hill (replaced by Sgt G B Wood) this crew was lost over Holland on the 29/30 July 1942 in Whitley Z9230 NF-N. The Whitley in the photograph (Z9282) was lost over France on the 24/25 July 1942. The badge on the aircraft shows a 'Gremlin' performing a hand-stand on the 'man in the moon', the motto, 'Quo Vadis'! (R Wilkin via K A Merrick)

* * *

From the 28/29 July until the end of the month saw 161 Squadron still flying bombing sorties. Five Whitley's being detailed to bomb the tank farm at Gien in the wake of the previous night's Halifax attack by 138 Squadron. Two only managed to get as far as Tangmere where they landed with engine trouble (one of whom was P/O Boothby newly commissioned from the rank of W/O) the remaining three completing the operation successfully. Four Lysanders decided to conduct a bombing war on their own. Three bombing Serqueux (3km north of Forges-les-Eaux, (Seine-Maritime) marshalling yard, the other, F/Lt Huntley, bombing a railway yard 8km NW of Abbeville. Four more Whitley sorties to Gien the following night reported 'large fires were started' and the operation was said to have been very successful. Two Lysanders continued their war with Sequeux but failed because of the weather, jettisoning their bombs into the sea at St-Valéry-sur-Somme, on the coast NE of Abbeville. The last night of the month five Whitleys were to be sent to Cholet but the ORB says two failed to take-off, which leaves one at the end of the runway wondering what happened! Only two bombed the primary target. The remaining one bombed the railway line 32km NE of Rennes.

Both Squadrons were well into August before they started to operate again. No.161 Squadron got going again on the night of 23/24th with two Lysander bombing operations, P/O Bridger dropping 2 x 100lb bombs on a railway train 5km west of Mézidon (approximately 20km SE of Caen). The other was an SIS sortie flown by S/L Lockhart, operation MERCURY, when he put down one agent with a package and picked another one up. This was the first conventional Lysander operation since May 29/30th.

The same night F/Sgt Cresswell flew an SIS operation BARK/BRUIN to France. He was unable to complete because of low cloud in the target area. It was completed by F/Sgt Wynn the following evening by parachuting into the pinpoint two agents. The remaining Whitley sortie for this night was flown by P/O Boothby to France, an SIS operation BEAGLE/BUSKER/BIJOU. He took-off at 20.26 and reports that he found the target easily from the coast after pinpointing the junction of the River Meuse and the canal. (Clearly seen on a map as being halfway between Charleville-Mézières and Sedan). Following the canal in a southerly direction they found their pinpoint, a lake in the vicinity showing up well (most probably Lac de Bairon). Here Boothby dropped three agents blind. His return flight wasn't so tranquil. At a height of 3,000 feet in the Cambrai area he was met with eight searchlights and light flak hit the starboard wing. He landed at Tangmere at 01.10 hours.

There is a mystery about this flight. In the remarks section of the operational report is written, 'owing to a misunderstanding these agents were dropped 40 miles (65km) from where they should have been'.

There is little doubt that P/O Boothby and his crew knew exactly where they were when the drop was made. Their track is easily followed on a map. The 'misunderstanding' could only have arisen from the wrong map co-ordinates for the pinpoint having been given to the navigator.

A similar mystery arose on the 1/2nd June and reported on page 196 of Professor Foot's book *SOE in France* in which he tells of two agents B H Cowburn and E M Wilkinson being parachuted in the Limousin 40 miles (65km) from the intended spot. The only two agents dropped in France that night were by F/O Walczak and his crew flying operation PALM/SPRUCE. This operation was certainly not completed 40 miles from the intended spot.

The next night the 24/25th three Lysanders flown by P/O Bridger, W/O Kingham and F/Lt Huntley continued their private war with French Railways. P/O Smith joined them flying a Whitley. W/O Kingham reported stopping a train, his bombs bursting among the trucks in the marshalling yard of Mézidon (Calvados). Huntley bombed an engine towing some 40 trucks between Lisieux and Bernay, causing a cloud of steam to come from the engine. These bombing sorties were to be the last carried out by Lysanders. I imagine the Lysander pilots taking part in these sorties found them diverting, probably better than sitting on the ground doing nothing. However I cannot imagine the Squadron engineering officer was too pleased having his valuable Lysander engine and airframe hours dissipated in this manner.

The 27/28th saw S/Ldr Gunn flying a successful Whitley SIS operation JOKER to France. Parachuting two agents, two containers and two packages onto the target. His report is a model of brevity. Selsey Bill 2,000 feet–Cabourg 2,000 feet–Châteauroux–to target. Reception flashed 'B'. Aircraft replied with 'A' and lights came on immediately. Made a complete circuit dropped load from 900 feet above ground. Three chutes seen to open. Aircraft flashed 'Z'. Green lights went out first. To Châteauroux–West to Cabourg at 3,000 feet–Coast at Tangmere–Benson–Base. Took off 20.11 landed 03.10.

W/Cdr Fielden that night flew TURQUOISE/SYRINGA XII dropping an agent on the former but leaving SYRINGA uncompleted. P/O Boothby had a successful trip to Belgium clearing up the three outstanding operations of BALACLAVA/WALLABY/ SPRINGBOK.

In the meantime F/Sgt Cresswell was flying Whitley Z9218 in an endeavour to parachute an agent, six containers and 32 Pigeons (report says two of them were special!) into France. This would complete operation MANFRIDAY/PLATYPUS partly left outstanding by W/O Walker of 138 Squadron on the 29/30th July. He took-off at 20.31 hours crossing the French coast in good weather at Pointe du Haute-Banc, (Berck) flying at 2,000 feet. At 23.34 hours while flying between 2,000 to 1,000 feet he met with light flak and searchlights which were nearly continuous from Hesdin (Pas-de-Calais) to Arleux (a small village 25km east of Arras). They pinpointed on a wood SE of Valenciennes and easily found their target. The reception flashed 'I' and they saw the red lights and dropped the agent and containers from 550 feet above the ground – the lights then went off. They set course for Berck (the way they came in) and from 23.50 until 00.14 hours they met with continuous flak and searchlights. A line of searchlights on the port side of the aircraft drove them north and they crossed the French coast at Boulogne taking continuous evasive action at a height of 500 feet. Once past the coast he climbed to 2,000 feet when one engine stopped and the other began to overheat.

After crossing the English coast although they saw Manston beacon flashing they were unable to make the aerodrome. They landed with their wheels up in a small field near Sandwich the time was 00.45 hours. After the crash Cresswell advised Tempsford by telephone his whereabouts having first organised a guard of local army privates in charge of an officer to watch over his wrecked aeroplane. In spite of this in the morning he found that a gold watch, a cap badge, all the flying rations, a pair of gauntlets, a flying helmet and the emergency rations had been stolen. Which I think was a poor show and if I had not read this in the operations report I would never have believed it possible. There were no injuries and the aeroplane was repaired to finish its days at No.42 OTU.

161 Squadron finished the month flying a further eight bombing sorties on railway communications. Sgt Readhead having dropped all of his 4 x 500 and 6 x 250lb bombs reported, among other things, 13km east of Angers, a goods train blew up with a tremendous explosion . P/O Smith attacked a train in the station at Meung-sur-Loire between Blois and Orléans with a 'terrific green flash'. Reports published in the press from Vichy stated that the Bordeaux to Paris express had been attacked. Also there were reports of bombing railway sheds, tracks, railway bridges and of making a thorough nuisance of themselves. These were the very last bombing sorties to be carried out by 161 Squadron.

Two Lysander sorties continued the serious side of operations. P/O McIndoe failing to complete CATFISH a series of dots being flashed from a torch on the ground warning him not land. S/Ldr W G Lockhart, DFC, flying an SIS sortie operation BOREAS II, ended with him taxying his Lysander V9597 into a ditch on the ground 1.8 km NNW Arbigny (Ain), which is some 20 km NNE of Mâcon, and having to set fire to it. He walked to the south of France and was taken to Gibraltar by felucca, arriving back at Tempsford on the 13th September. Lockhart flew his next Lysander sortie on the 18/19th November 1942.

CHAPTER NINE

138 Squadron Operations end of August–September 1942

Like her sister Squadron 138 started to operate again late into August. Two operations to Belgium on the 23/24th were uncompleted. F/O Wilkin was unable to find a reception at his LUCKYSHOT 6 target and P/O Newport-Tinley was unable to complete for a different reason. He took-off Whitley Z9287 at 20.41 hours for operation BALACLAVA/WALLABY/SPRINGBOK with two agents six containers, ten pigeons and a package of nickels to scatter. His reception would be three white lights and one red flashing 'C'. They crossed the English coast at Littlehampton at a height of 2,000 feet (where they were fired upon by a Bofors gun) and the French coast at Berck-sur-Mer at 22.19 hours still at a height of 2,000 feet. The weather was clear with a slight ground haze. From the coast they set course for the target area. Still at an altitude of 2,000 feet they were met with 12 searchlights and accurate light flak from several points at the southern edge of Cambrai. The flak hit them fraying a rudder cable, puncturing the hydraulic pipe leading to the rear turret and penetrating the agents' parachutes. They turned back dropping their pigeons 16km from the coast east of Berck-sur-Mer and landed at Tangmere at 01.05 hours. W/Cdr Hockey wrote on the operations report, '…fortunately agents were not injured'.

F/O Boothby of 161 Squadron successfully completed this operation on the 27/28th August.

The 24/25th saw four Halifaxes and four Whitleys off to France. F/Lt Sutton flying his first Halifax sortie having converted during the dark period. His target SYRINGA 10 was unpopular with him, finding it but reporting 'target inaccessible'. It was west of Nevers, which he identified, but the reception lights were very faint, without a flashing signal and could only be seen when he was vertically over them. To make matters more difficult the intercom failed just at this time, his WOp/AG endeavoured to repair it but without success. Sutton reported seeing an aircraft circling a factory, it then followed them passing behind at 3,500 feet.

All the sorties this night were supply drops to France, five operations coded SYRINGA (7,10,11,12 and 13). Of these SYRINGA 7 was being flown in Whitley Z9232 by S/Ldr H A Outram and his crew.

Unfortunately they went missing, crashing near the tiny hamlet of St-Loup on the south bank of the River Cher. St-Loup is roughly 10km SE of Romorantin-Lamthenay (Loir-et-Cher) which in turn is approximately 40km SE of Blois. There were no injuries and all five crew evaded capture making their way through Spain to Gibraltar from where they went home. P/O Wilson, S/Ldr Outram's second-pilot was a new 161 squadron pilot flying with this crew for operational experience.

Outram's MI9 interrogation gives no idea what happened he just says:

> None of us was hurt when our aircraft crash-landed near St-Loup on the unoccupied side of the line of Demarcation (on the River Cher) about 12 miles (20km) NW of Vierzon. We stayed beside the aircraft for about half an hour 'till it completely burnt out.

They decided to stick together and eventually met the French wife of a Welshman whose determination resulted in their repatriation. Outram arrived home via Gibraltar on the 28th September 1942. The others took longer!

F/Sgt Freeland flew SYRINGA 7 successfully two nights later dropping six containers onto the target.

The following night, 25/26th four successful French operations were flown. Three were supply drops and one involved an agent dropped by S/Ldr Boxer from a Whitley, operations DETECTIVE & BLACKTHORN. The weather he described as 'thick' when reaching the French coast at Cabourg at 7,000 feet where below the cloud was 10/10ths at 6,000 feet. (80km inland he reported the weather perfect). From Cabourg he set course for Vouvray (Indre-et-Loire) then direct to the first pinpoint, DETECTIVE. Here three parachutes were seen to open, probably the agent together with his two packages. However it is not clear from the report since at the next pinpoint BLACKTHORN, which appears to have been nearby, no parachutes were seen to open! The latter DZ is reported to have had 'water all around and would have been a difficult drop without reception lights'. Both drops were made from a height of 600 feet. He dropped his leaflets over Loches. The return trip home was made without difficulty, crossing the English coast at Selsey Bill.

The agent parachuted in was Henri Sevenet his mission was to try and bring out Phillipe de Vomecourt for a rest and for further training. De Vomecourt refused to go!

Probably one of the better known agents in the UK was Peter Churchill largely due to the public interest shown in his romance and post war marriage to a Frenchwoman Odette Sansom, whom he met in the field. On the night of 27/28th the responsibility of parachuting Peter Churchill into France (he had been landed in France on previous occasions by submarine) was given to a Polish airman F/O Walczak and his crew (F/Sgt Yenson was the pilot) Regrettably his report lacks detail and it is difficult to follow his route and actions when he got to his targets SUPPLY & SPINDLE.

Halifax W7775 took-off from Tempsford at 20.05 hours crossing the coast at Selsey Bill. At a height of 3,000 feet the French coast was crossed at Isigny thirty-five minutes later. Here they set course for Montsoreau (Maine-et-Loire) a small village on the south of the Loire where the River Vienne flows into it. It was a well chosen track keeping them clear of trouble and giving them an excellent pinpoint for setting course for their target. At 00.40 hours a triangle of red lights and a white light flashing 'Z' was seen – the DZ for SUPPLY. After dropping three packages from 600 feet the red triangle of lights went out. Another circuit was flown and the remaining two packages were dropped on the white light. The reception for SPINDLE could not have been very far away. He reports that he set course SPINDLE and completed this. Over the target at 00.55 hours, with the reception signal flashing 'D' Peter Churchill was parachuted in.

M R D Foot writes that Adolphe Rabinovitch, a young Russo-Egyptian Jew, a wireless operator, was dropped with him. Squadron records show only one agent, five packages and 24 pigeons were dropped on this operation. The pigeons being dropped 25-30km south of Pointe de la Percée.

While Cookridge writes that shortly after Peter Churchill's arrival twenty-six year old 'Alec' Rabinovitch was parachuted in north of Grenoble, the Polish pilot of his aircraft missing the prearranged DZ.

The next French operation involving a Polish crew and the parachuting of an agent took place the following night, the 28/29th. F/O Wodzicki and his pilot P/O Pieniszek flying a Halifax, operation CATALPHA. His instructions were to drop within 2/3km of the pin-point, there were to be no reception arrangements. From the French coast at Isigny P/O Pieniszek set course for the River Loire and then to Meximieux (some 20km east of Lyon). From here they went to the target. The estimated dropping point was 3km south of la Frette and 200 metres east of the road from la Frette to St-Étienne-de-St-Geoirs (Isere) (north of Grenoble). In fine weather the 'agent jumped very willingly and was quite happy and he flashed a torch when he reached the ground to show he was OK'. So much for missing the prearranged DZ. Six minutes from the French coast in the Channel on their way home they were attacked, flying at 6,000 feet, with accurate light and heavy flak from a convoy. They landed safely at Tempsford after being 7.50 hours in the air. This was the last Polish/French operation until the end of September.

There were six other operations to France that night, all supply drops, four of which were successful and two without reception. 18 containers and two packages were dropped.

No.138 Squadron finished the month of August with two Whitley sorties to Belgium. F/O Wilkin dropping an agent, six containers and 43 pigeons on operation MINK/OCELOT and W/O Walker completing SYRINGA 9. The remaining three operations were to France. The only Halifax sortie was flown by P/O Rymills on the 31/1st dropping an agent on operation AMETHYST but was unable to complete the second half of his operation DIRECTOR 2 through

Operations and Intelligence staff, RAF Tempsford 3 September 1942, including (front row left to right) W/Cdr E H Fielden, MVO, AFC (OC 161 Squadron), G/Capt A H MacDonald (Station Commander), W/Cdr R C Hockey, DFC, Czech War Cross (OC No 138 Squadron). (Imperial War Museum)

the lack of a reception. There had been five DIRECTOR operations during the month of August only one, a supply drop flown by P/O Rymills a week before, had been successful. The others failed being without a reception. This target is only mentioned once more in the operation book. P/O Rymills failing to complete DIRECTOR 13 the 23/24th September for the same reason. The use of Halifaxes on all these targets suggest that they were deep into France. The lack of receptions also suggests that this was the start of the penetration and break up of the circuit by the Germans.

The only other sortie this night involving the dropping of an agent was P/O Newport-Tinley flying operation CLAM/OUTCLASS. He had a busy night also attending to five containers, one package, three packs of nickels and 12 pigeons.

During the month of August the Squadron dropped 267 pigeons, in July 255, and one wonders where they came from and where they went!

*   *   *

No.161 Squadron started September with three unusual sorties to Holland. F/Sgt Wynne, Sgt Readhead and P/O Smith flying Whitley operations GASPER I, II and III respectively. They were each carrying 66 packages inside of which were cigarettes. Ken Merrick says they were to provide the Dutch underground with a much-needed black market commodity – a commodity to purchase information and to convert into currency. Strangely enough it was a year to the very day that a similar operation had been carried out in 1941, a half a million cigarettes having been dropped from a Wellington. The difference between the two operations was in 1941 the Dutch were operating the DZ. Now by the summer of 1942 the Germans had 30 SOE dropping zones in Holland under their control. There is little doubt these cigarettes fell directly into their hands as had all the agents dropped into Holland since March. There were, however, a small number of undetected Dutch SIS sites. I wonder where those cigarettes finally went?

Ken Merrick mentions a flight to Gibraltar by W/Cdr Fielden taking place on the 8th September and another on the 19th by F/Sgt Cresswell. There is little to be said about these two flights in the ORB except they both started from Portreath in Cornwall. 161 Squadron did not have any Halifaxes at this time so they must have been flown by Whitley. Fielden took-off from Portreath at 02.40 hours and landed at Gibraltar at 09.15 returning the same day at 23.08, and landing at base at 08.10. F/Sgt Cresswell carried three passengers and took 09.53 hours to get to Gibraltar. There is a letter dated 16th July 1942 tucked away in file Air 20/8451 (1942 Special Operations: despatch of personnel and stores) which says that aircraft from Tempsford would be required to transport agents to and from Gibraltar. Which solves this mystery.

The next moon period began on the 19/20th September, and 161 were to have a number of unsuccessful sorties due mainly to the weather. They were also to suffer a number of unfortunate losses, two on the opening night of operations. F/Sgt J D Walls and his crew flying Whitley Z6940 on operation TERRIER to Belgium crashed in the vicinity of Boulogne. There were no survivors. This was the crews ninth operation but only their second parachute sortie, the others were bombing.

P/O Boothby that night was flying operation LUCKYSHOT 7 to Belgium. Although crossing the English coast at Beachy Head at a height of 6,000 feet he decided to lose height to 2,000 feet when crossing the French coast at Haut-Banc (just south of Berck-sur-Mer). He then set course for Guise and from there went to the bend in the river Meuse south of Givet (unmistakable on a map!). From here they progressed to the target which they identified, but no reception was to be seen. However, they saw a dozen fires in the area, like burning haystacks, the nearest being 3km from the pinpoint. They decided to abandon the operation and set course for a bend in the River Somme south of Abbeville then crossing the French coast at 1,000 feet.

Five minutes after leaving the coast behind them the coolant temperature in one of the engines began to rise (he doesn't say which one). Mid-Channel the cabin filled with smoke, the oil temperature going up with the oil pressure dropping. The engine began to vibrate so it was shut down and at the same time jettisoning the containers, they were now down to 1,500 feet. They crossed the coast at Hove, the wireless operator working Pulham sending WJR (engine trouble) and homing on Tangmere. When over the Downs they lost height rapidly and decided they would not be able to reach Tangmere. So they turned south planning to land on a beach or in the water, Boothby warning the rear gunner to prepare the dinghy for launching.

In the moonlight, Boothby saw hills above his own height and switched on his landing lights to assist him. This had little effect other than dazzling him from the reflection of ground haze. Pulling back on the control column he stalled the aircraft, wheels up, onto the ground striking a tree with his port wing. The aircraft slithered to a halt between two high tension pylons four miles south of Storrington. The crew were uninjured with the exception of the rear gunner P/O McGuire who was shaken and bruised, when the rear turret fell off the aeroplane, and it was later found that he had broken his arm.

The wireless operator contacted Tangmere and told them that they had crashed. He also contacted the headquarters of No.7 Canadian Brigade Headquarters and they came out to put an armed guard around the aircraft. It would appear that they had quite a pyrotechnic display before having fired off all the very cartridges and marine distress flares to attract attention to themselves. From here they went to Tangmere taking their pigeons with them. The aeroplane, Z6814, was repaired and finished its days with No.81 OTU.

There was one other comment on the operations report that was interesting, it said:

> Apparently the Germans were holding manoeuvres in the vicinity of the pinpoint!

All three Whitley sorties to Belgium flown by 161 Squadron on the night of 23/24th failed because of the weather conditions. A Lysander SIS flight operation VESTA flown by F/Lt Huntley to France also failed for the same reason.

The next night was almost as bad, P/O Wynne was the only one out of four Whitley sorties to Belgium completing. This was his second attempt to complete SECUNDO & LUCKYSHOT 7, failing the night before. He completed SECUNDO first by dropping two agents blind in the Dinant area and then flew to la Roche and in that area completed LUCKYSHOT 7 by dropping six containers onto a triangle of white lights. It was a model operation – without fault.

P/O D C Boothby was to have another nightmare of a mission on the 24/25th taking a Whitley again to Belgium this time flying operation MONGOOSE/PRIMO. There is a note in the rough operations book that he and his crew safely baled out over France after he had dropped two agents and six containers. W R Chorley reports that the aircraft crashed near Sevigny-Waleppe (Ardennes) 23km WNW of Rethel in France. P/O Boothby, and two others evaded, three were made PoW and Sgt R E Franklin died of his wounds.

The MI9 interrogation of the evaders P/O Boothby, P/O Reed and Sgt Blyth states that all three landed near Rheims on the 25th. No reason is given why they abandoned their Whitley. Boothby walked for a half an hour to reach le Thuel (Aisne) which is just north of where the aircraft crashed. He progressed to Dizy-le-Gros (Aisne) where he found shelter in a farm and was given food, civilian clothes and a Michelin map. He was led to Sissone on a cycle were a railway ticket was bought for him via Rheims to Dijon (Cote-d'Or). This was the 26th. A priest took him to the Red Cross canteen where he was fed and slept under a table. In the morning he was advised by a porter to cross the line of demarcation at Seurre. He left the train at Seurre and walked until he came to a river (the Duobs) at Longepierrc. He attracted the attention of two Frenchmen in a boat who when told who he was took him across. He then walked to St-Bonnet-en-Presse (Soane-et-Loire) where he found shelter for the night. The next day the 28th September his host took him by car to Lyon where he was put in touch with an organisation. He arrived home via Gibraltar on the 19th October 1942. A real saga of determination and co-operation.

Reed and Blyth's story is much the same (but perhaps they did more walking!) however, they stated, 'we believe all the members of the crew except Sgt Franklin baled out successfully'. They got in touch with 'the organisation' in Marseilles and arrived home on the 19th October 1942.

161 Squadron finished flying for the month of September on the 25/26th with two Lysander sorties. P/O Bridger completing the outstanding SIS operation VESTA, having to dig out his bogged aircraft and P/O Vaughan-Fowler turning back from his SOE sortie CATFISH due to bad weather. He eventually landed at Exeter which is quite a long way from his Tangmere objective.

*   *   *

The month of September with its longer nights opened for 138 Squadron by flying a veritable plague to Poland. Halifaxes flying CHICKENPOX, SMALLPOX, RHEUMATISM and MEASLES. Only F/O Krol's operation RHEUMATISM, presumably piloted by the legendary F/Sgt Klosowski, failed because of the weather. They however completed this sortie on the night of the 3/4th dropping six men and four containers. F/O Walczac's Halifax was damaged by flak but not before he had dropped five men and three containers into CHICKENPOX. F/O Wodzicki was the other captain successfully flying two of the operations, SMALLPOX and MEASLES on the 1/2nd and on the night of the 3/4th. It looks as if he was highly contagious! He dropped six men and four containers each sortie. It was with regret that I found that all the operation reports for these sorties (as with all subsequent sorties to Poland flown by Polish crews) had been removed from the files. Which was a pity as most reports were now being typed and were readable!

However I found the Transport Form 28 (operation instructions for despatch of personnel by air) dated 29th August 1942, the DZ for RHEUMATISM was 90km ENE Glowno, 20km WNW Skierniewice, the DZ for MEASLES was 29km SW Sochacken (Sochaczew?), 12km SSE Louroy and SMALLPOX 31km E Mszczonow, 15km NE Grojec. Judging by the pattern of lights used by the reception committees they seemed to have been well manned. They used an eight light configuration pointing into wind:-

S/Ldr A H C Boxer, a New Zealander, seen here in the cockpit of his Halifax which bore his personal Maori arms. After his first tour with 138 Squadron he returned to Tempsford, in March 1944, to take command of 161 Squadron. He retired from the Royal Air Force as Air Vice-Marshal Sir Alan Boxer, KCVO, CB, DSO, DFC. (R Wilkin via K A Merrick)

```
                          o6
         o1  o2  o3  o4  o5  o7
                          o8
```

All the above DZs were within a radius of approximately 70-80km of Warsaw. A long and hazardous flight by moonlight, Warsaw being some 315 miles (500km) west of Berlin. A long and hazardous night for those supporting these operations from the ground.

The same night S/Ldr Boxer had his aircraft damaged by flak flying Operation MONGOOSE 1 to Belgium. His task was to drop eight containers, three packs of nickels (B.21) and two special pigeons and ten to scatter (I never found out what these special pigeons were). He set course from Tempsford for Orfordness, crossing the coast at height of 3,000 feet. Maintaining this height across the North Sea until

approaching the East Schelde estuary when he reduced it to 1,500 feet. The weather was good with a slight haze, no cloud and a visibility of 5 to 8km. Enemy opposition was first met shortly after passing the Dutch coast at Haamstede inaccurate light flak attacking them opposite Zierikzee, they were still at 1,500 feet. Nine minutes later three searchlights and four or five accurate light flak guns from the aerodrome at Woensdrecht attacked them. Flying on they encountered more light flak and searchlights south of Bergen op Zoom which according to the report, 'forced the aircraft off course'. They appeared to identify Turnhout canal (NE Antwerp) 'or probably east of Turnhout' but they were unable to identify Turnhout itself or Breda in Holland to the north. They proceeded via the Haringvliet where at Hellevoetsluis they were again attacked by light flak from three guns and two searchlights. They were at a height of between 1,000/300 feet when they aborted and finally crossed the English coast north of Orfordness. Before landing at Tempsford they jettisoned their containers on the airfield and landed without hydraulics and flaps. A less experienced pilot and crew might have lost their aeroplane under such circumstances.

This operation was completed successfully by P/O Turnham on the 18/19th September by dropping six containers on the target and scattering 22 pigeons.

P/O Turnham flew a Dutch operation MANGOLD/PARSLEY on the 1/2nd September. His task was to deliver two agents, four containers and a package. He took-off his Whitley at 23.15 hours and crossed the coast north of Sheringham making for the Isle of Vlieland off the Dutch coast. He crossed the island at a height of 1,500 feet at 01.15 hours. Conditions are reported as perfect. From here he flew on course for Stavoren crossing at a small village, Possen east of Stavoren. They proceeded eastwards and easily found Assen from which they went in the direction of the pinpoint where they expected to find the reception lights. Instead, he reports, there were about six vehicles with their lights on in a north, west and southerly direction. The lights went out as the aircraft passed over them. Flying a wide circuit and when he again approached the DZ area the lights went on again but again were dowsed when the aircraft approached. He then flew up the railway line to Assen and circled the town returning to the dropping zone passing over the area where, this time, the vehicle lights remained on.

Returning to Assen which he circled once more and then set course for Enkhuizen scattering his leaflets on the way at Oldemarkt. From Enkhuizen on his way to the coast flying at a height of 1,500 feet he was met with searchlights and light flak from the German aerodrome at Alkmaar. He crossed the coast south of Alkmaar at 500 feet and the English coast ten miles north of Southwold landing at Tempsford at 04.50. On board were his two agents four containers and five of the ten pigeons he had failed to parachute out. In the space reserved for remarks in his operations report were the words, 'target seems to be compromised'.

A group taken outside 138 Squadron crew room in June 1942. (Left to right) W/O Charlie ? (surname not known), P/O G F B Newport-Tinley (lost over Holland during Operation MARROW, 22/23 December 1942). F/Sgt John ?, F/Sgt H R Walker (who finished his second tour with the Squadron as a F/Lt in June 1944). P/O J E Turnham (lost over France during Operation PRODUCE 2, 1 November 1943). (John Button)

It would appear that the warning given by P/O Turnham went unheeded as F/O Wilkin attempted to complete the operation on 18/19th September. It failed being without reception. On the 24/25th P/O Newport-Tinley once again flew operation MANGOLD/PARSLEY. It was an eventful trip being attacked on the way in by light flak from three 'Bofors type' guns. They were flying at between 1,500 to 800 feet on the western point of Vlieland from here setting course for Stavoren and the target. They cruised round for five minutes until the reception lights were seen. Two runs were made, all the containers 'hanging up' on the first, They finally dropped two agents, four containers and a package from a height of 450 feet. After the second run the lights went out and he made for the coast, 3km south of Alkmaar a searchlight and a gun opened up on him. Here he also reported, 'much thunder and lightning with rain in places'. The weather fortunately cleared and arriving at the English coast they found that the guns in the rear turret were not working! This had been the third attempt to complete this sortie and at the time the agents had dropped into the hands of the Germans they had spent a total of approximately 13.30 hours in the air.

On the same night F/Sgt Freeland flew to Holland operation KALE/ CAULIFLOWER/LETTUCE 6 dropping two agents and six containers on a site 80km NNE of Wijk bij Duurstede and 40km NW Amerongen. From these two operations Cornelius Drooglever-Fortuyn, Captain Carl Beukema-toe-Water, Adriaan Mooy and Ralph Jongelie, together with an eighth transmitter, fell into the hands of Giskes. A third Dutch sortie the same night, operation MARROW 1 was flown

by P/O Kingsford-Smith depositing a further six containers into Giskes hands – he had had a good night! A further six containers arrived from MARROW 2 flown in by W/O Walker two nights later.

The 6/7th and the 12/13th September saw two Halifax sorties mounted to Norway. F/Lt Sutton flying CHAFFINCH, uncompleted 'no reception' and F/O Walczac flying GROUSE 2, engine trouble causing its failure. This operation was the start of positioning the advance parties for the destruction of the heavy water plant at Vemork in Telemark.

The 18/19th, 19/20th and the 22/23rd the Squadron's effort was devoted to Belgium. The exception was F/O Wilkin flying his Dutch operation MANGOLD/ PARSLEY and HAGFISH flown by F/Lt Russell to France. Five of the seven Whitley sorties were successful.

On the night of the 23/24th September the Squadron's effort returned to France, twelve sorties being flown until the end of the month. Fifty percent of the operations failed, three due to the weather, two due to no reception and one due to 'wrong reception'. However, six agents, 13 containers and nine packages were delivered.

The operation that failed due to the 'wrong reception' was WHITEBEAM/MONKEYPUZZLE 1/ARTIST first flown to France by P/O Turnham on the 23/24th September. The instructions on the form 28 dated 18th September 1942 says that two men, three packages and one container were to be dropped on a triangle of three red lights with a white one on the apex flashing 'F' for Freddie. The DZ would be 8km NE of Chambord and 6 1/4km WNW la Ferté-St-Cyr (Loire-et-Cher). The timing of the drop was to be between the hours of 22.00 and 02.00. I imagine the reason he reported 'wrong reception' was the colour of the triangle lights had been changed from red to white as reported by F/O Wilkin below.

There was little time wasted in mounting this operation again and the following night, the 24/25th F/O Wilkin, in Whitley Z9428 (NF-W), took-off at 20.50 in an endeavour to complete this operation. It was a straight forward trip leaving the UK at Bognor and crossing the

138 Squadron Whitley Z9428 NF-F (July – October 1942). Among the agents parachuted from this aircraft were the first two women FANY agents (Lisé de Baissac and Andrée Borell) on the 24/25 September 1942, three Dutch agents (Operation CELERY A, etc.) on the 21/22 October 1942 and four Dutch agents (Operation MARROW 7, etc.) on the 24/25 October 1942. All seven Dutch agents parachuted into German hands. Z9428 exploded in mid-air while on a training flight with No. 24 OTU on the 26 September 1943. (via Air Britain)

French coast at Pte de la Percée at 22.34 hours flying at 2,500 feet. Flying south they pinpointed Orléans and the Loire and made their way down to the target area reaching it at 00.35. They were now flying in low broken cumulus with a ceiling of 500 feet. The DZ was found without trouble but instead of a triangle of red lights, as expected, they were white, but the flashing light was OK. Making two runs over the target at 01.00 hours the drop was made from 500 feet, the despatcher reporting, 'agents jumped when told – everything OK'.

The agents were two women. A twenty-two year old Andrée Borrel returning again to France having previously been engaged for two years on an escape line and a thirty-seven year old Lisé de Baissac. They were the first women agents serving with FANY to be dropped by parachute into France. Andrée Borrel was to make her way north to Paris to work as courier to PROSPER (F A Suttill) She was eventually arrested in January 1944 and executed in Natzveiler in July 1944. Lise de Baissac went south to Poitiers where she would set up and run a reception *reseau* for incoming agents. She was lifted out on the 16/17th August 1943 by a Lysander piloted by S/Ldr Verity.

At the coast Wilkin flying at 6,000 feet was attacked by eight searchlights and light flak from Caen. He switched on his IFF and the searchlights went out! He landed at Tempsford at 04.00 hours.

The last 138 Squadron operations of the month of September took place on the 26/27th during which they were to be unfortunate to lose an experienced and successful crew. F/Sgt D H Freeland and his crew had flown their first Squadron operation in May. On this night they were flying to Belgium (their fourth operation within eight days) in an endeavour to complete IMCOMPARABLE 1 which bad weather had thwarted three nights previous. Their aircraft, Whitley Z9275, came down in the vicinity of Merville (Nord) in Flanders approximately 18km SW of Armentières. F/Sgt Freeland and two of his crew were killed and two taken PoW. There was a German airfield at Merville and possibly they flew over it and this may have contributed to their loss.

CHAPTER TEN

October 1942

On the 1st October 1942, Wing Commander E H Fielden, MVO, AFC, was promoted Group Captain to Command RAF Tempsford. Wing Commander P C Pickard, DSO, DFC, taking command of No.161 Squadron.

October 1942 opened with a full programme for 138 Squadron nine sorties being attempted on the night of 1/2nd, seven being successful and two uncompleted due to the weather. 161 Squadron solitary sortie operation CHESTNUT 1 to France flown by P/O Smith was also successful.

Three of 138's Whitley sorties were to Holland. W/O Walker's MARROW 5 meeting with ground fog, P/O Turnham's MARROW 3 receiving six containers and P/O Newport-Tinley having the misfortune to parachute yet another agent into German hands. His target CABBAGE/CATARRH 9 the agent being Aat van der Giessen, a young Dutch naval lieutenant.

France received two sorties not the least of these was F/O Anderle's Halifax operation CRAB 3 & PHYSICIAN/CHEMIST. He first disposed of three containers onto operation CRAB, situated in the Vire area in Normandy, then made track for Châteauroux and Bourges which they pin-pointed. From Bourges fog covered the ground, but they identified the target from a bend in the River Loire. F/O Anderle told his passengers because of the fog they may have to be dropped 5km from the pinpoint. At first they refused to jump but he made four further circuits pinpointing each time on the river and persuaded the passengers that the aircraft was in the target area, so they jumped. The two agents parachuted were F A Suttill (PROSPER) and J F Amps his assistant. Suttill's task was to form a new *reseau* in and around Paris taking his own code name for its identity (regrettably they were arrested in June 1943 and the circuit PROSPER collapsed). F/O Anderle reported on his way home some 30km south of Amiens two large flares were fired up from the ground exploding at 1,000 feet with a terrific flash, followed by innumerable stars which floated to the ground – this could have been 'Scarecrow', a flare used later against Bomber Command crews. He landed at St Eval.

The second of the French sorties aroused my interest when I found an undated Form 28 which was headed REDCROSS. It said that two

Nº 161 Squadron - October 1942

P/O · P/O · F/O · P/O · P/O · P/O · P/O · P/O
Bridger Jenkins Wotton MacIndoe Vaughan Stephens Mackenzie Russell
-Fowler

F/L · S/L · S/L · W/Cdr · S/L · F/L · F/L · A/S/O
Atkins · Boxer · Gunn · Fielden · Lockhart · Powell · Harcourt-Wood Johnson

On the 1 October 1942 W/Cdr E H Fielden was promoted G/Capt to command RAF Tempsford. F/O R G McIndoe flew his first Lysander sortie on the 31 August 1942, P/O J C Bridger and P/O P E Fowler flew theirs on the 25/26 September 1942. S/Ldr A H C Boxer, S/Ldr Gunn, OC Whitleys (they had no Halifaxes). S/Ldr W G Lockhart was OC Lysanders. It is probable W/Cdr Fielden had this photograph taken on the eve of his promotion to Group Captain. (via John Reid)

packages each weighing 104 lbs each would be dropped by 24 parachutes which may cause them to drift and allowances were to be made for this. Each package would be prominently marked with a red cross. They were to be dropped in a valley between Tullins and Rovon (Isrere – the file says Roven) and the villagers would collect them the following day. Tullins is roughly 20km NNW of Grenoble.

F/Lt Russell flew a partly successful Halifax operation consisting of three targets TIGER, REDCROSS & BLACKTHORN dropping five containers and two packages on the night of the 1/2nd October. TIGER an SIS target lacked a reception and was not completed. Regrettably the operations report is missing from the file.

Three further Halifax sorties were despatched this night to Poland. Again the Polish operational reports are missing. However, the Form 28 gives a good insight to these operations. The instructions on this form for operation GIMLET/SPANNER had been altered on a number of occasions but F/O Krol's crew this night were to drop six men and four containers (the men to be dropped separately from the containers). The site was 13½km NW Irena and 3kms NE Pawlowice. The reception committee would be displaying one red and one white light. In the original instructions it was requested 'as many bombs and incendiaries as possible be carried' and gave two targets. The target, if bombed, was to be the railway station at Warka. Krol and his crew successfully dropped six men and four containers. I do not know if they bombed the railway station.

Operation CHISEL was flown by F/O Wodzicki and his crew, the pilot being F/O Pieniszek, the aircraft Halifax W7776. Their instructions were to drop four men and four containers on either, 13_km SE Minsk Mazowiecki, 3km ESE of Siennica or 10km SW Losice, 3km N Prochenki. There were also two alternative railway bombing targets. They achieved the drop but on the way home ran out of fuel. The aircraft forced landing two miles south west of Goldsborough, north of Whitby in Yorkshire. There were no injuries, they had been in the air 13.30 hours!

The problem with identifying the pilot of the Polish crews at Tempsford is the ranking officer, if he was the observer, was the captain of the aircraft.

The final Polish sortie was HAMMER flown by F/O Walczac. It was a similar operation as that of CHISEL dropping four men and four containers which he completed successfully.

On the 2/3rd October another Polish crew entered the operational scene led by F/O Kuzmicki who flew a Halifax on operation LATHE to Poland, successfully dropping three agents and four containers. F/O Anderle completed TIGER outstanding from the previous night. They had little trouble finding their DZ after circuiting Givors south of Lyon and dropping an agent with two packages over a reception which they thought was a quarter of a mile SW of the pin-point given! They returned to Tangmere. Two other sorties went to Holland, one a supply drop and the other 'not completed' no reason being given.

No.161 Squadron also despatched two sorties to Holland losing P/O E Edge flying Whitley Z6653 on operation LETTUCE 7. He

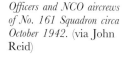

Officers and NCO aircrews of No. 161 Squadron circa October 1942. (via John Reid)

apparently had engine trouble and ditched into the sea off the Dutch coast. P/O E Edge and Sgt D L Taafe were picked up and taken prisoner. The four remaining crew members were lost at sea. There was no reception to meet the other Dutch operation MARROW 4 flown by F/Lt Marriot.

On the 3/4th 138 Squadron sent F/Lt Sutton in a Halifax to Norway on operation BITTERN. This was a mission, we are told, of trained assassins to 'liquidate known denouncers', in Norway. 'brought about due to the fears of the local population about reprisals'! The Form 28 was dated 24/9/42 and said it was to be a blind drop 21km ESE Honefossea and 23km ENE Hole. The pilot was to chose a suitable drop point in the event of the primary point not being suitable. Agents may be dropped in an area of 5km radius from pinpoint providing they know whereabouts. The pilot must be convinced he is in the dropping area, then drop. This operation is not to take place on Saturday nights owing to people taking walks in the dropping area!

F/Lt Sutton took off from Tempsford at 23.05 hours in a haze giving forward visibility of 1,000 yards (half the length of the main runway!) and a base of 1,000 feet. He crossed coast at Wells-next-the-Sea in Norfolk 28 minutes later. It remained cloudy and hazy with occasional showers half way across the sea. Reaching the Danish coast the visibility became good. They had set course for Hemstead which they easily identified. Here they saw an enemy aircraft circling a searchlight. They crossed the Norwegian coast at Jumfrulan (which I have been unable to trace). They had little difficulty pinpointing a bridge on the north east corner of a lake close to their target. At 23.05 the three agents 'seemed quite satisfied' and jumped from a height of 700 feet. Six containers were also dropped. They returned by the same route as they came. meeting with rain half way across the North Sea on their way to Flambrough Head. They were diverted to Acklington where they

Halifax W7776 NF-B converted for Special Duty work by A & A E E. It was the first of three aircraft (W7773, W7774, W7776) to be lost on Polish operations during October 1942. W7776 ran out of fuel and crash landed ½ mile SW Goldsborough near Whitby, Yorkshire, following Operation CHISEL to Poland on the 1 October 1942. F/Sgt Klosowski was the pilot, F/O M Wodzicki the navigator and captain. W7773 and W7774 were lost on the same night in October and the last of this series, W7775, was lost over Holland in December 1942. (Crown copyright)

landed at 07.10 hours.

On the 4th October F/O M Wodzicki and F/O L M Anderle were awarded the DFC and F/Sgt J Pieniszek was awarded the DFM although, by now, he had been commissioned.

* * *

In the meantime a new type of operation appeared in the operational diary for 161 Squadron. The 12th, 13th and 14th October shows F/Lt Whinney and P/O Kingham flying ASCENSION operations in Douglas Havoc aircraft.

During February F/Lt Whinney had demonstrated to the NID in a Wellington that it was possible to handle the NID Breton fishing boat radio link more efficiently from the air. In April with a crew that included foreign language speakers and agents, they were making flights at 22,000 feet in daylight during which they made radio telephone contact with the resistance. During January F/Lt Whinney had visited the High Altitude Flight at Boscombe Down and made his acquaintance with the Havoc which he thought was ideally suited for this work. However, after demonstrations and training, in July he took delivery of two Havoc I's AW399 and BJ477 from Burtonwood. These aircraft were fitted with aerials at Farnborough and the radio telephone at Cranfield. This radio communication system was devised as a quick training method for agents entering the field without the six months training needed to make them a proficient wireless operator using morse. Communication could be established using this method, with a French speaking crew member in the aircraft, up to a range of 160 miles. In addition, because of the very high frequency they were using, the agent transmitting on the ground was difficult to intercept. F/Lt Whinney called themselves a flying telephone exchange!

Crew of Whitley Z9428 NF-F, F/O R P Wilkin (pilot), Sgt Reardon (second pilot), P/O W Gliddon (navigator), P/O H Burke (WOp/AG), F/Sgt Hughes (AG). The aerial suggests an early 'Rebecca' receiver. S/Ldr Wilkin, DFC, P/O Burke, DFM and F/Sgt Hughes were lost in September 1943 over Holland. (R Wilkin via K A Merrick)

The Havocs were duly attached to 161 Squadron and operated out of St Eval. On the 13th October F/O Kingham flying Havoc BJ447 took off from St Eval at 07.20 hours. The route he took was St Eval–Bishops Rock – continue on the track as far as Longitude 7 degrees west to a patrol area approximately 40 miles (65km) west of Brest (during this time the French coast was in sight from 20,000 feet) –Lizard Point–St Eval. His duty was to establish R/T contact with a ship and receive reports on enemy shipping in the Brest–Lorient area. The weather was fair, patches of thundery cloud, no cloud above 5,000 feet. No enemy opposition encountered. F/O Kingham landed at 10.05 hours.

Prior to the departure of the ship on this operation all R/T contacts were OK. Of the three operational flights that took place on the 12th/13th/14th no contact was made with the ship. Because of the proximity of the French coast and to other shipping the Captain deemed it unwise to hoist and set his aerial during daylight for fear of being observed. As a result of these initial operations arrangements were made to fit these ships with permanently concealed aerials.

The complete record of these operations are in a thick file, AIR 20/8317. The file starts with the above operations and the information on them diminishes as they progress, finally only giving the pilot's name, aircraft, time up, time down and whether contact was made. On the 24th March 1943 these operations were flown from Tempsford, Hudsons taking over from the Havocs on the 29th October 1943. F/O Affleck flying the last Havoc sortie on BJ447 and the next day flying the first Hudson sortie. The file finishes on the 17th January 1945 with a Hudson sortie being flown by F/Lt Helfer who two days previous had made an emergency landing at Woodbridge on his starboard engine during operation WESTMINSTER.

The night of the 18/19th October saw 138 Squadron flying three Halifax sorties to Norway and a Whitley sortie to Denmark. F/Lt Russell flying to Norway declared that the DZ area for operation ORION was unsuitable and returned with his load. W/Cdr Hockey flew GROUSE 2 and dropped four agents, Claus Helberg, Jens Poulson, Arne Kjelstrup and Knut Haugland into the wastes of Hardanger Vidda 'on to a small mountain plateau at Flarfeit above the Sogne valley'. With them were dropped six containers and two packages, this operation was adding to the advance party for the eventual assault on the heavy water plant at Vemork. P/O Rymills dropped two agents and two packages on operation CASTER/CORONA.

The Whitley sortie TABLETOP A to Denmark flown by P/O Kingsford-Smith appears to be that mentioned by Cookridge as being the first of the water jumps. Dressed in a newly developed waterproof suit, which was worn over ordinary civilian clothing, Morgans Hammer was successfully parachuted into the waters of the Kattegat off the coast of Tisvilde, Zealand. Hammer's duty was to take over the TABLE Group, the method of his delivery into Denmark was caused by London having lost contact with the Danish SOE.

Eight of the nine sorties flown by No.138 Squadron on the night of the 21/22nd were to France. W/Cdr Hockey making a rare failure to complete in the absence of a reception. Of those remaining, five were successful. F/O Wilkin flew a Whitley sortie, operation CELERY A/PUMPKIN/MARROW 9/TOMATO A to Holland. Sadly there were no problems in parachuting Peter Kamphorst, Meinart Koolstra and a W/T operator Michael Pals into the hands of the Germans. After making two circuits of the DZ the despatcher reported 'they jumped when told'. Six containers had preceded them.

*   *   *

The new Commanding Officer of No.161 Squadron W/Cdr Pickard lost no time in flying his first official operation with his new Squadron. Flying operation MONKEYPUZZLE 2 on the 21/22nd in Whitley BD363 to France. They were carrying a crew of seven in all, which included two observers, P/O Broadley his regular observer, and F/O Taylor. They took-off from Tempsford at 20.15 hours and flew to Tangmere to top up their fuel tanks, taking-off for Cabourg at 21.11 hours, They crossed the French coast at an altitude of 5,000 feet, then meeting the Loire 6km to the west of the islands, east of Blois (these islands in the Loire were a very popular pinpoint and were used by most of us when down in that direction). At 13.18 hours they saw a bright static white light which went out as they approached it. They circled for 15 minutes and the light came on again flashing 'L' and then remainder of the reception lights came on. From a height of 500 feet four containers were dropped over lights that were only visible from overhead, He continues in his report 'but owing to a misconception, the packages were not dropped on the pinpoint but at Marchenoir (Loire-et-Cher), as they were thought to be GRANTHAM'S'. The three packages referred to, were dropped just west of the village. With that he returned home the way he came and landed at Tempsford at 02.45 hours.

During his briefing Pickard had been given, in error, two targets MONKEYPUZZLE 2 and GRANTHAM. The co-ordinates given for MONKEYPUZZLE 2 in the operational report (47° 40′ 10″N and 01° 35′ 39″E) when plotted puts it roughly 7km SE of Mer (Loir-et-Cher), on the south side of the Loire. Marchenoir is approximately 15km NW of Mer. 161 Squadron were flying two GRANTHAM sorties to Belgium that night. S/Ldr Gunn flying PERIWIG 6/GRANTHAM 2 which he completed, P/O Smith flying LUCKYSHOT 8/GRANTHAM 1 where there was no reception. All very confusing I wonder what Pickard thought!

Both Squadrons lost a Whitley that night, 161 Squadron losing BD228 returning from operation LUCKYSHOT 8/GRANTHAM 1 crashed on landing at Tempsford and burnt out killing the pilot P/O W W S Smith, DFC. two other members of the crew, were injured. No.138 Squadron lost P5029, one of the first of two Whitleys allocated to 419 Flight almost two years to the day. P/O G F B Newport-Tinley having completed, dropping eight containers, on operation SPRUCE 2 in France, lost an engine and ditched off Eastbourne Pier in Sussex. It must have been a text book ditching no one injured and all were picked up by the Royal Navy.

The 24/25th October was to be a busy night for Tempsford. No.138 Squadron flying a mixture of operations involving four Halifaxes and four Whitleys. Two Halifax operations to Norway failing because of the severity of the weather.

F/O Wodzicki and his crew had a unique sortie to Estonia, operation BLUNDERHEAD. The undated Form 28 said the operation would take place from Peterhead and it would be a blind drop between Leesi and Kiiu Aabla. The drop would be made in a clear area preferably near to a wood and the DZ should be shown to the agent so that he could orientate himself. One man and three containers were to be dropped and the agent would manhandle the containers himself. On the 18th October the Form 28 was altered to one package.

What actually happened, was a remarkable feat of piloting and navigation. Halifax W7773 piloted by F/Sgt Sobkowiak with W/O Zaremba as his second pilot took-off from Linton-on-Ouse at 17.55 hours and crossed the coast at Scarborough flying at 2,000 feet, (cloud restricted the altitude throughout the flight to 2,000 feet). Here they set course for The Skaw which was reached at 22.00 hours, from there to Gotska Sandon (a tiny island in the middle of the Baltic north of the larger island of Gotland). Still flying at 2,000 feet at 23.05 hours they reached Naissaar Island (about 17km NW Tallinn). Ten minutes later they were over the target area (Kiiu is about 30km east of Tallinn, Leesi a further 16km to the north). The passenger did not wish to be dropped over the pinpoint as the ground below was definitely marshy so another point was selected with the agents approval 'on the western side of the base of the Leesi promontory in a clearing between woods'. He 'jumped without hesitation' from 800 feet signalling the aircraft from the ground with a torch to indicate his safe landing. I should add in spite of the amendment to the Form 28, three containers were dropped with him.

They had dropped an Englishman, Roland Seth, who says he had the misfortune of having his parachute entangled in telegraph wires and a tree. He was immediately surrounded by Germans having fallen close to their field post. (I wonder how he managed to signal the aircraft of his safe arrival on the ground as reported by Wodzicki?) He escaped but was re-captured again shortly afterwards having been betrayed. He was incredibly lucky to survive captivity and the war.

Sobkowiak returned the same way as they came in crossing the Danish coast north of Ringkøbing making a landfall north of Sheringham and landing at Tempsford at 07.08 hours. They were without intercom soon after leaving the Danish Coast. They had been in the air 13.13 hours. If a track is drawn on a map from Gotska Sandon to Ringkøbing it will be seen that a considerable flying time must have been spent over neutral Sweden.

There were three Whitley sorties to Holland, P/O Kingsford-Smith flying operation MARROW 4, F/O Wilkin flying MARROW 7/CELERY B & C and P/O Turnman flying MARROW 6/TOMATO B & C. As a resurgence of these difficult and dangerous flights the macabre saga of treachery and betrayal continued. Four agents, Jan Hofstede and Horst Steeksma and two W/T operators Max Macare and Charles Pouwels and 18 containers were parachuted into the hands of the Gestapo. Giskes now had eleven radio links with Baker Street and the Germans were complaining that the flow of agents arriving in their hands was giving them so much additional work!

The remaining Halifax operation of this night was flown by F/O Anderle and his crew to their native Czechoslovakia, operation ANTIMONY. Anderle took-off at 18.42 hours. On board were the three agents and in the bomb bays, four 250lb and two 500lb bombs, each with a time fuse of 11 seconds. East Wittering on the Suffolk coast was crossed at a height of 6,000 feet just 48 minutes later. At 21.00 hours they were north of the River Somme at a height of 9,800 feet. They were now flying over 10/10ths cloud and heading for Strasbourg, the cloud below preventing them from identifying it. However they turned on ETA at 21.24 hours now at 11,000 feet. The first pin-point they obtained was Terezin on the River Elbe (roughly 50km north of Prague). From here they flew to Roudnice nad Labem (approx. 12km to the south), thence to Melnik (some 24km north of Prague) and to dropping point No.1. Haze preventing them from identifying the DZ clearly they proceeded to dropping point No.2. After consultation with the passengers all three, Frantisek Zavorka, Stanislav Srazil and Lubomir Jasinek, jumped from 400 feet above the ground (they were probably using the new large 'A' type parachute) – 'very nice jumping', said the despatcher! The estimated dropping point was east of Cineves (?) Lake the time 23.08 hours.

Ten minutes later they made their first attack from a height of 300 feet on Pardubice aerodrome (some 80km due east of Prague). Having first circled the town, on the first run they dropped one 500lb and two 250lb bombs on the hangars, the bursts were seen. On the second run they dropped an identical load onto the barracks, these bursts were not seen. A further two runs across the field were made, the report saying 'for the benefit of the front, rear and side gunners who fired several thousand rounds into aircraft parked on the aerodrome'. On the last run in they were hit by accurate return fire from the ground. Four low level runs at the target in moonlight was really asking to be shot down and this was the first and only time I have heard of side guns being used in a Halifax. They returned home across Germany, in the waning moon, at an altitude of 9,000 feet by the same outward route, landing at 05.21 hours. A truly remarkable operation. The purpose of the agents mission was to re-establish communication with the Home Army and to establish the fate of operation SILVER A. They remained free until January 1943 when Zavorka and Jasinek committed suicide and Srazil collaborated with the Germans.

P/O Prior of No.161 Squadron had an eventful Whitley SIS sortie, ORION I to Norway. He took-off at 18.27 hours meeting with severe electrical storms over the North Sea and a wind from the west that was stronger than calculated. The cloud at the Norwegian coast was 7/10ths strato-cumulus with base at 2,400 feet. Not satisfied with his landfall the pilot turned about and crossed the coast again at Hille Island at 4,000 feet, running into cloud and icing conditions inland. He turned about again this time making a wide sweep out to sea and approaching land again just west of Mandel. He crossed the coast flying at 2,000 feet when several guns opened fire on him holing the aircraft in several places and severing the control cable to the trimmer tabs making the aircraft very nose heavy. His evasive action brought him down to 100 feet and it became necessary to stabilise the aircraft by moving the two passengers and crew aft. The operation was then aborted and they landed at 02.58 hours. The damaged aircraft Z6828 was repaired and eventually found its way to No.42 OTU.

Bad weather forced F/O McIndoe to abort his Lysander operation CATFISH/GIBEL but two successful Lysander sorties took place the following night, the 26/27th. F/O Bridger flying an SIS operation ACHILLES and P/O Vaughan-Fowler an SOE operation SADLER/ELECTRICIAN.

No.161 Squadron finished the month with bad weather failing eight of their sorties. W/Cdr Pickard attempting to fly his first Lysander operation SQUID and SQUID B meeting with low cloud on both occasions. F/O McIndoe made his fourth Lysander attempt to complete CATFISH/GIBEL bad weather thwarting him again. The remaining five uncompleted operations for the month were Whitley sorties to France and Holland.

No.138 Squadron's end of October activities were also to be curtailed by the weather. However, On the night of the 27/28th they despatched three Whitleys to Holland. W/O Walker flying MARROW 10/CUCUMBER A & B, F/O Wilkin MARROW 11 and P/O Turnham MARROW 8. Two agents, the CUCUMBER team, Captain Jan Dane and Jacob Bakker together with 18 containers dropped into German hands. *SS Sturmbannführer* Schreieder of the SD (*Sicherheitspolizei* – the security police section of the SS) and working in conjunction with Giskes was reputed to have callously written in his diary 'our kitchen garden is thriving marvellously'. Four other sorties to France failed that night either because of the weather or the lack of receptions.

Operations for the 29/30th October were equally unproductive. Three Halifax sorties were briefed for Poland. BRACE for F/O Walczac, WRENCH for F/Lt Krol, and PLIERS for F/O Wodzicki. The Form 28 for BRACE, dated 22/10/42, suggests that the Gestapo Headquarters in Warsaw be bombed in addition to dropping six men, four containers and two packages. This order was rescinded by GHQ but a new operation RIVET was mounted, again recommending the bombing of the Gestapo HQ! A third Form 28, operation WRENCH says Bombs only, Gestapo HQ Warsaw, alternative targets Railway stations at Lowicz, Warka or Siedlice.

F/O M Wodzicki, 'Virtuti Militari', 'Krzyz Walecznych' (Order of Military Valour and the Polish War Cross), DFC, PAF, was lost over Norway in Halifax W7773 NF-S during the night of 29/20 October 1942 on Operation WRENCH to Poland. (via John Button)

As usual the Polish operational reports are missing from the files. However, operation RIVET never took place under that code name. F/Lt Krol's aeroplane piloted by W/O Klosowski was the aircraft carrying the bombs (4 x 250lbs and 2 x 500lbs). Ken Merrick says there was a plan in August (operation TUXEDO) for a one way mission by a Whitley (to be flown by Krol's crew), the aircraft to be abandoned over the target and allowed to crash onto the Gestapo HQ. W/Cdr Hockey advised strongly against it and asked in letter dated 16/6/42 that it be called off. Later he wrote asking if there was a self destructing device in the aircraft and if so that it be removed. It would appear that preparation for this operation had gone a long way to being completed.

Halifax W7774, piloted by W/O S Klosowski, PAF and captained by F/Lt S Krol, PAF, took-off at 17.54 for Poland on Operation WRENCH. Over Warsaw Krol decided, after several bombing runs, that he was more likely to cause greater casualties to his fellow countrymen than to the Gestapo and so they bombed an alternative target, not the railway stations as recommended but the German airfield in Okecia, Warsaw. On the way back they were attacked by two Me 110's some 65km from the Danish coast, damaging the engines, intercom, petrol tanks, and the dinghy. They ditched within sight of the English coast at 06.40 hours. Fortunately having been observed by the coastguard they were soon rescued by the Sheringham Lifeboat. This was the second wrecked Halifax that Krol had left behind him! F/Sgt Wasilewski was awarded a bar to his DFM for his part in this action.

There was no reception to welcome operation BRACE so it was abandoned, arriving home after being 14 hours in the air.

F/O Wodzicki and his crew flying Halifax W7773 failed to return from operation PLIERS having been shot down and crashing between Helleran and Refsland in southern Norway. All of the Polish crew were killed. F/O M Wodzicki, DFC, and his crew flew their first 138 Squadron sortie in March 1942. (remember he was an observer captain, his pilot on this operation was W/O F Zaremba). Such an experienced crew would undoubtedly be missed.

Three Whitley sorties were uncompleted this night due to weather and the lack of a reception. W/O Walker flying his sixth sortie of the month, operations TABLETOP & TABLEMAT to Denmark. In spite of circling both locations for ten minutes, no lights were seen. The 10/10ths cloud was down to 2,500 feet and below it was raining. Enemy ships shot at him through the cloud. Diverted to Bodney, Norfolk, he finally landed with his agent after a ten hour flight.

The last night of the month the 31/1st was to see P/O Rymills, DFM, finish his tour with 138 Squadron by flying operation GARTERFISH/MONKEYPUZZLE/ACTOR/ BUTCHER to France dropping three agents, four containers and four packages. He was to return to No.161 Squadron in January 1943 and to complete another successful tour, this time flying the Lysander.

On the down side the Squadron was to lose another aircraft, Whitley Z9159. P/O J E Turnham failing to return from France on his sixth operational flight of the month, operation PRODUCER 2. There are little details available other than the crew are buried in Abbeville.

October 1942 was not a very happy month for Tempsford.

CHAPTER ELEVEN

November–December 1942

It was 138 Squadron that opened the innings for November with F/O Walczac flying a Halifax on the 7th November to France, operation NEPTUNE 1. I cannot think of a more aptly coded operation, the agent was to be dropped into a lake. It is not said whether or not he appeared on the shore holding a trident!

Early during September two Armstrong Whitworth Albermarle Mk.1's, P1378 and P1390 had been added to 161 Squadron's inventory. Their purpose was to join the Royal Navy's NID boat operations as escort aircraft. The first of these operations took-off from St-Eval at 13.30 hours on November 9th and was flown by F/Lt Marriot in P1378. There were three crew on board plus Lt Bell-Scott, RNVR. Their duty 'to contact vessel, carry out escort duties on outward journey, maintain security from friendly aircraft and to check and photograph turn-out of vessel'.

They reported the vessel was picked up as she was leaving base at Scillies, photographed and several faults in her turn-out noted. Two Liberator aircraft showed interest but these were led away before they had any chance to identify the vessel. Escort duties were carried out until shortly after dusk. They landed at 17.15 hours after a flight of 3.45 hours.

A Havoc operation Ascension FOIBLE was successfully flown by F/Lt Whinney on the same day.

The dark period brought little rest as both Squadrons were called upon to fly. On the 7th when P/O Cresswell and P/O Readhead, from 161 Squadron, took-off Whitleys from Portreath in Cornwall and set course for Gibraltar on a ferry flight presumably carrying agents.

Following Operation TORCH, the Anglo/American landings in North Africa on the 8th November, No.138 Squadron were ordered to fly urgent supplies to Maison Blanche in Algeria. The 138 Squadron detachment detailed was: W/Cdr Hockey flying Halifax L9613, F/Lt Russell W1007, F/O Anderle W1002, P/O Pieniszek (Captain, F/O Walczac) W1229, S/Ldr Boxer DG252, W/O Klosowski (Captain, F/Lt Krol) W1012 and F/O Dobromirski (Captain, F/O Idzikowski) L9618. All aircraft were carrying ground crew.

S/Ldr Boxer with P/O Kingsford-Smith as co-pilot flew out to Gibraltar on the 16th arriving on the 17th. Kingsford-Smith is recalled by Merrick as saying: 'we carried some type of light artillery that could be carried by camel. It must have been urgently required as it was picked up by a type of jeep as soon as we unloaded it'.

W/Cdr Hockey with F/O Wilkin as second pilot followed from Tempsford to Hurn then on the 17th flew Hurn to Gibraltar in 8.20 hours and Gibraltar to Maison Blanche in 3.30 hours on the same day. During their flight the port-inner failed. On the 19th they left Algiers for Gibraltar the port-inner failing again. At Gibraltar attention was given to the engine and Hockey flew a 35 minute air test, before taking off on the same day for Tempsford arriving after a flight of 9.45 hours.

While this operation took place, Hitler, on the 11th November ordered the occupation of the Vichy Zone and German troops swiftly moved to occupy Lyon, Clermont-Ferrand, Limoges, Montpellier and Toulouse (in an attempt to capture what remained of the sabotaged French fleet), while Mussolini's troops occupied Savoy and the Côte d'Azure. Mass arrests among the Resistance leaders began, the town lights went out, the blackout over France was now complete.

In the meantime on the 18th November a 161 Squadron Whitley, Z9160, which due to engine failure had been left behind at Gibraltar on the 13th October, was picked up by P/O O A Cussen and flown out for home. A persistent engine problem compelled the crew to turn back, force landing near Armacao de Pera, (Algarve) 40km WNW of Faro. The crew was interned. The engine failure was doubtless brought about by the replacement made at Gibraltar. Merrick says, replacement Merlin X engines at Gibraltar were noted for their main bearing failures.

The MI9 interrogation of Cussen disclosed when 20 miles (32km) off Cape St Vincent engine trouble developed. They carried on to Cape Finisterre but the problem got worse and they decided to return to Gibraltar but they were compelled to force land at Armacao de Pera. They were taken to Elvas, staying at the Pensao Internacional Hotel until the 15th January 1943, flying home via Lisbon on the 17th.

The night of the 15/16th saw P/O Readhead, recently returned from Gibraltar, and F/Lt Prior both flying 161 Squadron SIS Whitley operations TERTIO and FRANCOISE to France dropping three agents between them and P/O Foster dropping two agents on LEMUR/TOAD in Belgium. The Lysander detachment left Tempsford the following day for Tangmere.

A lone Whitley operation by 138 Squadron on the 16/17th to France was followed on the 17/18th by a further three, one of which was flown by W/O Walker. He must have been a very popular airman, dropping two agents and ten cases of coffee during operation BABOON & DINGO in Belgium. The same night 161 Squadron Whitleys were over Holland where P/O Foster delivered stores onto TURNIP 6, and F/Sgt Gray not finding a reception for LEEK 3. P/O Bridger successfully flew a Lysander sortie, the fifth attempt to complete GIBEL/CATFISH. W/Cdr Pickard failed at his third attempt to complete a Lysander sortie (SKATE/SQUID) no reason was given.

The 18/19th saw 161 Squadron out alone, two Whitley sorties, weather preventing Sgt Hey completing a Dutch trip and F/Lt Prior flying operations SCIENTIST 2 & FARMER/MUSICIAN/BAKER to France. Prior parachuted in Captain Gustave Bieler (GUY), a French Canadian, who landed onto a rocky surface injuring his spine badly enough to put him into a Paris hospital. In spite of this serious injury he continued his valuable work until his arrest in St-Quentin on the 13th December 1943 causing the demise of the *reseau* MUSICIAN. He was eventually shot. Dropped with him were Captain Michael Trotobas (SYLVESTRE) and his wireless operator Albert Staggs. This was Trotobas's second tour and with Staggs was to set up the *reseau* FARMER. The former was to be shot by the Gestapo avoiding arrest on the 27th November 1943, the latter was arrested a month later and eventually released.

The operations report says Prior was flying Whitley BD276 and talks of setting course for Cabourg on the French coast but a change in wind found him over le Havre at 2,400 feet where he was attacked by flak 'from many positions'. He then made for 'the islands' (on the Loire) east of Blois thence to bend in the Loire south of Orléans. In weather that was 'very hazy' he followed the railway to his first target. The starboard engine had been losing revolutions after leaving the French coast and after completing the drop it became worse so he decided to return by the same route leaving SCIENTIST 2 uncompleted. In the UK Prior was diverted to Tangmere.

The Lysanders attempted their first double landing operation SKATE/SQUID which failed. S/Ldr Lockhart is recorded to have been attacked by seven plus FW 190's and abandoned his sortie. F/O Vaughan-Fowler failing to locate the landing ground.

The following night SCIENTIST 2 was completed F/Sgt Hey dropping the four containers brought back by Prior. Two supply sorties, one from each Squadron were also completed. W/O Walker's sortie for 138 Squadron appears to be his last, having finished his tour. He was to return to Tempsford with a commission and a second tour of duty.

The next time the two Squadrons flew was the night of 22/23rd, among the five Whitley sorties flown by No.161 Squadron the name of S/Ldr Hodges appears for the first time. (the rest period for his first operational tour being over, a tour which included a walk home through France). His first SD sortie was GORILLA & SYLVESTRE in France. Flying Whitley BD363 he crossed the French coast at Trouville flying at an altitude of 400 feet and headed for the islands in the Loire thence to the DZ of GORILLA dropping two agents and two packages from 550 feet, four parachutes were seen on the ground. They then proceeded to the second pinpoint SYLVESTRE (an SIS target) where they unloaded six containers. He diverted to Tangmere landing after 7.40 hours in the air.

Regrettably F/Sgt J A Hey of 161 Squadron in Whitley Z6629 and flying two operations to Belgium, PERIWIG 7 & QUINTRO (the latter an SIS sortie), failed to return. Presumably lost at sea, there were no survivors including the agent for QUINTRO, Lt Fernand de Bisschop.

Another Belgium sortie LUCKYSHOT 8 that night failed because of the weather. The Lysanders successfully flew their first double operation SKATE/SQUID. P/O Bridger and W/Cdr Pickard were the pilots. Pickard had at last completed his first Lysander operation.

The night of the 25/26th saw three 138 Squadron Halifax sorties flown to Norway, operation ORION 1 flown by F/O Walczac and his crew, THRUSH by F/O Anderle and GANNET by S/Ldr Boxer. Anderle successfully dropped two agents and six containers. The agent in S/Ldr Boxer's aircraft said the wind was too high and refused to jump. P/O Szrajer was the pilot on F/O Walczac's aircraft for

This photograph of P/O L McD Hodges was taken at Upper Heyford in 1940. On the 4/5 September 1940 he was shot down while flying a Hampden of No. 49 Squadron. Escaping after capture, he arrived home via Gibraltar on the 31 July 1941. He was posted to No. 161 Squadron in November 1942 and, as a Wing Commander, took command during May 1943. He retired from the RAF, Air Chief Marshal Sir Lewis Hodges, KCB, CBE, DSO & bar, DFC & bar. (ACM Sir Lewis Hodges)

operation ORION 1. They had two agents and one package to drop blind. A twin engined aeroplane came and looked at them at Farsund when flying at 4,000 feet. Evasive action soon lost it. They met with accurate flak from about ten guns shortly afterwards. Flying in good visibility at 2,500 feet they made a good pinpoint at Flekkefjord and made straight to the target. They pinpointed the hill on which the target was located but decided it was too rough for parachuting so they selected 'a flat place' about 3km to the east and dropped from about 800 feet. The rear gunner saw the parachutes land safely. The lakes were frozen and there was snow on the nearby mountains. (it must have been a bitterly cold night). They were diverted to Waterbeach for landing.

161 Squadron on the other hand flew three uncompleted sorties to France, lack of reception and bad weather were the cause of their failures. The Lysanders were out successfully, P/O McCairns, MM, flying PIKE/CARP his first of 36 such operations and P/O Vaughan-Fowler flying APOLLO. There was also another 'first' that night a Hudson sortie, operation STEWARD, the first attempt to land a Hudson in France. Flown by G/Capt Fielden operation STEWARD failed due to fog. He made a further unsuccessful attempt on the 23/24th December. Operation STEWARD was completed by W/Cdr Pickard on the 20/21st February 1943, landing a Hudson in the Arles (Bouches-du-Rhône) area. A double Lysander SIS sortie on the 28/29th operation PERRY flown by P/O McCairns and P/O Vaughan-Fowler put 161 Squadron into December.

From the 26/27th November until the end of the month the weather hampered 138 Squadron operations over France. However, on the 29/30th F/O Walczac's crew flown by P/O Szrajer again attempted to complete the SIS operation ORION 2 in Norway. Crossing the North Sea on the way out they met with heavy rain showers, and extremely rough flying conditions with the cloud base down to 2,000 feet. Near the Norwegian coast the aircraft was struck by lightning which temporarily blinded the crew. Once through this front the weather was clear. Deep snow covered the high ground and visibility was exceptional – 50km. They map read their way in the moonlight to the DZ without any problem, it was covered with deep snow, not surprisingly there was no reception. Abandoning the operation they flew back to Tempsford with the three containers they were intended to drop. F/Lt Russell also flying to Norway, operation GANNET had more success. In spite of low cloud over the North Sea they too found the DZ, and two agents recognising the country below, were dropped blind.

However, during this period six successful sorties were flown to Holland and four more agents were parachuted into Giskes net. On the 28/29th F/Sgt Weatherstone flying operation TURNIPS/BROCCOLI/MUSTARD dropped Lt. Johann de Kruyff and his radio operator George Russell. The following night Sgt Reardon flying operation LETTUCE 4/CHIVE/CRESS dropped Hermann Overes and Johan Bernard Ubbink, (it was he who escaped on the 30th August 1943,

reached Berne and informed London). Giskes now controlled fourteen different radio channels and by now forty-three British agents had fallen into his hands. It is horrific to think that no action was taken in London in spite of repeated warnings from a number of captured radio operators that they had been compromised . The negligence and complacency shown by Baker Street, which enabled this situation to develop, certainly sealed the fate of the agents dropped and for that matter many of the aircrews that were sent to deliver them.

My records show yet another agent was dropped with a package into Holland on the 29/30th November by P/O Bunting during operation SAUTERNS. I cannot find any reference to this operation in any reference book, it was probably for the SIS.

Sgt Reardon and P/O Bunting flew the last of the 138 Squadron Whitley sorties, the remaining crews, in the meantime, were converting to Halifaxes.

This photograph, taken facing due north, shows a T2 type hangar of which Tempsford had six. One, after the war, was dismantled and reassembled at Duxford where it can still be seen today. The building on the right housed the 'Squadron Offices'. The watch tower and shelters for the fire engine and night flying equipment can be seen to the left. (L Dibin via S Tomlin)

*   *   *

An urgent requirement for the transportation of approximately 71,000 lbs of supplies to Egypt found seven 138 and two 161 crews on attachment to No.511 Squadron, a long range transport Squadron operating Liberators from Lyneham. It was an operation similar to that of November to North Africa and could only be looked forward to with confidence of success by the selected crews. It was to turn out a disaster for No.138 Squadron.

The first two 138 Squadron Halifaxes left Tempsford on the 3rd December 1942: –
DT543, captained by F/Lt Krol, PAF, (pilot W/O Klosowski, PAF).
W1229, captained by F/O Walczak, PAF, (pilot P/O Szrajer, PAF) to Malta only. Leaving on the 6th: – L9618 F/Lt Sutton. Leaving on the

7th: – L9613 W/Cdr Hockey, DT542 captained by F/O Idzikowski, PAF, (pilot F/O Dobromirski, PAF).W1007 F/Lt Russell who was recalled. W1002 F/O Anderle. Two 161 Squadron Halifaxes also left on the 7th: – DG244 S/Ldr Hodges and DG245 F/Lt Prior.[2]

W/Cdr Hockey was in overall command of the force and his log book reads as follows:

L9613	7th December 1942	Tempsford – Lyneham	.50
	7th	Lyneham – Hurn	.40
	8th	Hurn – Malta (Luqa)	9.35
	8th	Malta – Cairo (LG224)	6.20
	10th	Cairo – Fayid	.50
Hart	(10th	Fayid – Heliopolis	.45
K6421	(13th	Heliopolis – Fayid	.45
L9613	13th	Fayid – LG224	.50
	15th	Cairo – Malta	6.40
	20th	Malta, Test flight	.50
	21st	Malta – Gibraltar	6.40
	22nd	Gibraltar – Tempsford	8.30

W/Cdr Hockey says he found one of the tyres on L9613 was in bad shape and he flew the aircraft to Fayid (a maintenance base on the Suez Canal) to get the wheel changed. Here he borrowed the Hawker Hart to fly back to Cairo. LG224 Kilo 26/Cairo West/Mena Road to give its full title.

Returning to Malta on the 15th, F/O Anderle flying Halifax L9618 went missing before reaching the island. He and his Czech crew were never heard of again, he was also carrying two ground crew in his aircraft. Their names appear on the Alamein Memorial. F/O L M Anderle, DFC, was the first and longest serving Czech pilot on 138 Squadron.

W/Cdr Hockey arrived at Malta on the 15th his intention was to refuel and fly through the night to the UK. However the weather report over England compelled him to delay his flight a further 24 hours by which time he found himself in hospital with sandfly fever. He ordered the rest of the force to continue flying home via Gibraltar. Having the additional responsibility of Air Marshal D'Albiac and Lord Apsley to fly home he reallocated these two passengers to other aircraft.

F/O K L Dobromirski, PAF, together with his Polish crew (he had an English Flight Engineer) on the 17th took-off Halifax DT542 from Luqa bound for Gibraltar. At 02.30 hours and barely airborne he crashed beyond the runway. All 16 persons on board were killed. Among the nine passengers killed were Major Lord Apsley, DSO, and Dobromirski's three ground crew. A Halifax flying with this number of passengers should not present any problem provided they were seated in a manner not to upset the aircraft's centre of gravity.

---

[2] The information is taken from the movements order but not all the crews returned home in the same aircraft.

L to R: F/O R P Wilkin, S/Ldr A H C Boxer and F/O L M Andrele circa August 1942. Sadly only S/Ldr Boxer was to survive. Wilkin was a Canadian, Boxer a New Zealander and Andrele a Czech. (R Wilkin via K A Merrick)

In the meantime F/Lt J C K Sutton decided to fly Halifax W1002 to Gibraltar taking the overland route rather than hug the North African coast. They took off from Luqa's uneven and goose neck flared runway and headed for Sousse in Tunisia anxious to put Malta behind them in the dark before the Luftwaffe's daylight patrols covered the island. They were well into Algeria and over the desert when the oil pressure on one engine began to drop. It was decided shut it down and to feather the airscrew. It was not long before the oil pressure started to drop on the other three engines so much so that they restarted the feathered engine in an attempt to maintain height. One engine then caught fire and Sutton advised his crew to stand by to bale out. Two baled out anyway. They were now low and just before they made a wheels up landing Sutton saw some buildings ahead in the dawn light. It was a successful landing everyone leaving the wreck safely but the remaining fuel in the belly tanks caught fire and with it the aeroplane. In daylight they were greeted by a soldier, a German *Legionaire* who had come from a nearby French Foreign Legion fort in the middle of the desert at le Kreider some 200 miles south of Oran. Sutton with his engineer examined the oil filters and found them clogged up, the oil tanks had been filled with the wrong type of oil. The wind forecast given to them at Malta wasn't very good either. They returned home on the 21st December. Prior's DG245 was delayed for five days at Gibraltar waiting for an engine change. He returned home on the 20th.

While W/Cdr Hockey's team was in action on the 9/10th December S/Ldr Boxer flew a Halifax operation during the dark period to Holland, operation PARSLEY A. From the report filed by him one wonders if his aircraft was being tracked to the target. The despatcher reported that several searchlights were to be seen which appeared to go out as they passed only to be replaced by others. Twin engined enemy aircraft (he did not say how many) passed 200 feet overhead going in the opposite direction and they also saw balloons at 400 feet – the same altitude as they were flying. Visibility was 6km but the wind over the target was 40 mph, it was very dark. Boxer, abandoning the operation, concluded it was not considered practicable during the dark period owing to difficulty in pinpointing on the coast and inland. G/Capt Fielden's remarks penned on the operational report concluded that the operation failed because of a high wind being stronger than predicted and also that this was the first operational effort employing TR 1335 (could this mean that the Germans had managed to get the 'Rebecca/Eureka' set working?). In spite of S/Ldr Boxer's experienced recommendations he went on to say 'I consider that with more experience of this apparatus this type of operation should be practicable during the dark period'.

Form 28 raised for operation PARSLEY A dated 4/11/42 gave the dropping zone as 6¼km ESE Hoorn, 2km SW Wijdenes, 250 metres from the coast. It said 'reception will stand on the shore one red light will be shown either side of the dropping point. The easterly red light to be doubled with a white intermittent light. Agent to be dropped approximately 200-250 metres off-shore at point opposite centre of lighting system'. I imagine this agent was a powerful swimmer!

On the night of the 20/21st December F/O Kuzmicki's crew, piloted by W/O Jensen, flew operation COCKLE (another water jump!) to France. An operation, due to bad weather, aborted by P/O Newport-Tinley two nights before. The thinking behind a water jump was that if the agent was too elderly to withstand a land jump he would avoid injury by landing in water. Jensen flew via Tangmere, Pointe de la Percée and Avranches, thence to the target which they overshot. Quickly pinpointing themselves on a river they soon picked up the lake where on the northern end of it parachuted in two agents, G Chartier and A Rapin. Jensen made another circuit and one passenger was seen wading ashore and another swimming towards land. For the elderly they must have been very fit swimmers! Report map co-ordinates show this lake to be Etang au Duc, just north of Ploërmel (Morbihan) some 50km or more to the WSW of Rennes. Leaflets were dropped on Montauban.

P/O Newport-Tinley was out this night too, flying CARACAL/ SHREW/PERIWIG 7 to Belgium. He had just instructed the despatcher to prepare for jumping in ten minutes when the despatcher turning to make his preparations was just in time to see his second passenger disappearing through the hole! It must have been a rough jump for them. They were flying at 900 feet at a ground speed of 200 mph at the time.

W/Cdr Hockey arrived back at Tempsford on the 22nd December declaring that Malta was not the healthiest place to be trapped on the ground having been bombed most days, his ground crew patching up the shrapnel holes in Halifax L9613 whenever they appeared.

That night four Halifax sorties for Holland were laid on. F/O Wilkin and P/O Kingsford-Smith parachuting in 12 containers each. F/Lt Russell flying MARROW 13 was, in brilliant moonlight, attacked when flying in the middle of Texal Island at an astounding altitude of 75 feet. Several guns of 20mm calibre as well as machine guns opening up hitting the aircraft, knocking out the forward bomb bay petrol tank, damaging the bomb doors, starboard flaps and the port inner engine. Half way across the island the port inner failed through loss of glycol. When at 200 feet he found it necessary to jettison his containers into the Zuider Zee. He was attacked again by a ship on the way home flying between 1,000 and 1,500 feet. With the port outer engine threatening to fail he sent out an SOS, but crossed the coast south of Southwold and landed at 02.35 hours.

He also reported that he saw near Texel at 00.05 to 00.10 hours heavy flak being fired at an unseen aircraft.

The last Dutch sortie that night was F/O G F B Newport-Tinley, DFC, flying Halifax W7775 on operation MARROW 12, he crashed in the area of Meppel. Of the eight on board only two survived to be taken PoW. This was probably the aircraft that F/Lt Russell reported as seen being attacked.

The night of 23/24th December was a complete failure. Six sorties taking off and all beaten back by the widespread atrocious weather. S/Ldr Gibson flew the last successful 138 Squadron sortie for the year, operation GLAZIER/TOBACCONIST the 29/30th dropping two agents and two packages in France. The remaining Squadron sortie flown by F/O Kuzmicki on the same night failed because of the weather.

The fourteen intended No.161 Squadron operations for the month of December were decimated by the weather. S/Ldr Lockhart completed an SIS Lysander operation CHUB/MINNOW/STARFISH on the 17/18th December, surviving the return flight by exceptional flying skill

Standing in front of Halifax DG253 NF-F are (L to R): first three ground crew, F/Sgt A Hughes, F/O Gliddon, F/Lt R P Wilkin, P/O H Burke, two ground crew, F/Sgt Risson. The remainder are ground crew. S/Ldr R P Wilkin, DFC, was lost flying Halifax DG252 NF-B over Holland in September 1943. (R Wilkin via K A Merrick)

having damaged his tailplane when landing in France. Two attempts were made to complete AJAX and JAGUAR, fog over the landing area prevented success. JAGUAR was the first Lysander sortie to be flown by S/Ldr Verity the new 'A' Flight Commander. The other completed Lysander sortie was operation LOBSTER/CUTTLEFISH flown by W/Cdr Pickard on the 22/23rd.

P/O Foster on the 29/30th flew the last 161 December completed sortie, a Halifax operation, BOOKMAKER & SCIENTIST 1. Foster reporting Northern France covered with snow, 9/10th cloud to the River Loire, broken cloud north east of Bordeaux with 5/10ths low cloud and a base of 1,000 feet. They pinpointed east of Saumur at the junction of the rivers (the meeting of the Loire and the Vienne). From here they made their way to the la Rochelle area where they pinpointed their BOOKMAKER DZ and parachuted in two agents blind, J A P Lodwick, a young novelist who in 1940 fought with the Foreign Legion, and Oscar Heimann a forty year old Czech Jewish dentist. His hesitation when jumping meant they were separated in the darkness and their mission, to destroy a factory working for the Germans was never completed. They returned home via Spain. Weather prevented the completion of the second target SCIENTIST 1.

Punctuated with non operational losses and operations decimated by appalling weather thus ended December, and the year of 1942. A year during which Tempsford lost 30 aircraft; 19 Whitleys, eight Halifaxes and three Lysanders at a cost of 111 lives and ten PoW's.

CHAPTER TWELVE

January 1943

The aircrews at Tempsford must have been pleased to have been given leave for New Year having worked so hard over Christmas. No.138 Squadron flew eight Halifax sorties when the year's first new moon had risen on the night of the 14/15th January. None were completed owing to the weather conditions, a duplication of the last sorties to be flown in 1942. One pilot, F/Lt Austin flying operation KER/GUDGEON, to France reported that the area where the DZ was situated was flooded. No.161 Squadron faired a little better. Of three Lysander SIS sorties two were completed, F/O Bridger flying AJAX and S/Ldr Verity flying CORINNE to the east of Lyon a prodigious return flight of 8.20 hours, possibly one of the longest single engine night flights of the war. It is well reported in his book *We Landed by Moonlight*. The other Lysander sortie ATALA flown by F/O Vaughan-Fowler was abandoned because of heavy cloud. F/Lt Prior and P/O Wynne flew two Halifax sorties to Belgium. Wynne dropping two agents and four cartons of coffee onto MISTLETOE. His second target GIBBON was uncompleted like that of Prior's operation because of the weather.

The following night, the 15/16th, 161 Squadron despatched two Halifax sorties to France and one to Belgium. F/Lt Prior endeavouring to complete his previous night's work SEXTO/LUCKYSHOT 8 again failed because of the weather. P/O Cresswell flying BUTTERCUP & PERCH 15 to France in the Blois area, dropped two SIS agents and three packages on BUTTERCUP, an engine failing as he did so. Undeterred they proceeded to PERCH 15 but arrived too early and decided to drop their leaflets elsewhere. Returning they found the lights of the DZ now lit and the correct signal flashing so they dropped four containers from a height of 1,400 feet not daring to come lower because of their engine problem. They landed at Tangmere.

In the meantime P/O Readhead and his crew were flying Halifax DG285 on operation KER/CRAB 6. The former an SIS operation and according to the provisional operation report prepared for his return, he was to drop a parcel on a pin point 47° 42′ 05″N, 01° 49′ 25″W, which is just south of a village called Sion-les-Mines (Loire-Atlantique) some 16km west of Châteaubriant in Northern France. There were no co-ordinates given for CRAB 6, a container drop. Regrettably P/O H S Readhead and his crew failed to return. Merrick reports that the French underground found a four engined aircraft burnt out, south of

Rennes. Seven unidentified bodies were found in the wreckage, all were interred in Rennes.

Four Halifax sorties arranged for 138 Squadron to France on the same night reported that they were unable to complete as there was 'no reception'. Thus it would appear that they all reached their target area but having to return home, not for the first time this new year, very tired and frustrated crews.

The 18/19th was a little better for the Squadron when eight sorties were carried out. Three to France were completed while another failed and two to Belgium were partly finished. Two sorties that failed are worthy of mention, the first flown by F/O Wilkin operation TABLEMAT/TABLEMANNERS a rare Halifax sortie to Denmark. He was carrying four passengers. Three and a half hours into their flight and 20km inland from the Danish coast flying at an altitude of 600 feet they met their first flak aided by four searchlights. Thirteen minutes later at a height of 500 feet searchlights aided accurate fire from a Bofors type gun. A further forty five minutes later still flying at 500 feet a Ju88 flying at 450 feet followed them on the port side. They then took violent evasive action, the rear gunner firing two bursts the results of which were not seen but neither was that Ju88 seen again! In spite of good visibility they were unable to get a pinpoint owing to the large amount of snow and ice on the ground, they abandoned the operation and returned home on a reciprocal track.

The other No.138 Squadron Halifax sortie that failed because of the weather was to Czechoslovakia, operation MERCURY flown by S/Ldr Boxer. This was flown in conjunction with operation IRIDIUM to Czechoslovakia flown by S/Ldr Hodges from No.161 Squadron. They took-off from Tempsford within nine minutes of each other, Boxer leading the way at 19.00 hours. Each were carrying four agents and ten bundles of leaflets (edition C1). Each were to make a blind drop within an area roughly 30km of each other. They were both instructed to return with their agents if they could not identify the exact pinpoint for dropping.

S/Ldr Boxer crossed the English coast at Beachy Head flying at a height of 4,000 feet; there was layer cloud over the Channel and the French coast where he crossed at Cayeaux flying at 7,000 feet. The cloud thickened considerably 30km inland. At 00.47 hours at an altitude of 6,000 feet over Paris they were attacked by heavy flak. To North West France he found icing started in cloud at an altitude of 6,000 feet, then deciding to fly above it at 8,000 feet as it was forecast that the cloud would disperse to the east. However, he says it thickened considerably, breaking in one or two places in the Rhine area. They were unable to get a definite pinpoint. He dare not come below cloud because of the approaching high ground and when they did reach the high ground they found that the valleys were filled with fog up to 5,000 feet. In an attempt to make a pinpoint they 'stooged in the Alps area' trying to locate Lake Constance. This was impossible and as his petrol

consumption was high he decided to abandon the operation and return home. He crossed the English coast at Newhaven and landed at 03.15 hours.

S/Ldr Hodges on the other hand, after leaving Beachy Head flying at 2,000 feet, crossed the French coast at Cayeaux at an altitude of 1,000 feet to a reception of two searchlights and inaccurate light flak. He then flew at 1,000 feet to la Ferté which they pinpointed. After leaving Troyes they climbed steadily to 4,500 feet at which height they stayed throughout the operation. They managed to pinpoint Mulhouse and Regensburg in spite of low lying fog after the Rhine. Here near the Czechoslovakian border they met with very thick fog and they decided to return when SW of Pilsen (owing to the very heavy fog this must have been a dead reckoning position that is to say the calculated position of the aircraft on the navigators chart). In the Troyes area on the way home they met with low cloud and rain. They pinpointed Manston on the English coast and landed at Tempsford 05.50.

It should be remembered the moon was full and these flights were routed across Germany. The tactics adopted by both crews were different but both operations failed because of thick fog. To have flown all that way and having to return with their passengers knowing that someone would have to try again must have added to their extreme disappointment and fatigue.

Louise Atherton says in the **PRO** publication *SOE in Eastern Europe*:

IRIDIUM Czechoslovakia 1942. Air transport plans for the bombing of Policka and the dropping of agents, as well as propaganda leaflets on Prague. There is no clue as to whether the operation, which was to include MERCURY, took place, or if it was combined with the bombing of the Skoda factories.

In so far as the air operations are concerned the following sorties from Tempsford were attempted. All failed because of the weather:

Halifax DG245 seen here in 138 Squadron NF markings. Transferred to 161 Squadron, under markings MA-W, it was lost on the 15 march 1943 on Operation IRIDIUM to Czechoslovakia. The pilot was F/Lt A E Prior, DFM, and there were no survivors. (P.R.O.)

18/19th Jan	S/Ldr Hodges	(161 Sqn)	IRIDIUM
18/19th Jan	S/Ldr Boxer	(138 Sqn)	MERCURY
26/27th Jan	P/O Foster	(161 Sqn)	IRIDIUM
26/27th Jan	P/O Wynne	(161 Sqn)	MERCURY

P/O Foster had his passengers reduced to three. He pinpointed Lake Constance, reporting the cloud was 10/10 from 2,000 to 8,000 feet with heavy icing. From here to Czechoslovakia they were unable to pinpoint owing to the difficult weather conditions and poor visibility causing them to abandon the operation. On their return, flying at 4,000 feet, they were coned by searchlights at Igolstadt (report says Ingeldstat) just 65km north of Munich but a diving turn proved successful evasive action. They landed after nine hours in the air.

P/O Wynne took off ten minutes after Foster reporting 10/10 cloud, tops 6,000 to 9,000 feet icing in cloud. He flew all the way on DR but as the target area was covered in 10/10 cloud he could not identify DZ and returned. His aircraft was coned by searchlights at 8,000 feet over, he believed Pilsen. The heavy flak that followed was inaccurate. When they landed they had been flying 9.05 hours.

13/14th Feb	F/O Kuzmicki	(138 Sqn)	IRIDIUM
13/14th Feb	F/O Walczac	(138 Sqn)	MERCURY
19/20th Feb	F/O Ruttledge	(138 Sqn)	MERCURY
19/20th Feb	F/Lt Wilkin	(138 Sqn)	IRIDIUM
24/25th Feb	F/O Kuzmicki	(138 Sqn)	IRIDIUM
14/15th Mar	F/O Clow	(138 Sqn)	MERCURY
14/15th Mar	F/Lt Prior	(161 Sqn)	IRIDIUM

F/O Clow came the nearest to completing their operation. Off at 19.08 hours taking the route Beachy Head–Point Haute Banc–Laval–Lake Constance–Regensburg–Target. They reached the target area recognising the Moldeau River, the lakes and the woods but haze, poor visibility and darkness made it impossible to identify the exact pinpoint. The passengers recognised the district but were not sufficiently sure of their exact position to want to be dropped (it was to be a blind drop). Leaflets were dropped three minutes after leaving the target area at Klatovy some 55km south of Pilsen.

On the way to the target at 5,000 feet north of Augsburg they passed through a belt of searchlights which was reported to be about 25km deep and coning above the aircraft at 10,000 feet. The heavy flak that ensued was accurate and intense. On the way home at approximately 33km north east of Lake Constance, at 5,000 feet they were met by a Ju88 which stood off, for roughly two minutes about 800 yards on the starboard side of their aircraft. 'It then weaved underneath and away to a port astern position' where it closed to 150 yards and opened fire with a short burst 'which did no damage'. The rear gunner opened fire and appeared to hit the enemy aircraft. It was not seen again. They landed at Tangmere having been airborne for ten hours. It was discovered that the aircraft had been hit by a cannon shell in the starboard wing.

F/Lt A E Prior, DFM, and his crew flying Halifax DG245 took off 52 minutes after Clow and regrettably failed to return from this operation. They are buried in Durnbach War Cemetery in the town of Bad Tölz some 40km south of Munich. It is likely that the four agents flying with them were also killed.

S/Ldr C F Gibson, DFC, and his crew were also lost this night flying operation BRONZE to Czechoslovakia and this event is recorded more fully later.

No further SIS, IRIDIUM, or SOE, MERCURY, operations were flown again, possibly because half of the team had been lost. It is interesting to conjecture that each of those Czech agents spent the best part of 40 hours or more passenger time in the air, freezing, waiting, thinking, watching, there was not much else they could do. No further Czech operations were to fly from Tempsford.

Air Chief Marshal Sir Lewis Hodges commenting on Czechoslovakian sorties said 'It was a miracle that we didn't loose more crews bearing in mind that we had such a very long flight over Germany'.

*   *   *

Back to the 22/23rd January S/Ldr Boxer was flying a 138 Squadron operation CRAB 11 & JUGGLER/FARRIER. He took-off at 21.10 hours crossing into France at Pte de la Percée at 5,000 feet. From here they had no problem pinpointing the Loire. The weather 'gradually cleared to practically clear skies over the target'. They identified Montargis (Loiret), approximately 55km east of Orléans. This was shown to the two passengers, who satisfied, were parachuted blind with two packages, 2km to the SW of the pinpoint at a height of 500 feet and at an airspeed of 125 mph. The despatcher remarked they jumped immediately when told. Thus parachuted in for the first time, H A E Déricourt, air movements officer for Northern France and double agent – the name of the person who dropped with him is unidentified. Boxer then proceeded to CRAB 11 via Châteauneuf-sur-Cher (Cher) (about 28km south of Bourges) and here after making two circuits over the reception lights from a height of 450 feet, dropped six containers. He landed at Exeter. A Major Beir flew with them on this operation and 'was very impressed with the way the operation was carried out'. He, whoever he was, should have been, it was carried out by a skilled crew during a break in the atrocious weather.

The 23/24th January saw 161 Squadron completing four successful Halifax sorties, a 100% effort, while two Lysander sorties, MINER and ATALA failed for the lack of a reception. Operation MINER flown by P/O McCairns was to have landed on an unused airfield at Périgueux. Luckily it was discovered earlier that the Germans were waiting for this landing.

F/O Foster flying an SIS operation VIRGO 2 was to complement four other 138 Squadron Norwegian sorties flown that night. Leaving the UK at North Coates Foster crossed the Norwegian Coast 2.33

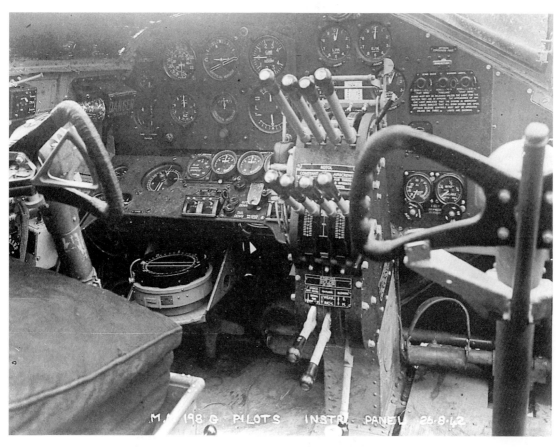

Handley Page Halifax cockpit, albeit fitted with dual control for conversion training. Normally the area, occupied in this case by the instructor, was open and one could see the Navigator and Bomb Aimer's position in the nose of the aircraft. The WOp/AG sat beneath the Pilot and the Flight Engineer stood behind him. The latter's instrument panel was fixed to the bulkhead and when he was unoccupied kept lookout for enemy aircraft through the astrodome above. (Imperial War Museum)

hours later at Grimstad (approximately 35km east of Kristiansand) thence to Lillehammer (approximately 135km north of Oslo). They identified Randsfjord to the west and altered course for the target, Samajelien(?). They made several runs over the pinpoint and from a height of 1,000 feet dropping the agent blind, together with a package consisting of a pair of skis and ski-sticks, they were seen to land close together. Foster remarked that he had little difficulty finding the target but dropping was difficult since over the surrounding high ground was isolated low cloud. He also recommended that future agents be dressed in white and that white parachutes be used since those used could clearly be seen. They landed at Kinloss having flown 10.20 hours.

P/O Kingsford-Smith, flying operation CHEESE 3 a mission to establish W/T contacts and secret army links in South Norway, met with low cloud with a base of 1,000 feet. Unable to make a pinpoint he returned the two packages and six containers to Harwell where he had been diverted.

F/O Kuzmicki and his crew dropped seven containers on GANNET 1. His fellow Polish colleague F/O Walczac and his crew flew CHAFFINCH leaving the UK via Blakeney in Norfolk making a landfall on the Norwegian coast in good visibility 2.50 hours later at Begndal(?). They pinpointed their way forward identifying lakes until reaching the target area. Here they circled for 25 minutes looking for the reception lights. They informed their three passengers that they knew where they were and asked if they would like to jump blind. The passengers agreed and all three were parachuted in from 600 feet above the ground together with three packages and six containers. At the same time the rear gunner reported seeing reception lights on the slope of a hill 1,000 yards away. The agents signalled from the ground signifying that they had landed safely. Walczac was diverted to Kinloss landing after flying for 8.15 hours. The captain reported he considered the reception lights were in the wrong place.

Also on the 23/24th January S/Ldr Gibson flew operation GUNNERSIDE to Norway, which, in retrospect, could have been the most important of all the SOE operations flown during the war. A mission to drop a party of saboteurs for the destruction of a plant producing heavy water by electrolysis, at Vermork in Telemark. If this mission was successful it would bring to an end Germany's preparations to manufacture an atomic bomb.

This was a less ambitious operation than that of two Halifaxes towing Horsa gliders ending in disaster on the 19th November. One Halifax crashing into a mountainside killing the crew and the other broke its frozen tow rope. The Commando survivors from the two Horsas were murdered by the SS and buried on the shore beside Wodzicki and his crew who were lost on the 29/30th October 1942.

Gibson's instructions were to drop a team of six blind within 20 kms radius of the pinpoint if the reception lights could not be seen. The team was; Joachim Ronneberg, Knut Haukelid, Kasper Idland, Fredrik Kayser, Birger Strømsheim and Hans Storhaug. Gibson found the southern tip of Norway covered in low cloud with fog in the valleys north of the target area. After making landfall on the Norwegian coast south of Kragero they failed to make any immediate recognisable pinpoint. However, they eventually pinpointed the Naze and from there set course to Lake Tinn, they had now been over Norway over an hour and a half. Ice and snow on the lakes made it difficult to recognise exactly where they were, setting course to the target area from a village they thought was Gjuvvik. Not being sure Gibson asked his passengers if they recognised the terrain below, unable to do so, the operation was abandoned. Light flak met them on the way out at Farsund. They too landed at Kinloss having been airborne for 8.50 hours.

Although there is no mention of this in the operational report, Merrick observes that Gibson had one engine badly damaged and another on fire when he landed at Kinloss. However, since this aircraft, NF-O, did not fly on operations again until three weeks later, this would probably confirm Merrick's report.

New instructions were issued for the next attempt to complete GUNNERSIDE. The ATF6 (Air Transport Form replacing the old Form 28) dated 6/2/43 indicated the dropping zone would be 11½km SW Stegarvis Saeter, 199½km south Maarbu. 'Rebecca' would be used if available and the operation would be carried out between the 11th and 25th February 1943. A plan of the DZ was shown as being:

oRed

oR oR oR oR

o White flashing

The load was to be six men, six containers and five packages. The instructions were that the full load was to be dropped on one run:

1) Danger area – Should not approach (DZ) from the South or leave it South of the 60 degree line of Latitude.
2) Dummy Circuit – A feint circuit should be made 40-50m from dropping point (m – probably metres, hardly miles)
3) Dropping order – All Containers. three men, three packages, three men, two packages.

S/Ldr Gibson, on the 16th/17th February again flew NF-O, in an effort to complete this important mission. It would appear that the carefully made preparations went by the board. They were led to the original reception area 16km out by a 'Rebecca' signal but passed to the north of it. In accordance with the amended instructions Gibson, as required, dropped blind from a height of 700 feet, the team and their supplies. The team landed safely on the frozen surface of Bjornos Fiord but Knut Haukelid was fortunate to escape serious injury having landed among the descending containers.

On the 27/28th February the GUNNERSIDE team met up with the now exhausted GROUSE team. It was claimed they were able to inflict such damage to the Norsk Hydro heavy water plant as to prevent the Germans ever again from using it to its full capacity. Later this target was to be bombed.

Cookridge records that the Norwegian winter of 1942/43 was considered one of the severest in living memory.

The 25/26th January saw 138 Squadron launching four sorties to Poland. S/Ldr Boxer flying operation VICE unable to identify his target returned after engine failure over Poland. F/L Krol and his crew flying BRACE dropping four agents only, returning with his containers. F/O Kuzmicki flying SPOKESHAVE reporting that his agents would not jump, there being no answer from the ground to the aircraft's signal. They landed after 12.40 hours in the air.

However, P/O Kingsford-Smith and his crew were given operation SCREWDRIVER to fly and an operational report available, albeit one from which I cannot trace any of the locations mentioned in it. According to his debriefing his route was; Cromer–Lodbjaarg (Denmark)–Sameo–Koton (Swedish Coast) then 'followed neutrality down coast'–Jamunder See–Wloki–Plotak–Target (at 16km SE Lowicz). He circled the target area for ten minutes looking for the reception lights and then went to a 'safe area' where he dropped his four passengers from 800 feet. (One of whom carried $243,000 in a money belt). Circling after the drop he saw a light flash from the ground and a car coming at speed down the road past the pinpoint. His six containers he brought back to Tempsford where he landed after 12.20 hours in the air, as all these Polish operations were, it had been a long flight.

On the next night the 26/27th F/O Walczac flew operation GAUGE to Poland dropping another team of four passengers. Their mission was to endeavour to explain to the Polish Home Army why it was not possible at that moment to give them the assistance they so dearly wanted. There was an operations report for this sortie. The pilot F/Sgt Twaderwa took the route Wells–Bovojaerg (probably Bovingbjerg on the Danish coast),–Stevns Klint (33km south of Copenhagen)–Bornholm–Jamunder See. They had so far been flying on DR navigation, making their first visual pinpoint on the River Vistula at Gruziadz from where they flew to Fordon. Here they contacted their target arriving over the reception lights to drop their four passengers and six containers (so they thought) from 600 feet. The rear gunner was asked how many parachutes did he see and replied 'four'. The tested switches indicated that the containers had gone but when they arrived back at Tempsford it was found that they had hung up. A disappointing finish to a superbly flown operation that had taken 13 hours to complete.

On Walczac's return he had hardly got into bed when he was sent off to Norway on the night of 29/30th to unsuccessfully attempt another important operation CARHAMPTON. Bad weather was to blame. Two other sorties on the previous night, one to Denmark and the other to France failed due to the lack of receptions. These were 138 Squadron's final sorties for January – it had been a difficult month for them.

From the 25/26/27th No.161 Squadron finished their month with S/Ldr Hodges returning from France with a u/s intercom and F/Lt Prior flying operations DESIGNER/STATIONER & CRAB 12 to France. Flying down to the Loire islands and map reading his way to Givors (Rhône) some 25km south west of Lyon he parachuted six containers onto the reception lights of CRAB 12. He reported that high ground in the area made it difficult for his run-in. From here he flew west to drop blind DESIGNER/STATIONER. The pinpoint is described as 'positively identified by the railway, road, river and the town'. The report states that the town was 'Bleale', however, there is no such place in the *Code Postal*, but, clearly fitting this description on a map, is Brioude (Haute-Loire). The two passengers were told where they were and Jacqueline Nearne a member of FANY was the first to jump followed by S/Ldr Maurice Southgate who was to take over the leadership of the new STATIONER circuit. Prior estimated they were dropped about a mile to the north of the pinpoint, his instructions were to drop 'within 3km of the pinpoint'. The two met upon the ground (not without a fright!) and some little time later Southgate's brilliant SOE career nearly finished abruptly when he asked a woman cyclist the way to Brioude – in English – she thought they were German! Jacqueline was the fourth woman, (remember the NKVD agent), to land by parachute in France. A Lysander airlifted her out in April 1944, Southgate was fortunate to survive Buchenwald.

Three Halifax sorties, S/Ldr Hodges to France and Foster and Wynne to Czechoslovakia (already recorded), and four Lysander sorties, one unsuccessful, finished the month of January for 161 Squadron. W/Cdr Pickard flying an SIS operation ATALA brought out Pierre Brossolette. Pickard, spent nearly two hours over the landing area waiting for the flare path to be laid, returning to Predannock with his fuel tanks dry.

CHAPTER THIRTEEN

February 1943

Approval for two dual controlled Halifaxes had now been granted together with the maintenance crews. Tempsford was to convert their own Halifax crews. Still under consideration was the establishment for the instructors!

F/O R C Hogg took off from Tangmere for Tempsford on the 4th February. His 138 Squadron Halifax DG271 had the misfortune of swinging, collapsing the undercarriage to write the aeroplane off, there were no injuries.

The 13th/14th of February started the month's operations for 161 with the first Hudson pick up sortie. W/Cdr Pickard flying operation SIRENE/BERENICE landing at the aerodrome of St-Yan, bordered by the Loire, 6km south of Digoin (Sôane-et-Loire). Here he landed five persons and returned with mail. The landing field was ploughed up, shortly after, by the Germans. Two other successful Lysander sorties were completed that night, Jean Moulin being one of the passengers brought to the UK. S/Ldr Verity flying a third Lysander was not required to land.

The Chiefs of Staff decided that it would use five long range Halifaxes from No.161 Squadron and one in reserve from No.138 Squadron for operation PULLOVER an operation of such importance as to justify the diversion of these resources from SOE work. It involved the dropping of 20 men in the north of Norway, near the Swedish border, to destroy a viaduct carrying a railway to Narvik on which vital iron ore supplies were being shipped to Germany. The commander of this operation was Major Baird but whether this was the mysterious Major Beir, who flew with S/Ldr Boxer on the 22/23rd January, is not recorded.

The operation was to commence at Kinloss. The route was to be Kinloss-Unst (the northern most part of the Shetland Islands) − a small island west of Vega Island just off the Norwegian Lofoten Islands and thence to a DR position between the southern tip of the Lofoten Islands and Seines Fjord. They would be flying at 7,000 feet, from which height the Lofoten Islands and the fjords along the coast would be clearly visible. From here they would track to a new pinpoint on the frozen Sitas Lake and then to the target Alt Lake, two miles (3 km) from the Swedish border and fifty miles (80 km) from Narvik. The flying distance was calculated at 2,150 miles (3,440 km). There was no margin for error.

Lockheed Hudson cockpit. (Imperial War Museum)

In retrospect it must be considered a compliment to the aircrews of 161 Squadron that they could fly to such fine limits. Why I ask, couldn't Bomber Command bomb the viaduct? Nevertheless six Halifaxes and their ground crews departed for Kinloss on the 13th February. The operation was eventually cancelled because of adverse weather conditions.

On the 22nd the last 161 Squadron Whitley operation was recorded, an aircraft borrowed from No.502 Squadron to complete an ESCORT sortie, RODNEY. Flown by F/Lt Marriot, the Albermarle in which he should have flown this sortie having made a wheels up landing a few days before.

While the Halifaxes were in Scotland five pick-up flights were attempted of which two were unsuccessful because of the weather. On the 24/25th S/Ldr Verity flew a Lysander on an SIS operation ECLIPSE to return the legendary Jean Moulin to France. Meeting with thick fog over the landing field he was forced to return to Tangmere which was now covered by a thick fog. He and his passenger were lucky to survive uninjured a shattering crash. From the accident report it is unbelievable that the aeroplane (V9674) would ever fly again. However, the extensive damage was repaired and the aeroplane returned to 161

Squadron. That night W/Cdr Pickard bogged down a Hudson in France for two hours during an SIS operation PAMPAS, requiring an additional two horse power to pull him onto firm ground. He brought out seven passengers.

Halifax operations for 161 Squadron recommenced on the 26/27th February with four proposed sorties to France. Three failed because of the weather. The fourth flown by P/O Foster operations PAULINE & PHYSICIAN 8 (both SIS and SOE) to France. Crossing the French coast at a height of 500 feet at Cabourg he set course for, and pinpointed les Andelys (on the Seine south east of Rouen). The DZ of PAULINE was 49° 24′ 35″N, 01° 35′ 05″E roughly 20km NE les Andelys (Eure) in the area of the small village of Morgny (Eure). First making a dummy run over the target of a triangle of red lights with a white flashing 'R' he then from 600 feet parachuted two important agents Col. Passy (André Dewavrin) chief of the BCRA (*Bureau Central de Renseignements et d'Action*) and F/Lt Yeo-Thomas of the SOE.

Their important mission was to assess the resistance forces in France; obtain their allegiance to de Gaulle; co-ordinate their military and intelligence activities and to consider if it would be possible and to set up a 'central management committee'.

With them were dropped four packages, three for PAULINE and one for PITINETTE (says the report). Six parachutes were seen to open. Foster continued eight minutes away to PHYSICIAN 8 in the area of NE Gisors. Here on a reception flashing 'F' dropped three containers and a package. They went home crossing the coast 8km west of St-Valéry their height given in the operation report was three feet. They landed at Abingdon of all places. An accolade appeared on the operations report; 'Once again a good effort by a first class crew' and signed by the OC No.161 Squadron

Yeo-Thomas is reported in Bruce Marshall's book, *The White Rabbit*, of flying out on a weather aborted sortie the previous night. There was a 138 Squadron sortie PITINETTE aborted through weather and flown by F/Lt Dodkin on the night of 24/25th February. This must have been it, but I cannot find that operation PAULINE had ever been flown before.

No.138 Squadron on the other hand unhindered by the demands of other services had a full and varied programme for February. Some 63 sorties being planned, 27 failing because of the appalling weather and seven lacking a reception, doubtless for the same reason.

The beginning of February saw 14 sorties attempted by 138 Squadron only one being completely successful. On the 13/14th. F/O Gebik dropped two agents into operation SEXTO in France. On the same night of the four operations that were partly successful, P/O Kingsford-Smith parachuted two agents, four containers and two packages into Belgium, He did not attempt to complete his third target. One sortie to Holland flown by S/Ldr Gibson, MARROW 16/CATARRH 10/CHICORY again was partially completed, six containers, four packages and four boxes of chocolate together with a

On the left is P/O Kingsford-Smith, RAAF, with his crew. They were shot down over Tours, France, on 19/20 February 1943 in Halifax W1012 NF-Z and all became PoWs. (via K A Merrick)

young woman, Beatrix Terwindt, a former stewardess of KLM, were parachuted. She was working on behalf of MI9 in an attempt to start an escape route between Holland and Belgium. Although landing on a German site she survived the war and became one of the few agents to testify before the Dutch Commission of Inquiry that took place after the war.

Also on the 13/14th IRIDIUM and MERCURY went to Czechoslovakia as already mentioned. Two sorties to Belgium were partially successful, P/O Kingsford-Smith dropping two agents, four containers and two packages into two of a three target operation.

F/O Ruttledge flew operation TONIC, a PICKAXE mission to drop an NKVD agent into Germany. The ATF6 was dated the 18th December 1942 and indicated that TONIC would be a blind drop consisting of two men and one package at a pinpoint situated 4km SSE Endingen, 5½km SSW Riegel, 16km NW Freiburg. Specific instructions were: 'In accordance with the cover story this operation should preferably take place over a weekend.'

Ruttledge took-off from Tempsford at 20.05 hours. Taking the route Beachy Head–Pointe du Haut-Banc–A large wood south west of Valenciennes–Lake Lachaussée (approx. 30km SW of Metz)–Target. They pinpointed 'junction of canal with river Rhine near Sundhouse'. This must have been the junction of the Leopolds Canal and the river Rhine just 12km north of both Endingen and Riegel. Here they spent three quarters of an hour over the target area, poor ground visibility preventing them from pinpointing their exact position. This coupled with a calculated ground wind of 30mph decided them against the drop and they abandoned the operation. They returned home by the same route landing after some 7.30 hours in the air. There had been no enemy opposition and apart from ground haze weather conditions were good.

F/O Wilkin and his crew on the 16/17th February were the next to attempt completing operation TONIC. He too made his way to that mysterious wood SW of Valenciennes. However, having made a pinpoint on the River Meuse, they flew to Lake Lachaussée and made a DR run from there. Stratus cloud 10/10ths down to the ground caused them to abandon the operation. They logged 6.10 hours flying when they touched down at Tempsford. Our NKVD agents had now spent 13.40 hours in the air.

On the 18/19th F/Lt Dodkin should have flown operation TONIC but it was cancelled at the last minute.

Operation TONIC was brought to a successful conclusion on the 24/25th February by a Polish crew seemingly flying their first SD operation. Captained by F/Lt Gryglewicz the navigator and piloted by F/Sgt Twardarwa they crossed the French coast at a height of 500 feet and afterwards set course for a large wood south of Valenciennes, which they reached on DR. They pinpointed the lakes west of Sarrebourg (some 55km east of Nancy), (Meurthe-et-Moselle) and pinpointed the canal joining the River Rhine. From here because of bad visibility they made several runs to the target eventually parachuting load from 1,900 feet indicated, flying due north. Three parachutes were seen to open. The agents must have been relieved to have jumped at last having logged 17.25 hours in the air when they finally left the aeroplane.

The 15/16th February saw four sorties arranged for France only one being completely finished although P/O Clow on his partially completed operation dropped two agents on BREWER. He could not complete PHYSICIAN 2 & 8 due to the weather.

The 16th/17th saw ten aircraft 'laid on' to fly operations ranging from Holland, Poland, Denmark, Norway and Germany (TONIC). The other sortie to Norway, (other than GUNNERSIDE), was operation CARHAMPTON previously attempted on the 29/30th January. The original purpose of this ambitious mission was to seize a convoy of merchant ships near Abelsnes in Flekkefjord. It failed but the mission decided to remain in Norway and attempt further operations until finally evacuated by sea. F/Lt Austin flew the operation dropping 12 containers and four packages onto the target.

Four sorties were conducted to Poland, none of the operation reports are available. Operations RASP, VICE and SAW (the latter two flown by Polish crews) were all successful and in all 12 personnel and 12 containers were dropped. F/O Kuzmicki and his crew flying operation SPOKESHAVE were forced to jettison their load when the two starboard engines cut. This operation was completed by F/O Kuzmicki on the 19/20th dropping four passengers and six containers into this target.

Two operations to Holland took place on the same night F/Lt Hooper having the misfortune to drop three agents, Klaas Bor,

Cornelius van Hulsteyn and Cornelius Braggaar into operation TURNIP/ENDIVE/PARSLEY A/RADISH and the arms of the waiting Germans. P/O Clow flew operation MARROW 23, PARSNIP 3 & CALVADOS, a three target mission. First he dropped seven containers into MARROW 23 and then from 500 feet dropped another seven containers and four boxes of chocolate into PARSNIP 3 – once more into the hands of the Germans! He had yet to complete his night's work by finding CALVADOS in Germany.

The ATP6 for CALVADOS was dated the 10th February 1943 and said the operation was to be a blind drop on a pinpoint 11½km WNW of Lingen, 4¼km WSW of Dalum. It was reported that 'the drop was to be made as near to the pinpoint as possible, providing the agent knows where he is' and that 'this operation should, if possible, coincide with a bombing raid in NW Germany'. This appears to be an incredible request, not only optimistic, but without the knowledge that Bomber Command operated in the dark, outside the moon period.

Clow says in his report that after PARSNIP 3 they set course for CALVADOS and easily map read their way to the target. However, as they were approaching the pinpoint there was a misunderstanding between the flight engineer and the despatcher causing the agent to be dropped sooner than intended. The airspeed at the time was 145 mph and their height was 700 feet. They calculated that they had dropped him 5km NE of Neuenhaus (just inside Germany from the Dutch border) and about seven miles (11km) SW of pinpoint. The map co-ordinates show the pinpoint was to have been close to the meeting of three roads to the west of Lingen. Having dropped they headed for Hoorn and home crossing the Dutch coast 11km south of Egmond at a height of 200 feet. This could have been another PICKAXE operation.

The last unaccounted operation for this night was TABLEMAT/TABLE-MANNERS to Denmark which had remained uncompleted since the end of January. The ATP6 for this operation said that this was to be a blind drop 17km ENE of Mariager, 1½km N Overgaard. The drop should take place between 21.00 and 21.30 GMT. Camouflaged parachutes required for all.

S/Ldr Boxer had been entrusted with this sortie taking-off from Tempsford at 18.38 hours. It was to be a blind drop of a team of four consisting of; Ole Geisler, Hans Hendrik Larsen, Adolf Larsen and the radio operator (TABLEMAT) Gunnar Christiansen. Their route was Tempsford–Cromer–Ringkøbing–Beder from here they map read their way to the target. The weather, from seven degrees east, had been clear skies with excellent visibility in bright moonlight. They crossed the Danish coast at 500 feet. The target area was reached at 22.41 hours and the pinpoint easily found, the passengers positively identifying ground detail. They were then parachuted in from a height of 700 feet, four parachutes were seen to open. The despatcher reported after the drop he had to cut away and jettison the straps of the four 'A' type parachutes as they became entangled in the tail. They crossed the

Danish coast at Stadil flying at 100 feet and the English coast Holkam Bay at 2,000 feet. Landing at Tempsford 02.05 hours. Boxer's final report said 'although the pinpoint was good and easy to find he considers that it is unsuitable as it is completely surrounded by detached houses'. From the map co-ordinates given (55° 49′ 10″N, 10° 15′ 05″E) it would appear it was situated in the back yards of north Copenhagen!

The very next night the 17/18th S/Ldr Boxer flew operation FLOOR to Poland dropping into it four passengers and six containers. Likewise F/O Kuzmicki who dropped the same load into operation WALL. F/Lt Dodkin could not find ELKHOUND/GOLFER in Belgium. The 18/19th saw one sortie to France which failed because of the weather, likewise one to Holland failing because of fog. Two other sorties to Holland, MARROW 19/MARROW 20/HOCKEY/TENNIS were flown by Sgt Smith. The Dutch section in London had now switched from vegetables to sport for their operation names. More the pity that they did not pay more attention to the more important details of their operations. The other MARROW 18/PARSNIP 4/ BROADBEAN/GOLF was flown by F/Lt Austin. Between them they dropped into German hands four agents, Gerard van Os, William and Peter van der Wilden and Captain John Kist. Also 20 containers, four packages and eight boxes of chocolate. An additional two transmitters also fell into Giskes's hands making now, sixteen in all.

The next night 19/20th four sorties flew to France P/O Clow dropping 13 containers and three packages into three targets LIME 1/2/3. They were tackled in numerical order. They had hardly crossed the French coast when at a railway junction 17km south of Isigny flying at 1,500 feet they were met with two searchlights and accurate red tracers from about eight guns. It was a demoralising way to start a sortie, believe me! However, they set course for the Loire, then Limoges and to LIME 1. In clear skies and bright moonlight they dropped, from 600 feet on a reception flashing 'C', four containers and two packages. LIME 2, they said, was easy to find and they saw the reception committee moving towards the five containers as they dropped from 1,500 feet. They had difficulty in finding LIME 3 due to the position of the site in relation to the surrounding countryside. Here they delivered four more containers and a package. They had no problems coming home

S/Ldr Gibson likewise with three targets STOCKBROKER, GOAT/RAT & PRUNUS 3/STONEMASON. He had one agent and one package to drop at STOCKBROKER and reported he was certain he passed over the pinpoint but no reception was in place. He then took the one agent and one package intended for PRUNUS to their destination via Toulouse. Here, flying at 1,000 feet, a searchlight held them and coloured tracer was fired accurately from about six guns which damaged the port outer engine. Continuing and recognising ground detail of the PRUNUS dropping zone they again passed over the DZ without a reception in position. Reduced to three engines and still carrying a large payload they were unable to stay in the area any longer and returned home. They did not attempt to drop the two agents and one package that were destined for GOAT/RAT. After a flight of 10.20 hours they landed at Tempsford..

F/Lt Dodkin, flying another three target sortie, dropped a passenger onto BEAUNE his other two targets, CRAB 4 and PERCH 6 lacked receptions. The final French sortie was flown by P/O P Kingsford-Smith, BURGUNDY, BUTTERCUP 2 & DIRECTOR 4, the first two being SIS operations. Although not recorded it is thought that these targets were near Lyon. Coming home, and trying to find a pinpoint in fog, they drifted over the aerodrome at Tours and were promptly shot up by light flak knocking out the two starboard engines. Unable to bale out, because of the low altitude at which they were flying, he crashed landed Halifax W1012 into a field 20km south of Tours. The agent, they were carrying, disappeared the next day and Kingsford-Smith and his crew were eventually taken PoW.

In the meantime S/Ldr Boxer was flying operation SODAWATER, a PICKAXE operation with two NKVD agents and a package to drop blind into Austria. The route he chose was Beachy Head–Point du Haut–Banc–Leval–Lake Lachaussée–pinpoint on Rhine Marne Canal. From here they set course for Lake Constance. On this course the temperature of the port outer engine started to rise and it was decided

W/Cdr K S Batchelor, DFC, who took command of 138 Squadron on the 28 February 1943. He flew a Wellington on the first bombing raid of the war and in May 1941 commanded No. 311 Squadron. On the 24 May 1943 he was posted to command RAF Stradishall, achieving the rank of Group Captain at the age of 29. (Mrs D Batchelor)

to feather the engine and return home. Unable to maintain height they jettisoned their package from a height of 2,300 feet, it dropped into a wood 16km NE Freiburg. 65kms east of Lake Lachaussée they saw, on the starboard side at 3,000 feet, an unidentified twin engined aircraft flying on a reciprocal course and flashing a white light. They landed safely at Tempsford having been airborne for 7.45 hours.

This operation was completed five days later on the 24/25th and flown, ironically by a Polish crew, lead by F/O Gebik. They used much the same route out as S/Ldr Boxer. At Lake Constance they turned on ETA for Neusiedler See (Lake) having first made a pinpoint on Chiem See (approximately 50km west of Salzberg). Neusiedler See is about the same distance SE of Vienna. It was in this area that they parachuted from 700 feet, the two NKVD agents and their parcel. On the way home 24 minutes after leaving the target area flying at 6,000 feet they met with accurate heavy flak from four guns at Steyr (south of Linz). From Lake Constance the weather had been clear with good visibility. They landed at Tempsford at 05.30 having been flying for 10.40 hours. The remarks by the OC No.138 Squadron on the report was 'Good show'! G/Capt Fielden was more forthcoming with 'Very creditable'!

Two successful Polish sorties were flown on the 20/21st F/O Walczac and F/O Gebik flying operation RIVET and FILE respectively. Each dropped four passengers and six containers on their respective targets.

Apart from the two successful sorties to Austria and Germany, the remaining 14 sorties (nine to France and five to Holland) for this moon period and the remainder of February were to fail. The dedicated effort by the ground and aircrews went un-rewarded through the vagary of the weather.

On the 2nd February W/Cdr R C Hockey, DSO, DFC, had been posted to Air Ministry ACAS 1. W/Cdr K S Batchelor, DFC, a regular officer, had acceded command of No.138 Squadron in his place. W/Cdr Batchelor, on September 4th 1939, took part in the first RAF bombing raid of the war, flying a Wellington of No.9 Squadron.

CHAPTER FOURTEEN

March 1943

March opened for 138 Squadron with a flurry of six sorties to Poland. Two on the 3/4th three on the 8/9th and one on the night of the 9/10th. All were cargo drops, four were flown by Polish crews. F/Lt Gryglewicz and his crew failing LILY because of 'insufficient petrol'. He landed at Docking in Norfolk having been in the air 14 hours, no wonder he ran out of fuel! F/O Ruttledge trying to complete LILY the following night failed due to 'ground mist'. F/Sgt Smith flew an SIS sortie TULIP dropping six containers and four packages. All these Polish targets were named after flowers, ROSE, LILY, ASTER, and DAISY which was unusual. They were to revert to more functional names of tools or building materials! The operational reports are, as usual, not available but one must assume that reception committees were used since dropping stores blind would not have achieved very much.

One other sortie to Holland on the night of the 9/10th was flown by F/Lt Austin, operation SEAKALE/MARROW 17/SPROUT/KOLHRAB. Tragically three passengers, a radio operator Pieter Arendse and two SOE agents, Pieter Dourlein and Peter Bogaart were dropped into the hands of Giskes who now had 17 radio links with London. Six months later Dourlein was to escape and became the first Dutch SOE agent to reach England. Seven containers and four boxes of chocolate were also dropped.

The first 161 Squadron Halifax sortie for March was an SIS operation ADMIRAL to Holland completed on the 11/12th March by F/O Cresswell. He departed from England via Cromer for Vlieland, and in clear skies and good visibility, flying at 300 feet crossed the Dutch Coast, at Burg (which must be an error unless it was Den Burg on Texal and that means he was way south of track). From here they set course for Beilen, which they found and followed the railway north to the DZ. The co-ordinates of which was 52° 56' 25"N, 06° 33' 47"E. making it close to the small village of Hooghalen about 6km to the north of Beilen. Here from 700 feet at a speed of 132 mph they blind dropped an SIS agent. There is no mention of this drop in the history books, no name given, which leads me to believe it was totally successful and unobserved by the Germans. Cresswell flew out of Holland at a height of 300 feet at a position, he says, west of Edam, dropping four boxes of chocolate on the way. W/Cdr Pickard wrote on the operational report, amid ink blots for which he was probably responsible, 'This operation was very nicely carried out'.

That same night 138 Squadron sent two supply sorties to Holland, which dropped a total of 21 containers, six packages, eight boxes of chocolates, F/Lt Hooper's aircraft also carried 12 pigeons. He abandoned his sortie after completing half of it as there was a fighter nosing around in the target area, probably unleashed by Giskes.

A successful sortie to Denmark, TABLEGOSSIP & TABLETOP 1 was flown that night by S/Ldr Boxer with W/Cdr Batchelor as his second pilot. Captain Charles Tyce, the instructor and conducting officer of the agents, flew with them. They crossed the Danish coast at Svinklov flying at 500 feet and made for TABLEGOSSIP a target in an area south of Aalborg. Boxer had an option of two pinpoints on which to drop their agents, Flemming Muus, Einar Balling, Verner Johansen and Poul Jensen. The first pinpoint he considered 'rather a lot of woods' and proceeded to the second which 'appeared to be better'. Where from a height of 550 feet above the ground at an airspeed of 120 mph the four passengers were dropped blind about 2km NW of pinpoint which was identified by ground detail. Regrettably Poul Jensen was injured on landing. With them were dropped four packages which Cookridge says each contained a bicycle. He also added they were

A Halifax aircraft shedding its load over a Dropping Zone. The packages are being pushed out by the despatcher. (Crown copyright)

supposed to have been met by a reception committee, but the pilot missed the dropping zone. There is certainly no mention of a reception committee in the operational report and a pilot with the experience of Boxer knew exactly where he was. They then proceeded to the second target TABLETOP 1 where a reception committee waited beside their 'C' system lighting flashing 'R' to receive four containers. The aircraft flashed its recognition signal 'F' and from 700 feet dropped its load. They left the Danish coast flying at a height of 200 feet at Klitmøller approximately 85 kms due west of Aalborg and in clear skies over the North Sea crossed the English coast at Sheringham. They landed at Tempsford after 7.07 hours in the air unaware that they had put in position a man who was to become the SOE chief organiser in Denmark – Major Flemming Muus.

Only one of four Halifax sorties mounted by 161 Squadron on the 12/13th was partly successful being half completed. F/Lt Prior flying an SIS operation JALOUISE and PIMENTO 3 an SOE operation. Four containers were dropped. I know not where. Weather and no reception failed the other three sorties.

138 Squadron on the other hand had six aircraft in the air and faired little better. One French sortie failing and F/O Kuzmicki reporting no reception in Norway. Two others to Belgium and France were partly finished due to the weather.

Two Norwegian sorties were successful F/O Gebik and his Polish crew dropping three agents, five containers and three packages into operation PHEASANT. S/Ldr Gibson flew the other one, MARDONIUS, which was a mission mounted to attack shipping in Oslo harbour using local recruits and trained agents – three ships were successfully damaged.

Flying with S/Ldr Gibson's crew as rear gunner was F/Lt Putt, an elderly officer, in comparison to others on the Squadron's strength, having participated in the First World War. He was a great character and revelled under the nickname of 'Colonel'. He was also a great asset to the mess and, indeed, to W/Cdr Pickard when he bogged his Hudson in France during February! He must have had great powers of persuasion too, flying operationally at this time of his life.

However, MARDONIUS was to be a blind drop. Gibson flying in clear skies and good visibility, via Cromer-Jomfeuland-Tyrifjord-Kjiller-Enebakk-Target. A route which is difficult to trace, with the exception of Tyrifjord which is approximately 35km NW of Oslo and Enebakk. The target co-ordinates puts it roughly 15km to the SE of Oslo, which they identified as 'being by a large lake east of target' (probably Oreren). Here they dropped two agents, four containers and two packages from 600 feet. One of the agents was Max Manus, famous in the annals of Norwegian SOE operations for his underwater activities. Gibson flew home by the same route but when 8km from the Norwegian coast two medium heavy guns firing explosive shells, opened fire on them at 800 feet. They had been 8.55 hours in the air when they landed at Tempsford.

The night of the 13/14th March saw the commencement of a massive effort to Poland that was to last almost a week. Two Polish sorties from 161 Squadron saw P/O Wynne returning from YARD short of fuel and P/O Foster reporting no reception for his target SLATE. For 138 Squadron a mixture of Polish and RAF crews flew six successful sorties – operations AREA, STOCK, TILE, WINDOW, BRICK, and DOOR putting four passengers and six containers into each target.

The next night the 14/15th was tragic. Both Squadrons losing two aircraft. No.161 Squadron losing F/Lt A E Prior, DFM, and his crew during operation IRIDIUM to Czechoslovakia, the consequences of which I have already written. F/O G A Osborne, taking off Halifax DG283 for operation DIRECTOR 34, lost an engine half an hour into the flight, in spite of jettisoning his load he could not maintain height and crashed at Fawley three miles from Henley-on-Thames. Two crewmen were killed and the remainder injured. Osborne was later to receive the George Medal for his bravery in assisting crew members from the burning wreck. The two other missing aircraft from 138 Squadron were Halifax BB281, flown by S/Ldr C F Gibson, DFC, and Halifax DT620, flown by F/Sgt L R Smith. S/Ldr Gibson was flying SIS operation BRONZE to Czechoslovakia and crashed near Munich killing all of the crew. The fourth loss of the night was F/Sgt L R Smith, also on long range duty flying SLATE to Poland, who crashed Halifax DT620 at Store Heddinge 21km SE Køge in Denmark, all the crew were killed. The moon was almost full.

Intriguingly six sorties had been destined for DIRECTOR 34 in France that night. F/O Osborne, as previously stated, unfortunately met with engine failure. His colleague from No.161 Squadron F/O Cresswell reported no reception and the other four sorties from No.138 Squadron reported that they were unable to complete because of the weather.

W/Cdr Batchelor was flying DIRECTOR 34, his first SD operation as captain and his operations report said it was a straight forward 6.20 hour trip. Base-Tangmere- Cabourg-Blois-Nevers-Tournus (Soane-et-Loire). They had flown through a thick haze along the entire route with visibility down to a kilometre in places. At Tournus it was impossible to pinpoint below cloud. The target was east of Chalon. The reception was to be four bonfires and a light flashing 'P'. Batchelor was carrying 15 Containers and ten packages. They made their approach to the target and the foothills of the Alps flying blind below and in cloud. He abandoned the sortie returning the same way as he came in and landed at Tangmere. This must have been the same weather experienced by all the DIRECTOR 34 sorties.

One week later, on the 20/21st, DIRECTOR 35 was flown by four aircraft, with three completing, and dropping a total of 35 containers and 30 packages. A large amount of heavy hardware for the reception committee to remove and hide. F/Lt Hooper failed having been hit by flak.

The remaining operations completing the programme for the night of 14/15th March were three sorties to Poland, two successful and one PIPE failing due to 'insufficient petrol'. The two successes YARD and STEP received a total of three passengers, twelve containers and six packages. F/O Clow flew the second sortie of the night, MERCURY, to Czechoslovakia. To complete the nights work F/O Ruttledge flew a successful double operation IRIS & GUDGEON 1 to France, dropping an agent, six containers and three packages in all.

A hardworking but unrewarding night for both squadrons. Eleven sorties mounted by 138 Squadron and four by 161 Squadron, four aircraft, lost and only four sorties completed (one of those only partially).

On the nights of 16/17th and 19/20th No.138 Squadron flew eight sorties, seven to Poland. These operations were given the uninspiring names of PIPE, LOCK, ATTIC, KNOB, KEY, BEAM and CELLAR. The last one failed due to the lack of a reception. The outstanding PIPE was completed by S/Ldr Boxer. Six passengers, 42 containers and 24 packages were dropped in all. The exception to the Polish operations was a sortie flown to Norway by F/O Wrezien and CHAFFINCH 1 which failed lacking a reception.

During the same period of time, the 17/18th, 19/20th six 161 Squadron SIS Lysander sorties were carried out. All were successful with the exception of F/O Rymills flying operation HECTOR on the 19/20th who reported that he 'could not find the field'. TRAINER, a double Lysander sortie on the 17/18th, must have given F/O Vaughan-Fowler something to think about, the engine of his Lysander caught fire on the ground. However, both he and his landing partner, F/O Rymills both made it safely back to Tangmere. A Lysander flown by F/Lt Bridger on the 19/20th, operation SIRENE 2 returned Jean Moulin and General Delestraint to France. General Delestraint was arrested during the first two weeks in June. Jean Moulin was arrested on the 21st June and whilst under interrogation was brutally murdered by Klaus Barbie, the Gestapo chief of Lyon. His silence during his ordeal made him a national hero.

This night a 161 Squadron Halifax DG244 piloted by F/O H L Wynne, DFM, was flying an SIS operation VEGA 3 to Norway. Tragically he and his crew were lost without trace.

In the remaining days of March 161 flew two successful Halifax SIS sorties, F/O Foster flying LEO to Norway, and F/O Leggate, a triple operation to France YOLANDE, OAKTREE & DIDO, although OAKTREE went uncompleted for the second time. Two Lysander sorties were completed, S/Ldr Verity bringing home Peter Churchill on the 23/24th, operation JOCKEY/PLAYWRIGHT. On his way out Verity was attacked by a night fighter who fired tracer at him.

The 20/21st March saw 138 Squadron complete the four DIRECTOR 35 targets as reported. Two Polish sorties GLASS and BASIN saw F/O Gebik complete the former and F/O Kuzmicki returning because of 'shortage of petrol'. Sgt Cook having had an electrical failure could only complete half of his French operation LUCERNE/ DAFFODIL & GUDGEON 5 & 6. On the 23/24th March four sorties to France were attempted. F/Lt Austin had a fishy and a busy night with two French targets, ROACH 4/MUSSEL MINOR/WINKLE & GUDGEON 7/HADDOCK/SWORDFISH, parachuting two agents, four containers and three packages on the former, finding the reception by map reading their way in clear weather along a railway line from Chartres (Eure-et-Loire). The next target was some 320km to the south east near Roanne (Loire) in a bend of the River Loire where they dropped two agents, three packages and six containers on a reception flashing 'P'. On their return they dropped leaflets over Roanne and Nevers together with three pigeons. North east of Orléans they dropped twelve pigeons, which seemed a long, long way from home for them. Almost out of France flying at 500 feet they were engaged by two searchlights and four guns at Caen, their tracers being accurate enough to hit the fuselage. That exhausting effort took him 6.20 hours by the time he had landed at Tempsford.

F/Lt Gryglewicz and his crew also flew a twin operation to France, BUTLER/ BARBER/PUBLICAN & STATIONER 3, the latter objective was not completed as although they were certain they identified the pinpoint there was no reception to greet them. However, from a height of 900 feet, in the Saumur area, he parachuted, blind, Françoise Garel, the organiser of BUTLER, Marcel Rousset, and Marcel Fox. The drop wasn't entirely successful, the package dropped with them, containing their baggage and Rousset's wireless set, was lost. All three were arrested in Paris on 7th February 1943. Garel and Fox died in captivity while Rousset was said to have escaped. Shortly after their arrest the *reseau* BUTLER was penetrated and their dropping zones operated by the Germans.

W/Cdr Batchelor was operating again flying a double SIS target JALOUISE & LUPIN to France, dropping six containers into the former and failing to complete the latter, it would appear that the reception lights were the wrong colour and the white light was flashing the wrong letter. F/O Ruttledge flew OAKTREE, CRAB 8 & GUDGEON 2, to France dropping in all two agents, 14 containers and two packages onto his targets.

A unique sortie to Corsica operation SEA URCHIN was undertaken by Sgt Cook. He had been Kingsford-Smith's second pilot before he was shot down. Cook took-off at 19.12 hours. taking the route, Tempsford–Tangmere–Cabourg (crossing into France at 300 feet, then flying in 10/10ths medium cloud to the Loire)–Orléans–Nevers–Lyon, here at 2,000 feet they met with four searchlights and accurate light flak. The cloud was now 10/10ths from ground to 12,000 feet. At Cap Lardier, they were up to 8,000 feet setting course for Corsica in clear weather with a slight haze. They were able to pinpoint visually, the Gulf of Ajaccio, Propriano (on the coast 30km to the south) and shortly after Sartène. From here they had no difficulty in finding the target which they circled and crossed for 27 minutes. Unhappily there was no one there and they had to return with their cargo, six containers, dropping their leaflets near Dreux, roughly 50km west of Paris. They landed at Tempsford at 06.15 they had been in the air 11.13 hours.

G/Capt Fielden who that day had been awarded the DFC wrote on the operational report 'a long way to go to find no reception'. Eric Piquet-Wicks, in his book *Four in the Shadows*, describes the landing by submarine, in January 1943, of a Corsican, Fred Scamaroni and two others (one a W/T operator), onto a beach in Corsica. The operation was called SEA-URCHIN this solitary, unsuccessful, air drop to Corsica was obviously an extension of this operation. On the 20th March the OVRA (the Italian secret police who had taken over the island's security) arrested Scamaroni and shortly after he committed suicide.

The following night the 24/25th seven operations were mounted of which four, successfully, to Poland, STONE, CELLAR, BASIN, and DORIC. Most of them six container cargo sorties although F/Lt Gryglewicz dropped three passengers on CELLAR. The rear gunner, flying DORIC in F/O Wrezien's crew, claimed to have hit a Ju 88 and a Me 109 in combat. STONE was to be the last of S/Ldr Boxer's tour as he had flown five successful sorties that month, one to Denmark and four to Poland but he was to return to Tempsford one year later.

F/Lt Hooper was unable to complete a French sortie due to the weather. In two sorties to Holland F/O Ruttledge dropped 13 containers, a barrel of coffee and ten boxes of chocolates onto a German operated site PARSNIP 5/LETTUCE 10. The German Abwehr must have laughed their heads off at this deadly and bizarre situation. We, their enemy, dropping into their hands, agents, munitions, coffee, chocolate and at the same time exposing our aircrews to real and unnecessary danger. F/O E Clow, a New Zealander, was flying another Dutch sortie, his twelfth operation as captain, since joining the Squadron in early February. His Halifax HR665 was shot down and he made a skilful ditching in the Ijsselmeer near Enkhuizen. The crew were taken prisoner. It is thought the two agents on board were Bergman, who was drowned, and Gerbrands, who escaped. The draft operational report awaiting completion on their return confirms they had two passengers on board.

Apart from the unsuccessful operation FURZE to Poland the month ended with S/Ldr Robinson flying another unique sortie this time to Tunisia. The operations report gives little detail other than it was coded KIPLING (Rudyard had been crossed out on the report). In addition to Robinson's crew was a Major Wooler and S/Sgt Clark of the US Army. The operation started from Canrobert an airfield in Algeria, approximately 55km SE of Constantine – it is not recorded how they got there. They took-off at 23.00 hours and flew to Pichon and from there to the target 35° 11′N, 10° 41′E. which was approximately 55km due south of Sousse close to the railway line to Sfax, 8km north of la Hencha. The moon and the stars were just visible through thin high stratus and ground haze limited visibility to 5km into the moon. A searchlight came on as they neared la Hencha but made their run into the target which they could clearly see from ground detail. The starboard outer failed at the same time and the propeller was feathered. From a height of 500 feet, and at a speed of 138 mph, they dropped, blind, eight passengers and a container just west of a road and rail junction 8km north of la Hencha. They returned to Canrobert the same way, landing after 03.50 hours in the air, but this sortie could not have been as easy as it was made out to be and although they spent almost an hour over the target area there is, unfortunately, no record to reveal the purpose of this sortie other than the obvious interest the US Army had in it.

March had been a full working month for both Squadrons. Fifty percent of the 61 sorties flown by 138 Squadron had been sent to Poland. Adam Zamoyski, in his book *The Forgotten Few*, says there were only 55 flights to Poland in 1943. This is a grave error as 55 flights for the first three months of 1943 would have been nearer the mark. After March no further Polish sorties could be flown until September (when 23 sorties to Poland were flown) for the simple reason that Poland could not be reached under the cover of darkness. I have no wish to contest other Polish SOE figures mentioned in this book other than No.138 Squadron flew over 300 sorties including Poland in 1942.

The loss of three Halifaxes by No.161 Squadron severely cut their long range operational effectiveness. No.138 Squadron faired no better by losing the same number. Both Squadrons lost an aircraft on the same night flying to Czechoslovakia and a third was attacked by a night fighter and hit in the wing by a cannon shell. It looked as if the German defences had now caught up with those single sorties crossing Germany in moonlight to get to their Czechoslovakian targets.

The crews of S/Ldr Gibson and F/Lt Prior were buried at Durnbach War Cemetery and were joined after the war by the remains of W/Cdr Farley and his crew who had died a year before.

CHAPTER FIFTEEN

April 1943

By April 'Gee' had filtered down to the SD Squadrons No.161 Squadron having the first three aircraft at Tempsford fitted with this navigation aid. By this time the Germans had effectively jammed this equipment but it could still be used for accurate fixes on the coast. I remember the navigator of a crew I was flying with in early 1944 getting a 'freak' fix within 50 miles (80km) of the target area somewhere near Périgueux. It generated great enthusiasm within the crew when the navigator made his announcement!

The March moon period finished with two 138 Squadron Polish operations FLAX and NETTLE. F/O Polkowski returning from the former with an unserviceable petrol pump and F/O Izycki arriving too late over the target to drop. These were the last sorties to Poland until the nights grew longer in September.

The Albermarles had now been withdrawn from No.161 Squadron although from the 24th March to the 8th April the Havocs had been active, albeit with little success.

The moon rose again on the 11/12th April heralding another busy month for the Tempsford Squadrons, most of the targets being in France. No.161 Squadron regained the services of F/O Cussen who had returned from his November internment in Portugal and had converted to Halifaxes to fly PHYSICIAN 17 & STATIONER 1 to France. PHYSICIAN 17 was in the Selles-St-Denis area approximately 50km south of Orléans. Receiving an accurate 'Gee' fix he had little trouble locating the DZ flashing 'C' dropping five containers and one package. STATIONER 1 was thirty minutes away near Lothiers 14km south west of Châteauroux (Indre) but he was unable to find it. 'Gee' had now failed and he turned for home. Nearing the coast at 1,500 feet light flak came up at him from Caen.

F/Lt Foster was flying LUPIN, PIMENTO 18 & 10. LUPIN, outstanding since the 20/21st February, was in the Mâcon area and was identified by a DR run from the River Saône and a pinpoint from Bourg-en-Bresse. Stratus cloud at 4,000 feet covered the moon making conditions dark and the target difficult to find. Flying on a course of 060 degrees at 800 feet above the ground and at an airspeed of 135 mph they parachuted the agent plus one package on a triangle of white lights with an extra white flashing 'V'. The despatcher reported that the passenger hesitated for a few seconds. The pilot also reported 'owing to the slight hesitation of the passenger before jumping she may have dropped a short distance to the east of the reception'. He continued to PIMENTO 10 where he dropped four containers onto white lights, reporting although the site was easy to find it was very close to a river. His remaining five containers, destined for PIMENTO 18, were brought back since there was no reception. A seemingly routine operation, however, pinned to the report is a letter addressed to the Senior Intelligence Officer, Tempsford, from A.I.1(c). It is dated the 22nd April 1943, and headed OPERATION LUPIN, it says;

> We have now heard from the agent dropped in the above operation and she has given us the point where she landed, which is in the neighbourhood of the village of Perrex. The area where she landed at (and) the actual pin point are marked on the attached map.
> (Sgd) A COMPTON F/Lt for Wing Commander

Pinned to the letter was a large scale map (13cm:1km) of the area showing the location of the reception and where LUPIN landed. The distance between the two points is approximately 15km, the landing point being to the west of the DZ (the DZ appears on this map to be 2km to the North of Bourg). The terrain in between looks pretty rugged. There is something decidedly wrong here and I cannot see that it is the fault of Foster's crew. The only conclusion I can come to is that the reception site wasn't where it should have been. The map attached to the letter is an old French Army survey map dated 1889 (prix 1f.50) revised in 1897 and reproduced in 1940. In English at the base of it is written 'The longitudes refer to the meridian of Paris, which is 02° 20′ 14″E of Greenwich'. It was on this map that the co-ordinates of the DZ were plotted. I was totally confused, perhaps too was the person who plotted these co-ordinates!

Furthermore I have been unable to trace just who LUPIN was. No source records mention a woman being dropped this night; perhaps it was an SIS operation that has yet to come to light but Foster's second pilot, P/O Affleck is a name that would feature for some time in Tempsford operations.

No.138 Squadron were this night flying six sorties to France. Four by Polish crews. None of them were completely successful, mostly due to the lack of receptions. However, two of the partially completed operations parachuted a total of five agents and 14 containers.

Another seven sorties were attempted by the Squadron the following night, the 12/13th. Again four Polish crews participated. Regrettably Halifax BB340 flown by F/Lt J Izycki's crew, piloted by F/O B Korpowski, PAF, and flying operations DIRECTOR 22, REPORTER & SURGEON to France, was lost. They were crossing the French coast at 500 feet when a short burst of flak set fire to one engine. causing them to crash land at Douvres-la-Delivrande, 5km from the coast and 12km NNW Caen. Fire completely destroyed the aircraft. One of the crew died, four were taken PoW and three evaded, two of whom, the despatcher and the flight engineer, were RAF personnel. Two agents on board survived the crash, Claude Jumeau (his second tour) and Lee Graham were bound for the vicinity of Lyon. Regrettably they were soon to be arrested, Jumeau to die in prison and Graham to survive the war. The map co-ordinates of the target shown on the draft operations report waiting their return was 45° 25′ 00″N and 05° 02′ 07″E which approximates the pinpoint some 25km north of Aix-en-Provence in the Lubéron. On this target they were to drop two agents, five containers and two packages. Two of the evaders F/O Korpowski, who was badly burned, and Sgt Dent the flight engineer arrived home via Gibraltar on the 3rd June 1943

The crew of F/O Gebik, piloted by F/O Miszewski were flying operation PRUNUS 3/STONEMASON & GUDGEON 9. They took off from Tempsford at 20.56 crossing the Channel via Bognor and east of Pte de la Percée and into France at a height of 100 feet. From here they flew to Saumur and then direct to the pinpoint of PRUNUS situated at 43° 07′ 41″N and 00° 30′ 16″E. approximately 42km SE of Tarbes, the only town of any size in the area. The DZ was in the middle of nowhere (Toulouse being 100km to the NE) surrounded by mountains with heights up to 2,500 feet. No wonder Gebik reported it as a bad pinpoint, difficult to find. The reception was flashing 'C' and Gebik parachuted in, from 700 feet above the ground, a French-Canadian C J Duchalard. His main task was to work a 'Eureka' set — the ground transmitter for 'Rebecca'. They also dropped, four containers and a package. Afterwards Gebik made his way east for another 30 minutes to GUDGEON 9, approximately 13km NE of Foix (Ariege), where another five containers and two packages were dropped onto the target flashing 'G'. They returned home the same way as they came, landing at 04.56 after an eight hour flight.

M R D Foot says that Maurice Pertschuk, one of the leaders of PRUNUS, received Duchalard and settled him in a safe house before leaving for his lodgings in Toulouse. The journey from the reception area to Toulouse was a long way and one wonders how he made his way there. Regrettably the Germans were waiting for him. Within a week of Duchalard's drop the principle members of the circuit PRUNUS had been arrested. Duchalard remaining free made his way home through Spain. This operation is reported by Foot as having taken place a day earlier.

Of the remaining five 138 Squadron sorties that took place on the 12/13th April, three were supply drops and two were uncompleted. No.161 Squadron had two Halifax French sorties in the air that night, the lack of receptions prevented F/O Leggate from completing any of his three pronged mission. F/O Cussen on the other hand flying YANNICK,COCKLE 2 & COCKLE 3/BARACUDA had the reception lights turned out at YANNICK (an SIS target) as he was making his approach. A convoy of vehicles were seen from the aircraft travelling along a road close to the site. However, he dropped five containers on each of the other two sites.

F/O O A Cussen had flown Halifax DG409 on operations to France on the 11/12th and 12/13th of April. On the 13th April he was conducting an air test on this aeroplane when the port-inner engine failed on take-off, the aircraft swung causing the undercarriage to collapse, in turn writing it off. Fortunately there were no injuries but it was hardly the way to celebrate his recent return to the Squadron from internment!

Two No.161 Squadron Halifax and two Lysander sorties were flown on the 13/14th. However, 138 Squadron were flying four sorties to France, one to Belgium and one, of all places, to Italy. The Belgium sortie GIBBON 2, CARACAL 3 & PORCUPINE/MANDRILL was flown by a New Zealander, Sgt W A Cook, on Halifax BB363 and regrettably was lost. The aircraft was presumed to have come down in the sea with the loss of nine crew members, two under training. According to the ATF6, at GIBBON 2, situated approximately 8km SE of Nivelles (Belgium), they were to drop two packages. At CARACAL 3 about 12km south of Brussels, one container on a reception flashing 'C'. Finally at PORCUPINE/MANDRILL some 15km NE of Namur they were to drop two agents blind. It is not said whether or not the two agents were on board when the aircraft was lost.

A photocopy of the log book of Cook's flight engineer Sgt Edwin Hammett was sent to me by his brother Peter. Edwin was 21 years old when he was lost and, before he took the Flight Engineer's course at St Athens, was a Corporal fitter on a Spitfire Squadron at Tangmere, during the Battle of Britain. Amazingly Hammett's log book shows his initial air experience to be a 7.20 hour operational flight to France, as second engineer, in a Halifax flown by F/O Ruttledge on the 23/24th March. He added another 9.05 hours flying time to this before his next operational flight as Sgt Cook's flight engineer when they were both lost.

The night of the 13/14th had another of those strange flights of which there are no details other than an operations report. F/O Kuzmicki and his Polish crew flew operation LOGANBERRY to Italy. They took off at 21.00 and crossed the French coast at 400 feet at Point de la Percée where, from Caen, they saw heavy flak being directed at other aircraft. From here they flew direct to Nevers, thence Lac du Bourget (65km due east of Lyon). They had difficulty once they reached Mount Blanc when clear skies changed to 10/10ths cloud with a base of 8,000 feet. They circled for half an hour climbing above the cloud and then set course above it, descending on ETA, where in the target area visibility was poor due to the dark. The exact pinpoint, 45° 25' 00"N, 08° 02' 07"E, was found by identifying a lake into which (so the report says!) they dropped six containers from 250 feet above the ground. There being no reception arrangements. Heavy flak was seen coming from Turin 35 minutes later, firing at other aircraft at 12,000 feet. They had been airborne for ten hours when they landed.

The 14/15th saw nine Halifax sorties flown from Tempsford and double Lysander sortie from Tangmere. Only F/O McCairns superb airmanship, having struck a tree on take off in France, prevented a Lysander disaster. Three 161 Squadron Halifax sorties to France were completed. P/O Affleck, flying his first sortie as captain, completed YANNICK, an SIS operation, uncompleted from two nights earlier he dropped a package. Strangely he too reported motor traffic near his other target COCKLE 4 as had Cussen previously on the YANNICK operation.

*   *   *

Sgt E G Hammett, Flight Engineer to Sgt W A Cook, lost 13/14 April 1943 off Bournemouth in Halifax BB363 NF-T.
(P Hammett)

An important SOE operation was flown by a 161 Squadron crew to France that night. F/O Leggate flying PERCH 7 & SPINDLE A. After delivering five containers and two packages to PERCH 7 he then moved onto SPINDLE A. Here he dropped, it is said by Jerrard Tickle in his book *Odette*, Peter Churchill into the arms of Odette Sanson on a snow covered site on the summit of Mount Semnoz about 5km south of Annecy. Tickle says this site had been selected the previous day by Odette Sanson and her companion 'Arnaud' (Captain A Rabinovitch) who pronounced it suitable by pacing out 100 metres to the right and to the left. On the night of the drop a bonfire prepared the day before, was lit by them at the sound of the aircraft.

Leggate reports he had little trouble finding the target, the town of Annecy (Haute-Savoie) 'was lit up' and in addition to a DZ flashing 'F' a bonfire had been lit, 'which proved helpful'. At 00.52 hours from a height of 800 feet at an airspeed of 140 mph, Churchill was dropped. It was his fourth tour. Regrettably 24 hours later both had been arrested. They were fortunate enough to survive their terrible ordeals and to marry after the war.

No.138 Squadron were not as lucky as their sister Squadron, two of their operations failing because of the lack of receptions. One flown by a Polish crew led by F/O Polkowski and piloted by F/O Polnik is notable because of its ingenuity. They were flying PRUNUS 6 & STOCKBROKER/SHIPWRIGHT/STATIONER 2 and the two targets were in the Hautes-Pyrenees. The former has already been mentioned but the latter was in the Tarbes area. The route they took was Start Point in the UK–Ile d'Oussant (An island some 40km west of Brest). Then through the Bay of Biscay (where the cloud base was 500 feet), making a landfall at Léon (approx. 25km NW of Dax). From here they went to STOCKBROKER and parachuted two agents, a Frenchman Amédeé Maingard and Harry Rée (who spoke French with a Mancunian accent!), two containers and two packages on a site flashing 'J'. Then west to PRUNUS 6 where they dropped five containers, returning into the Bay via Léon (Landes). The height of this flight rarely exceeded 500 feet! They were airborne for 10.20 hours.

F/Lt Gryglewicz and his crew flying SCIENTIST 7/SCIENTIST A/WEAVER, & SCIENTIST 17 & SCIENTIST 22 in the Angoulême area was half an hour from the target when it was discovered that one of his passengers had left his papers behind. One only jumped the other was brought home!

The 15/16th brought another string of successes for both Squadrons with twelve completed sorties all to France except one supply SIS operation to Belgium flown by S/Ldr Hodges of 161 Squadron. They also flew four Lysander and one Hudson sortie. F/O Vaughan-Fowler and F/O McCairns bringing home Passy, Brossolette and Yeo-Thomas. Both S/Ldr Verity and F/Lt Bridger brought home damaged aircraft. Four sorties flown by 138 Squadron were also successful. In all one agent, 47 containers and ten packages were dropped.

The 16/17th showed a change in direction, both squadrons sending a sortie to Norway. F/O Leggate of 161 Squadron flew CHAFFINCH 1/CENTAUR dropping six containers and four packages onto reception which he said was near a lake. The agent he was carrying for CENTAUR, Oluf Reed-Olsen, although sitting on the edge of the exit hatch, was refused permission to jump as the surface wind was calculated to be in excess of 45 mph.

F/O Gebik and his crew were flying operation PUFFIN. Their operations report says they were to drop blind two agents, eight containers and three packages. Plotting the co-ordinates given the pinpoint was approximately 30km to the NW of Oslo near a large lake, Tyrifjord. In his report Gebik specifically mentions this lake as identified and from here so was the pinpoint where they dropped their load blind from 900 feet.

Another Polish crew led by F/O Polkowski flew operation TABLELAMP/TABLE-GOSSIP to Denmark. Flying from Cromer to cross the Danish coast north of Sondervig at 200 feet thence north of Holstebro and to Skals (north of Viburg). Finding the target flashing 'Q' it took four minutes to parachute in from 800 feet, Kai Lund, four containers and one package. They whipped out at 200 feet to the coast at Vorupor. On the way home picking up good fixes from the Eastern 'Gee' chain, the Northern chain was not working. They landed at 03.49 hours.

There were two other 138 Squadron French sorties this night. F/Lt Dodkin in clear skies and considerable ground haze could not find the large wood SE Valenciennes and reported he 'Got Lost'. It was concluded that there was a navigational error. S/Ldr Robinson flew the other sortie.

For No.161 Squadron three SIS French Lysander sorties were flown. F/Lt Bridger flying operation PETUNIA landing near Issoire (Puy-de-Dôme) south of Clermont-Ferrand. A long distance flight by any standards. Forced to take his engine to overshoot the narrow mountain plateau landing strip he struck some overhead electric cables after bouncing on a hill, and burst a tyre. On landing he decided to deflate the other tyre by firing his pistol into it in the hope that this would give him a straight take off run. Landing at Tangmere he found copper wire had wound round his propeller boss and was trailing behind his aircraft.

Two Halifax sorties were laid on by 161 Squadron that night. F/Lt Foster to fly one agent and two containers to Norway on operation ALGOL – he returned early having an oil leak in one of his engines. P/O Affleck was to have gone to France flying 15 containers to SPRUCE 9. He too returned early, his aeroplane unable to gain height.

The 17/18th saw nine Halifax sorties take-off for France. Only one flown by F/O Cussen, of the three flown by 161 Squadron was successful. Cussen in addition to dropping nine containers and six packages onto PERCH 6 & WHEELWRIGHT 1 scattered 50 pigeons.

All five of 138 Squadron's effort were completely successful. Unhappily Halifax DT725 flown by F/Lt B S Lawrenczuk's crew and piloted by F/O T Ginter, flying operation LIME 9 to France to drop eight Containers, was lost. (LIME 8 was in the Lons-le-Saunier area, east of Chalon-sur-Saône, presumably LIME 9 was in the same area) They crashed at Ussy, 8km NW Falaise, none of the crew survived.

The following night the 18/19th April, of the six operations mounted one was of particular interest, F/O Gebik and his crew flying SCULLION, & PIMENTO 14 to France. The first target was approximately 10km north of Autun (Saône-et-Loire), was positively identified and agreed with Hugh Dormer the leader of the group (Gebik had a 3km leeway). From 800 feet, at an airspeed of 120 mph, six passengers were dropped blind, the despatcher reporting 'all jumped very quickly and without hesitation'. With them went one container and a package. SCULLION was a sabotage party planned to attack a synthetic petrol plant near Autun but was found to be too heavily guarded, so the mission was aborted. Gebik then proceeded to PIMENTO 14, 40 minutes away and on a site flashing 'R' dropped four containers and two packages. It was a difficult site and due to high ground it was only possible to fly over it from North to South or vice versa. The reception lights were said to be 'very bad' but there was no enemy opposition. They landed after 7.13 hours in the air.

The night of the 19/20th saw two flights to Norway. A 161 Squadron Halifax flown by F/O Cussen flying operation ALGOL & CHAFFINCH 3. ALGOL was an SIS operation. They crossed the Norwegian coast at 5,000 feet recognising Flekkefjord in clear skies and good visibility. From here they went to Tinnsjo Lake and thence to the target which was all of 75km west of Oslo. Picking up an isosceles triangle of red lights with one white flashing 'K' from a height of 500 feet they dropped their agent. The despatcher reported although the passenger made a clean exit his parachute was not seen to open. He was seen to be struggling during his descent as if to free his parachute and then seen to hit the ground. S/Ldr Hodges wrote on the report that 'there seems to be no apparent reason why the parachute failed to open. The bag was examined and there was no sign of any defect'. Two containers were dropped with him. The wind at the pinpoint was estimated to be well under 20 mph. Cussen then moved onto CHAFFINCH 3 but without reception failed to drop the remaining nine containers. The flight took 8.15 hours.

F/O Kuzmicki and his crew flew the sole 138 Squadron sortie this night, likewise to Norway coded CENTAUR & CHAFFINCH 2. They crossed the coast at Jomfeuland flying at 200 feet! thence to Hollen and to the target. Here they parachuted one passenger blind at an estimated dropping point, 'slightly north of pinpoint'. This was undoubtedly Oluf Reed-Olsen's second attempt as described in his book *Two Eggs On My Plate*. The despatcher comments 'Jumped OK' but did not realise that Olsen was unconscious having struck the tailwheel and was swinging violently on the end of his static line, his parachute having failed to release. Olsen says in his book he regained consciousness looking up at the rear turret and then realised that his parachute had partially opened and he was dropping to the ground much too fast. He landed heavily,

Captain Oluf Reed-Olsen whose first parachute mission into Norway, 19/20 April 1943, nearly ended in disaster. (Oluf Reed-Olsen)

a tree breaking his fall, the canopy of his parachute spread in its upper branches. He had dislocated his right knee. The operations report says he was dropped from 800 feet above the ground at an airspeed of 130 mph. Kuzmicki then flew on to a reception 18 minutes away and dropped nine containers. Like Cussen the trip took 8.15 hours and completed the outstanding CENTAUR operation of the 16/17th. Olsen's pistol and suitcase wireless can be seen in the Imperial War Museum.

It was a terrible coincidence that there had been a problem with the parachutes fitted to those SIS agents that night. One asks if they had been packed by the same person?

With the moon on the wane the last of 138 squadron's April operations were to be flown on the 21/22nd April. F/Lt Hooper flew to Denmark, operation TABLETOP 2/ TABLEHABIT, his seventh sortie for the month. It took two hours to cross the North Sea before reaching the Danish coast at a height of 800 feet at Lodbjaarg. The location of the target was the same as the last Danish operation flown on the 16/17th April by F/O Polkowski. Hooper made two runs over the target dropping four containers at 00.33 hours on the first and the agent, Proben Lok-Lindblad at 00.36 on the second, thus, spending three minutes over the target.

Cookridge records that Muus in May sent a signal to Baker Street complaining that in both of these drops the aircraft flew too high, probably between 1,000 and 1,100 feet and the dispatch of the containers could probably be seen for miles. It was also dangerous for the aircraft to fly straight towards the DZ, drop the cargo and return in a beeline! Hooper was accused of remaining over the target too long making huge circles then dropping his containers, returning after six minutes to drop Lindblad after the DZ lights had been extinguished. It is hoped that Baker Street told Muus that Polkowski and his crew had since given their lives over Holland for the same cause that Muus himself was fighting and could not pass his complaint on to them. Hooper in his report did not mention that the lights had gone out when he dropped his agent.

Hooper on his 'beeline' for home had yet to overcome another danger, the weather worsened as they reached the English Coast and 30km from Cromer, they were diverted to Elsham Wolds in Lincolnshire. This airfield proved unfit and were diverted again, to Leeming landing after being airborne 7.10 hours.

Cookridge also says 'on balance, drops of men and material in Denmark were carried out with far fewer losses than in any other enemy occupied country'. A tactless conclusion to make as Tempsford alone lost 13 aircraft in or around Denmark. A memorial has been erected by the Danish people to Commemorate the 69 lives of Allied airmen lost supporting the Danish resistance. I am sure that no one would have wished a greater sacrifice to have been made.

In the meantime S/Ldr Robinson was flying to Holland NETBALL/GHERKIN/ MARROW 27 & 28. Flying at 1,000 feet on

the way out they met with light flak from an unseen ship 20km NW of Vlieland. Five minutes later flying at 50 feet flak came up at them from the north end of Texel. 'Rebecca' (the Germans had at last got this working!) from a height of 2-300 feet and 8 to 10km out led them to the target, MARROW 28. Here from 500 feet on the DZ flashing 'M' they parachuted, two agents, seven containers and two cases of chocolate. On their way to MARROW 27 they saw MARROW 29, which was F/Lt Dodkin's target, waiting to receive his 14 containers.

At '27' they dropped another seven containers and three packages one of which should have gone to their first target. Robinson reported on their way home they saw Soestenburg aerodrome, NW of Harderwijk, 'lit up with flarepath'. They calculated the wind over the North Sea had reached 50 mph.

F/O Cussen from No.161 Squadron also went to Holland that night flying operation LACROSSE & LEEK 6. Giskes from these three Dutch operations imprisoned three agents: Frederick Rouward, Ivo van Uytwang and Albert Wegner also receiving 35 containers, seven packages and four boxes of chocolate.

S/Ldr Verity flew a Lysander operation TOMY to France, it must have been quite dark. He brought back Déricourt for further training and a reprimand 'having endangered a Lysander through an ill placed flare path'.

CHAPTER SIXTEEN

May – June 1943

The first Halifax operation of May was flown on the 5/6th. S/Ldr Hodges with S/Ldr Verity as his second pilot repositioning Déricourt by parachuting him blind from 700 feet 'in bend of River Loire by St-Laurent'. The pinpoint was identified by the railway and the River Loire. This 161 Squadron operation FARRIER flown without the aid of the moon could not have been as easy as the report suggests. S/Ldr Hodges had already flown an ASCENSION operation ST JAMES 2 in a Havoc during the morning!

It was said following Déricourt's return, in addition to disclosing, in advance, pick up flights to the Germans, he was forced to hand over mail that came into his hands for onward transit.

May was another busy month for both Squadrons. The rising moon on the 11/12th saw 138 Squadron flying three cargo trips to Holland during which a Polish crew led by F/O J Polkowski was lost flying operations LEEK 7 & CATARRH 12 in Halifax DT725. They came down in the sea off the Dutch coast, there were no survivors.

F/Lt Austin flew TABLEJELLY/TABLEGOSSIP 2 to Denmark. Crossing the Danish coast at Vigso in clear skies and good visibility parachuted Captain Paul Hansen, one other and two containers with two packages on a reception flashing 'M'. It was the same site used twice before. They also scattered 25 pigeons. Before reaching the Danish coast the flaps crept down to 60 degrees and the aircraft began to fly in circles. Austin eventually got the flaps fully down, steadied the aircraft and flew home at a ground speed of 98 mph! It took him nearly four hours to reach the English coast.

The 12/13th May saw eight 138 Squadron sorties flown to France. Four were cargo drops. F/O Ruttledge flying ARARAT, CHESTNUT 3 and ROACH 16 & 17 in clear skies and good visibility at ARARAT dropped blind from 600 feet an agent with a package. Thence to CHESTNUT 3 eight minutes away in the Rambouillet area where onto a reception from 500 feet he dropped five containers. A further 45 minutes south he was in the Cosne (Nievre) area dropping his remaining ten containers. An easy, well conducted operation taking 5.15 hours flying time.

S/Ldr C G S R Robinson flying Halifax BB313 on operation DONKEYMAN 1/ROACH 10 & LIME 16 had the misfortune to be shot down by flak on the way home and crash landed near Troyes

(Aube). Records say he had completed LIME 16 dropping five containers onto this target. Five of the crew were made PoW and three managed to evade capture.

Sgt J C Tweed the second pilot who evaded explains more fully what happened during his MI9 interrogation. They flew over Romilly aerodrome (Romilly-sur-Seine [Aube] approximately 30km NW Troyes) and were hit by flak and set on fire. The pilot ordered the crew to abandon the aircraft but before they could do so he made a forced landing in a field. Although injured he and another member of the crew pulled the wireless operator clear and dragged him about 100 yards from the aircraft. Robinson coming out of the aircraft was dazed and cut about the face. Tweed then pulled the bomb-aimer clear but was unable to help the navigator as he was pinned under the wreckage. Deciding he could do no more made good his own escape, arriving in the UK on the 18th September 1943.

The two other evaders P/O J T Hutchinson, air gunner and Sgt W H Marshall flight engineer said they baled out from between 6,000 and 8,000 feet, not seeing any other crew member bale out after the order had been given. They heard that four members of the crew had been killed when the aircraft had crashed. This, however, proved not so although two others members of the crew had baled out and were captured, they both landed uninjured close to each other and buried their Mae West, parachute and helmet. The burning aircraft was seen falling and explosions were heard somewhere to the west of them. Contact was made with helpers and they both arrived in the UK via Gibraltar on the 6th August 1943. F/O F C Jeffrey, navigator, and P/O R G Johnson, the bomb aimer, were repatriated from PoW camp in February 1945.

Ten sorties took-off from Tempsford for France on the 13/14th 138 Squadron completing six of them, had the misfortune of losing another crew. F/O T Noble, flying Halifax BB328 on operation PHYSICIAN 10 & ROACH 6, his aircraft crashing at Pont-Audemer (30km SE of le Havre). Sadly there were no survivors. His was a cargo flight and his objective was to drop ten containers onto PHYSICIAN 10 and five onto ROACH 6.

F/O Affleck flying two SIS operations, FRESIA & CIRCLE, abandoned his sortie after having his aircraft damaged by flak from a convoy off the French coast. He was to have dropped one package on FRESIA about 10km SW Laon. The operations report gives no further details.

No.138 Squadron were extremely lucky not to lose another Halifax on the 14/15th. This was due to the flying skill of F/Lt Austin, who was flying operations LIME 8/ACROBAT/JUDGE/COTTON-WOOD & ROACH 31 with an extra navigator and despatcher on board for operational experience. His mission was to deliver three passengers and five containers to a site flashing 'A' approximately 12km SE of Lons le Saunier (Jura). From here he was expected to fly west to ROACH 31 flashing 'P' some 25km NW of Nevers where he was to have dropped a further ten containers.

Five minutes from the French coast at 600 feet a single gun fired at them from a field. Two minutes later two to three searchlights coned the aircraft and three to four light flak guns opened fire crippling the starboard outer engine. This they believe was at Lisieux (Calvados). Fifteen minutes later, unable to maintain height they jettisoned their containers from 2/300 feet south of Mézidon. They landed safely at Tempsford 2.22 hours later. France was far from becoming an easy sortie.

During the nights of 15/16th and 16/17th May sixteen Halifax cargo sorties to France were undertaken by 138 Squadron and six SIS cargo operations by 161 Squadron. The 15/16th saw G/Capt Fielden attempting to fly a Hudson sortie, operation TULIP to France. Fog in the landing area in the Florac (Lozere) region thwarting his effort. He completed this operation on the 19/20th taking his passengers, one of whom was General Georges, to Maison Blanche, near Algiers. Insufficient darkness prevented him returning to Tempsford.

F/Lt Foster also flew to Maison Blanche with a load of freight on the 15/16th. On his way he attempted to drop two packages on WISTERIA, an SIS target in the south of France. He took-off from Lyneham and flew to Lands End, then down the Bay of Biscay making a landfall at Biarritz thence to the target area. He made five passes at the DZ but the lights only came on as the aircraft passed over them. Being impossible to drop under these conditions he continued to Algeria. He landed at Maison Blanche after 9.15 hours in the air. Merrick says he delivered 3,515 lbs of freight returning with passengers.

The Station Sick Quarters report in the Tempsford ORB says that F/Lt J E Bartrum died of multiple injuries when Lysander R9106 stalled, crashed and burned on the airfield at 12.45 hours on the 16th May.

The 17/18th saw one of three 138 sorties, F/O Gebik and his crew flying TABLEMUSTARD/TABLEGOSSIP 3 to Denmark. Coming in from Ringkøbing thence to Silkeburg, Gebik was to use the same site (56° 33′ 20″N, 10° 03′ 25″E) as had Polkowski and Hooper in March and Austin on the 11/12th May. Fortunately it had not been compromised. Here they parachuted three agents and four containers from 700 feet. It would have been a text book operation except for one problem. Gebik had contacted the ground on his S-phone and all the operator on the ground could say was 'Hello, Hello'. Gebik had experienced this before with the same agent, a repeat performance was not appreciated.

On the 18th May F/Lt R W J Hooper overshot at Maison Blanche in Halifax JB802 and struck an Arab dwelling. The aeroplane was written off. Three aircrew were injured. It is presumed that he was taking cargo down there, but this is not recorded as part of an operation.

A further eight Halifax sorties took-off for France from Tempsford on the night of 18/19th May. Of the two successes from 161 Squadron, P/O Higgins completed the SIS operations FRESIA & CIRCLE, that

P/O Affleck was compelled to abandon five days before, and dropped two agents, a parcel and scattered 35 pigeons.

S/Ldr Griffiths flying operations ROACH 33/LING/INKFISH & CARMEN to France. CARMEN was to have five packages. The remaining targets in the Château-Thierry area, were to have two personnel, ten containers and three packages. At 1,500 feet they crossed the French coast at Cayeux, twelve minutes later roughly five guns of the Bofors type opened fire at them from Serqueux marshalling yard. The guns were mounted on three trains shunted side by side in the yard. Shells from them exploded inside the aircraft wounding two despatchers and one of the agents. Griffiths says while three to four guns engaged him one laid a carpet by spraying from side to side to prevent the aircraft from diving to take avoiding action. This action took place in bright moonlight, clear skies and good visibility. One hour twenty three minutes later he landed at Tempsford.

The SSQ report in the Tempsford ORB reads;   .

> 19.5.43. B Whitcombe, A/c (aircrew) 138 to Henlow. Gun shot wound of left lumber region. Multiple gun shot wounds of skull and left leg.

S/Ldr Verity flew his first Hudson pick-up operation, BLUNDERBUS, on the 19/20th. 138 Squadron had six airborne that night one flown by S/Ldr Griffiths. F/O Gebik, and his crew, were attempting to complete F/Lt Austin's operation of the 14/15th, now named LIME 8/ACROBAT/JUDGE/ACROBAT 1 & LIME 21. Fifteen minutes into France, flying at 200 feet, a machine gun opened up at them from behind. They pinpointed the River Loire and thence flew to a site in

Hudson N7221 MA-P making a low-level run over the runway at Tempsford in 1943. This aircraft was landed in France by S/Ldr Hugh Verity on his first Hudson sortie, Operation BLUNDERBUS, on 19/20 May 1943. (Note Halifaxes with triangular fins) (Imperial War Museum)

S/Ldr Verity's navigator on his first Hudson 'pick-up' flight was F/Lt Philippe Livry-Level seen here after the war as a Colonel in l'Armée de l'Air wearing the decorations of; Compagnons de la Libération, Croix de Guerre 1914–18 et 1939–45 (14 citations), Grand Croix de la Légion d'honneur, DSO, DFC & bar, DFC (US). (Courtesy Tilly-sur-Seulles Museum)

the Lons-le-Saunier area, flashing 'A'. From 700 feet Gebik dropped John Starr and his wireless operator John C Young (who spoke French with a strong Geordie accent!), in addition to five containers and two packages. Starr was betrayed by a double agent and arrested in July but survived, Young, arrested in November, died in Mauthausen Concentration Camp. Gebik then turned due south for eight minutes and on LIME 21, another site flashing 'A' dropped five containers in two sticks. They landed safely at Tempsford.

The following night the 20/21st, five Halifaxes flew to France from 138 Squadron dropping five agents (two SIS) and twenty two containers. Of the two Halifaxes from 161 only one completed when

P/O Higgins dropped one agent and ten containers.

On the 21/22nd another two SIS/SOE 161 Squadron Halifax sorties took to the air for France and Holland. P/O Affleck was flying operation GENERAL, LEEK 8 & CATARRH 12 to Holland. He crossed the English coast at Southwold at 1,500 feet making for the centre of Vlieland crossing at an altitude of 100 feet in haze and sea mist. Three minutes later, the aircraft hit the water and bounced off it, Affleck managing to pull the aircraft out of trouble. Throttling back the port outer engine which was vibrating, he feathered the airscrew. On the way out he again crossed Vlieland flying at 50 feet and reported seeing light flak in the direction of Texel. He returned to base on three engines in spite of the port inner having six inches off the end of the airscrew, landed safely. The OC of No.161 Squadron was not amused and wrote to this effect on the operations report. Fortunately this accident did not prevent Affleck from later becoming one of 161 Squadron's leading Hudson pilots. GENERAL was an SIS operation to drop an agent blind together with a package about 4km south of Meppel.

Three of the seven sorties launched by 138 Squadron that night, the 21/22nd, went to France, two to Belgium and two to Holland. F/Lt Dodkin flying MUSKRAT/VAMPIRE to Belgium. Most agents intended for Belgium were dropped in France near to the southern border and then made their way north into Belgium. Dodkin's instructions were to drop two agents and one package blind on a pinpoint approximately 16km north east of Antwerp in the proximity of Westmalle. He left the English coast at Orfordness but nearing the enemy coast decided to return to Orfordness in the hope that the light from the moon would improve. He again set course from Orfordness to the isle of Tholen on the Dutch coast, crossing at 700 feet. From here he went, still in Holland, to Roosendaal, thence to the target. Here, 'within three miles of pinpoint', he dropped his two agents in poor visibility from a height of 800 feet. The pinpoint had been identified by a bridge over the Antwerp Canal and a village nearby. On his way out a solitary searchlight from Haamstede on the Dutch island of Schouwen looked for them.

Sgt Brown flew to Holland on operation POLO/SQUASH/ CROQUET/ MARROW 34 & 37 flying at 50 feet across Vlieland, two guns from the southern tip of the island fired heavy flak at them bursting above the aircraft. In spite of a recent SIS warning that Dutch SOE networks had been penetrated they dropped three SOE agents, Anton Mink, Laurens Punt and Oscar de Brey into MARROW 34 and the hands of the Germans. They were later executed, yet another warning to London had been ignored. These were the last Dutch agents to be parachuted directly into the hands of the Gestapo. Brown went on to MARROW 27 where opening the bomb doors when running up to the target a container fell out. From the remarks on Brown's report it was suspected faulty manufacture of the release mechanism was the cause – it was not the first time this had happened.

The second Dutch sortie, to be flown that night, was F/Sgt P B Norris flying Halifax BB329 on operation MARROW 35 & 36. His task was to drop seven containers and two packages on each target. Hit by flak he crashed at 02.00 hours on polder Noordbeemster (Noord Holland) 14km ESE Alkmaar. Norris, and five of his crew, were taken PoW while two other crew members were killed.

On the 28th May a new unit, No.1575 Flight, was formed at Tempsford and was comprised of four Halifaxes and two Venturas to operate from Tunisia. Corsica was to be the priority target. Among the crews were two Halifax pilots, F/Lt Austin and F/O Ruttledge from 138 Squadron, and to fly the Ventura, F/O Boothby, a former Havoc pilot from 161 Squadron. They flew out in June.

During May No.138 Squadron flew 72 Halifax sorties from which five aircraft were lost (three over France and two over Holland); two were damaged on operations over France and three crews flew eight sorties each and three flew seven. On the other hand No.161 Squadron 25 Halifax sorties without loss. Two aircraft were damaged on operations (one over France and one over Holland). There were 16 Havoc sorties, six Lysander and three Hudson sorties (considerably less than April).

Also, during May, W/Cdr Pickard, DSO & two bars, DFC, was promoted to Group Captain and posted to Lisset as Station Commander whereupon W/Cdr Hodges took command of No.161 Squadron.

Unfortunately the No.138 Squadron file, containing the operation reports for the period 10th June to 7th August 1943, is missing and may never have reached the Public Records Office.

* * *

If May was a busy month for both squadrons June was to be busier. Operations for the June moon period began on the night of the 10/11th 161 Squadron dispatching one Halifax to France and two SIS sorties to Holland. P/O Higgins was flying operation LEMONTREE & MARROW 39 intending to drop blind LEMONTREE, an SIS agent plus his package, on a pinpoint approximately 12km NNE of Apeldoorn east of Epe. His track from Southwold was to the northern tip of Texel crossing here, flying at 50 feet, and making for Enkhuizen. He made his first run to the pinpoint from Elburg approximately 13km NW of the target. Unable to positively identify it he turned south identifying Harderwijk to make another run from there. Flying at 200 feet flak from two to three 20mm guns opened accurate fire on them. Three minutes later a twin engine fighter attacked them from astern and on the starboard quarter causing damage to the tailplane and the port engine nacelle. No further damage was done during three attacks lasting ten minutes made from 4 to 500 yards range dead astern. The rear gunner Sgt Cochrane was able to return fire and the fighter was last seen passing beneath the aircraft. Twenty minutes later still flying at 300 feet west of

Akersloot (about 5km south of Alkmaar) a single 20mm gun opened up on them with accurate fire. They arrived back at Tempsford at 02.59 hours and because of the damage to their aeroplane decided to circle the aerodrome until they could land in daylight first jettisoning the seven containers due for Giskes at MARROW 39. Their three bundles of leaflets (edition H22) and 20 pigeons had already been scattered over Holland at Harderwijk and Elberg. Higgins landed Halifax DJ996 safely with their agent at 05.30 hours. There is little doubt that Giskes was more interested in downing this aircraft than receiving his containers.

The following night the sole No.161 Squadron Halifax sortie to France, operations PHYSICIAN 32 & CHARLOTTE, was posted by Bomber Command as 'lost without trace'. F/Lt A F Foster, DFC, was flying Halifax DG406. One of the objectives was to drop ten containers on PHYSICIAN 32 (which Merrick says they achieved). Since the names of the crew appear on the Runnymead Memorial it is probable that they came down in the Channel. It was a sad loss of an experienced crew and S/Ldr A de Q Walker, DFC, who had just taken command of the Halifax flight, was flying with Foster as an observer

No.138 Squadron commenced their June operations on the 10/11th sending nine aircraft to France. F/Lt Hooper having dropped five containers on PHYSICIAN 54, due to engine trouble jettisoned the remaining ten destined for ROACH 47/48. Six sorties were failed or partially failed by lack of receptions. The following night the seven sorties despatched were decimated by the weather. F/O Malinowski reporting 'enemy opposition' prevented him, in France, from completing ROACH 54 & 40/ BLUEFISH.

On the 13/14th, in among the ten 138 Squadron Halifax sorties, the first American OSS agent was dropped by F/O Zbucki during operations SACRISTAN/CARDINAL, SCIENTIST 3 & BUTLER 1. The agent was E F Floege, born in Chicago in 1898 but ran a French bus company in the town of Angers. He was dropped near Tours and with him 'Olivier', a sabotage instructor, who took himself off to Lille. In spite of his eventual arrest by the Gestapo, Floege escaped and survived.

From the 12/13th to the 17/18th No.161 Squadron's twelve Halifax sorties had one failure due to the weather, they all went to France. F/Sgt Wilkinson flying an SIS operation TIPTREE with the aid of 'Gee' and the map, dropping blind two agents with a package in the Rennes area. He left France east of St-Brieuc (Côtes-d'Armor) and thence to west of the Channel Islands and home via Selsey Bill.

S/Ldr Verity flew a Hudson sortie, KNUCKLEDUSTER, on the 15/16th. He made three attempts to land near Macon in darkness and in rain, returning on the 18th via Algiers and Gibraltar.

The 17/18th took P/O Higgins, flying PHYSICIAN 49/LINKMAN an SOE operation, to France. Crossing the coast at Cabourg on the way in he was flying at 4,000 feet when red and white rockets were fired bursting above them at 6,000 feet. Higgins parachuted on a site flashing 'Q' roughly 11km east of Chambois (Orne), one agent, ten containers and a package. At his SIS target HERON he dropped one container and four packages.

P/O Higgins was again sent to Holland on the 19/20th in an attempt to complete LEMONTREE, the SIS operation that so nearly ended in disaster for him on the 10/11th. Like the other 161 Squadron Dutch operation that night it was doomed by the weather. A high surface wind made it impossible for Higgin's agent to jump.

Included in the nine 138 Squadron sorties of the 14/15th and 15/16th was a drop of two Canadians, Lieutenants Frank Pikersgill and John Macalister. This was made by F/O Downs on the 16th operation ARCHDEACON/PLUMBER/PHYSICIAN 55 & 56 in the Cher valley north of Valençay. Their objective was to set up a sub-circuit ARCHDEACON. Five days later they were both arrested.

The next thirteen Halifax operations spanned the 16/17th and 17/18th, on which night the organiser of PARSON, François Vallée was dropped in the Rennes area by F/O Kalkus and his crew who were flying the operation PARSON/SCIENTIST. Vallee had already received the Military Cross for his SOE work in Tunisia.

Halifax W1229 was lost at Tempsford, on the 19th June, while landing in a cross wind on a training flight. The pilot is recorded as W/O S Klosowski, PAF, and was probably the instructor.

No.138 Squadron joined its sister squadron on the 19/20th, with two cargo operations to Holland although one failed because of the weather. F/O Affleck, from No.161 Squadron, reported that at one of his French targets, SCIENTIST 35, three fires and a column of smoke arose after his load was dropped. It was assumed that some of the containers had ignited on impact.

Halifax DT727 was lost at Tempsford on a training flight on the 22nd June. During a three engine approach it swung on landing and crashed into hangar. The pilot is recorded as W/O S Klosowski, PAF, – his second similar accident within three days!

The remaining 22 sorties, through to 21/22nd, went to France. The new Commanding Officer of No.138 Squadron, W/Cdr R D 'Dickie' Speare, DSO, DFC & bar, recorded his first operational flight with the Squadron flying operations PHYSICIAN 70 & 50 on the 20/21st. He dropped 15 containers in all onto these targets. Sadly W/Cdr Speare was killed on 23rd November 1945, while flying an Anson. He is buried in Bournemouth North Cemetery.

The 21/22nd saw two 161 Squadron Halifax sorties failing because of the weather. P/O Wilkinson and F/O Cussen meeting the same 10/10th low cloud with rain to the ground in their target areas. On the way home Cussen's port outer engine failed after reaching the French coast and he was compelled to jettison his twelve containers in order to maintain height. He landed at Predannack. Returning to Tempsford the starboard outer failed. Cussen's comments are not recorded.

On the 22/23rd twelve operations were despatched by 138 Squadron, including one to Belgium and another to Holland both failing because of the weather The remaining ten flew to France. Of the

four 161 Squadron sorties two went to Holland. P/O Wilkinson making a third attempt to complete to LEMONTREE & PARSNIP 6. Nearing the Dutch Coast at 1,500 feet he was engaged by a flak ship firing six machine guns and four Bofors type guns. Fifteen minutes later flying at 150 feet in the Ijmuiden area he saw an aircraft at 8,000 feet being engaged by heavy flak, catching fire and falling to the ground. Boisterous weather and high cloud made conditions dark in the Zuider Zee. With a wind velocity of 25 mph he decided to abandon the operation. LEMONTREE, an SIS operation, was to have been a blind drop. He reported considerable flak was being fired from many points over eastern and southern Holland. Bomber Command were attacking Mulheim.

Wreckage of Halifax DT727 NF-K which, on the 26 June 1943, had swung violently after a three-engine landing. This was the second training accident within four days with W/O S Klosowski, PAF, and F/O J A Krzehlik. PAF, at the controls. (Air Britain)

Sadly one of the casualties that night was P/O R G Higgins and his crew flying their seventh trip of the month (their third to Holland). This crew had already fought for their lives over Holland twelve days ago. Their target, this night, a combined SIS/SOE operation, was ST PAUL/HARROW & CATARRH 13. The aircraft, Halifax DG405 crashed into the Ijsselmeer with the loss of eight lives. It is probable that Giskes had informed the Luftwaffe they were coming.

The last of the Halifax operations for the month were mounted by 138 Squadron on the 23/24th June. Three to France, two returning early because of engine failure and three to Holland. F/O Wilkinson returning early due to compass failure and S/Ldr Griffiths at last completing LEMONTREE & PARSNIP 6 at the fourth attempt, dropping the SIS agent, LEMONTREE and his packages, blind.

---

[3] In the February 1996 edition of the magazine *Flypast* there was a photograph of one of BB373's engines, found in 1994.

Giskes's PARSNIP 6 received seven containers and four boxes of chocolate.

F/O W S Kalkus, PAF, and his crew piloted by F/Sgt T Zabicki, PAF, flying the remaining targets of the Dutch operation TURNIP & LETTUCE, weren't so lucky. Their aircraft Halifax BB379,[3] hit by flak, crashed at Oostzaan and killing four of the crew. Oostzaan appears to be less than 2/3km from the northern suburbs of Amsterdam near to the entrance of the Coentunnel. F/O Kalkus was the son of General Brygady Wladyslaw Kalkus who died in Ormskirk Military Hospital on 25th February 1945.

On June 26th the Station Commander G/Capt E H Fielden was appointed CVO.

June had seen 117 Halifax sorties flown, 91 by 138 Squadron, many having multiple targets, 20 Havoc sorties, 13 without contact and 15 by Hudson/Lysander with a remarkable 11 successes. The cost was three crews and five aeroplanes, all Halifaxes. Of the 138 Squadron Halifax crews, one flew nine sorties, three eight and four seven. The weather greatly influenced operations not only in the air but presumably on the ground since many of the failures lacked receptions.

CHAPTER SEVENTEEN

July–August 1943

138 Squadron's July operations commenced on the 1/2nd by despatching Sgt Brown to France, operation TOMCOD 5, it failed being 'too dark'. The moon rose on the 12/13th and the July moon period began with S/Ldr Pitt flying a four target sortie to Belgium CLAUDIUS/POINTER, GIBBON 5, LABRADOR 3 & CARACAL 6, bad weather caused them all to fail. The remaining eleven sorties of the night were to France, thirteen targets involved the ROACH circuit, with only four successful. Sadly F/Lt N Lewicki, PAF, and his crew, flying only their fourth Squadron sortie, operation ROACH 94 & 92, in Halifax JD115, crashed at St-Paul-sur-Risle 4km SE Pont-Audemer (Eure). There were no survivors.

The lack of receptions caused half of 161 Squadron's nine Halifax sorties from 12/13th through to 14/15th to fail – a really frustrating time for both Squadrons.

No.138 Squadron's eleven aircraft effort for the 13/14th was more successful, ROACH targets, in spite of lacking one reception, receiving 68 containers. Continuing through to the 16/17th a further 19 sorties were flown. W/O Scott losing himself on the 15/16th flying ROACH 79/80 reporting that his 'Gee was U/S'.

On the 15/16th F/Lt Milne had three targets two in France ROACH 126 & 138 on which he dropped 15 containers and the other to Germany, operation HERD. The form ATF6 No.2047, dated 2nd July, says this was to be a blind drop on a pinpoint 8km SSE of Wittlich, 7¾km NW of Mulheim. 49° 56′ 15″N, 06° 56′ 15″E. The operation comprising of one man only (no packages), scheduled from 10th July to the 24th. If the dropping point was not found the agent was to be brought back to base. The special instructions were 'This operation should coincide as far as possible with a bombing raid over Western Germany'.

Bomber Command this night sent 165 Halifaxes to make an unsuccessful attack on the Peugeot factory at Montbéliard (Doubs) a French town near the Swiss Border. Unhappily Milne's operations report is missing so it is impossible to determine the route he took, or whether the air attack was of any assistance to HERD. The agent was dropped and Milne wasted no time, he was home after six hours.

The same night P/O Bown went to CLAUDIUS/POINTER in France and MUSICIAN 4 & OTHELLO 1 in Belgium dropping two agents and two packages. There was no one to meet him at OTHELLO 1.

161 Squadron produced three Halifax sorties one of which, flown by S/Ldr Ratcliff, had three targets to Belgium GAGS, PROPS & MANNINGTREE on which he dropped four agents and two packages. He also scattered 30 pigeons. The pigeons seem to have been working overtime, 150 having been dropped since the 13/14th July.

On the 16/17th W/Cdr Hodges flew a multi Halifax sortie ROACH 117 to France and to Belgium ROWNTREE & FLOATS. Only ROWNTREE was there to receive him on which he dropped two agents and a package. He must have spent half the night scattering his 50 pigeons

This night the Station Commander G/Capt Fielden flew a Hudson to France on operation BUCKLER, intending to land in a field approximately 30km east of Lyon. Unable to make contact at the target he flew to Algiers finally parking his Hudson T9465 at Blida. A Blenheim, forced to land having lost a propeller, swung into it, demolished the port wing and writing the Hudson off. S/Ldr Wagland, DFC, Fielden's navigator, went along to see the Blenheim pilot in hospital and found that he wasn't badly injured. G/Capt Fielden and his crew returned home in a Lancaster.

This particular Hudson had been presented to the RAF by the employees of Lockheed-Vega. It was already two years old when it came to No.161 Squadron in June and this was its one and only SD flight. A picture of this aircraft exists in the IWM files showing it badly damaged and being loaded on to a barge in the Arctic. The caption says that 'whilst on patrol in the Arctic circle it was forced to crash land in bad weather, it took seven weeks and two days to salvage it!

S/Ldr Ratcliff on the 17/18th had barely crossed the French coast at Cabourg when he lost his starboard outer engine over Mézidon. He decided to continue operations HADDOCK 7 & TRAINER 17 on three engines, neither of these sites had anyone to receive him. His SIS target WALLFLOWER however was up and about at 02.21 hours flashing 'D' and in spite of describing the lights as poor parachuted two agents and two packages on it from 600 feet. The site was surprisingly close to the west of Mâcon (Saône-et-Loire) and they received the benefit of his four packs of leaflets. He continued on three engines to Algeria via Montpellier crossing the French coast at Sète (Herault) (some 30km to the SW) flying at 5,000 feet. From here he flew to the island of Menorca thence to Algiers, landing at Maison Blanche on three engines 7.55 hours after leaving Tempsford. The report says he scattered his 30 pigeons at Villefranche. There are eleven towns/villages with this name in the Code Postal if it was the one some 35km south of Mâcon, those pigeons had a long way to fly home.

His dud engine replaced he left Algiers at 13.30 hours on the 22nd July arriving at Gibraltar at 16.40 waiting until 22.30 hours to depart. Landing at Boscombe Down at 05.56 on the 23rd July taking off again at 10.45 hours for the 40 minute flight to Tempsford.

W/O Scragg flew a faultless first trip DONKEYMAN 11 to the Seine near Mantes 30km NE Paris where he unloaded 15 containers. He met his baptism of fire at Vernon when three 20mm guns opened up on him with accurate fire bursting above the aeroplane. He was flying at 2,500 feet at the time. He scattered another 30 Pigeons.

Seventeen Halifax sorties were to be flown by 138 Squadron from the night of 16/17th through to the 22/23rd July. Thirteen were successful cargo flights. The fifteen sorties mounted on the 22/23rd included two to Denmark, F/Lt Malinowski dropping an agent and two packages on TABLESANDWICH. Weather prevented him from completing his three other targets. Another Danish target flown by F/O Zankowski and his crew dropped six containers into TABLEJAM 1. The weather was to interfere with ten of the sorties flown this night.

Operation PUBLICAN 2, ROACH 62 & BEVY was a three pronged mission to France to be flown by F/O Hart. The lack of receptions at the first two targets left only BEVY to complete. The ATF6 No.2246 dated 14th July gave the dropping point of BEVY as 14km SSW of Melun on the edge of Forêt de Fontainebleau, 2km SE of St-Martin-en-Biere. It was to be a blind drop and Hart was given leeway to 'drop agents at any suitable spot within five miles of pinpoint at the edge of the Forest of Fontainebleau. If no suitable point found within this radius, return to base with full load'. The operation was scheduled from 18 July 43 to 24 July 43. and was to comprise of two men and two packages. The two men were Guido Zembsch-Schreve, a Dutchman, and his wireless operator J M C Planel, an Anglo-Frenchman who had lived in the south of France. Their mission was to create the *reseau* PIERRE/JACQUES.

I first met Guido through my son Paul and his granddaughter

Above: *Lockheed Hudson III T9465 UA-N of No. 269 Squadron at Kaldadarnes, Iceland. This aircraft was presented to the RAF by the employees of the manufacturer and bore the legend 'SPIRIT OF LOCKHEED-VEGA EMPLOYEES'. On the 17 July 1943, as MA-T of 161 Squadron, it was wrecked when parked in Blida, Algeria and struck by a Blenheim that was attempting to land on one engine. (RAF Museum)*

Right: *Photocopy of Air Transport Form 6 No. 2246 for Operation BEVY. The aircraft was piloted by F/O Hart on the 22/23 July 1943 during which Guido Zembsch-Schreve and his wireless operator, Claude Panel, were dropped. (Public Record Office)*

Danielle who were both working at that time as Biologists in the Natural History Museum, London. He was a delightful person to meet and gave me a copy of a manuscript (now published by Leo Cooper, Pen & Sword Books entitled *Pierre Lalande*) and wrote in the fly leaf 'Freddy Clark. To one of those who from the air provided us with what we needed in the field'. In my case these words were extremely flattering but they were a well chosen epithet for all of us engaged in SD operations.

He described his departure from Tempsford as seeing the silhouette of a Halifax whilst changing. Then with his parachute on his back advancing to it with a beautiful moon rising above the horizon in the

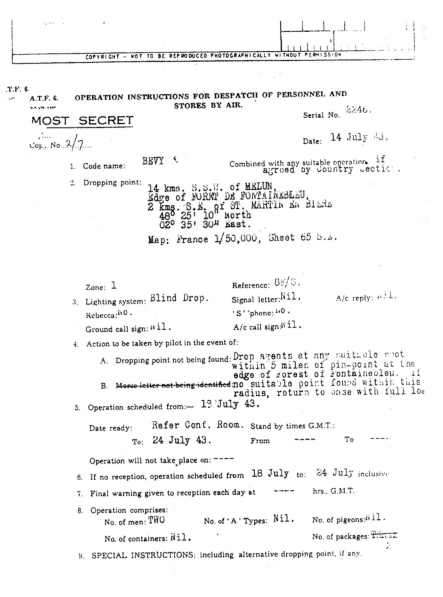

T.F. 6.

A.T.F. 6.   **OPERATION INSTRUCTIONS FOR DESPATCH OF PERSONNEL AND STORES BY AIR.**

Serial No. 2246.

MOST SECRET

Cop. No. 2/7.   Date: 14 July 43.

1. Code name: BEVY   Combined with any suitable operation if agreed by Country Section.

2. Dropping point: 14 kms. S.S.W. of MELUN.
   Edge of FORET DE FONTAINEBLEU,
   2 kms. S.E. of ST. MARTIN EN BIERE
   48° 25' 10" North
   02° 35' 30" East.

   Map: France 1/50,000, Sheet 65 S.E.

   Zone: 1   Reference: 85/5.

3. Lighting system: Blind Drop.   Signal letter: Nil.   A/c reply: Nil.
   Rebecca: No.   'S' 'phone: No.
   Ground call sign: Nil.   A/c call sign: Nil.

4. Action to be taken by pilot in the event of:

   A. Dropping point not being found: Drop agents at any suitable spot within 5 miles of pin-point at the edge of forest of Fontainebleu. If
   B. ~~Morse letter not being identified~~ no suitable point found within this radius, return to base with full load.

5. Operation scheduled from:— 18 July 43.

   Date ready: Refer Conf. Room.   Stand by times G.M.T.:
            To: 24 July 43.   From   ----   To   ----

   Operation will not take place on: ----

6. If no reception, operation scheduled from 18 July to: 24 July inclusive

7. Final warning given to reception each day at   ----   hrs., G.M.T.

8. Operation comprises:
   No. of men: TWO   No. of 'A' Types: Nil.   No. of pigeons: Nil.
   No. of containers: Nil.   No. of packages: Three.

9. SPECIAL INSTRUCTIONS: including alternative dropping point, if any.

Captain Guido Zembsch-Schreve seen here in the uniform of No. 10 Commando in 1945. (Guido Zembsch-Schreve)

east. A poignant memory that, a rising moon with a silhouetted Halifax. Guido was the first to leave the aircraft through the exit hole followed immediately by Jacques. Both landed safely in a field of uncut corn. They buried their parachutes under some dead leaves in a nearby wood and went to look for their packages which were eventually found later. It says much for F/O Hart's crew that they had landed close to their intended dropping point.

Guido Zembsch-Schreve was eventually arrested in April 1944 and the concentration camps he was sent to, Ravensbruck, Buchenwald and the dreaded Dora read like the battle honours of an Army Regiment. Dora was a concentration camp in the Hartz mountains housing the forced labour employed in assembling V2 rockets in granite caverns. Many were to die, firstly excavating the tunnels and later, for example, from lack of protection for their lungs which were inhaling toxic spray paints. 1,500 souls a month died. Zembsch-Schreve says in his book that due to sabotage only 54% of these rockets reached their ultimate target.

Our paths crossed, unbeknown to us, in Paris May 1944, when we

Exterior and interior of Fresnes Prison taken possibly before the first World War. It had not changed very much during the second!

10. Etablissement Pénitentiaire de Fresnes. Vue d'ensemble des Préaux cellulaires

1. - Établissement Pénitentiaire de Fresnes. - Le Château d'Eau

were both incarcerated at the same time in Fresnes prison. From what he told me my accommodation was five star compared to his.

* * *

One of the four No.161 Squadron Halifax sorties mounted this night failed to return. Sgt D A Crome flying Halifax DK119 to France on his fourth operation PRINCESS & TOMCOD 10/MISTRAL 3. The Bomb Aimer Sgt Patterson reported 'We suddenly crashed in comparatively flat country in the neighbourhood of St-Sauvier (Allier) 25km west of Montluçon'. At low altitude after finishing their drop, engine trouble had developed that was not due to enemy action. The aeroplane was very badly damaged, the rear gunner F/Sgt Lavallee dying in the crash. They removed Sgt Hathaway, the navigator, from the wreck but he was so badly injured they left him a few yards from it in the care of some Frenchmen who promised to destroy the aircraft. However, he recovered to become a PoW as did the despatcher Sgt Allen. The rest of the crew evaded, Sgt Patterson re-appeared in the UK a month later.

W/Cdr Hodges flew his first Hudson sortie, operation GAMEKEEPER landing on a hill north east of Angers. Among his passengers were Major N R Boddington and J C A Agazarian the purpose of their visit to France was to investigate the disaster of the reseau PROSPER. A toss of a coin sent Agazarian into the hands of the Gestapo, torture, which he endured silently, and death six weeks before the end of the war. Had the coin fallen on the other side Boddington would have suffered the same fate. He was the deputy of Col M J Buckmaster, head of F Section SOE in London. It is hard to fathom any good reason for allowing such a senior member of the organisation, with a mine of SOE information, to desert his London desk and so place his knowledge at risk in the field.

Twenty five Halifax sorties from the 24/25th were to finish the

The Hudson crew of W/Cdr L McD Hodges when OC No. 161 Squadron. (L to R) S/Ldr J Wagland, Navigation Leader, F/Lt L G A Reed, Signals Leader and F/Lt J Corner, Gunnery Leader. (ACM Sir Lewis Hodges)

months work for both Squadrons. With the exception of one success to Denmark the remainder flew to France. F/O Hart on the 24/25th flew SCIENTIST 50 & PARSON/DEACON/ DRIVER dropping, in the Rennes area, two joining members of the PARSON circuit, H H Gaillot and his wireless operator Georges Clement. Professor Foot describes Gaillot as a nearly fifty year old Belgium interior decorator known in London as *grandpere*. He was certainly old enough to be the father of most of the crews flying that night. Regrettably they were eventually arrested. Clement in November, Gaillot in January 1944 when PARSON was rolled up by the Germans.

P/O Affleck flying one of the five No.161 Squadron sorties had an engine problem on reaching the French coast. The starboard outer showing low oil pressure and a high temperature. He returned early to base jettisoning his load on the airfield before landing safely. S/Ldr Verity successfully concluded BUCKLER in a Hudson.

Thirteen of the final July sorties were successful, failures were due to the weather and the lack of receptions. It had been a busy month, Five crews from 138 Squadron flew six Halifax sorties each and also one from No.161 Squadron. Fourteen pick-up sorties were flown two failing because of the weather and one 'No Reception'. The Havoc was airborne 19 times one sortie flown by W/Cdr Hodges who also flew a Halifax and his first operational Hudson sortie during the month.

*   *   *

If it was thought July had been a busy month, August was to be even busier. The moon period started for 138 Squadron on the 8/9th August with three successful sorties to France followed by two to Denmark on the 10/11th all were cargo drops involving 69 containers.

The effort increased on the 11/12th, twelve Halifax sorties three of which were to Belgium (never considered easy) the remainder to France. F/O Hart flew a difficult sortie to Belgium involving three targets, operations TYBALT/HILLCAT/MAN DRILL 1 & BULLFROG 1, crossing into France flying at 100 feet at Haut-Banc then on to Guise. From here he flew to Givet on the France/Belgium border commencing a DR run eastward to the pinpoint. In spite of heavy rain and low cloud identified ground detail and parachuted blind from 700 feet two agents and two packages. MANDRILL then received two containers and BULLFROG, near St-Hubert, received five containers and two packages. Apart from the weather, clear patches fortunately coincided with target areas, it was a model trip. He again crossed the French coast at a height of 100 feet!

This was to be the start of a pigeon dropping frenzy, 510 of them would see themselves scattered into the winds by 138 Squadron and 550 by No.161 Squadron. The aircrews of Tempsford were not the only flyers required to work hard this August.

Sgt Brown returned early with engine trouble forcing him to jettison his containers. He should have dropped eight containers and three packages on DICK 22 and seven containers on TRAINER 12 in France. This was the third time since June his aeroplane 'Z-Zebra' had failed him.

Of the four 161 Squadron Halifax sorties that night the one involving Belgium was flown by F/Lt Cussen. His tactics were different to F/O Hart, crossing the French coast at Pointe du Haut-Banc at a height of 4,000 feet. He was opposed by one searchlight only at Valenciennes to drop three containers on the MOUFLON 2 reception SE of Tournai. His attempt to drop eight containers and two packages on TOM 4, east of Valenciennes and two containers on GIBBON 5 came to nothing, no receptions were present. They scattered 52 pigeons. His second pilot on this sortie was a Norwegian, Lt Per Hysing-Dahl flying his first operational sortie, more of whom later.

No.161 Squadron with an additional Halifax were able to increase their maximum effort to five aircraft, (they had nine trained crews). This they accomplished for the first time on the 12/13th. P/O Affleck taking Per Hysing-Dahl as his second pilot to Norway, an SIS operation METON/NJORD. It appeared to be an operation of urgency having to be undertaken at this time of year. The target was roughly 18km NNE of Kristiansand. The unusual reception arrangements were to be, 'two men 50 metres apart one holding a red torch in each hand. The second holding a white in one hand and red in the other'. They took off at 21.20 and 2.54 hours later they were flying at 5,000 feet towards the east of Kristiansand. Unfortunately Affleck had no reaction from 'Gee' and they were unable to find a pinpoint on the coast. It must have

Tempsford, August 1943. The crew of Lt Per Hysing-Dahl, RNoAF, 161 Squadron. Standing (L to R): Sgt Johan Erland, RNoAF, (Despatcher), Lt Hysing-Dahl (Pilot), Sgt 'Lucky' Foster (Rear Gunner), Sgt Ivor Galley (Bomb Aimer). Sitting: Sgt Dick Sutton (Navigator), Sgt 'Andy' Anderson (Flight Engineer), Sgt Edvard Rieber-Mohn, RNoAF, (WOp/AG). (Ivor Galley)

been a great disappointment to Hysing-Dahl that the flight was not an operational success. However, it finished the training for another Halifax captain.

No.138 Squadron's effort that night was a creditable fifteen sorties matched only once before in July. They were all destined for France but only four were totally unsuccessful, one of which was the loss of Halifax BB334. Flying his 27th operation W/O2 R A Scott, RCAF, was attempting to complete operations SPRUCE 20 & 21 unfinished from the previous night. The account given to Merrick, page 88 in *Flights of the Forgotten*, differs from that given to the MI9 interrogator, on the 6th November 1943, following a successful evasion. Briefly he tells Merrick having left the coast at Cabourg he set course for the Loire islands. Shortly after they descended to 1,000 feet, he was surprised by a searchlight and a single gun put their port outer engine on fire. At the same time they were attacked by a Me 110 resulting in the death of the rear gunner, whom it was later discovered had shot the fighter down. Air Ministry records say they crashed near Ecorcei (Orne) 6km SSW of l'Aigle with the loss of two lives.

Scott told the MI9 interrogator that they were hit by flak whilst flying just above tree top level catching the port outer engine on fire. He had no time to take up crash stations and crash-landed the aircraft in an open field surrounded by woods near Alençon (Orne). The aircraft burned furiously on the ground and the clothes of the flight engineer were burning when they left the aircraft. However, Scott subsequently met up with Sgt Trusty the dispatcher and together they made a long and successful evasion arriving home via Gibraltar on the 5th October 1943. No fighter attack was mentioned by either of them at the time of their MI9 interrogation, neither was it mentioned to Merrick that Scott had been scorched about the face. It is not surprising under the stress of his ordeal such detail had been overlooked.

F/Sgt James flew an interesting sortie SCULLION A, BOB 6 & TRAINER 21. 'No reception' failed the latter. BOB 6 received eight containers but SCULLION A received an OSS agent Lt G Demand, an American. His task was to prepare a suitable landing site for six agents to be delivered on the 16/17th August.

The only 138 Squadron French operation (of eight) on the 13/14th August to drop an agent was F/Lt Milne. He parachuted one (probably Eric Cauchi) and seven packages onto SCIENTIST 171 & STATIONER 17/DEAN. A site south of Châteauroux flashing 'S'. Reference is made in the report to 'roller device used for despatching parcels proved very satisfactory'. With seven parcels to deliver a 'device' like this was certainly necessary.

Of the four successful 161 Squadron sorties to France F/Lt Cussen was the only crew to drop an agent. His targets were MESSENGER & MOUSTACHE 1. The latter an SIS target which failed, lacking a reception. On MESSENGER he parachuted Eliane Plewman with a package on a site flashing 'K' to the SE of Lons-le-Saunier (The intended site was 46° 38′ 39″N–05° 42′ 12″E). Cussen reported that the reception was laid out about 2km to the SSW of the point briefed, the correct letter, however, was received. The despatcher says that Eliane jumped when told that her parcel was 'OK'. Her package was a briefcase, containing one million francs, She said that she did not drop on the intended reception. (Cussen confirms that). Since no one met her when she landed she hid her briefcase, it was found later empty. It must have been a terrible moment for her. Sadly she was arrested in March 1944, the traitor who betrayed her was tried after the war and executed, a fate that Eliane had met, in Dachau some months before.

Another 138 Squadron aircraft was lost on the night of the 14/15th when one out of the twelve aircraft dispatched to France failed to return. S/Ldr F C Griffiths, AFC, flying Halifax JD180 on operation PIMENTO 12, reported in his MI9 evasion debriefing they were shot down while dropping leaflets over the town of Annecy (Haute-Savoie) probably by machine gun fire hitting both engines. They crashed on the village of Meythet 1km NW Annecy killing all at their crash stations with the exception of Griffiths and Sgt Maden who was thrown from the aircraft. The front of the aircraft broke off with Griffiths in it and flew over the main street setting fire to a baker's shop, the rear part came down on two houses. Griffiths got out of the wreck in a semi-conscious state having fractured his right arm and left shoulder blade. He began to walk away from the fire when two Italian soldiers took hold of him, removing his Mae West and parachute harness. As they began to march him to a lorry a petrol tank blew up in the burning aircraft. The two Italians ran away shouting something about bombs. Griffiths walked off and hid in a ditch. There were a number of explosions and flying bullets. Griffiths thought this was the moment that Maden was shot (by Italian soldiers while trying to evade capture). Griffiths was eventually picked up by a Frenchman and later taken to Switzerland. On the 29th October he arrived in Spain. After a period of imprisonment he arrived in Gibraltar and home on the 29th November 1943. Five civilians died in the village.

That same night only two of the five 161 Squadron French sorties were successful. Tempsford was lucky not to lose another aeroplane when F/Sgt Line flying 15 containers to SCIENTIST 159 a target situated approximately 15km SE Saumur. The DZ appears to have been very close to a single railway line running SW from Saumur (it is not longer shown on modern maps). From three guns mounted on stationary flat wagons at the railway station of Courchamps (Aisne) (three km to the NE of the DZ) an accurate stream of coloured tracer came up at them hitting the aircraft. They had previously spotted the reception lights and lost them in the low cloud that covered the target area spending nearly an hour flying at 300 feet trying to find them again. Wisely, his aircraft damaged, Line decided to abandon the operation.

Flak trains, primarily used to defend trains against the attack of Typhoon 'train busters', were a menace to us, they were liable to 'pop up' anywhere. Being mobile their positions could not be recorded on the 'flak map' in the briefing room. This one at Courchamps was almost too close to the target to have been a coincidence.

F/Lt Hooper flew his first Lysander sortie failing because of the weather. Hooper completed his Halifax tour with 138 Squadron on the 13/14th June.

Another notable 'first' took place that night, Lt Hysing-Dahl flying his first operational sortie with his crew, SCIENTIST. A target some 100km south west of Saumur, 15km SE Chantonnay (Vendée). He too had made a pinpoint on Montsoreau at the joining on the Vienne and the Loire as had F/Sgt Line and met the same low cloud of 200 feet within the target area. An impossible task he returned home.

This was an unusual crew in that it contained three Norwegians, Per Hysing-Dahl the pilot, Edvard E Rieber-Mohn, the WOp/AG, who were at school together and Johan L Erland the despatcher. Erland also attended the same school albeit not during the same year as Hysing-Dahl and Rieber-Mohn.

Edvard's father, Fredrik W Rieber-Mohn, a solicitor, was an Army reserve Captain and when the Germans invaded Norway on the 9th April 1940 was called to command a company mobilised from Sogn and Hardanger. They fought bravely until they were finally overrun on the 30th April when there was a cease fire, Edvard's father was severely wounded by a bullet in the liver. During convalescence he contacted his former officers urging them to form cadres of resistance. Rieber-Mohn a former Scout Commissioner for the Bergen area formed the basis of his underground resistance organisation from scout leaders and older boy scouts. He was organising a pick up operation to take the former editor of a now banned Oslo newspaper to England. Per, Edvard and another, Louis Pettersen were invited to join them.

The operation failed and three weeks passed before another boat could be organised. Finally twenty-seven persons were assembled to board a 27 foot boat said to be the heaviest loaded boat to cross the North Sea during the war. High winds heavy seas, engine failure, sickness, hull leakage and constant use of the hand-pump to keep the vessel afloat made the two day voyage a nightmare. They landed at Baltasound on the northern most tip of the Shetlands. Edvard said they were lucky not to have missed the island entirely. His first impression of freedom was eating white bread and New Zealand butter a change after the black 'war bread' of Norway. A few were asked to take the boat to Lerwick which they did – pumping all the way. At Lerwick it sank over-night, no one was pumping. This was a typical voyage for the large number of Norwegians who came to this country to join the fighting forces.

Eventually Per and Edvard having volunteered for the Royal Norwegian Air Force found themselves at 'Little Norway', Toronto, Canada for flying training. Louis Pettersen having elected to join the SOE found himself making several boat trips to Norway with arms and explosives. He was to parachute out of a Halifax into Norway during the Winter of 1943/44. Edvard had the misfortune to be 'washed out'

after 50 hours of initial pilot training and decided to muster as a WOp/AG returning to the UK during the winter of 1943.

Per, on the other hand, continued pilot training, 82 hours on the Fairchild Cornell PT-19 then to No.34 SFTS Airspeed Oxfords at Medicine Hat, receiving his flying badge on the 31st July 1942. He was then fortunate enough to take a two month navigation course on the Ansons of No.34 General Reconnaissance School at Charlottetown. Then to the UK to No.11 AFU Shawbury to acclimatise him with UK flying conditions.

I imagine both he and Edvard were pleased to see each other at No.24 OTU Honeybourne (and later with Johan Erland now a mid-upper gunner) to form the nucleus of a Whitley crew. They were joined by three RAF Sergeants Dick Sutton as Navigator, Ivor Galley as Bomb-aimer and Lucky Forster a rear gunner. It was a six week course

On the left is Louis Petterson who crossed the North Sea with Hysing-Dahl and Rieber-Mohn, a journey he was to make, as a Norwegian agent, five times in all. He also parachuted twice into Norway. Once on the 21 September, on Operation REDWING, with his radio operator, Gunnar Wiig-Andersen (seen here on the right),

finishing on the 20th May 1943.

During the latter part of this course unbeknown to Edvard his father Fredrik W Rieber-Mohn, one of the pioneers of the Norwegian resistance, was arrested in May by the Gestapo, tortured and imprisoned in a concentration camp at Natzweiler in Alsace. Here he endured a terrible year dying on the 30th May 1944. One of Edvard's most treasured possessions is a letter from his father dated April 1943 brought, against all orders, to him in England by Louis Pettersen.

After a six week detachment to St Eval where they flew 72 hours of anti submarine sweeps in Whitleys with patrols of up to eleven hours endurance (they were not quick enough to catch one they saw on the surface). On the 10th July 1943 they arrived at Tempsford for Halifax conversion by 'B' Flight, No.161 Squadron. Their instructor was F/Lt Wilkin and the aircraft BB364. The course took 57 hours flying time within the period of the 16th July to the 11th August 1943.

The 16/17th August saw six French Halifax sorties mounted by 161 Squadron to France. F/Lt Cussen dropping two agents (possibly SIS) and two packages on HONEYSUCKLE and scattering a record 80 pigeons. F/Sgt Line was the only failure flying a SCIENTIST 59 target without reception. For the second time this month 138 Squadron launched fifteen sorties, a magnificent effort by the air and ground crews. Resulting in a record delivery to France of 14 parachuted agents plus 184 containers. Four sorties failed, two without reception, one early return with engine trouble and one aeroplane failing to return.

F/Sgt Armstrong, flying BOB 3/MARIOTE/AMPERE/GALLER & BOB 11, crossed the coast at Cabourg flying at 9,500 feet then to Blois-Cosne-les-Laumes (Côte-d'Or). In clear moonlight dropping three agents together with six packages and one sinker (whatever that may have been) on a target some 28km north of Dijon flashing 'R'. It cannot be determined just who the three agents MARIOTE/AMPERE/GALLER were or the purpose of their mission. Ten minutes later from height of 600 feet he was dropping 15 containers on BOB 11.

A similar operation was flown by F/Lt Milne taking off within minutes of Armstrong. He decided to deliver his 15 containers first onto SCIENTIST 175 a target some 30km due south Aubusson (Creuse). Three minutes before crossing the coast at Pt de la Percée flying at 4,000 feet two flak ships were seen at Port-en-Bassin, a further three minutes saw light inaccurate tracer coming up at them. 33 minutes later, flying at 1,000 feet some 8km to the NE of Sablé-sur-Sarthe (Sarthe) (SE Laval) they reported at 22.26 hours seeing an aircraft engaged by light flak at about 2,000 feet, catching alight and then crashing into the ground. None of the three Bomber Command Turin losses came down in this area and neither did the No.138 Squadron loss, to which this incident was attributed. S/Ldr Verity flying a Lysander reported seeing an aircraft shot down in flames at 22.25 obviously the same aeroplane, although he reports it to the north of the co-ordinates given by Milne. Whose aeroplane it was will remain a mystery.

who operated his radio in the field for twenty months. Operation REDWING was carried out by a 161 Squadron aircraft piloted by F/O Bell. Both Norwegian agents were seventy years old when this photograph was taken in 1989 Petterson sadly died in 1996. (Orjan Deisz via Edvard Rieber-Mohn)

After completing SCIENTIST 175, Milne then headed north east for 55 minutes to his second target PETER 1/TRIREM/LOUGRE/ COTRE, flashing 'D' in an area approximately 30km SE Montluçon (Allier). Here he dropped, from 600 feet three personnel and five packages plus one 'sinker'. The second agent was slow in parachuting making it necessary for a second run to drop the third agent and a third run for the packages. The 'Eureka' beacon was not working and they landed at Tempsford at 03.53 hours. Again the identity of these three agents is not recorded..

WHEELWRIGHT 17 & 24 were the intended targets for F/O K Zankowski, PAF, and his crew. F/O J Krzehlik, the pilot flying Halifax JD312, took off from Tempsford at 20.15 hours, 25 minutes before Milne. When a half an hour from their target Krzehlik had to reduce

The portrait of Hugh Dormer that hangs in the Officer's Mess at the Irish Guards Regimental HQ, Wellington Barracks. (Courtesy of the Regimental Lieutenant-Colonel, Irish Guards)

power on one overheating engine. Their mission completed but, 'due to severe trouble which had now developed in the engine', Krzehlik was compelled to make a forced landing at 23.30 hours not far from their DZ (3km E Arx (Landes) some 32km NEE of Roquefort well south of Bordeaux). Within ten minutes they were approached by six or seven Frenchmen who asked them not to burn the aircraft until they had removed the petrol, this done the aircraft was then burnt! The whole crew then evaded through Spain arriving home at Bournemouth, via Gibraltar, on the 23rd October.

This could not have been the burning aeroplane reported seen by Milne and Verity.

F/Sgt James was given the task of putting the six man team SCULLION B into position, a second opportunity for the Irish Guardsman Lt Hugh Dormer and his team to destroy the synthetic oil plant near Autun (near le Creusot), the previous attempt in April having failed. James, in addition, had 15 containers to deliver to SCIENTIST 180 and a package to an SIS site, WHITSUN, all of which he completed successfully. He crossed the French coast at Cabourg flying at 6,000 feet, down to the Loire islands, across to Cosne and then to the target about 12km to the north of Autun (Saône-et-Loire). The team in April were dropped blind, this team was parachuted on a site flashing 'R' at almost the identical pinpoint. All six parachuted out safely from a height of 600 feet and with them went a container and a package. James went on to Nevers (Nievre) and SCIENTIST 180, WHITSUN was a DR run from Nogent-le-Rotrou (Eure-et-Loire). On the way home nineteen minutes from the coast flying at 400 feet two to three guns opened fire at them from an aerodrome (possibly Conches) north of Breteuil (Eure). The tracers were well behind their aeroplane. James landed safely after 6.27 hours in the air.

M R D Foot reports that Dormer and his team 'managed to plant their bombs but did hardly any damage'. All but Dormer and his wireless operator, Sgt Birch, were arrested. Lt H E J Dormer, DSO, rejoined his regiment on his return and was later promoted to the rank of captain. He was killed, during a tank battle in Normandy, on 1st August 1944.[4]

S/Ldr Pitt in the meantime was flying PENNY/FARTHING a blind drop in the Clermont-Ferrand area of two OSS agents, a success after two previous failures. Pitt then flew on to deliver 15 containers onto SCIENTIST 125.

The following night, the 17/18th August, 161 Squadron's five Halifax operations were almost completely successful, however two targets of double operations lacked reception. S/Ldr Ratcliff completed the SIS operations NJORD & METON in Norway left unfinished five days earlier. He had little problem identifying his

---

[4] Strangely both crews who flew the SCULLION operations were shot down over Poland on the 14/15th September 1943. Gebik and crew died and only two of James' crew survived.

pinpoint on the shore of Lake Eikeren (SW Oslo) and at the requested
of his passenger dropped him blind into the clearing of a nearby wood
from a height of 700 feet. Two containers and a package followed him
down. Ratcliff was over the target for three minutes. He then flew to
METON and dropped seven containers. The remaining four 161

sorties went to France.

Of 138 Squadron's nine sorties, eight were successful, one failed to return. F/Sgt N W Hayter, RAAF, flying Halifax JD179 on operations BOB 43 & BOB 34, crashed at Ecorcei (Orne) 6km SSW of l'Aigle. Sadly there were no survivors.

P/O Bown had an unusual task, two blind drops in the south of France DRESSMAKER A & DRESSMAKER B. The former pinpoint was identified some 16km SW of Albi (Tarn) and here they parachuted blind two passengers and a package. Sixteen minutes later Bown found his second pinpoint DRESSMAKER B, some 6km east of Mazamet and dropped, again blind, two passengers and one package. Bown then flew to SCIENTIST 169 and delivered 13 containers. The purpose of DRESSMAKER was to attack the tanneries at Mazamet. It was found that they were disused. Bown's flight took 8.20 hours.

August the 18/19th for 138 Squadron started with a near disaster. P/O K H C Brown, recently commissioned from the rank of F/Sgt, took-off from Tempsford at 20.14 hours in Halifax DG253. Fifteen minutes later he returned to base with a strong smell of petrol coming from the bomb-bay fuel tank (says the F1180 accident report). He landed too fast and subsequently ran off the end of the runway onto scrubland, wrecking the aeroplane. There were no injuries and Brown was flying again the following night. Of the remaining ten sorties that night seven were completed two lacked receptions and one 'nil visibility at ground level', these were cargo flights to France.

161 Squadron flew five successful Halifax sorties to France. There seemed to be some misunderstanding by P/O Affleck's crew flying BOB 16/PONTON/SOLDAT & TRAINER 14 via the Loire–Joinville to

Halifax DG253 NF-F was written-off when it overshot the runway at Tempsford 18/19 August 1943.
(R Wilkin via K A Merrick)

the target area 10km south of Verdun. The lights of BOB 16 were bad and switched off when Affleck made his first circuit. It was 27 minutes after arrival before he was able to make his first run to drop two passengers and two packages. The second run took place eight minutes later when from 400 feet, three packages and three containers were dropped. Five minutes later the navigator asked Affleck to make a third run who concluded the previous run had failed. In error, 12 containers that should have gone to TRAINER 24 were dropped. Affleck had made eight circuits lasting 40 minutes. Under the circumstances it was not surprising that an error should have happened. It was not thought so by the Officer signing the operation report.

The Squadron's Halifax activities for the 19/20th resulted in three successful French sorties out of four. W/Cdr Hodges flew a Hudson sortie DYER lifting out ten passengers, one of whom was Tony Brooks of PIMENTO.

The 16 French Halifax sorties that finished this moon period for No.161 Squadron resulted in 13 successes. Two were noteworthy, S/Ldr Ratcliff flying two targets on the 22/23rd parachuted a WAAF wireless operator Yvonne Cormeau onto WHEELWRIGHT 19, which was near the village of St-Antoine-de-Queyret in the Gironde, roughly 44km to the east of Bordeaux. With her were dropped eight containers. She was to work with George Starr and was eventually over-run in the field by Allied forces. Having operated continuously for 13 months she was probably the most outstanding wireless operator of them all. Ratcliff dropped seven containers and three packages onto his secondary target SCIENTIST 108. It was an uncomplicated flight that took 6.35 hours.

On the same night F/Sgt Line was flying a cargo drop DONKEYMAN 25 in the Gien area. West of Cabourg he was met with tracer and medium flak from four guns, bursting behind them. At the same time at 6,000 feet they believed they saw an aircraft shot down in the Port-en-Bassin area. Almost an hour later at Mer (on the Loire 30km SW Orléans) they reported another aircraft seen shot down by flak from Orléans catching fire and crashing to the ground in flames. A mystery, Bomber Command were attacking Leverkusen in Germany.

Nine Halifax sorties from No.138 Squadron on the 19/20th went to France, eight were successful. A tenth went successfully to Belgium when F/Sgt James, flying LEAR/BUCKHOUND, SAMOYEDE 1/LABRADOR 5, GIBBON 5 & CARACAL 6, four separate targets, dropped two agents and twelve containers in all.

Of the eight sorties flown for the 20/21st one went successfully to Belgium. Of the other seven to France F/O Hart flying operation SACRISTAN/JOINER & DICK 30 dropped Andre Bouchardon, a wireless operator, for Ernest Floegge. He escaped arrest in December but received a German bullet in his thorax before returning, overland, to the UK with Floege in February. It has been said this drop occurred on the 19th.

F/Lt Wilkinson dropped two agents, fifteen containers and five packages onto PETER 4.

The 22/23rd ten sorties took-off for France, seven were completed. F/O Freyer flew PETER 5 & SCIENTIST 112 but there was no reception.

The 23/24th August finished this moon period, 12 sorties flew to France only 50% were successful.

August, for Tempsford, was a busy month, having flown 179 Halifax sorties most of which had two or more targets. 138 Squadron accounted for 124 and lost five aircraft. Eleven Halifax crews flew seven sorties each, three in excess of seven. Pick-up flights totalled 16, only two failing because of the weather. The Havoc flew 19 sorties.

With the disappearance of the moon, as was the practice, most of the aircrews disappeared from Tempsford for a well earned leave.

CHAPTER EIGHTEEN

September–October 1943

The Polish 'C' Flight of No.138 Squadron had, in August, been allocated three Liberator BIII's and the Squadron's Halifax establishment was accordingly reduced. The eight Halifax losses to be suffered by the Squadron during September would somewhat decimate it.

The September moon rose on the 8/9th with both Squadrons flying their Halifax force to France. All four sorties from 161 Squadron were cargo drops, one only being completely successful. Of the eight from 138 Squadron only three were completely successful. Lack of receptions for both Squadrons were responsible for all failures.

The 9/10th saw 138 Squadron mounting six sorties to Poland, all flown by Polish crews. S/Ldr Krol's crew flying NEON 4, having dropped three agents, one package and six containers they were attacked and hit by a Me 110. F/Lt Zbucki's crew flying NEON 1 ran out of time and had to abort the mission. F/Lt Kuzmicki's crew flying FLAT 6 had the misfortune to be hit by flak from a ship in the Great Belt causing him to abort the operation. The remaining three targets had six containers and six packages dropped on each of them.

With two aircraft under repair from the previous night's operations, twelve 138 Squadron sorties were mounted on the 14/15th. One Polish crew went unsuccessfully to France, the remainder to Poland, of these, six were flown by Polish crews and five by the RAF. At great cost seven targets were successfully completed. Of the Polish crews F/O Krywda's aircraft was hit by flak in the port wing making it Category 'C'. F/Lt Malinowski had his aircraft damaged and his bomb bay fuel tank hit. Tragically F/Lt K Gebik, DFC, PAF, flying operation FLAT 22 in Halifax JD154 and piloted by F/Lt Jakusz-Gostomski, DFC, PAF, struck a block of flats and exploded at Skalmierzyce Nowe, 10km SW Kalisz, Poland. There were no survivors.

Of the RAF crews S/Ldr Pitt, flying FLAT 23, successfully dropped six containers and six packages. F/Lt Perrins lacked a reception for his target FLAT 12 and three other crews failed to return. F/O E C Hart, flying Halifax JN910 on operation FLAT 12, crashed homeward bound in the Baltic near Rugenwalde. With the exception of one crew member taken prisoner there were no other survivors. F/Sgt W H James, flying Halifax HR666 on operation FLAT 12A, crashed into the sea off Korsor in Denmark. There were two survivors. F/Lt A J M Milne,

DFC, flying Halifax JD269 on operation NEON 9, crashed on the railway 6km N Esbjerg in Denmark. Ten died in this incident which included three officers of the Polish Liberation Army.

To drop 12 agents, 22 packages and 42 containers the aircrew cost was 28 lives.

Of the six cargo drops despatched to France this night by 161 Squadron only one was completely successful the remainder were either hampered by the lack of receptions or the weather. Fortunately the 14 pick-up flights flown so far this month were meeting with more success.

The 15/16th seven of the eight French sorties from 138 Squadron were completely successful, F/O Bartter having a partial success with his three target sortie, on DETECTIVE 4 he dropped an agent, the other two lacked receptions. S/Ldr Wilkin had one of those mysterious sorties BOB 58, BOB 62/PIQUIER/IROQUIS/FLAM- AN/BROPS where a small team of four agents together with six packages were dropped on BOB 62, some 25km north of Dijon (we had dropped here before). The purpose of this mission is unknown and, eight minutes away, he dropped 15 containers on BOB 58.

Four cargo drops over France by 161 Squadron on the 16/17th September were partially successful. Lt Hysing-Dahl completing SCIENTIST 132, in the Langon area south east of Bordeaux, by dropping eight containers and two packages. He was carrying an extra crewman a S-phone operator, who was in communication 8km from the target but switched off as soon as the load was dropped. He reported his helmet was not the correct type and impeded communication. There was no reception to receive Hysing-Dahl's second drop SCIENTIST 87. On the way home, approaching the coast at 6,500 feet, flak was seen bursting at 8/10,000 feet and two red fires were seen on the ground, thought to be aircraft shot down.

No.138 Squadron, on the other hand, sent five successful sorties to France with its OC, W/Cdr Speare, dropping an agent on MUSTER. There were also four Polish sorties manned by three Polish and one RAF crew. Two were successful, three agents, six containers and one package each being dropped on NEON 1 and NEON 2.

Sadly the crew of Halifax BB309 flying operation NEON 3 and captained by F/Lt W Wasilewski, PAF, was shot down by a night fighter, crashing at Slaglille 4km ENE Soro, Denmark. They were homeward bound and had already dropped their load of two agents, six containers and one package on the target. The pilot, F/Sgt T Miecznik, PAF, managed to evade and, during his MI9 interrogation, disclosed that while over Zealand, in Denmark, with the second pilot, Sgt E Kasprzak, PAF, at the controls, they were attacked by a Ju88. This they shot down. The aircraft was hit and as they were now at 200 feet they were forced to make a crash-landing. Unfortunately it crashed into a farmhouse with five people (three adults and two children) in it, setting it on fire. Miecznik was thrown out of the aeroplane breaking his leg and his arm. He, the second pilot and the rear gunner, Sgt Puchala, were taken to a hospital in Ringsted. Kasprzak died shortly afterwards but Miecznik stayed in hospital until the 1st November when, from that date, his 'journey was arranged for him'. He arrived in the UK, via Stockholm, on the 24th January 1944.

FLAT 5, the target of F/Sgt L A Trotter flying Halifax JD156, was not reached and, flying at a height of 1,000 feet, they were shot down by a night fighter, ditching in the sea 16km off the Jutland peninsula. Three lives were lost and four made PoW. There is an excellent description of this action in Ken Merrick's *Flights of the Forgotten*, in which, it states, that the round trip was expected to take 14_ hours in clear skies and bright moonlight.

On the 18/19th September a total of six agents were dropped by 161 Squadron from seven sorties to France, one failing because of the weather. Lt Hysing-Dahl and his crew contributing three to this total. F/Sgt Line operating NW of Bordeaux SCIENTIST 70 dropped his 15 containers but not his agent as his instructions were not to drop him unless he could identify the site code letter. On the way home flying at 1,500 feet over Montsoreau (Maine-et-Loire) his aircraft was hit by light flak in the tail. This could not have been very serious as he landed at Ford and proceeded to Tempsford ten hours later. There was a heavy thunderstorm over the Channel and a Lysander, returning Yeo-Thomas and Brossolette to France, landed near Angoulême (Charente). Only three sorties were mounted by 138 Squadron this night, F/O Freyer flying FLAT 20 to Poland.

Two Stirlings, from No.214 Squadron, started operations this night from Tempsford. F/Sgt Gallop and F/O Eddy failing in their attempt to complete. Both Stirlings were carrying 24 containers (nine more than a Halifax), fog covered the surface within their target area.

During the night of 19/20th No.161 Squadron flew mainly Halifax sorties, six, of which, covered France, Belgium, Germany and Holland. Lt Hysing-Dahl flying TOM 15 to France and GRATIANO/TYBALT 1, a target in Belgium, dropping an agent five packages and two containers onto a site flashing 'C' – S-phone told him the drop had been successful. W/O Scragg flew operation RIGI, a blind drop onto a pinpoint 50° 30′ 37″N, 06° 24′ 44″E in Germany, and TOM 27 to France. Fog in Germany, and no reception in France, thwarted his efforts. W/Cdr Hodges flew a Halifax SIS operation to Holland, IRENE/LANCING, parachuting two agents and five containers onto one light flashing 'D-W'. One 20 mm cannon engaged him at Lamberscheeg whilst flying at 600 feet.

Only three sorties were mounted by 138 Squadron. The first Liberator (BZ860) sortie was flown by F/Lt Malinowski and his crew on operation TRAINER 42 or 40 to France, a target 20km east of Vichy. They pinpointed 'two tunnels NE of target', which can be clearly identified on a map, but there was no reception at either of the targets. Twenty minutes on their way home, flying at 2,000 feet, an unidentified aircraft followed them for a short time, they lost it by diving into cloud. At Cabourg on the coast flying at 6,000 feet light flak firing at them burst well below the aircraft.

A CARPETBAGGER
Liberator B-24D
'Strange Cargo' which
completed fifty operations.
This type was assigned
to the Polish contingent
at Tempsford and carried
twelve containers.
(Harrington
Carpetbagger
Museum)

The remaining two sorties flew to Holland to targets manned by the Germans. S/Ldr R P Wilkin, DFC, flying operations CATARRH 14 & LEEK 9 in Halifax DG252 with, strangely enough, a five man crew. They were hit by flak and crashed into the sea off the Frisian Islands. There were no survivors. F/Sgt N L Sherwood, flying Halifax BB317 on operations PARSNIP 7 & LETTUCE 12, ditched in the North Sea having been hit by flak after dropping 14 containers and one package onto his targets. Three of the crew were killed and four were made PoW.

While 161 Squadron continued to successfully service SIS targets in Holland, SOE targets flown by 138 Squadron were still meeting fatal conclusions, probably because the Germans were aware of them coming.

Only six more sorties, five to France one to Poland, finished the September moon period for 138 Squadron. One notable sortie taking place on the 22/23rd when F/Sgt Cole flew first to DETECTIVE 1, a target flashing 'F' roughly 30km SE of Tours where he dropped 15 containers and five packages. Then proceeding to WRESTLER/STATIONER 12 where on, sixteen minutes later and a target flashing 'D', approximately 17km SSW of Châteauroux, Pearl Witherington, a WAAF, was parachuted. She eventually became the circuit commander of WRESTLER until France was liberated by the Allied Forces.

Nine minutes from the French coast F/Lt Zbucki's pilot W/O Ziollsowski flying a Liberator became ill. Operation STATIONER 20 or 11 was abandoned when it was decided to turn back. They were carrying six containers.

Thirteen more sorties finished the months' work for No.161 Squadron. Those to France being decimated by the weather, four flown to Norway faired better. F/Sgt Buchanan, flying SWALLOW 2 and GUNNERSIDE support operations, dropped 12 containers onto the target. F/O Bell dropped two agents and five containers onto REDWING and Lt Hysing-Dahl, flying his first successful trip to Norway, when he made a DR run from Lake Ossjoen to parachute blind two agents, two packages and eight containers, onto GOSHAWK.

Halifax sorties for September numbered 98 considering the size of No.161 Squadron's Halifax force their contribution of 43 sorties was certainly the lions share. Four of their crews flew six sorties each, 16 of the 19 pick-up flights were successful, and nine Havoc sorties flown. Eight aircraft were lost but the longer nights had brought Poland and Norway within range

*   *   *

October's operations opened on the 4/5th. 161 Squadron flying 23 sorties through to the 15/16th only six were successful. Among them F/O Bell completed an SIS operation, LEATHERHEAD & ST MARTIN, to Holland on the 8/9th dropping blind two agents and two packages from a height of 700 feet. He crossed the Dutch coast at Tholen, (approximately 40km south of Rotterdam) flying at 300 feet, to Geertruidenberg on the Maas – NE to Rossum – due east to a bridge crossing the Maas at Raverstien and from there they made a DR run to the pinpoint (virtually into the suburbs of Nijmegen). There is mention in the report of a power station with two chimneys with a height of 350 feet, it is not clear where they were but possibly they were mixed in with the flak and searchlight activity at Nijmegen. They went home the same way as they came crossing Tholen at 100 feet, a brilliant example of precision flying over extremely hostile territory. They also found time to scatter 40 pigeons.

That same night Lt Hysing-Dahl flew, again, to Norway but the weather prevented him from completing LAPWING. He was sent again the following night successfully dropping blind four agents, five packages and eight containers, by the lakes NW of Kjoligrube. He landed at Kinloss. The weather washed out two other 161 Squadron Norwegian targets that night. In fact the weather was responsible for washing out 14 of the 23 sorties, four had no reception although F/O Harborow managed successfully to work TABLEJAM 10 in Denmark on the 11/12th dropping nine containers.

No.138 Squadron met with the same appalling weather. Through to the 8/9th October only three out of 15 sorties were completed. F/Sgt Cole flying OSRIC 1 & CARACAL 7 to Belgium on the 7/8th. His target was approximately 4km NW of Waterloo. 'Gee' fixes assisted him in the identification of Hal, a town to the west of the target, but visibility was very poor with high cloud obscuring the moon and low stratus covering the ground, so no reception was seen. Returning home at Cambrai, they were flying at 800 feet, a Very cartridge, three reds, was fired at them from the aerodrome,. Reaching the coast at Haut-Banc at a height of 1,500 feet the aircraft was coned and engaged by 20 mm flak from both sides of the estuary but the rear gunner returned fire and doused one of the searchlights. Flak had set the cargo on fire and this was jettisoned into the sea before they landed at Tempsford just before midnight. The same night the crew of F/O Pretnkiewicz reported seeing, when ten miles (15km) from English coast, an aircraft engaged by gunfire and fall in flames into the sea.

More support for GUNNERSIDE was delivered by F/O Bown onto SWALLOW 1 in Norway. Two nights later on the 10/11th he went to Norway again flying operation FEATHER and dropping blind seven passengers, five containers and packages near Dordalen to the west of Orkla, an area SW of Trondheim. This team was lead by Peter Deinboll and their mission was to sabotage the Orkla pyrites mines – direct sabotage proved impossible. Bown reported 'Orkedalsoren' 22.08 hours at 3,000 feet. Five single engined aircraft, with fixed undercarriages (probably Ju 87s), were seen flying east to west at about 3,000 feet and were being fired at from the direction of Orkedal Fjord and Gaulosen. Bown landed at Kinloss.

On the 9/10th a single sortie took-off from Tempsford, a Liberator BZ858 on operation COTTAGE 7, for Poland and piloted by W/O B Hulas, DFC, PAF. The third Liberator operation attempted by 138 Squadron. The captain and navigator F/Lt M Malinowski PAF in his MI9 interrogation tells us that before arriving at the target the flight engineer informed him the fuel consumption was too high to return to base. They were over the Baltic in daylight on their return journey and when over the Kattegat it was decided to head for Sweden instead of trying to cross Denmark. Crossing the Swedish coast they abandoned the aircraft some 30km north of Varberg. Malinowski was directed by a farmer to the main road where the Swedish Home Guard picked him up. He arrived in the UK via Stockholm on the 11th June 1944.

The original story was they were hit by flak on the way out which damaged the fuel tanks and then dropped six containers onto their target. On the way home they abandoned their aircraft over Sweden, the crew were interned. There was no mention during the interrogation of all the crew members of any flak attack or arriving at their target. It would appear that someone hadn't done their homework on the aircraft fuel/range limits.

There followed seven sorties in good weather to Norway and one to Denmark all of which were completed. Norway received 24 agents, 32 containers and 23 packages. A team of four, on the 11/12th, dropped blind on BUNDLE in the Oslo area by S/Ldr Cooke. The agents refusing to jump, before a second parcel went out, resulted in two runs and considered about two miles apart. The agents did not seem to mind the delay having seen where the seven containers had landed. This was a further attempt to destroy shipping in Oslo and Fredrikstad.

The next night the 13/14th F/O Blazewski and his crew piloted by F/O Dziedzic flew to a target JOCKEY 10, some 15km south of Avignon and approximately 8km east of St-Rémy. Fourteen minutes from the target, flying at 1,500 feet, two searchlights 'flicked over' the aircraft and coloured tracer was fired at them 'from a few light guns'. They pinpointed the Rhône, north of Arles near Fontvieille, and started a DR run over the target site but turned at Cavaillon to make a second run flying at 1,000 feet. Light flak opened fire at them from Cavaillon, Cheval Blanc (Vaucluse) and the railway running north to Noves. Over the small village of Eygalières, just 5km south of the target, heavy flak burst around them at the same height as the aircraft which, from the flashes on the ground, they thought came from either Tarascon, to the west of them, or Avignon to the north. (they were still flying at 1,000 feet and there is a spot height of 365 metres in the vicinity). No reception was seen and they left the area immediately. Plotting these locations on a map the target was completely surrounded with flak sites and they were very lucky to survive. They landed at Exeter after 9.15 hours in the air.

Two remarkable operations took place on the 16/17th when F/Lt Perrins, of 138 Squadron, took-off from Kinloss at 19.08 hours and made for the Shetlands. Reaching them at 20.12, he made for Ros Lake in Norway and from here to Torne Lake (which appears to be in Sweden) from which three DR runs were made to the target BRUNHILD. On the third run the reception lights flashing 'K' were seen through a momentary break in the low cloud and one agent six containers and three packages were parachuted in from 800 feet. The agent flashed 'B', a pre-arranged signal, to show he had arrived safely. Almost two hours later they were over Vega and well on their way to Kinloss where they landed at 07.35 after 12.27 hours flying. The exact location of the pinpoint was 68° 23′ 30″N, 19° 48′ 35″E, which is either in Sweden or very close to it!

On this night F/O Bell, of 161 Squadron, flew SIS operation BALDUR to Sweden, taking off from Kinloss and arriving 18 minutes later after Perrins. After 4.14 hours, flying at 8,000 feet, he made his Norwegian landfall at the isle of Viga and from here he 'lake hopped' through the Arctic Circle via Ros Lake, Vire Lake to Katsak lake in Sweden. Between here and Sitas Lake (approx. 65km south of Narvik) at a height of 700 feet above the ground (there are spot heights of up to 1,577 metres here) he parachuted one agent, two packages and a container. All four parachutes were seen to open and the passenger flashed an 'OK' signal on landing in this remote area. Bell landed at Kinloss after 11.09 hours in the air. Possibly he was able to use the Northern 'Gee' chain but there is no mention of this in his report on which was written 'A very good effort, this was the most difficult operation ever attempted'. Bell's pinpoint was 67° 50″N, 17° 40″E.

(There was no such remark on Perrins report!)

F/Lt Grey continued No.161 Squadron's effort flying SACRISTAN 2 where he dropped 15 containers. Moving to his second target SCIENTIST B/VERGER, roughly SE of le Mans, his agent refused to jump as it was 15 minutes before his scheduled jump time. Grey flew away for 17 minutes and, returning, found the lights again but, running into a heavy rain storm, they were quickly obliterated from his view. Had the agent jumped as soon as they had arrived the operation would have been successful.

Through to the 18/19th the weather improved and more operations were completed. Although on the 18/19th one non-completion is recorded by F/Sgt Buchanan flying PLAYBILL, an SIS operation, and TOM 26 to France. At Cambrai four blue searchlights coned them at 1,500 feet and light flak from three guns opened fire. Thirty minutes later they made their first DR to the target from Étreux (Aisne) but although they recognised ground detail they could see no lights. They, therefore, made a turn to starboard and started to make a DR run from Maubeuge (Nord) when they spotted a twin engined enemy aircraft approaching from the starboard quarter at 1,200 yards. It followed them down to ground level and closed to 600 yards but was lost due to the violent evasive action taken by Buchanan. By now their position was uncertain, circling the area for 20 minutes without success they decided to abort.

F/O Affleck flew his first successful Hudson pick-up, operation HELM, to France.

F/Sgt T W Lewis was given an SIS Belgium operation, PLAYBILL, to complete together with MOUFLON 3 & CARACAL 7 on the 20/21st October. His Halifax EB239 crashed at Valenciennes (Nord) in France resulting in the death of all the crew. The last three 161 Squadron Halifax sorties for the October moon period took place on the 21/22nd. None of them were successful, weather and engine failure were responsible for their failure.

During the same period No.138 Squadron, following their successful run on Norway and Denmark, met with bad weather. On the 14/15th S/Ldr Krol's crew flew a Liberator for 15.05 hours to drop, in Poland, four containers onto COTTAGE and landed at Kinloss on completion. The next night five out of eight sorties were completed. Two of the failures were caused by bomb doors failing to open on F/Sgt Pick's aircraft when over his French target SCIENTIST and S/Ldr Cooke, flying TRAINER 96, had to abandon because 'Fire developed in the aircraft'. This was said to have been due to flak but there is no mention of a flak strike in the operations report.

The 18/19th included an attempt by F/O Bailey, to complete the German operation RIGI but he was unable to pinpoint. Regrettably S/Ldr C W Passey, DFC, flying operations BADMINTON, RUGGER & MUSKRAT 3/4 to Belgium and Holland in Halifax LW281, failed to return. Sgt Healey, RCAF, in his evasion report said:

While searching for our target (MUSKRAT 3/4) we were flying very low probably about 400 feet when German machine guns hit our starboard outer and inner engines. We started to climb but the aircraft was burning fiercely so the pilot crash-landed between Herenthals and Gheel (some 30km east of Antwerp).

Healey then walked for three hours with the Belgian agent who had been a passenger in the aircraft. He finally reported to Allied troops in Brussels about the 15th September 1944. A Dutch agent on board, Jan van Schelle, also evaded and after contact with a 'safe house' in Brussels was, unbeknown to him, aided by a German agent, Christmann, who had penetrated the French escape line VIC causing considerable casualties to the Resistance. Van Schelle evaded to Spain and of the other crew members, one was taken PoW while the remainder managed to evade capture.

The first 'Old Bill' NF-V with its crew (L to R): E Williamson (WOp/AG), W Williams (Bomb Aimer), J Ackroyd (Air Gunner), F/Lt 'Bill' Bailey (Pilot), Jack ? (Despatcher), Mac ? (Navigator), Frank ? (flight Engineer. This photograph was taken in October 1943. The second 'Old Bill' NF-F crashed on take-off 1 June 1944.
(E Williamson via John Button)

One of the eleven sorties, on the 20/21st, was flown by S/Ldr Krol on operation COTTAGE to Poland and this was to be his last from Tempsford.

Bad weather over France on the 21/22nd failed the final four 138 Squadron sorties to finish their October moon period.

On the 25th October No.1586 (SD) Flight was formed, a separate Polish Flight to which all surplus Polish personnel were posted. It had an establishment of three Liberators and three Halifaxes reducing the establishment of No.138 Squadron to ten Halifaxes with two in reserve.

'OLD BILL' and his MERRY MEN.
ERIC - Wireless Operator
MYSELF - Air Bomber
JOHNNY - Rear Gunner
OLD BILL - Skipper
JACK - Mid-upper Gunner
MAC - Navigator
FRANK - Flight Engineer

F/Lt K J Szrajer, Virtuti Militari, Krzyz Walecznych (Order of Military Valour and the Polish War Cross), DFC, PAF, who left Tempsford on the 25 October 1943 to join the newly formed Polish Flight No. 1586 at Tunis. He flew Wellingtons at Hemswell from October 1941, joined 138 squadron in May 1942, eventually completing three tours and 100 operations. On the 15 July 1944 he was second pilot of Dakota KG447 that landed in Poland to retrieve technical information and parts of the V2 rocket. (K J Szrajer)

Polish Airmen, flying with Tempsford squadrons had served SOE/SIS, throughout Europe, well. No.1586 Flight flew out to Tunis, and later to Brindisi, where they continued their magnificent SOE work.

There had been considerable Polish political pressure, since February 1942, to bring this about and a Polish report (PRO HS4/173), dated February 1942 and prepared for General Sikorsky, severely criticised the organisation and technical ability of 138 Squadron. It came to the conclusion that only a Polish Flight, under the command of a Polish officer and with Polish technicians, plus Liberator aircraft when available, would be a suitable solution. An adequate reply was given at the time by a memo to the CAS (which can be seen in AIR19/815). It states that one Polish crew had diverted 200 miles (320km) to view their home town!

Over fifty percent of the total of 120 Halifax sorties flown by the two Squadrons in October ended in failure. Five Hudson pick-up sorties were flown with one failing and sixteen Lysander operations with seven failing. Weather conditions had severely curtailed all operations, however, 639 pigeons were dropped! The Havoc had now been replaced by a Hudson and No.214 Squadron Stirlings had again operated from Tempsford during the moon period.

Photograph of S-phone ground equipment which was used to make ground to air contact with the aircraft from roughly six miles. With the aerial pointed at the aircraft two way conversation could then take place. (Photo: Harrington Carpetbagger Museum)

CHAPTER NINETEEN

November—December 1943

Bad weather continued through to the 3/4th November when, as the moon rose, the first Halifax sorties took off for France. Bad weather caused the failure of four out of the five mounted by 138 Squadron, and one of three mounted by 161 Squadron. S/Ldr Ratcliff failed on his operation JOHN 26 where he was to drop two agents, 15 containers and five packages onto a target approximately 23km north of Lyon in an area covered with small lakes. On the way to the target approximately 17km west of Châteaudun, (here was a German airfield) they saw an unidentified aircraft hit the ground and explode. They stayed in the target area for 20 minutes. Thick ground fog and receiving no signal from 'Rebecca' he decided to return home, landing at Tangmere.

Flying a 138 Squadron sortie that night was newly commissioned P/O H F Hodges in Halifax DT726 on operation JOHN 13. He crashed 18km NW Privas at a village called Marcols-les-Eaux (Ardèche) the only one saved evaded. Among those killed was Capt J A Estes, USAAF, attached to the Squadron for operational experience before joining the USAAF's newly formed CARPETBAGGER force. This regrettable loss could not have been the one reported by S/Ldr Ratcliff as has been suggested.

The sole survivor and evader was the rear gunner Sgt J F Brough and his MI9 interrogation disclosed that they had crashed into a mountain, about 3km from Marcols-les-Eaux, and immediately caught fire. All other members of the crew were killed. Brough was thrown clear when his turret broke off, he was stunned and had sprained his ankle but otherwise was uninjured. He stayed on the mountain side near the aircraft until the morning, at daylight he examined the aircraft and found that everything had been destroyed. Brough then walked to a farm house were he was given shelter and put in touch with an organisation that were to arrange his journey home where he arrived on the 9th February 1944.

There are map spot heights of 1,165 and 1,031 metres close to this village and one wonders how many other Tempsford losses occurred in this manner.

The 5/6th November saw both Squadrons despatching five sorties, 138 Squadron completing only one. S/Ldr Cooke finished the outstanding operation RIGI to Germany dropping an agent blind, his parachute was seen to open. Ground mist prevented Cooke from delivering 15 containers onto TYBALT 4 in Belgium. F/O Cole flew a cargo trip to France for operation TOM 32. Nine minutes after crossing the French coast at Haut Banc three searchlights and light flak from starboard opened up on him, probably from Crécy-en-Ponthieu. At Doullens he set course for Guise and from here made a DR run, in poor visibility, to the target, roughly 6km SE of Maubeuge (Nord). One minute from ETA target at 800 feet three searchlights came on in front of them, one illuminating the aircraft, while three light 20mm guns opened fire. They took evasive action and wisely abandoned their mission. F/O Bailey was another meeting flak near his reception, TABLEJAM 15 & 16 in Denmark. Weather and no receptions failed two Belgium sorties.

161 Squadron fared no better. F/Lt S N Gray made a spectacular start to operation SACRISTAN 5 when, taking-off in Halifax DK232, he swung onto the grass and ran over a sodium flare which caused the undercarriage to collapse. The aircraft became a total write-off although no one was seriously injured. P/O Scragg flew an SIS operation, ST PETER/ST HENRY, to Holland. He used the same basic route as F/O Bell had done three weeks earlier; Tholen, at 500 feet, Geertruidenberg – Reek, and then the target which was approximately 8km SW Nijmegen (not far from where Bell dropped). Low cloud and mist made visibility poor and Scragg made to return home, however, he decided to make a second attempt during which the Maas was identified and the pinpoint found. Two agents were parachuted blind, from 600 feet, with a container and a package. The second agent was a little slow in getting out having been airsick but was estimated to have dropped within 100 yards of the first. On the way back Scragg's crew scattered five packs of leaflets (H17) – rather like dropping a paper chase for the Luftwaffe!

From 6/7th through to the 9th November seventeen sorties were flown by 138 and six by 161 to France, fewer than half were completed. F/Sgt K R Copas, flying Halifax JN921 on operation TOM 6 to France, crashed near Liesse-Notre-Dame (Aisne), 15km NE Laon. There were no survivors. An old RAF map shows three German airfields, all north and close to Laon, and Copas, probably, flew over one of them.

No.161 Squadron suffered a loss on the 8/9th November. F/O J M McBride, having completed SIS operation CANADA, landed at Tangmere in Lysander V9723 at 02.50 hours. Bursting a tyre, the aircraft swung and was damaged beyond repair but, fortunately, there were no injuries.

On the 9th November their Majesties, King George VI and Queen Elizabeth, visited Tempsford. They were met, at Sandy Station, by AVM R Harrison, AOC No.3 Group, G/Capt E H Fielden, W/Cdr J Corby and Commander Willis, RN, the Chief Constable of Bedfordshire.

They toured the camp and inspected aircrews from both Squadrons.

Their Majesties King George VI and Queen Elizabeth inspecting the WAAF at RAF Tempsford on the 9 November 1943. Far left is G/Capt E W Fielden, Station Commander. (via K A Merrick)

W/Cdr Hodges was among those presented and he was to fly a Lysander that night to France on operation ORIEL from Tangmere. The Royal Party left Sandy at 6.00 pm. having taken tea in the mess.

That night six of the eight sorties mounted by 138 Squadron went to TRAINER 95, a target situated in the Vercors some 30km SW of Grenoble (Isère). At this time the largest single *Maquis* unit was based there among the high mountains. Each aircraft carried 15 containers and eight packages. F/O Bartter reported dropping on a triangle of bonfires. Only four aircraft completed, dropping 60 containers and 32 packages only – a mere drop in the ocean. In June 1944 the Vercors was to be the scene of brutal carnage.

Of the 25 sorties (only two outside France) flown by the Squadron from the 10/11th to the 17/18th November, only eight were completed with the weather and lack of reception committees causing the failures. F/O Bartter, flying TRAINER 14 to France on the 10/11th, abandoned the sortie as 'unforeseen wind strengths and bad visibility' caused a petrol shortage. On the 15/16th W/O Kennedy flew BOB 47/SLING, a cargo drop to France. He took a well proven route by way of Cabourg-Bellême-Isles in Loire-Sully-Sens and then to the target, which was close to the small village of Villenauxe-la-Grande (Aube) some 50km NE of Sens. They met with 10/10th cloud, over the French coast, clearing to the Loire but, over Sens and the target area flying at 1,500 feet, they had 10/10ths cloud below the aircraft making visual pinpointing impossible. They decided to abandon the sortie and return home the same way as they came. Nearing the Loire, in the vicinity of Orléans, the aircraft received several bursts of light flak, one shell exploding in the engineer's compartment wounding the engineer, the pilot and the WOp/AG. They brought their load safely back to Tempsford and W/O Kennedy flew operationally again on the 4/5th January 1944.

With the moon on the wane only seven more 138 Squadron sorties were flown to finish the month. One to Holland failed because of the weather, the other that failed was P/O Brown's Norwegian operation, FIELDFARE, during which the two agents, he was to drop blind, refused. Brown spent 20 minutes over the target area, snow and ice making it difficult to pinpoint but when he was finally certain that he had found the target the agents said they had been too long in the target area and refused to jump. They were brought back, understandably Tempsford were none too pleased.

*   *   *

No.161 Squadron's 20 Halifax operations, from the 9/10th to the end of the November moon period, met with fifty percent success. Once again the weather played a great part in failure but F/O Harborow and Lt Hysing-Dahl returned early with engine trouble and F/Lt Gray had a problem with his ASI. Unhappily on the 10/11th P/O M A Line, RAAF, flying Halifax EB129 to France on operations PENNYFARTHING, TRAINER 38 & MALPHOMENE, crashed at Brunelles some 45km west of Chartres, killing all the crew with the exception of one who was taken PoW. Among those killed was Lt B W Gross, USAAF, bombardier of the CARPETBAGGER force – PENNYFARTHING being an OSS target. On the 16/17th a Lysander, V9548, was lost when flown by F/Lt R J W Hooper on operation SCENERY. His aircraft was bogged down on the ground and so he set it on fire and successfully evaded capture. Four nights earlier he had called off two other landings, the landing field being too soft. The 15/16th saw François Mitterrand airlifted out in a Hudson flown by W/Cdr Hodges, his second airlift of a future President of France, his first was Vincent Auriol who was airlifted in October.

On the 17/18th P/O Scragg flew PEMBROKE, a successful SIS blind drop of an agent in Holland. Flying at 50 feet over Vlieland he had time to report the sighting of a single funnelled vessel, of about 4,000 tons, which was beached on the south side of the island. Fog topping at 300 feet obscured his vision thereafter until he reached land.

F/Lt Gray's aircraft, flying in the Angoulême area in low cloud from 500 to 3,000 feet and in rain, was struck by lightning 'breaking the Bomb Aimer's panel'. 'Rebecca' was picked up 33km out from target at a height of 4,000 feet and S-phone confirmed that the drop onto PAUL 5/ FAUX went well. However one of the 15 containers hung up and was brought back.

With the Halifax establishment of No.138 Squadron now reduced to ten it is not surprising that only once during the month of November did they manage to get nine aircraft into the air. They flew 67 sorties, completing only 24. Likewise No.161 Squadron only completed 17 of the 34 Halifax sorties they dispatched. Low level flying in such weather as these crews were experiencing must have been exhausting. Pick-up operations airlifted out some 48 passengers and put down 24. One Hudson picked ten up and put down five. Seven of the ten agents dropped by 138 Squadron were in Norway, three of the six parachuted in by 161 Squadron were in Holland. In all, four Halifaxes and two Lysanders were lost. Six Stirlings of No.214 Squadron participated in November operations as they did in December.

It was hardly conceivable that December would prove a worse month than November. Halifax operations commencing on the 10/11th, two of seven operations mounted by 138 Squadron were completed, the weather decimated the rest. F/Sgt Watson flew operation OSPREY 1 to Norway, dropping four agents, ten containers and six packages. F/Sgt Thomas flew one of the two sorties to Denmark operation SPAGHETTI/TABLEJAM dropping two agents, nine containers and two packages on to the target. The other sortie to Denmark, flown by F/Lt A C Bartter in Halifax, BB378, on operation TABLEJAM 18/19, was shot down by a Ju 88 and crash landed near Tostrup. Three of the crew evaded and four were taken PoW. Fortunately, for the Danish SOE, Dr Flemming Muus, the senior SOE agent in Denmark who, having spent a period in the UK, was to parachute, survived uninjured. The report made by F/Lt Bartter on this incident (PRO file AIR20/8249) differs from other published descriptions.

The flight was delayed by frost on the aircraft. It had been cleared from the wings and was being cleared from the rear turret, which had been badly frosted. Although the turret had not been cleared of frost they were ordered into the air because the latest permissible time for take-off had passed. They were told the turret would defrost once airborne – which it didn't. They crossed Jutland at about 300 feet dropping to 100 feet to cross the sea for Zealand. Flying in bright moonlight and perfect visibility Bartter climbed to 800 feet to 'carry out his task' (which suggests that Muus was readied to jump) when the Bomb Aimer (F/Sgt B H Atkins who was commissioned after capture) saw the shadow of another aeroplane cross their track. The Flight Engineer in the astrodome reported that a Ju 88 had turned and was coming in level from astern out of the moon. The first attack made at tree top height damaged the nose, and put the intercom out of action. Bartter could no longer receive instructions for evasive action. A second attack damaged the elevator and aileron controls and set fire to the wing. The crew were ordered to crash stations as they crashed into a frozen field between Tostrup and Banderup some 20km south of Holbeck. A final attack was made just as the aircraft was touching down, Bartter called him a very daring pilot. The rear gunner got in the last of his four bursts as he broke away. After leaving the aircraft fire spread rapidly and fifteen minutes later exploded. A picture in a local paper showed the aircraft completely destroyed. Bartter believed that the bad visibility from the rear turret was partly responsible for the loss of his aircraft.

Bartter's MI9 interrogation says after they landed they decided to split up, the four NCO's setting off in an easterly direction and into captivity. The three officers walked all night due north receiving assistance the following day and arriving home via Stockholm on the 5th January 1944. Cookridge wrote that all the crew baled out and were all back in the UK within ten days. It will be seen that no assistance was forthcoming from Dr Muus as implied.

Three Lancasters, from No.617 Squadron, flew into Tempsford on the 8th December. They were ED906, flown by F/Lt Clayton, ED825, by F/O Weeden, RCAF ,and ED886 (an aeroplane that survived the Dam Raid), flown by W/O Bull. On the 10/11th they were given SOE targets to fly but Clayton was the only one who successfully completed. F/O G H Weeden, RCAF, was shot down by flak and crashed near Méharicourt (Somme) – there were no survivors. W/O G F Bull was hit by flak and crashed at Terramesnil (Somme), 6km SSE of Doullens. Two crew were killed, four PoW and one evaded. It is said the OC of No.617

The wreckage of Halifax BB378 NF-D after being shot down by a Ju 88 at Tostrup in Denmark on the 10/11 December 1943. The pilot, F/Lt A C Bartter was flying Operation TABLEJAM 18/19. (via K A Merrick)

Squadron, W/Cdr Leonard Cheshire, was not pleased to have lost two of his aeroplanes which were, unbeknown to him, on SD operations.

Of the six Halifax sorties flown by No.161 Squadron this night only three were successful and were Norwegian. F/O Bell dropping four agents, eleven containers and six packages on SANDPIPER 1 and Lt Hysing-Dahl and P/O Scragg completing the other two. A flight to Germany, JUNGFRAU, flown by W/O Caldwell failed because of the weather. Lysander V9673 was lost when F/O J R G Bathgate, DFC, RNZAF, flying operation STEN, was shot down and crashed at La-Ville-aux-Bois-lès-Pontavert (Aisne) some 20km SE Laon, his passenger Capt Claudius Four died with him.

On the 16/17th December 138 Squadron despatched six aircraft to France. A petrol leak caused P/O Brown to return early and divert to Woodbridge landing safely amid growing confusion of main force Squadrons diverting upon their return from Berlin. S/Ldr Wilding returned early landed at Tempsford before the weather closed in. W/O Pick flying MARC 1, a target in the Arcachon (Gironde) area, attempted to find the primary and the alternative in the Figeac area (some 230km to the east) but there was no response from either 'Rebecca' or S-phone. Thick fog covered the Angoulême area and the secondary target, making it difficult to pinpoint. He landed at Chivenor after 9.25 hours in the air.

Of the other three sorties F/Sgt T M Thomas was also flying MARC 1 but had taken off 15 minutes before Pick in Halifax LW280. Unable to land on his return he baled his crew out, his aircraft crashing into the sea off Harwich. Four lives were lost.

F/Sgt J G A Watson flying Halifax LL115 on operation DETECTIVE 3, a target in the hills roughly 25km SE of Carcassonne, should have dropped twelve containers and five packages. He had been in the air 9.44 hours when he crashed at Capel Green near Woodbridge at 05.30 hours. Of the eight crew on board only one survived.

F/O R W Johnson, returning from operation WHEELWRIGHT 36 in Halifax LL119, was unable to land and abandoned his aeroplane, it crashed into the sea off Felixstowe. There were no casualties.

The three Halifax sorties mounted by No.161 Squadron this night also met with disaster. W/O W A Caldwell took-off from Tempsford at 21.15 in Halifax LL120 to fly a cargo drop on WHEELWRIGHT 47. They went down to Angoulême and in the target area met with high patchy cloud, rain showers and thick fog covered the ground. There was no response on 'Rebecca' from the target or from two special 'Eureka' beacons that were set up in this area. On the way back they flew over a well lit aerodrome, SE of Thouars (35km south of Saumur), where night flying was taking place – 'No action developed'. With bad weather at base and at the two given diversions, Swinderby and Woodbridge, Caldwell decided to bale out his crew in the Spilsby area at 05.45 hours, all landed safely (including their pet Fox terrier) but the navigator broke his ankle. The aircraft crashed into the sea near Skegness after they had been airborne 8.30 hours.

F/Lt S N Gray also flew WHEELWRIGHT 50 in Halifax DK206. In an endeavour to get under the cloud at his landing diversion Woodbridge, the aircraft struck the ground and crashed 05.05 hours at Tangham Forest in Capel St Andrews, killing the pilot and two others, and seriously injuring another three (strangely enough this was a six man crew). Two agents walked away from the crash. They had been airborne 8.28 hours.

F/O D R Harborow, DFC, flying Halifax LK899 to WHEELWRIGHT 37, met with similar weather as the other crews flying in this area. A report, written from memory as the aircraft logs had been lost when the aircraft crashed at 05.25 in the River Debden at Bawdsey, indicates that their 'Rebecca' appeared to be a little more active. Professor M. Gaskin, who was the Flight Engineer in LK899 at the time of the crash, provided the following:

> The aircraft was first directed to Little Staughton, which had FIDO, but conditions were equally difficult and they were sent to Woodbridge joining the circuit turn 4 or 5. It was bright moonlight above unbroken cloud. The first aircraft down broadcast a 'Gee' fix from the runway. Those ahead just went off the air one by one as they were called down. Control told Harborow the cloud base was 200 feet and that they could safely descend to that height anywhere in the locality. Everyone took up landing positions, Gaskin beside the pilot, the Navigator F/O McMaster remained in the nose, to home them on 'Gee'. They circled out to sea and broke cloud at 200 feet. Looking up as they crossed the coast Gaskin saw what appeared to be a large white post looming ahead. It was one of the masts of Bawdsey radar station. This they struck with their port wing taking away the port engine and the whole outboard section of the wing, slewing the aircraft to port. The pilot opened up the port throttles and the aircraft levelled up and then they stopped surrounded with water. They had 'belly landed' in the mud on the south side of the River Debden. Gaskin says he felt no impact. The crew evacuated the aircraft, Harborow needing assistance. When it was realised the Navigator was missing Gaskin and Charlton, the Wireless Operator, went back inside the aircraft via the astro-hatch to look for him, they failed to find him. He was found in the water 20-30 minutes later by a boatman having arrived from Bawdsey landing stage. The boatman took him, Gaskin and Charlton to the station Sick Quarters of RAF Bawdsey. In spite of two Medical Officers trying to resuscitate him McMaster did not regain consciousness. F/O W F McMaster, DFM, was buried at Colchester.

Blanketed in thick fog Tangmere had already suffered its losses. F/O J M McBride, returning from operation DIABLE in Lysander V9367, was killed attempting a ZZ landing. Two agents Marcel Sandeyron and, it is said, a woman survived. F/Lt S Hankey, flying Lysander V9373 and returning from the same operation, was diverted to Ford and crashed at nearby Yapton. He died with his two passengers Albert Kohan and Jacques Tayar.

An hour or so previously W/Cdr Hodges had landed a Lysander at Tangmere bringing back F/Lt Hooper.

Although recorded as a 138 Squadron Mk V Halifax this is, in fact a 148 Squadron Mk II Halifax (note the Messier undercarriage). It does, however, show how the fifteen containers, nine in the main bomb bay and six in the wing bays, were loaded. This aircraft also has four-bladed airscrew on the outer engines. (via K A Merrick)

No.138 Squadron still had to fly eight operational sorties to finish their year. In the meantime another disaster struck the Squadron, a new crew, captained by Sgt H G Williams flew his Halifax, BB368, into a brickwork's chimney a mile SE Henlow where he was practising container dropping on the airfield. All nine crew members died. It was surprising this hadn't happened before, there were numerous brick chimneys in the vicinity of both airfields scattered about the countryside like underfed skittles.

The year ended with three amazing 'Special Pigeon Operations' taking place on the 29/30th. Each aircraft carrying 191 pigeons. W/Cdr Speare flew at 12,000 feet SW of Dieppe, Bacqueville-Clères-Rouen-Bolbec-Golderville-Cany-Bacqueville, making 'Gee' fixes at turning points. He was over the area for 17 minutes dropping pigeons at the rate of 12 a minute. F/O Ashley flew St-Omer–Arras–Doullens–St-Omer and S/Ldr Wilding flew Blangy–Grandvilliers–Gournay–Buchy–St-Saëns–Blangy. It can only be imagined that, being dropped from a height of 12,000 feet, they were well and truly scattered, out of oxygen and frozen stiff when they landed on winter's landscape below – there could not have been many, if any, that survived these conditions to return home to the UK.

December 1943 had been an appalling month, the loss of eight

Halifaxes from Tempsford during this month was a large percentage of its small available force. It was fortunate it cost only 21 aircrew lives. The loss of two 161 Squadron Lysanders cost another four lives. The further loss of two Lancasters from No.617 Squadron at a cost of nine lives regrettably added to the months' casualties. Fortunately the assistance given by the Stirlings of No.214 Squadron was without loss.

CHAPTER TWENTY

January–February 1944

The appalling weather continued into January. Of the twelve Halifax sorties launched by No.138 Squadron on the 4/5th January to start the new year's operation only four succeeded. F/Lt Stiles flying TYBALT 9 to Belgium a target some 22km SW of Givet, found no reception. From thence he flew to Gerolstein and made a DR run to JUNGFRAU a target in Germany near Koblenz. Here in clear visibility he dropped blind from 600 feet a NKVD agent with a package (said to be a folding bicycle) which was delayed a second or two since it became 'caught in the hole'. This operation had been outstanding since 10th December.

Two other NKVD operations to Germany this night failed because of the weather. P/O Cole flying BOB 54 & EIGER was able to drop 12 containers onto BOB 54, 22 km south of Châtillon before cloud and icing in the target area of EIGER compelled him to return with his two NKVD agents. W/O Pick flying TRAINER 101 & SQUAD 1 encountered 10/10th cloud on his way to his French target in the Sancerre area where there was no reception. Snow and aircraft icing prevented him from making a visual pinpoint at 48° 24′ 15″N, 07° 51′ 48″E to blind drop SQUAD 1 in Germany.

F/O Johnson lost an engine and returned early jettisoning his load near Arundel, landing at Tangmere with his two agents concluded operation BATCH 1/JOHN 22. The nights' one success went to Norway, GOLDFINCH 3 a cargo flight flown by P/O Brown. The B-24's of CARPETBAGGER force also launched their inaugural operations from Tempsford. Six Liberators having been on attachment from Alconbury since the 2nd January.

161 Squadron crews were more successful on their opening night of the new year, five out of seven Halifax sorties being completed. Lt Hysing-Dahl flying his last Halifax sortie to Norway, SIS operation ARQUEBUS 1 a reception in the bottom of a narrow valley situated 59° 50′ 04″N, 06° 28′ 02″E, a cargo drop supporting the radio contact based in Hangesund. P/O Buchanan flew WHEELWRIGHT 50 to France. Near Angoulême they saw a twin engined aeroplane with its navigation lights on. After pinpointing Langon (Gironde), 10km from the target they picked up 'Rebecca' and in clear skies and good visibility dropped from 700 feet in addition to Claude Arnault and a WAAF, Anne-Marie Walters, 15 containers and four packages. The site appears to have been situated near Gabarret (Landes) a small village some 40km east of Mont-de-Marsan.

The use of modified Hudsons for dropping on certain targets was now considered more economical than using Halifaxes. The first such sortie was flown by F/Sgt Smith, an SIS operation VIENNE, delivery of two packages to a site in the Fontainebleau area south of Paris. In spite of a 2,000 feet cloud base and ground haze in the target area he completed.

Three out of four MARC targets situated south of Arcachon (Gironde) were completed, receiving four agents, 39 containers and 18 packages. Two MARC 1 sorties had been outstanding since that disastrous night of the 16/17th December 1943. S/Ldr Ratcliff reported the S-phone operator was very excited. F/Sgt Bransden approaching MARC 4 saw the reception lights switch off.

On the 6/7th sixteen Halifax sorties took-off nine were completed. Once again the lack of receptions caused the failures. P/O Scragg of 161 Squadron on his way to PAUL 9 north of Figeac had his port-outer fail some 35km W of Poitiers. He aborted and reaching the Loire jettisoned his 14 containers returning with his five agents and 4 packages. Of the seven 138 Squadron successes F/Lt Perrins flew an NKVD sortie EVEREST 1 situated in Austria. A remarkable flight by any standards taking off at 20.03 hours he went via Bognor–Cabourg–Loire (isles)–Nevers–Lake Bourget (east of Lyon)–Châttilon (some 25km east of Aosta, Italy)–Lake Como (north of Milan, Italy)–Lake Ossiacher (west of Klagenfurt, Austria)–St Polten–EVEREST 1 (48° 08′ 30″N, 15° 39′ 00″E)–position 44° 10′N, 15° 02′E–Viesta (?)–Ptealice (?)–Malta. The weather had been clear until the target, where a heavy storm made conditions dark. He pinpointed St Polten and made a DR run to the target but as there appeared to be an internment camp on the pinpoint itself he flew 8km to the east and dropped his two agents and two packages from 800 feet. He finally landed Malta at 07.40 hours, an 11.17 hour flight.

W/O Pick parachuted the first of the Inter-Allied Missions coded UNION consisting of H H A Thackthwaite, P J Oritz and C F Monnier onto the target JOHN 38 in the area of Romans-sur-Isère (Drôme). 'Rebecca' assisted and one of the passengers conversed on the S-phone. Fifteen containers and five packages went down with them. Pick complained that the site was too near high ground and had to make a steep turn to avoid it. The mission's task was to impress on the *Maquis* leaders the need of organised guerrilla activity on and after 'D' day.

The 7/8th January saw Lt Hysing-Dhal flying a difficult double sortie to finish his first tour, operation MESSENGER 2 to France and EIGER to Germany. The route to the French target was, Cabourg–Loire islands–Cosne–St-Jean-de-Losne (some 30km SE Dijon). From here they pinpointed on the River Doubs and made for MESSENGER 2 a target near the village of Lemuy (Jura) some 35km south of Besançon, intending to drop nine containers. Spending seven minutes over an identified target area, without any reception lights seen they turned north for Germany via Besançon–Lure–then east pinpointing on the Rhine–Ludwigshafen (Lake Constance)–from here north to EIGER (48° 20′ 31″N, 09° 05′ 00″E) 8km E. Hechingen, some 16km SW of Reutlingen. Having positive ground identification from 800 feet they dropped blind two NKVD agents (the crew thought one was a woman) and their package. On the way home flying at 1,500 feet near the Loire they saw two Ju 88s flying a reciprocal course 500 feet above them. They landed after 8.55 hours in the air. Having finished his Halifax tour Lt Hysing-Dhal now joined the Lysander flight.

Of the ten 138 Squadron sorties on the 7/8th only five were completed. One of which S/Ldr Wilding flew BOB 18 to France dropping 12 containers and then to SQUAD a German target. They pinpointed Kenzingen and although this was some 20km south of the dropping point (48° 24′ 15″N, 07° 51′ 48″E) they dropped as the agent specifically asked to be dropped between Offenburg and Freiburg. P/O H M Kennedy, newly commissioned from Warrant Officer, took-off Halifax LK743 for operations TYBALT 3 & THERSITES 4, Belgium. Re-joining the Tempsford circuit 4 hours 43 minutes later, without his port-outer engine which would not feather, his overloaded aircraft crashed at nearby Tetworth Hill and caught fire. All seven crew members were killed. Sadly, Bill Chorley reports, there were three agents on board to be dropped in Belgium namely, Capt. H P Verhaegen, Sgt H Goffin and Sgt Michaux.[5] This terrible tragedy was caused by engine failure.

Seven Halifax sorties were flown on the 10/11th. Technical problems were encountered by F/Lt Stiles, whose bomb doors failed to open as he ran up to a Belgium target SAMOYEDE 2. It was found that the main hydraulic pipe had been severed. They dropped three parcels and it was thought that one of them struck the tailwheel. The reception lights were extinguished as he made a second run to deliver the remaining parcels. F/Sgt Gregory had nine containers hang up at TYBALT 3. P/O Cole dropped three agents and six packages on TYBALT 11. All these targets were in Belgium. F/O Johnson flying two French targets was fortunate not to find a reception at ARCHDEACON 8 now worked by the Germans. However, making a DR run from Guise dropped an agent on MUSICIAN 11 a site flashing 'J' some 23km NE St-Quentin a site also worked by the Germans. One of 161 Squadron's three Halifax sorties went to Holland. P/O Buchanan flying operation SEDBURGH crossed the coast at 200 feet at Tholen, parachuting blind two SIS agents with two packages between woods near Breda.

On the 23rd January two 161 Squadron Halifaxes were lost conducting an air/sea rescue search. F/Sgt J W Robertson, flying

---

[5] Bill Chorley also reports that two agents were dropped in Belgium the same night, Wilfred Waddington (who was thought to have been in the Halifax flown by Kennedy) and Philippe de Liedekerke. The only other Belgian sortie from Tempsford was PLAY-BILL II, an SIS sortie flown by P/O Buchanan of 161 squadron. This failed because of bad weather and, in view of this, it is likely that P/O Kennedy dropped these agents before returning home.

Halifax LL182 and F/O K F Smith flying Halifax DG272. Taking off within six minutes of each other it was thought the aircraft collided, there were no survivors.

Seventeen sorties finished the month on the 29/30th, thirteen were successful. During the month a total of 48 agents had been dropped. Bad weather had prevented Lysander or Hudson pick up operations.

On the 27th January I arrived at Tempsford from 1659 HCU posted to No.138 Squadron. With me came the crews of Sgt M F Ratcliffe and Sgt K R Tattersall, posted to No.161 Squadron. (both of whom were to be commissioned, Ken Tattersall receiving the DFC). It had been snowing and was bitterly cold. In the distance I could see silhouetted against a white background Halifaxes with four bladed airscrews and without mid-upper turrets. I thought this strange and Tempsford a cold and desolate place – I was unaware what was going on here. Fortunately the mess was warm and friendly. I was soon in the air P/O Pick taking me twice to Henlow warning me about the chimneys and F/O Ashley taking me there by night.

The Tempsford ORB records that there were three 'Air Raid Red' alerts in January. There must have been others later since I well remember flares dropping and shadows of low flying German aircraft turning towards London. Wisely the defences of Tempsford kept as quiet as a mouse. They were using the cooling tower to the north of the aerodrome as a turning point and the railway line to London as their 'Iron Beam'.

*   *   *

On the 3/4th February F/Sgt Murray took me on my first operational flight BUTLER 14. I remember we had superb visibility and the moonlight was so brilliant we had difficulty seeing the lights of our target flashing 'Z'. (It was situated about 30km NW Angers). Here Murray from 800 feet dropped 15 containers on a site operated by the Germans. Our leaflets were dropped in the Laval area. We landed after 4.55 hours in the air. My introduction to the air war, could not have been more peaceful, unhappily this state of affairs was not to continue. Two other German operated sites were included in the sorties mounted by 161 Squadron that night. P/O Buchanan flew PHONO 8 which was situated 12km SW Fontainbleau, (his third target, the other two, SIS, lacked receptions). F/Sgt Smith was unable to complete PHONO 6 until the following night his target situated, 30km SW Pithiviers (Loiret). Both dropped eight containers.

Between the 4/5th February and the 5/6th 25 sorties were mounted by 138 Squadron of which 21 were successful, among them three to Denmark and Norway. Among the failures on the 4/5th was F/O Ashley taking me on my second operation AUTHOR 9 in France. We shared the long runway with B-24's of CARPETBAGGER force. On the way out Ashley pointed out a small square of bright lights in the Angoulême area. 'A prison camp' he said, I was to see it again. We found both the primary and alternative targets but no reception. On the way home flying at 2,000 feet we saw a Stirling coned by two searchlights and attacked by light and heavy flak from St-Florent the aerodrome at Saumur. It crossed our track some 300 feet ahead and 200 higher. We had flown 7.20 hours when we landed.

The same night F/Lt Downes failed to find his target PAUL 29 in the south of France in spite of circling for 17 minutes, 10/10ths cloud obscuring the moon. On his way home at 1,000 feet two machine guns opened fire about 13km east of Vire in Normandy hitting the nose and rear turret of his aircraft. He landed safely after 8.37 hours in the air.

F/Sgt Murray on the 5/6th flew to France his operations report lacking detail. PETER 50 lacked a reception but two agents in good visibility were parachuted blind from 700 feet onto operation SPIRITUALIST 1. These were undoubtedly Rene Dumont-Guillemet and H L Diacono his wireless operator who went to work in the Paris region. Foot says they were dropped in Touraine. F/Sgt Hayman flew TINKER 4 in the Clérey area some 10km SE Troyes. A red flare was dropped from above as they neared the Loire isles. It was raining and visibility poor when they reached the target flashing 'G'. Although they dropped 15 containers the agent was too sick to jump and was brought back.

Of the nine Halifax sorties flown by 161 Squadron during the same period six were successful. Ken Tattersall flying his first operational flight as captain on the 5/6th. BOB 104 & MIGNONE an SIS target on which he dropped three containers and two packages. There was no reception at BOB 104. Wg/Cdr Hodges flew three SIS targets BRUXELLES, CALANGUE & NARCISUS. His route was, Cabourg–Loire–Sully-sur-Loire, where he made a DR run from Boisseaux (Loiret) and parachuted blind from 600 feet four agents and two packages, operation NARCISUS. Returning to Sully thence to Nevers wherein the area dropped, from a height of 4,200 feet indicated (there is high ground NE Nevers), one agent, six containers and three packages, operation BRUXELLES. Turning due west to Issoudun proceeded to Blois where his DR run to CALANGUE was fruitless, lacking reception. He returned to base with four agents, nine containers and two packages that were intended for CALANGUE.

F/Lt Parker completed operation CALANGUE on the 8/9th making his DR run from the Loire and dropping, on a site flashing 'H', four agents, nine containers and two packages. On the way to the target he met with light flak from Châteaudun. His second target MIRAGE 1 near Nevers was uncompleted, no reception, and for his pains he was shot at from Bourges. Certain sources said operation CALANGUE was an SIS pathfinder force dropped into the Châteauroux region for 'Sussex' operations, an intelligence gathering operation for the forthcoming invasion.

Two 161 sorties sent to France on the 7/8th returned early, one due to the weather the other from an intercom problem. Of the four operations dispatched by 138 Squadron two failed to return from

France. S/Ldr T C Cooke, DFC, AFC, DFM, 'A' Flight Commander flying LW275 on operation JOCKEY 5 above cloud on the outward flight suffered an engine fire in the starboard inner. This was extinguished but they could not maintain height and when dropping into cloud they iced up. It was decided to bale out and landed 6km south of Hauterives (37km NNE Valance). They were able to evade capture and, by May, all were back in England.

F/O G D Carroll on the other hand, flying Halifax LL114 on his fifth operation JOHN 35 crashed at Autrans 14km west Grenoble, there were no survivors. I knew Dennis Carroll well, we had trained together in South Africa and were pleased to renew our friendship when I arrived at Tempsford. Two nights before his loss we had been out drinking in a small pub at Gamlingay.

I flew my first solo operation on the 8/9th February a cargo flight to BOB 78. On the fourth of our DR runs from Châtillon-en-Bazois (Morbihan) three bonfires were lit in front of us and we dropped from 600 feet through a snow shower. I was amazed to see a reception committee out in weather like this. We were one of eight successful operations out of ten.

Three others, flown by F/Lt Mill, F/Sgt Baker and F/O Thomas were dropping on German controlled sites ARCHDEACON & PHONO. Mill's operation ARCHDEACON 10 was washed out by the weather. Prior to this he had dropped blind two agents on MONTAND 1 near the Belgium border and three agents on IAGOI near Arquennes south of Brussels.

Baker was flying FLAVIUS 2 to Belgium dropping blind two agents from 6-700 feet having made a DR run from Guise. 15 containers went to the Germans onto ARCHDEACON 11. Thomas had PHONO 5 & TRAINER 101 and it was on PHONO 5 a site near Sully sur Loire flashing 'D' that four agents R E J Alexandre, J P H Ledoux (two Frenchmen), F A Deniset (a Canadian) and R Byerly (an American W/T operator), were dropped into the hands of the Gestapo (none of whom survived the war), together with eight containers. He also dropped seven containers onto TRAINER 101. The *reseau* PHONO had now been in German hands for five months. This night 138 Squadron dropped 18 agents and 102 containers.

The following day I was given a brand new Halifax V – LL252, 'K'-King. It was the only new aeroplane I was ever to fly and a great joy to have.

The 8/9th saw 161 Squadron flying five Halifax sorties dropping six agents and 34 containers. The classic Hudson sortie operation BLUDGEON flown by F/O Affleck took place this night. He became stuck in the mud for two and half hours in a field near Bletterans. An incredible feat of guts and determination got him airborne and home. I remember congratulating him in the mess on the award of his Distinguished Service Order (DSO).

The next night 10/11th F/O J W McDonald, RAAF, was lost flying Lysander V9822 (an aeroplane, it is said, that had been originally built and delivered with target towing equipment installed), on operation

SERBIE. After making two unsuccessful attempts at landing in a field at la Chaussée (5km north Dun-sur-Auron, SE Bourges), his approach for his final landing was too fast and after touching down he nosed over beyond the flare path and caught fire. Hugh Verity reasons that the pilot left the mixture control in 'weak' and thus was unable to fully close the throttle. I wonder if the removal of the towing equipment from this aeroplane contributed to this unfortunate accident by seriously altering its trim?

It is interesting to note that F/O McDonald was buried at Farges-en-Septaine some 18 km to the north of la Chaussée and very close to the German airfield of St-Avord. It would appear that both the wreck and McDonald were taken there for further examination. His two passengers Jean Lacroix and Willy Josset were said to have been saved albeit, Lacroix being badly burned, nursed in hospital in Bourges and flown home on the 3/4th March. P/O Scragg flew a Hudson to the Blois area parachuting two SIS agents onto CANNA.

Thirty-four 138 Squadron sorties were flown from the 10/11th to the end of the month, four to Belgium the remainder to France. Weather and the lack of receptions reduced successes to 50%. One is worthy of mention, F/Lt Johnson flew BUTLER 12 on the 29/1st March dropping two agents, eight containers and seven packages onto the German operated site flashing 'A'. From the coast at Pte de la Percée, a forty minute DR run to the target was made meeting with flak at Bayeux. The agents dropped were J T J Detal, a Belgian, and P F Dulcos, a twenty year old, they died in Gross Rosen camp.

During the same period 161 Squadron flew 17 Halifax operations, ten of which were successful. W/Cdr Hodges flew the final operation of this command, a Hudson pick-up sortie CORPUS to France on the 15/16th, the weather preventing final success. The same night Capt Halle, RNoAF, a replacement for Hysing-Dahl, flew his first operation, a cargo drop onto WHEELWRIGHT 36 in the Marmande area (Lot-et-Garonne), the only successful operation out of eight mounted by 161 Squadron that night.

On the 24/25th February S/Ldr Ratcliff, flew PETER 16 a target situated at 46° 28′ 14″N, 02° 43′ 56″E some 17km NNE Montluçon. They picked up 'Rebecca' some 45km from the target and made a DR run from St-Amand-Montrond (Cher). In the darkness, there was no moon, they found the DZ (reporting 'possibly also a triangle of torches/flares') and on the first run in from a height of 600 feet dropped three agents. Two of them were W/Cdr F F E Yeo-Thomas and his companion Maurice Lostrie (Trieur) the third parachutist's code name was 'Africain' whom I have been unable to identify. This was the second Inter-Allied Mission, ASYMPTOTE, it is said that Lostrie was a saboteur. It was unfortunate that Yeo-Thomas was injured on landing. The operations report says the third agent was slow jumping and in doing so accidentally released the parachute of a package in the aircraft. 15 containers and eight packages were delivered from 400 feet on the second run. No enemy action was reported. This was Yeo-

Thomas's third mission to France, his second using a parachute. The citation for his George Cross said for 'the most amazing fortitude and devotion to duty'. He died in 1964 aged 62 his life undoubtedly shortened by Gestapo brutality he received during captivity.

The last four 161 Halifax sorties of the month, the 29/1st, included another new Norwegian Pilot Lt Piltingsrud flying DICK 62 to France failing through lack of a reception. P/O Caldwell met with a pyrotechnic display at Ouistreham on the French coast, light flak falling short of his aircraft mingled with searchlight and red and orange flare activity. He pinpointed Angerville (40km SE Chartres) and made a DR run to complete PHONO 4, a German site, where he had the misfortune to parachute from 700 feet three agents J F A Antelme, L Lee (W/T operator) and Madeleine Damerment. Both men had been in the field before. None were to survive the war. Piltingstrud reported that the reception lights followed the aircraft's circuit. M R D Foot says 'Mlle Damerment's *ordre de mission* gives the dropping zone as 3km SE Sainville, 31 km ESE of Chartres', some 12km NW Angerville from where Caldwell made his DR run. Caldwell then continued to GARDENIA, an SIS target in the vicinity of Sully, dropping six containers and four packages. At the Loire the weather was hazy with 10/10th cloud at 3,000 feet.

F/Lt Affleck completed a Hudson parachuting sortie by dropping blind two SIS agents in Holland. He crossed the Dutch coast at

The crew of Captain Gunner Halle, RNoAF, 161 Squadron, February 1944. (L to R): Sgt Bill Angel (Ground crew), ? (Flight Engineer), Capt Halle (Pilot), F/O Ivor Galley (Bomb Aimer), F/O ? (WOp/AG), ?, RCAF (Despatcher), Sgt Hall (Navigator), F/O ? (Air Gunner). Seated: Ground crew. (Ivor Galley)

The Power Station at Great Barford. It was situated 3.5 miles to the north of the airfield. The height of the camouflaged chimneys was 150 feet and could come into play if you hooked your take-off from runway 01! It also acted as a turning point for Luftwaffe raids on London.
(Photo: IWM HU60536)

Tholen flying at 300 feet, made for Breda with a DR run from here completed MARLBOROUGH by dropping from 650 feet. Compass failure had prevented him from completing this operation earlier in the month.

In spite of the difficult flying conditions during the month of February seven crews flew five or more operations. With an additional six Halifaxes added to the inventory of No.138 Squadron no doubt greater demands would be made on them during the next moon period. However, the logistics for the supply dropping requirements of SOE had now exceeded the capacity of the two Tempsford Squadrons. It was pleasing to discover that No.38 Group, with their paratrooping, supply dropping and glider towing aircraft, were to assist the SOE from their own bases.

March 1944

In the meantime W/Cdr A C Boxer had been posted in to command No.161 Squadron.

From the beginning of March the practice of including the map co-ordinates of dropping zones in operational reports ceased, making it impossible to give their precise location.

With the moon already risen March did not start off at all well. The 1st/2nd March saw only two of seven operations mounted by 138 Squadron successful, however, all three attempted by 161 were completed. Aided by a 'Gee' fix from the Loire, F/Lt Parker dropped from 600 feet, in low cloud, thirteen containers on the German operated site BUTLER 3. The reception for his second target BATTERN 2 (SIS) was incorrectly laid out and consequently he did not drop.

Two other German operated sites were serviced the following night, the 2/3rd. Michael Foot records six agents were dropped onto German operated ARCHDEACON reception. Squadron records show these were dropped three at a time from two aircraft. Taking off at 20.21 hours F/Lt Downes of 138 Squadron made a DR run from Guise (Allier) to parachute three agents and six packages onto MUSICIAN 12 (an ARCHDEACON site). Downes reported it was a very good site (flashing 'L') and said there was a 'strong smell of cordite in the aircraft from Albert (the town of!) and a large amount of smoke in the target area'. He then proceeded some 30km NE Albert to deliver a cargo drop to TOM 5. With so much air activity in the area it was not surprising that there was no reception.

P/O Buchanan of 161 Squadron took-off five minutes after Downes, flew to Guise and made a DR run from there to MUSICIAN 7 parachuting in eight containers, a signal from the ground confirmed their safe arrival. He returned to Guise making another DR run, this time, to ARCHDEACON 6 where he dropped three agents, seven containers and eight packages. Buchanan reporting 'fires seen in the direction of Albert'.

The six agents parachuted in were G B McBain, D H Finlayson (a W/T operator), M Lepage (OSS) and E Lesout (OSS) and their mission, LIONTAMER, was to start a new circuit near Valenciennes. A Rabinovitch, a W/T operator on his second mission, and R Sabourin, a French Canadian. Rabinovitch was to start a new circuit BARGEE near Nancy. Regrettably all were captured on landing and

Air Vice-Marshal Sir Alan Boxer, KCVO, CB, DSO, DFC, seen here as an Air Commodore when serving with No. 1 Group, Bomber Command. In addition to commanding No. 161 Squadron in March 1944 he went on to command a Vickers Valiant (nuclear deterrent) unit, No. 7 Squadron, in November 1956. (AVM Sir Alan Boxer)

later died in concentration camps.

This night fifteen Lancasters of No.617 Squadron bombed an aircraft factory at Albert.

From June 1943 until May 1944 ARCHDEACON sites received by parachute some 2,320,000 French Francs.

P/O Cole and P/O Pick, both 138 crews, also dropped two agents each. Cole using a fixed 'Rebecca' site BOOT near his target in the Aiguillon area SE Bordeaux dropped onto STATIONER 31 Roger Landes and A L J Sirois, a W/T operator. Landes managed to organise and arm over 2,000 men by D-day. Pick dropped east of Paris into BOB 136 in the area of Sézanne (Marne).

I flew BOB 55 dropping in the Dijon area some 15 containers and six packages. On our return we wandered over the railway marshalling yards at Orléans and were illuminated by a predicted searchlight. Squadron records say we were hit in the starboard outer engine. I remember looking at the oil slick on the engine cowling surmising there could be a few days leave in this. It was not to be, damage repaired, we flew the same aeroplane the following night.

Weather was now affecting operations, especially those to France. Both Squadrons had the misfortune to lose an aeroplane on the 3/4th. F/O D S Bell, DFC, now a Lysander pilot flying V9605, having crossed the coast at Hermanville engine trouble forced him to return. Turning back, when about 10km out to sea, he re-crossed the coast at 600 feet and made a crash landing due east of Plumetot, approximately 8km north of Caen, in Normandy. He and his two passengers were uninjured and evaded. Bell was flown back on the 15th March.

Lt Hysing-Dhal flew his first Lysander sortie this night also to the same target FRAMBOISE. Six of the seven Halifax sorties flown by 161 Squadron were a success, five of them had multiple targets, most for the SIS.

No.138 Squadron flew 17 operations this night (Belgium accounting for five) only eight were successful. Halifax LL279 flown by F/O W C Kingsley, RCAF, to JOHN 23, France, crashed in the Bernay (Eure) area killing Kingsley and four of the crew, two were PoW. Those who died were buried at Bernay, St-Croix communal cemetery. There was a German airfield, St-Martin, to the NW of Bernay, and one wonders if they had flown over it. It was only their second operation.

Operations flown by 138 Squadron from the 4/5th, 5/6th, 6/7th amounted to 34 with only 16 successful, lack of receptions causing most of the failures. S/Ldr Russell the new 'A' Flight Commander flew a successful first operation, BOB 142.

Several operations for the night of the 5/6th appear to have been intercepted by the enemy, possibly those aircraft using the Haut-Banc area for their entry into France. The enemy activity appeared to have been concentrated in the Hesdin/Frévent area of the Pas-de-Calais. (a German airfield, Nuncq, was based 4km N Frévent).

F/Lt Ashley, abandoned his French sortie TOM 35 having been hit many times by flak at 50° 20'N, 02° 30'E (approximately half way between Hesdin and Arras). Heading for home, flying at 500 feet reported when at 10km SW Hesdin, 'many searchlights (presumed predicted) constantly illuminated the aircraft on track for about 10 minutes'. Three sorties to Belgium also met with enemy opposition. F/Sgt Baker flying TYBALT 28 reported 'many blue coloured searchlights' illuminated his aircraft and attempted to pass him from one light to another. Flying at 500 feet in the Frévent area several light flak guns opened up hitting the aircraft. Probably on the way home having reported 'no reception' at his target.

F/Sgt Ratcliffe flying TYBALT 29 reported searchlights and flak from 16km inside the coast until the Guise area. He too said the searchlights appeared to pass him on from one to another. Ratcliffe switched on his IFF during his evasive action and this appeared to stop the flak for a while. He was unable to identify his target in the Sedan area through poor visibility and snow on the ground.

F/Lt Johnson also reported 'no reception' having found the pinpoint for his target TYBALT 18 in 'clear skies, ground covered with snow'.

On the return journey he was flying at 100 feet in the Frévant area when several searchlights illuminated the aircraft and light flak opened up on him.

S/Ldr Wilding on his way to his Belgium targets CAWDOR & TYBALT 12 reported while flying at 200 feet 'many searchlights on track and flak in the Frévant area'. He made his DR runs from Givet on the French border of Belgium parachuting blind three agents and three packages onto the pinpoint CAWDOR. On his second target TYBALT 12 he dropped 15 containers and three packages reporting 'snow on the ground'. Gaining height to 8,000 feet, SW Arras, a Me 410 made an attack from starboard, a burst from it hitting the aircraft causing substantial damage and wounding the despatcher. The rear gunner managed to get off 200 rounds as the enemy aircraft passed by below them. Wilding landed at Tangmere.

Merrick reports that a Stirling of 214 Squadron out of Sculthorpe, flown by F/O Triplow servicing a target near Hirson close to the Belgium border encountered accurate flak soon after entry into France. The damage suffered by the aircraft was sufficient to earn Triplow a DFC. The route to Hirson could have conceivably been via Pas-de-Calais. No.90 Squadron also lost a Stirling EF147 flown by W/O B Edinborough, flak setting fire to containers in the bomb bay and parachute flares inside the fuselage. Edinborough crash landed SE Abbeville, all the crew evaded.

Bomber Command Diaries report that 49 Stirlings and 17 Halifaxes were flying Resistance flights that night.

The sixteen Halifax sorties flown by 161 Squadron during the same period met with 50% success. There were also five Hudson parachute sorties flown. P/O Scragg flew one of them to France, dropping two agents and a package onto an SIS target, operation CHARDIN – the only one successful. One of the agents told Scragg before take-off the reception lights may be white instead of red. He was right!

Capt Halle was kept busy dropping three agents and twelve containers on WHEELWRIGHT 84 & DARENTH 1 in France and the next night the 6/7th March flew his first sortie to Norway, his home country, attempting two SIS operations. His first target AQUARIUS was a triangle of red lights with a white flashing 'K'. In clear weather from 650 feet he dropped one agent and six containers. From a DR position on the coast north of Egersund they flew some 165km or more to Sandesome 25 km S Drammen) where they made a DR run to OCTANS. Thick cloud preventing them from dropping. They returned to land at Downham Market. The following night Lt Piltingsrud, also flying his first Norwegian operation, completed OCTANS by dropping, in clear weather, two agents and four containers.

On the night of 5th March a Stirling EE944 of No.218 Squadron flown by P/O E H Edwards returned from operations with its port outer engine u/s. He attempted to over-shoot a fully laden aircraft (having been refused permission to jettison his load on the airfield) and struck the ground with his wing. There were two survivors. I remember the control tower's refusal to Edwards' request alarmed us all. In retrospect nothing had been learned from P/O Kennedy's tragic accident of the 7/8th January.

The only agents dropped in France on the night of 7/8th of March were three on PAUL 54 near Angoulême by F/Lt Stiles of 138 Squadron. He says he picked up 'Rebecca' 55km out and on his first run dropped 15 containers, three agents and three packages from 700 feet, four more packages were dropped during the second run. Two of these agents must have been the brothers P E and E P Mayer, the third remains unnamed. Six other agents were dropped in Norway that night from two aircraft. Operations DAG & MANI and FIELDFARE.

Thirteen aircraft from 138 Squadron were dispatched to France on the 10/11th to a series of dropping zones in the mountains south of Geneva, *Maquis* country, operation UNION 3. Our instructions were simple, get into the area and if you couldn't find the DZ you were given, drop where you saw one. We were to take off as a Squadron and saturate the target area by arriving over it at the same time. Not our scene at all! I remember slowly taxying, in a queue, to the threshold of runway 25, a strong side wind attempting to weather-cock the aeroplane into wind and into the morass that edged the taxy track. When I received the green light to take-off, to my chagrin, I found I had dissipated my brake pressure to zero. We were fortunate there was no traffic on the railway line at the precise moment we flew over it.

We pinpointed Dijon and flew to Lake Bourget (north of Chambéry). Low cloud and snow obliterating ground detail prevented us from recognising it. We turned towards Moutiers (Savoie), our next pinpoint. In the middle distance we could see the unmistakable shape of Mount Blanc glistening in the moonlight. At ETA Moutiers we picked up a 'Rebecca' signal and circled for 15 minutes to see if we could find the lights of a DZ. Through a gap in the clouds we saw a triangle of fires in a valley and dropped our 15 containers and six packages. The altimeter was reading 5,000 feet. On reflection it was hardly likely that our cargo dropped on its target. I couldn't climb out of there fast enough there were still peaks above us. We had been airborne eight hours when we landed.

Eleven aircraft found targets and 165 containers and 66 packages were dropped. One aircraft failed to find a DZ and one gave MARKSMAN 20 an unexpected bonus of 15 containers and six packages which could not have pleased them.

The 18/19th F/Lt Downes flying at 3,000 feet picked up WHEELWRIGHT 64's 'Rebecca' 40km away. He parachuted in, a WAAF, Yvonne Baseden (a W/T operator who survived Ravensbrück) and Baron Gonzagues de St-Geniès. Evidence points to the DZ being in the Marmande area (Lot-et-Garonne). Four packages and 15 containers followed. P/O Thomas dropped three agents on PAUL 9 picking up 'Rebecca' over 100km from the site. He reported when crossing the French coast at Pt de la Percée seeing 12 fighter flares drop ahead of his aircraft but could not identify the aircraft they illuminated. Downes had also reported yellow fighter flares. Both pilots reported

Maureen Patricia O'Sullivan (Simonet -aka Paddy), now Mrs Alvey, an Irish wireless operator who was parachuted into France on the 22/23 March 1944. She was a WAAF. (Courtesy Special Forces Club)

large fires and explosions in the Bergerac area (Dordogne). Thomas seeing red markers and Downes reporting that he saw it 100 miles away, smoke reaching 5,000 feet. F/Sgt Jones also flying PAUL 9 reported these explosions, as did I flying WHEELWRIGHT 61.

That night thirteen Lancasters from 617 Squadron plus another six from 5 Group made 'an accurate raid of an explosives factory at Bergerac in France'.

On the 30/31st five most experienced 138 Squadron crews were sent to Belgium. W/O Gregory flew TYBALT 22 & BALTHASAR 1 and S/Ldr Russell flew TYBALT 11 both taking the Northern route via Holland both met with enemy opposition from almost the identical spot off Tholen. Gregory crossing the coast at 300 feet dived to 50 feet to shake off the searchlight and three light guns firing at him. Russell's rear gunner at a height of 400 feet shot out two of the three searchlights illuminating them, the flak then ceased. Both had the benefit of 'Rebecca' from over 50km. (probably the same one picked up out at sea, Russell says from 4,000 feet, he also had S-phone working on his target from roughly 10km). Gregory dropped 12 containers onto

TYBALT flashing 'C' near Espierres (east of Roubaix) and, 37 minutes later, three agents, three containers and two packages on BALTHASAR flashing 'A' near Peruwelz (SE of Tournai). Russell, on his, dropped 15 containers.

Of the remaining targets two had 'no reception' and F/Lt B B Mill flying Halifax LL287 on operation OSRIC 27 was shot down by flak and ditched in a river 2km west of Hansweert, Zeeland, Holland. Mill evaded but three crew were killed and four made PoW (there was a second pilot). Two Belgium agents on board, Lt R Deprez and Lt A Giroulle, were drowned.

The last day of March the 31/1st saw 138 Squadron launch 14 sorties. Three crews, including my own, were flying their tenth operation of the month. I have no doubt that the other two, P/O Pick (promoted F/Lt) and F/Sgt Jones, felt clapped out like myself. Having sneaked a look at the night's fuel loads we calculated we were going to Norway. Four crews in fact did. F/Lt Johnson dropped three agents and 12 containers onto THRUSHRED 2. F/Sgt Jones was successful with operation GREBERED dropping 12 containers. F/Lt Stiles went to service two SIS targets HAMMOND & BETA. Making two runs on the former he dropped five containers and two packages but the agent refused to jump maintaining that a stationary car on the road showing powerful headlights made it unsafe for him to do so. Six containers were dropped on the latter target. F/Lt Pick met with no reception. Other than one sortie to Denmark where S/Ldr Wilding dropped an agent and 12 containers onto TABLEJAM 43, the remainder went to France.

F/Sgt Mackay was one of them flying MARREE (SIS) & PETER 58 had hardly crossed the French coast when flying at 4-5,000 feet over

Le Cimtiere de la Gaudier, Nantes, where ninety-two airmen and fifteen soldiers are interred. In the foreground the first headstone is that of Sgt R G Thompson and next is that of Sgt E M Keep. (Author)

Crew of Halifax LL252 NF-K lost over Tours, France, on the 1 April 1944. (L to R): Sgt E Wilkinson (Despatcher), Sgt R G Thompson (WOp/AG), Sgt E M Keep (Bomb Aimer), Author (Pilot), F/O R J Carson, RCAF, (Navigator), Sgt W R McBurney, RCAF, (Flight Engineer), Sgt D W L Brown, RCAF, (Air Gunner). (Author)

Lisieux light flak struck his aircraft. He says from 'probably ten accurate guns', while taking violent evasive action his gyro compass toppled. A ground haze prevented him from finding his targets.

I was caught off balance at briefing finding we were taking Halifax LL252 to France to drop six containers, two packages onto an SIS target ORAGE and nine containers, six packages onto PETER 5. Even more disturbing our normal entry to France via Cabourg was denied us. The Americans had banned all air traffic from the area. Thus a new route had to be plotted into territory which lacked knowledge of known flak sites. Our briefing was explicit, we had a special package to deliver to ORAGE an SIS target in the vicinity of Châteauroux. We were not under any circumstances to drop this unless the correct answer was given from the site to our aldis signal. PETER 5 we would pick up on the way in and if we missed it we could make another pass at it on the way out.

There was no reception on PETER 5, SW of Tours, so we moved onto ORAGE finding a triangle of fires. Circling we flashed the identification letter. They did not reply. We flew away and twice returned, they still did not answer our signal. We decided we could not wait any longer for fear of compromising the site by our engine noise, so we left for a second stab at PETER 5. Again there were no reception lights but as we were leaving for home I thought I saw a torch light flash at us on our port beam. Foolishly I went to investigate.

We turned for home, my fruitless investigation causing us to fly across the aerodrome at St-Symphorien, Tours. A searchlight illuminated us, unlike previous occasions when this had happened Lloyd Brown, my rear gunner, was unable to bring his guns to bear to extinguish it. I was now down to 300 feet and taking flak hits into the port inner engine which caught fire. Feathering the propeller and operating the fire extinguisher had no effect and I climbed for height for the crew to bale out during which time the port wheel fell out of its housing and we began gently to turn left into the ground. I had time to straighten the aircraft up, illuminate the landing light, close the throttles and pull back on the control column to make a crash landing into a vineyard at the Vallée de Cousse, 8km east of the airfield. Sadly Sgt E M Keep, the A/B, and Sgt R G Thompson, the WOp/AG, were killed and the Navigator, F/O R J Carson, RCAF, was injured. The rest of us were fortunate to survive.

March had been a busy month for No.138 Squadron, 27 crews flying 153 individual sorties, dropping 30 agents, 1,216 containers, 488 packages and scattering 581 packs of leaflets and 651 pigeons. Over eleven crews flew seven or more operations each. Three crews were lost.

Halifax operations for 161 Squadron for the period from the 10/11th March until the end of the month were also numerous and successful, 25 sorties out of 38 succeeding. Although the Hudsons took their part in parachuting and SIS wireless operations, none flew pick-up flights during the month of March.

On the 10/11th F/Sgt Bransden attempted a double operation to Germany and France ELM & BOB 153 bad weather prevented its success. On the 14/15th F/O Bell was brought back from France in a Lysander flown by F/Lt Anderson, he had been away 11 days. The same night Lt Piltingsrud flew a lone cargo sortie to Norway dropping

Wreckage of author's Halifax LL252 NF-K being dismantled by the Luftwaffe in a Vouvray vineyard. Sgt R G Thompson and Sgt E M Keep lost their lives in this crash on the 1 April 1944. Photograph taken by the local Resistance. (Author)

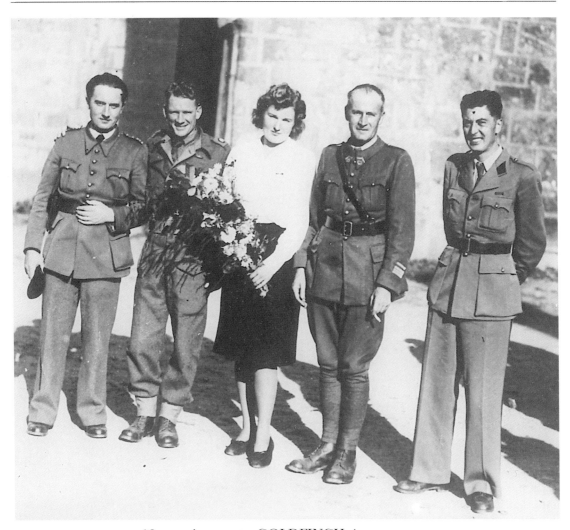

On the right of Paddy O'Sullivan is Major Percy Edward Mayer, the leader of the FIREMAN circuit, together with other French officers. (Courtesy Special Forces Club)

12 containers onto GOLDFINCH 4.

During the night of 22/23rd March Patricia O'Sullivan (Simonet), a WAAF W/T operator, was parachuted in to join the Mayer brothers (dropped near Angoulême two weeks earlier by 138 Squadron). Squadron records are not clear whether she was dropped by P/O Smith, of 161 Squadron, during Operation JOHN 72 or by P/O Pick, of 138 Squadron, on Operation JOHN 59. Both had dropped one agent each that night. Patricia O'Sullivan was eventually overrun by our own forces.

On the night of the 28th March, Hudson FK767 flown by F/O R L Baugham was making a low level training parachute drop at Henlow. It was dark, there was no moon. He failed to find the lights on his first pass and it was thought that he was looking out of the cockpit for the lights when the aircraft, turning steeply, stalled and crashed into the ground. Sadly all four crew on board were killed.

The last day of the month was a mixed bag for 161. Lt Halle and Lt

Piltingsrud taking their crews for successful cargo drops to Norway, operations LAPWING and GIRTH 2. F/Sgt Tattersall flew TABLEJAM 47 to Denmark dropping an agent and 12 containers. He was flying an aeroplane in which a few nights previously he had returned early with engine failure.

P/O Smith flying at a height of 2,000 feet made a DR run from the junction of the canal and the Somme (6km W Péronne) to his target TOM 47. At Bouvincourt-en-Vermandos (Somme) some 40 light flak guns opened fire on him. He could see the reception lights of his target but as he turned towards them he was once again engaged by flak and a searchlight. Wisely he decided to abandon his mission. Six minutes later flying away from the target area over Béthencourt-sur-Somme (some 8km NW Ham) 15 to 20 light flak guns together with a searchlight further engaged him. Bouvincourt was 2½ km north of a heavily defended German airfield (Péronne). Smith and his crew were extremely fortunate to survive.

Holland and operation FARO was F/O Caldwell's task, crossing Vlieland at a height of 50 feet (!) noting that night flying was taking place at Texal aerodrome. Making a DR run from the coast and ground detail being clear, dropped four agents blind, N J Celosse (Faro), A M J Cnoops (Cricket), H A J Sanders (Swale), J H Seyben (Ping Pong) and three packages near Wieringermeer. Caldwell landing at Waterbeach reported one agent brought back, refused to jump saying his papers were not in order. F/O Ibbot was also over Holland flying a Hudson crossing the coast at Tholen flying at 100 feet. He made a DR run from Breda, as he approached Breda the airfield lights at Gilze-Rijen came on. He parachuted blind, near Etten-Leur, SIS operation FENCING 1, consisting of T Biallosterski and J A Steman. He landed at Foulsham in Norfolk.

Of the eleven Halifax crews operating with 161 Squadron in March, four had flown ten operations namely, F/Sgt Tattersall, F/Sgt. Bransden, P/O Smith, and F/Sgt Ratcliffe. (ten operations was roughly 65 flying hours). Four crews flew six or more sorties. Let it be said Harris did not work his crews this hard. Each Squadron dropped 30 agents. It is only possible now to record a few of the names of the many being dropped. March Lysander sorties amounted to 13.

.

CHAPTER TWENTY-TWO

April 1944

April started with 138 Squadron flying 18 sorties between 1/2nd and 5/6th, only two failed. Targets included Norway four, Denmark two, Belgium one and France eleven. On the 5/6th April Tempsford parachuted into France some sixteen agents. F/Lt Walker dropped a single and six packages onto DITCHER 37 making a DR run from a lake near Marizy (Saône-et-Loire) some 12km SSE of Montceau-les-Mines. Returning to the lake he made another DR run to drop 15 containers onto JOHN 34. Bad weather at base forced him to land at Chivenor. F/Lt Downes made his DR run from Chauray (4/5km NE Niort) dropping four agents, 15 containers and six packages from 600 feet onto 'four reds in a row', the DZ for DICK 45. He was forced to land at Exeter. DICK 45 had a busy night, W/O Yardley visiting them with another 15 containers.

Three 161 Squadron Halifax sorties were mounted to STATIONER targets. Professor Foot commented 'As many as sixteen agents were sent in April and May to receptions by STATIONER (organised by Major M Southgate)'. He considered it a questionable decision of 'F' section 'pouring agents into France through this one channel'.

F/Sgt Bransden flew two targets, he was unable to complete STATIONER 56, lacking reception. Making a DR run from le Blanc (Indre) (some 45km SE Châtellerault) for his second target he found VYGELIA flashing the correct signal on a single red light and in excellent visibility he parachuted onto it five agents, five containers and seven packages. He landed at Lyneham, and found one container had hung up. Sgt McGibbon flew STATIONER 48 & 51. He too made his DR run from le Blanc and on 48 flashing 'L' made three circuits at 700 feet parachuting in three agents and three packages on the first, two further circuits were made for another six packages. With ground detail clear he returned to le Blanc and went to 51 where he dropped 15 containers. He also landed at Lyneham.

The third Halifax sortie involved F/O Morris who flew STATIONER 59, first to le Blanc but then eastward to la Châtre (Indre) from here making his first target DR run. He must have overflown it since he pinpoints Ardentes (some 12km SE Châteauroux) and returns to la Châtre to make another. At the edge of a wood, between wood and village, he found the site flashing 'B', parachuting three agents and three packages. Morris landed at Middle Wallop. This drop was sufficiently far south east for it to have been Capt M Leccia

Charles Staunton was
Violette Szabo's leader on
both her missions.

and Lt E A L Allard, two Frenchmen and a Belgian, Lt P A H Geelen.
After delivering a large sum of money to a nearby safe house they were
contacted by a double agent who betrayed them to the Gestapo in
Paris. Shortly afterwards Southgate suffered the same fate.

Tempsford was fogbound.

It was the night of the 5/6th Violette Szabo, together with Philippe
Liewer (Staunton), were taken to France. There seems to be some
confusion among the historians as to whether they were parachuted in
or flown in by Lysander .

Cookridge says they landed by Lysander on the 15th April but there were no Lysander operations that night. Minney, Violette Szabo's biographer, says the Lysander which took off from Tempsford was spotted by a German fighter (this sounds fictitious) near the landing field between Chartres and Orléans.

F/Lt Taylor and F/Lt Whittaker both flying Lysanders took off from Tempsford (returning to Tangmere) each taking two agents, on operation UMPIRE, both landing in a field 1.5km ENE Azay-sur-Cher some 7km ESE Tours. Verity names three of the passengers. The 161 Squadron diary records that Lt Hysing-Dahl took three agents with 4 packages on operation LILAC, Verity says the field was 1.5km W Baudreville some 30km ESE Chartres but does not mention that passengers were taken out. It could have been possible the Norwegian, Hysing-Dahl flew them in, the landing field was certainly between Chartres and Orléans and a train to Paris could have been caught at nearby Angerville.[6]

M R D Foot says they were parachuted in, it is questionable if they were included in the Tempsford parachute operations that night which were, as it can be seen, way to the south and Szabo and Liewer were going to Rouen. However, Vera Atkins, the intelligence officer who worked closely with the women of 'F' Section, SOE, was recently kind enough to clarify this mystery by saying that she remembered escorting Violette Szabo to an awaiting CARPETBAGGER B-24 sent to collect her from Tempsford.[7]

However, at Rouen Szabo and Liewer realised they would be unable to accomplish their mission to re-establish contact with the agents of the penetrated *reseau* SALESMAN. They were air-lifted out on the 30th April/1st May by F/Lt Large flying a Lysander. This did land at Tempsford with a flat tyre punctured by a piece of flak. This was Violete Szabo's first mission, her courage during her second was to merit the award of a posthumous George Cross

Of the sixteen French sorties launched by 138 on the 9/10th, only seven succeeded, lack of receptions accounted for the failures. In addition to being without reception at STATIONER 43, W/O Yardley collected a number of holes in the tail of his aircraft at 2,000 feet near Parcoul (Dordogne) a village (some 36km NE Libourne) reporting six machine guns firing from a road at 23.57 hours. Strangely P/O Baker also reported at the same time, same place, the same guns firing tracer! Baker went on to complete WHEELWRIGHT 51 in the Auch area (Gers). Yardley went on to Périgueux turning north east some 55km to make a DR run from St-Yrieix-la-Perche (Haute-Vienne). He saw another site flashing 'U' when searching for his own and, when he returned, saw roughly 15 containers and parachutes in the edge of wood. This could have been F/Sgt Hayman flying STATIONER 44.

---

[6] The author has since established, from the operational report, that Hysing-Dahl went out empty and two other Lysander sorties flown by F/Lt Whitaker and F/Lt Anderson were not completed.

[7] An aerial photograph of Tempsford dated 'April 1944' shows two B-24s parked close to the 161 Squadron hanger.

F/Lt Stiles parachuted two agents, 15 containers and eight packages onto HARRY 28 also scattering five pigeons and four packs of leaflets.

On the 9/10th April, 161 despatched seven Halifaxes and four Hudsons to France dropping sixteen agents, seven from the Hudsons. P/O Caldwell dropping six onto TEMPETE in the Vatan area had the misfortune of failing to drop his three containers. On his second target PETER 38 some 16 minutes away he made DR run from Vallon-en-Sully (Allier) but only six of his twelve containers were released. It was found on his return that his bomb release equipment had failed. Lack of receptions caused three of the 161 sorties to fail.

Between the 10/11th and the 11/12th 161 Squadron mounted ten Halifax and three Hudson sorties, only two failing. Capt Halle flew to Belgium dropping two agents on OSRIC 28 and S/Ldr Parker dropping blind a further two on ELM in Germany. Parker met accurate fire from six to eight guns in the Aube area (some 40km E Argentan) having had a searchlight flick onto them at 4,000 feet. He took the route into Germany via Belfort and made a DR run from Lake Constance, during which they saw clearly Horb, the River Naglad and the road to Naglad village, identifying the pinpoint by a wooded slope and a road they dropped from 900 feet. The remaining Halifaxes went to France. Two Hudsons flew French SIS operations DATCHWORTH and CHRISTS. A third flown by F/Sgt Morris going to Holland operation BRADFIELD dropping blind two SIS agents. Making his DR run from a flooded Tholen at 500 feet and pinpointing the junction of the Maas and Waal at Rossum. On the night of 10/11th a total of 12 agents were dropped in all.

Regrettably, the night 10/11th, F/Sgt J E McGibbon, RCAF, flying

Halifax Mk V NF-D and crew. (L to R): W/O R Bode, Sgt A G Smith, Sgt C F Wills, Sgt E G Baker, P/O W Yardley (Pilot), Sgt S Stephens. Inset: Sgt J Beale, DFM. The badge on the nose (which they inherited) is a winged Elsan. There were forty-two miniature Elsans on the nose when the crew finished their tour and Jack Beale had flown on thirty-three. Gibraltar Farm is on the extreme left. (Jack Beale)

Opposite: *The operations board in the control tower for the night of 9/10 April 1944. However, Hale, Ibbot and Ferris were parachuting agents from Hudsons. All sorties went to France and a total of seventeen agents were dropped. In less than a month eight of these crews were lost*

(K-McKay, H-Jones,
P-Hayman, V-
Williamson, Q-Thomas,
L-McMullen,
Y-McGibbon and
S-Hale). W/Cdr Brogan
was lost in March 1945
and E-Stiles and his
crew survived an
horrendous take-off crash
in June 1944. The
WAAF is Sgt Lintott.
(via K A Merrick)

Halifax LK738 to France on operations JOHN 98 & BREUGEL, crashed into a wood about 3km west of St-Hilaire-sur-Risle (Orne) (Rille says the Bomber Command casualty card) there were no survivors. F/Sgt Hayman flying a 138 Squadron aeroplane reported seeing an aircraft shot down by flak when flying at 4,000 feet in the Bellême area, bearing 340 degrees, 10 miles (17km). If plotted from Bellême there, further north than ten miles and to the right is a small village, St-Hilaire-sur-Risle. Hayman, I am sure was witnessing the sad demise of F/Sgt McGibbon and his crew. Hayman went on to drop in two runs from 700 feet four agents and fifteen containers on to JOHN 38. He made his DR run from Condrieu (Rhône) reporting this site should not be used in bad weather – it was too near high ground.

Bomber Command were bombing railway yards in the north east of France this night. A small force of 180 Lancasters also bombed Tours. I had just finished a meal in a house where I was hiding nearby the target, St-Pierre-des-Corps, when the first bomb exploded!

During the same period 138 Squadron flew twelve sorties on the 10/11th and eleven on the 11/12th, four to Belgium the remainder to France. A Stirling flown by F/Lt Bailey is mentioned twice in 138 operation reports. His first (10/11th), operation DONKEYMAN 38, making a DR run from St-Julien-du-Sault (Yonne). The second

Date	Pilot		Code	Target	Country		Result
2/10th	F/Sgt Lawrence		C	STATIONER 53	FRANCE	N.C	No Reception
	F/Sgt Hayman		P	" 44	FRANCE	C	
	F/Sgt Jones		H	" 36	FRANCE	N.C	No Reception.
	W/O Palmer		N	" 52	FRANCE	C	
	P/O Baker		O	WHEELWRIGHT 51	FRANCE	C	
	W/O Gregory		R.	STATIONER 43.	FRANCE	N.C	No Reception
	F/Sgt Williamson		V	PIMENTO 78	FRANCE	N.C	" "
	W/O Yardley		D	WHEELWRIGHT 73/TERMOOLLE FRANCE		N.C	Wireless Equipment c
	F/L Ashley		A	WHEELWRIGHT 90.	FRANCE	N.C	No Reception
	F/L Johnson		M	SCIENTIST 52.	FRANCE	N.C	No Reception.
	F/L Stiles.		E	HARRY 28	FRANCE	C	
	F/Sgt Mackay		K	PIMENTO/ AUBRETIA.	FRANCE	C	P.78 . N.C N.R.
	S/L Wilding.		J	STATIONER 53/ DAR WENI	FRANCE	C	St.33. N.C.N.R.
	F/L Ack		F	TOM 35	FRANCE	N.C	No Reception.
	F/L Thomas.		Q	TOM 51	FRANCE	C	
	F/O Mc Mullan.		L	DICK 7.	FRANCE.	N.C	No Reception.
9/10th	P/O Caldwell	HALIFAX.	U	TEMPETE // PETER 38.	FRANCE	C	
	P/O Smith.		W	PACK 60.	FRANCE	C	
	Lt Piltingsrud.		X	TOM 42	FRANCE	NC	No Reception.
	F/Sgt Tattersall.		T.	STATIONER 14½	FRANCE	C	
	F/Sgt Bransden.		Z	" "	FRANCE,	C	
	F/Sgt Mc Gibbon.		Y	SYRINGA // DICK 8	FRANCE.	C	
	Sgt Benfiet.		Y	STATIONER 50.	FRANCE.	NC	No Reception.
	F/L Hale.	HUDSON.	M	AUTHOR 31	FRANCE	C	
	F/O Ibbot.		P	DAVIDSTOWE.	FRANCE	C	
	F/O Ferris.		N	STATIONER 46.	FRANCE.	C	
	F/Sgt Morris.		R	BOB 165.	FRANCE	N.C	No Reception

(11/12th) PIMENTO 71 & JOHN 6 making a DR run from Bourg. Neither were completed and reported on the latter target 'W/Op twitching (!) against packages sent five parcels, already on rollers, out and damaged the floor'. F/Lt Bailey went back to flying Halifaxes next time out.

Of the 26 agents dropped, seven were in Belgium. The most notable drops in France were F/Sgt Jones dropping six on OURAGON, an SIS, target making his DR run from le Blanc. The agents parachute straps became tangled after the drop and had to be jettisoned. He went on to complete a cargo drop onto PETER 52, and F/Sgt Hayman, dropping four onto JOHN 38. On the 11/12th F/Lt Thomas made a DR run from Conde dropping five onto BOB 165. ARCHDEACON, his second target (operated by the Germans), was in the Vervins (Aisne)

Although it has been said that the names on the operations board were chalked up at random (for photographic purposes) the above extract from the operations diary of 138 (top) and 161 (bottom) Squadrons show that they were genuine operations mounted on the 9 April 1944 – which is surprising in view of their very nature. (PRO).

area and here he dropped twelve containers. On the way home he met four guns and two searchlights at Aube. At a height of 2,000 feet and 40 miles (65km) from Tempsford the airfield 'Rebecca' signal was picked up. I wonder why it took so long to install?

Ken Merrick, describes the magnificent contribution made on the night of 11/12th of 55 aircraft from No.38 Group and 14 from No.90 Squadron. Regrettably five Stirlings were lost. Two of three from No.90 Squadron, and one from No.190 Squadron, were lost over the UK.

The moon period finished on the 12/13th April with both Squadrons concentrating on Belgium. The six cargo sorties dispatched by 138 Squadron flew via Tholen, Holland. F/Sgt Hayman was first off at 00.19hrs for OSRIC 2 crossing the Dutch coast at Tholen, height 100 feet. His rear gunner replying to one searchlight and machine gun fire. He was unable to complete as there was no reception near Colfontaine (SW of Mons). F/Lt Pick off at 01.24hrs, crossed Tholen at 200 feet proceeding south pinpointing the River Sambre and making a DR run to OSRIC 37 near Binche (some 20km W Charleroi) dropping 15 containers. F/Sgt Jones off at 01.35hrs was high crossing Tholen at 500 feet, picking up the River Schelde and making his DR run to OSRIC 35 and dropping. A searchlight disturbed him at Kibbendijke. W/O Yardley flying OSRIC 22 failed to pinpoint over Tholen reporting low tide had uncovered mud banks, his time off was 01.44 hrs. P/O Baker off at 01.48hrs met with two searchlights at Tholen but made a successful drop onto OSRIC 41 having found a bend in the Schelde from which to make his DR run. The last to take off, at 02.02 hrs, was F/Sgt Williamson for OSRIC 30 he was at 600 feet when he saw Tholen but went down to sea level turning south to

A No. 38 Group Halifax MK V of No. 644 Squadron, based at Tarrant Rushton, that towed Hamilcars and Horsas at D-Day, Arnhem and Operation VARSITY. They started SOE operations in March 1944. The symbols on this aircraft show that it had completed ten operations. This was the same type of Halifax used at Tempsford during 1944. (Phillip Jarret)

make a successful DR run from Wichelen east of Gent. He bolted back via Tholen at zero feet reporting that visibility was bad.

Only one of four Halifax sorties launched by 161 to Belgium was successful, OSRIC 24, flown by F/Sgt Bransden, receptions failed to materialise for the other three – a frustrating experience for crews flying these difficult and dangerous operations.

At 13.00 hours on the 19th April Sgt K E Vear, RCAF, took off a No.161 Squadron Hudson T9439 on a cross country exercise to Wales via Cornwall. Steering on a gyro compass set zero at take-off, a u/s radio, and frontal conditions resulted in the aircraft becoming lost. Swedish fighters eventually forced them to land at a Gothenburg military airfield. The crew were interned and repatriated a little more than six months later.

With the moon rising on the 20/21st and through to the 26/27th a total of 38 cargo sorties were flown to France, only five failing. The 27/28th saw both Squadrons out in numbers, fifteen from 138 and six from 161. It would have been better if they had all stayed on the ground. Of the ten 138 failures F/O McMullen on his way to OSRIC 32 met three flak ships at the entrance to the Oosterschelde. Flying at 100 feet at the time intensive and accurate light flak hit his starboard outer engine which he feathered, with his Gee set also out of action he returned to base. Unhappily Halifax LL356 flown by F/Sgt G H Williamson, RAAF, was lost on a Belgium operation OSRIC 59. They were taking the southern route via Holland and came down into the sea. One body of the crew was recovered on the beach of the Isle of Terschelling. There were no survivors.

Four other 138 aircraft flew operations STATIONER 35, 37, 42 and 44 none were completed. Although lights were seen it was reported that a low moon and haze made it very dark.

Of the five 161 Squadron failures F/Sgt Tattersall flying BOB 169 reported 'very dark moon in target area made it impossible to map read'. W/O Ratcliffe flying BOB 177 was approaching his target when three flares came up at him – he left at once! Both made DR runs from Cosne (Nievre). Another Belgium operation OSRIC 36 was flown by Lt Piltingsrud, RNoAF. At 0015hrs flying at zero feet reported that light flak was attacking another aeroplane 10 miles south. He gave his position as 51° 28'N, 04° 00'E, some 8km SE Goes on Zuid Beveland. The aircraft seen attacked could have been that of F/Sgt Williamson. Piltingsrud then turned out to sea to get a 'Gee' fix, coming in again at 01.01hrs flying 100 feet over Tholen. Here he flew over several light flak guns which hit both inner engines, damaging the propeller and spinner of the starboard inner, the port inner engine and the trailing edge. The aircraft was now difficult to control, neither engine would feather. The W/Op was also hit in the right leg by a small piece of shrapnel. However Piltingsrud had sufficient control flying homeward at 200 feet to report seeing the identical flak ships that had shot at McMullen. A skilful emergency landing was made at Woodbridge after 2.37 hours in the air.

The night of the 28/29th was devoted entirely to Norway, Six Halifax sorties from No.161 Squadron and nine from 138. Each Squadron completed four and five agents were dropped. Lack of receptions being the main cause of failure, although the weather had now begun to interfere, a front moving south east across southern Norway. For 138 S/Ldr Russell flew MAKIR, an SIS operation, with Oluf Olsen and Lars Larsen on board. Making their DR run from Lake Eikeren (59° 36'N, 10° 00'E this had been used before) ground detail was clearly recognised and the DZ site was pinpointed but no lights were seen. Russell flew away for half an hour in the direction of Oslo where from 10 miles (18km) watched the target markers, flares and explosions from a small force of 51 Lancasters bombing an airframe factory. Returning to the pinpoint there again being no reception he turned for home. P/O Baker flying HUMNAH 1 & HUMNAH 2 to Norway met with 10/10th cloud with a base at 2,000 feet and tops at 6,000. Well into his flight he found that fuel was not transferring from the bomb bay tank and had to abort, there would not have been sufficient petrol to complete.

France this night was serviced by 10 Halifaxes and 13 Stirlings from 38 Group and an additional 13 Stirlings from 90 Squadron. Only one failure – a remarkable effort, regrettably a Stirling was lost over the UK from bad weather.

Another wasted effort occurred on the 29/30th when five 138 Squadron aircraft were sent to STATIONER 70. P/O Baker was the only one to beat the weather, dropping 14 containers.

April finished with 161 Squadron mounting six French sorties on the 30/1st with 100% success and 138 mounting thirteen to France with nine successes. One solitary operation OSRIC 26 was flown to Belgium by F/O Hayman who parachuted in three agents fifteen containers and four packages. Two new crews, led by F/O G D Kidd (Service number 152341) and F/O J A Kidd (152342), appeared in the operations book both flying MASON 1 to France. They were to fly the same target on a number of future occasions and were promoted to the rank of Flight Lieutenant at the same time, They were twin brothers.

April was another month of great demand on Tempsford Halifax crews, 13 of them flew in excess of seven operations each. Concern was expressed over crews completing operational tours. From 205 Halifax and 11 Hudson sorties were dropped, 71 agents, 1,800 containers, 715 packages and 531 pigeons. Coupled with the effort from No.38 Group and No.90 Squadron the April build up for the approaching 'D' Day was enormous but sadly not without loss. 13 Lysander pick-up sorties were flown.

CHAPTER TWENTY-THREE

May 1944

No.138 Squadron opened the month of May on the 1/2nd, by mounting four sorties to Belgium and seven to France. S/Ldr Wilding was to combine his Belgium operation, OSRIC 2, with one to Germany, DENVER 1, weather prevented him from completing either of them. F/Lt Bailey had instrument problems flying to OSRIC 42 and aborted. F/O Coldridge, F/O McMullen and F/Lt Walker were targeted onto TOM 45. They flew south to the Loire, then Sully-sur-Loire turning north east to the target area east of Paris. Walker had no problem dropping his fifteen containers. McMullen at 01.12 hrs, reported seeing 'something burning on the ground after falling in flames'. He proceeded via Misy-sur-Yonne (Seine-et-Marne) (10km E Montereau) making his final DR run, from la Ferté (possibly la-Ferté-sous-Jouarre there is another la Ferté-Gaucher, to the south but this had an airfield close to it). The target was close to a small river and McMullen expressed concern that future loads might fall into it.

Coldridge went via Bray-sur-Seine (Seine-et-Marne) making for Charly (NE la Ferté-sous-Jouarre) to make his DR run. During his second run flying at 2,000 feet ten plus light flak guns together with an 'uncertain number of machine guns' opened fire on him hitting the aircraft in the belly, the side of the fuselage and the port outer and port inner engines (he gave his position at this time as 48° 50′N, 03° 00′E the site of a German aerodrome at Coulommiers). He dived to 200 feet, got away, and recovered to 2,000 feet. Discovering that he was losing petrol badly he abandoned the operation and made for home. W/O Yardley down to fly DIRECTOR 54 must have had a problem on the ground he is simply reported as 'did not take-off'. The next 30 sorties through to the 6/7th were all French cargo drops, eight failing mostly due to no reception.

Bomber Command were to lose 42 Lancasters from a force of 362, on May 3/4th, bombing a tank depot at Mailly-le-Camp (Aube) in brilliant moonlight. A further 84 Lancasters plus four Mosquitoes bombed an airfield at Montdidier about 160km to the north west and almost on the same track. There was also a minor raid of 14 Mosquitoes to bomb an ammunition dump at Châteaudun. Fourteen Halifax cargo drops were dispatched by 138 Squadron to France, four failing through lack of receptions. Most of them flew west, Angoulême is mentioned in a number of reports. F/Sgt Lawrence flying

Three unknown Tempsford WAAFs included not only for their beauty but also for the poem found written on the back of the original photograph.

'If we could take the tiny freckles on your nose,
Each one to be as a million years and more,
Then multiply, as far as multiplying goes,
Add the stars; then total up the score,
We would have for all the world to see,
And envy too,
Half the years my dear, that I shall be;
In love with you.'
'At Tempsford WAAFERY'
(Harrington Carpetbagger Museum)

VENTRILOQUIST 31 reported seeing the Halifax of W/O Yardley flying VENTRILOQUIST 5, Yardley in turn reported, when flying home at 2,000 feet, 'a large amount of fire and explosions' at Châteaudun.

F/O G Kidd and F/O J Kidd were both working the same target, MASON 2 the former on his way home, saw an explosion in the Chartres area. J Kidd on his way to the target reported at 02.40 hours red target indicators in the Chartres area and on his way home, explosions and smoke in the same area. He also reported seeing his brother's Halifax in the target area!

My good friend F/O McMullen was flying DIGGER 1 that night, being an Australian he must have laughed at the irony of it. He reported seeing a patch of oil in the Channel, this information was communicated to No.3 Group HQ.

Of the five Halifax sorties dispatched to France by 161 Squadron only one, Capt Halle, RNoAF, flying DONALD 8 & HYPATICA, reported seeing any enemy air activity. Making his way at 2,000 feet in good, clear weather, with good visibility, to Pithiviers (Loiret), from where he was to make his DR run to DONALD 8 he saw 3km to starboard what he believed was a fighter shot down (no flak). Turning north at Pithiviers for DONALD 8, his first target, at 01.06 hours saw 1km ahead what he believed to be a heavy aircraft falling in flames and exploding (no flak). Still at 2,000 feet and three minutes from his DZ at 01.56 hours he reports from a position 48° 22′N, 02° 20′E, 10 to 15 miles (16km/24km) on his port side an aircraft shot down by light flak. When plotted this sighting was over the German airfield at Mondesir. Halle went on to drop eight containers and two packages on DONALD 8. Climbing again to 2,000 feet he set course for HYPATICA, here there would not be a reception. At a position roughly 20km south of Châteaudun he saw at 02.53 hours about 15 miles (24km) to starboard another aircraft shot down by light flak. He landed at Tempsford at 05.10.

That night F/Lt L L Whittaker, DFC, was sitting in his Lysander V9664 (SIS operation FORSYTHIA) in a field near Ouarville (Eure-et-Loire) (some 22km SE Chartres). A developing RAF air attack was said to have caused him to take-off hurriedly. Sadly he flew due east and shortly after was shot down, over Mondesir airfield 10km SSW Étampes (Essonne), and killed. This was the third incident witnessed by Capt Halle. The receptionists for FORSYTHIA said it was brilliant moonlight.

It would appear that Bomber Command did not bother to inform Tempsford of its intentions. It is probable that they were using Châteaudun as a turning point.

There was a change in pattern on the 6/7th, half of the 12 sorties mounted flying to Norway, one only failing. F/O Hayman dropping two agents and eight containers on OTTO 2. P/O Jones flew PIMENTO 67 to France identifying in moderate visibility Sancerre and Digoin and making his DR run to the target from Mâcon (Saône-et-Loire). There were three receptions in the area all flashing 'R'. He took the one he thought was in the correct position and once the aircraft was committed the lights of the other two went out and he dropped his fifteen containers and eight packages without further ado. On the way home he reported at 02.42hrs large explosions and smoke from Tours and at 03.05hrs seeing an aircraft fall in flames and crash two miles on their port quarter when some 6km NW Mamers. Whilst Bomber Command were operating over France that night there were no losses in this area, nor any attack on Tours.

M R D Foot writes that Tony Brooks, working a PIMENTO DZ in May, had a container full of grenades explode when it hit the ground alarming a nearby SS unit. The reception fled leaving Brooks, like King Charles II, hiding in a tree. Jones flew the only PIMENTO operation in May, there is no reference of an explosion on the DZ in his report. Perhaps this was the end product of a visit by a B-24.

F/Sgt Lawrence flew a target coded HALIFAX! F/O Coldridge flying at 2,000 feet was again attacked on his way down to HISTORIAN, a target in the Cher, this time by a machine gun from the railway east of Vire. His rear gunner silenced it.

Halifax operations flown by 161 for the same period followed a similar pattern. Opening with two successful sorties to Belgium and followed by seventeen to France with two failures. Three SIS Hudson targets in France received four agents.

The 6/7th saw 161 Squadron complete three Norwegian sorties. Lt Piltingsrud completing MAKIR outstanding from 28/29th April. Oluf Olsen knew the pilot well and unlike his first parachute drop into Norway this was 'the easiest', Lars Larsen jumped with him. Piltingsrud made his DR run from Berg, parachuting them from 500 feet onto a triangle of red lights with a white signalling 'K', also dropped were nine containers. Piltingsrud's regular aeroplane 'X' badly damaged on his Dutch flight at the end of April would not fly again for another four days. He must have been pleased with the ease that this flight was concluded. F/Lt Caldwell parachuted another Norwegian agent onto CRUPPER 3.

'Three Hudsons went to France dropping five agents' – so said the Squadron diary. However, the operation reports states that the three SIS operations had, instead, gone to Holland. F/Lt Menzies, F/Sgt Morris and S/Ldr Wilkinson, flying operation BLUNDELLS, ST VALENTINE'S and MENECRATES respectively. All crossed the Coast at Tholen at a height of 200 feet, all dropped blind. Menzies 10km to the east of his pinpoint at the request of his two agents. Morris made his DR run from Breda dropping one agent but bringing his pigeons back since 'they had French markings'! Wilkinson dropped a further two agents, map reading his way from Wichelin. Unusually, no enemy action was reported.

On the 7/8th P/O Smith made another attempt to complete the outstanding German operation DENVER coupled with TYBALT 15 in Belgium, it failed, the pinpoint could not be found. He went again the next night when at 4,500 feet met with four to five accurate light flak guns which damaged his starboard inner undercarriage door. His given position plots yet another aeroplane from Tempsford over the German airfield at Pérrone. From here to Étreux (10km N Guise) they appeared to have been harassed by yellow searchlights and one or two chandelier fighter flares. In the Étreux area they circled searching for a pinpoint, without success. They said probably high winds forced them off track, getting within 'Gee' range they actually found themselves to be 62 miles (95km) south of track. Both targets remained uncompleted.

Through to the 10/11th, 21 successful Halifax/Hudson sorties were flown, nearly all to France. W/Cdr Boxer on the 7/8th set out for France in a Hudson to fly LALAIE & MINISTER 3, returning early on one engine. Seven agents were dropped during this period.

For the same period 138 were not so fortunate. The night of the 7/8th saw six sorties out to France and two to Denmark. Halifax LL280 flown by W/Cdr W McF Russell, DFC & Bar, was shot down by a night-fighter on its way to his target CITRONELLE 1 in France. They crashed at St-Denis-d'Orques (Sarthe) 40km west of le Mans. Only three of the seven crew buried at le Mans could be identified. When W/Cdr Russell, now CO of No.138 Squadron, arrived at Tempsford to take over 'A' flight he asked me to collect his crew from 1654 HCU at Wigsley, which I did. They were all looking forward to commencing their second tour, it was a tragedy that none of them would survive.

The same night F/O H H McMullen, RAAF, flying Halifax LL192 to Denmark on operation TABLEJAM 46, was lost crashing into the Kattegat off Northern Jutland. None of the crew survived. 'Mac' wore the distinctive dark blue uniform of the RAAF and was a particular friend of mine. Against all advice we flew the station Tiger Moth, T7351, (they said it was jinxed!) to Waterbeach to meet some of his Australian friends. I often wondered what he thought when I went missing the following night.

On the 8/9th eleven sorties flew to France. The ten successes included P/O Hayman flying operation ARCHDEACON 14 and P/O Jones flying operation MUSICIAN 7 & ARCHDEACON 8. Both ARCHDEACON targets were under German control. In bright moonlight and industrial haze, Hayman made his DR run from le Cateau-Cambrésis (some 22km SE Cambrai) dropping fifteen containers and six packages. Jones made both his DR runs from Guise, the Germans receiving eight containers and a further six packages.

Five crews were sent to PERCY 3 on the night of 9/10th. A target in the Brive-la-Gaillarde (Correze) area south of Limoges and 65km east of Périgueux. Four crews completed successfully but F/O A S Coldridge, RCAF, and his crew flying Halifax LL183 were 'forced to bale out on their way to the target, landing 2km east Rochechouart (Haut Vienne) some 30km west Limoges. However, their luck held out, all the crew survived, six evaded and one made PoW on the 11th May. Coldridge and Medland arrived home via Paris, Madrid and Gibraltar on the 6th September, Evans, Jones and Blacknet who after helping to repulse a German attack on a *Maquis* base stayed with the *Maquis* for three months instructing on arms and receptions. On the 28th August they contacted an English Captain who arranged through the Americans at Limoges to fly them back to Tempsford.

All thirty 138 Squadron operations through to the 28/29th were to France and all but nine completed. On the 10/11th F/Lt Walker flew MINISTER 4 making his DR run from Montereau-faut-Yonne giving his drop position of 48° 32′N, 03° 10′E some 25km to the north east. He made 'Rebecca' and S-phone contact when instructions came from the ground to drop 'one boy' and his personal luggage. Since the Germans had been around they were not prepared to accept containers.

During Walker's circuit he was told 'please hurry'. A successful drop from 600 feet was confirmed from the ground. This must have been J L de Ganay, a saboteur, who operated successfully disrupting canal and railway traffic from nearby Nangis (Seine-et-Marne). There were no other agents dropped this night from Tempsford based aircraft.

On the 17th May F/Sgt W M Strathern took off Halifax LK736 on a training flight when an engine caught fire and they crash landed at Great Barford, killing the bomb aimer. This was a terrible aeroplane and could barely fly on four engines. I flew it twice on operations, all pilots who flew it complained bitterly of its performance.

Before the moon rose again, on the 23/24th May, S/Ldr Wilding dropped five agents onto DITCHER 40 in the Digoin (Soane-et-Loire) area although I cannot find what their mission was. During the day of the 23rd Halifax DG286 was lost. F/Lt J V Perrins was instructing F/O N L St G Pleasance on circuits and landings when taking off the port tyre burst at 90 mph. The aircraft swung, collapsing the undercarriage, writing off the aeroplane but there were no injuries.

The 27/28th saw F/Lt Thomas assisted by 'Rebecca' on both his targets in the Chateauneuf area parachuted three agents and six packages on VENTRILOQUIST 5 and making three circuits on his second target VENTRILOQUIST 8 before delivering twelve containers on a site making it difficult for him, in that they extinguished its lights during two of his runs.

P/O Yardley had a frustrating flight, making a DR run from le Blanc to PERCY 7, delivering ten packages after they had jammed the hole and finding the lights laid cross-wind. Landing at Tempsford he found his fifteen containers had hung up.

Of the sixteen French cargo sorties mounted by 138 Squadron on the 28/29th no less than seven targets were under the control of the Germans. All sites received 15 containers and at least five packages in hazy conditions and varying visibility. Operations DELEGATE 2, 3, 4, & 5 were flown respectively by F/Lt Johnson, P/O Jones, F/Lt Stiles and F/Lt Walker.

Johnson came down south via Fougères to his DR run from Ingrandes (on the Loire some 28km west of Angers) two of his container parachutes failing to open (laconically reported, 'considered fell into reception'). Jones made his DR run from the coast of Bretagne at Cap d'Erquy (some 35km west St-Malo) Poor visibility and mist making lining up the target difficult. Stiles started at Cap d'Erquy pinpointing Jugon-les-Lacs, some 50km NW of Rennes, dropping leaflets in the St-Méen-le-Grand (Ille-et-Vilaine) and Broons (Côte-d'Armor) area (in that order which suggests he was coming home). Three fighter flares dropping in this area (48° 06'N, 02° 12'W) must have given him a fright. Another DR run from Cap d'Erquy by Wilding on 'Gee' caused little difficulty but poor visibility forced him to make two runs.

Three other German operated sites serviced that night were BUTLER 20, 21 & 24 flown by S/Ldr Brogan, Lt. Piltingsrud of No.161 Squadron and S/Ldr Wilding. Like the DELEGATE targets all were showing the correct signal all were virtually in the same area.

Brogan making a DR run from Domfront reporting 'the moon partially obscured' and Wilding making a second run using the jettison bar to release his seven hung up containers. It seems strange that so many German operated sites were serviced on the same night!

What a cat and mouse game this was, think of the radio traffic there must have been to put the logistics into operation. M R D Foot says during May 1944 ARCHDEACON received FF 500,000 and BUTLER French Francs 250,000. In June DELEGATE received FF 500,000. There was of course a further cost, human lives, of those dropped onto German operated sites.

The 31st May/1st June was a disastrous night for Tempsford. Of the six Belgium 138 Squadron operations and three from 161 Squadron, three aircraft failed to return. In addition to the now normal hazard of enemy activity during Belgium trips, this night a severe storm over the North Sea was reported.

F/O J P Gallagher, RCAF, flying operation OSRIC 78 in Halifax LL419 was shot down by a nightfighter and crashed in southern Holland at Tholen-Lepelstraat. There were no survivors .

138 Squadron's other loss was W/O H F G Murray flying Halifax LL276 on operation OSRIC 74. Near to the Island of Tholen in southern Holland they were intercepted, it is thought, by a Me 110 who set the port wing ablaze. It crashed near Halsteren. Three of the crew baled out and were taken prisoner. Murray and the rest of the crew were lost including F/O J L Solomon an additional navigator. Murray when a F/Sgt took me on my first operational sortie in February.

A Hudson V9155 flying a Dutch SIS operation BEZIQUEZ piloted by F/Lt W M Hale, RCAF, was shot down by flak from the airfield at Gilze-Rijen (10km E of Breda) the wreckage falling in a nearby cornfield near the Ridder Street and the Warande. Regrettably all four crew and two Dutch agents on board, C M Dekkers (Poker) and J Kuenen (Football) were killed.

Like 138 Squadron there were few Halifax/Hudson operations conducted by 161 Squadron during the period 15/16th to the 31/1st June. The Hudsons spent most of their time during the dark period flying ten SIS wireless operations, not without mechanical problems due to oxygen and petrol pump failures. Most of the ten of twelve successful Halifax sorties to France were flown on the 28/29th. Three STATIONER targets getting the attention of four sorties. The only agents dropped during this period were two from a Hudson flown by F/Sgt Morris to OVERTURE II two containers and packages went with them. On the 30th a 161 Squadron Halifax LL300 caught fire while being serviced in a hangar and was damaged beyond repair.

Tempsford's May finished with 189 Halifax and fifteen Hudson dropping sorties, one Hudson and eight Lysander pick-up sorties. One Lysander, one Hudson and seven Halifaxes (two non-operational) were lost. In excess of 800 pigeons were also dropped. A difficult month for all.

June–July 1944

June 1944, had already opened with Tempsford suffering three losses, another seven would occur before the month ended. Judging by the number of successful operations mounted by both Squadrons leading up to the eve of 'D Day' one would never have expected the further destruction of another three aeroplanes.

On the 1/2nd 161 Squadron mounted nine sorties to France all of which were completed. The most notable being a Hudson sortie flown by S/Ldr Wilkinson dropping four SIS agents from 600 feet onto a good reception RAGEUR in the Nevers area. The navigator of F/O Ibbott's Hudson had the misfortune of dropping his navigation calculator and breaking it, making it necessary for him to plot manually. Low cloud made it impossible to identify pinpoints and they decided to return early bringing back the seven packages intended for HALS, an SIS target in France.

No.138 Squadron on the other hand launched 17 French cargo drops. F/Sgt Lawrence, flying STATIONER 108, dropped three of his four agents but, in addition to the remaining agent, brought back a container that had hung up. P/O Yardley, F/O Lyne and P/O D A Hayman flying PERCY 7. Both making DR runs from le Blanc (Indre). Yardley first over target reported seeing another Halifax circling in the area. Lyne next to drop reported parachutes seen on the ground south of the lights. Halifax LL289, flown by Hayman, was set on fire and crashed in the area of Longué-Jumelles (Maine-et-Loire), (13km NNW Saumur) where five of the crew are buried. Two of the crew were taken PoW but one, Sgt A Lyall was injured badly enough to have been repatriated. It was the loss of a very experienced crew.

The following night, the 2/3rd, of the 21 Halifax sorties despatched from Tempsford, five went to Belgium. Of the two Belgium successes from 161 Squadron, Capt Piltingsrud flying via Givet dropped two agents and two packages blind on his pinpoint FLAVIUS. His second target, a reception OSRIC 58, received a further two agents fifteen containers and three packages. S-phone contact was made with the ground but transmissions from the aircraft went unheard. W/Cdr Boxer flew a lone Hudson to France, completing HALS, outstanding from the previous night. In clear weather on a reception flashing 'S' he was forced to drop his five packages downwind from 500 feet.

The only success from three 138 Squadron Belgium sorties was flown by F/Lt Johnson, with him, making his operational debut, was

F/O Pleasance. In good visibility they made their first DR run from the lake north of Chimay to PLAYBILL 4 where they dropped two agents and three containers. From here they made a DR run to TYBALT 12 to drop the remainder of their load, twelve containers and two packages.

F/Lt T M Thomas flying operations RODERIGO 1 & OSRIC 77 in Halifax LL307 took the southern Holland route to Belgium crashing 1km SW Stavenisse on the tip of the Island of Tholen. All the crew and two, Sgt H Filot and Sgt Stroobants, of the three Belgian agents on board died. The third, G Masereel, survived the crash but was wounded and although captured he did survive the war.

F/Lt H Stiles, DFC, three minutes into his flight after taking off Halifax LL284 in the half light of dusk, lost his port inner engine at an altitude of 100 feet. Unable to maintain height he made a skilful crash landing close to the airfield at Sandy. (There is mention in the accident report that the port outer may have also lost power). The aircraft caught fire, although the crew survived, four were seriously injured. His intended target was TYBALT 29, in Belgium. This was F/Lt Stiles 59th operation and the last of his second tour.

Seventeen French cargo drops were completed on the 4/5th, three failing from 138 Squadron. F/Sgt Mackay had an engine failure after take-off, made a circuit of the airfield and successfully landed. He was to have flown an SIS target ORANGE. F/Sgt Paterson having made two DR runs from the islands in the Loire to his 'no reception' target VENTRILOQUIST 5 was hit by flak on the way home. He lost an engine just inside the UK coast compelling him also to make a fully laden three engine landing at base.

The nose of the wreckage of Halifax LL284 NF-E which crashed taking-off from Tempsford for Belgium on the 2 June 1944. The words 'Old Bill' can just be seen. Miraculously the crew survived, albeit with injuries. The pilot was F/Lt H Stiles, DFC. (H Stiles via K A Merrick)

Above: *Wreckage of LL284 looking back from the nose.* (H Stiles via K A Merrick)

Right: *F/Lt H Stiles, DFC.* (H Stiles via K A Merrick)

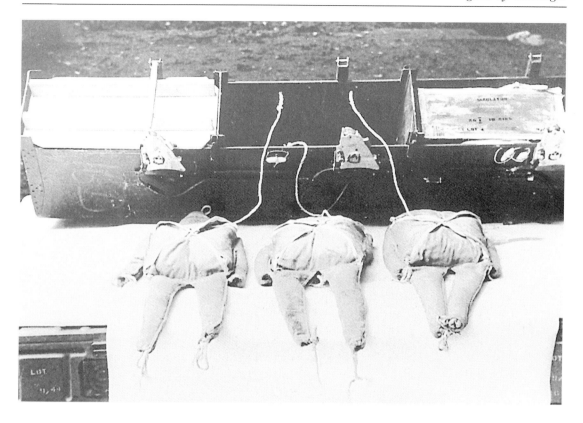

AATDC/828/1/Tech/A700.
Sheet 8.

Gingerbread Men
Above: As delivered by
container
Left: Stacked ready for
delivery by despatcher
through hole in fuselage.
(Courtesy Airborne
Museum)

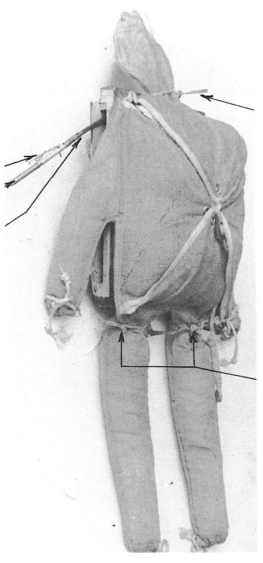

A Gingerbread Man
(Courtesy Airborne
Museum)

Six STATIONER sorties flown by 161 Squadron, were all successful.
The 5/6th June 1944, 'D-Day', saw seven 138 Squadron aircraft and
four from 161 Squadron take off on operation TITANIC 1 to drop a
phantom army of dummy parachutists with packages that simulated gun
fire. Operation TASK 2 was to drop 'Window' metal strips to confuse
the German radar. Stirlings from No.149 Squadron were also involved
in this deception taking place in the Yvetot (Seine-et-Maritime) area,
inland some 40km E of le Havre. Some low cloud, base 1,000 feet, over
the target area was discernible but 'Gee' fixes and ground detail enabled
the area to be identified. Little enemy action was encountered although
P/O Jones reported a searchlight and small arms fire from the St-Pierre
area (probably St-Pierre-Lávis, 10km NW of Yvetot). He also
commented 'six large and six small brought back, no time'. It would

appear that only two minutes were allowed for the drop. P/O Smith (161 Squadron) reporting, 'Window dropped as briefed but a few parcels of smaller type left due to insufficient time'. F/Lt Kidd (138 Squadron) said 'Drop made as ordered, window later'.

These dummy parachutists were known as 'Gingerbread Men' and were made of hessian, stuffed with straw (says the Airborne Forces Museum, where an example can be seen – more likely stuffed with kapok) and carried a rifle fire simulator. They were about 30 inches tall and looked like a pigmy scarecrow. Forty were launched from inside a Halifax fuselage by the despatcher and each bomb bay container probably carried another eight. The American equivalent was made of rubber and was inflatable, it looked aggressive and weighed a lot more. The despatcher, also dispensing 'window', had a very busy night.

F/Lt Johnson flew TITANIC 4. With the cloud base at 1,000 feet and visibility fairly good, 'Gee' and ground detail fixing their position on the corner of the marsh north of le Mesnil-Vigot (some 14km NE St-Lô, south of the Cherbourg peninsula), at 00.43 hours. From 800 feet they dropped two three man parties of the 1st SAS Regiment. These consisted of one officer and two other ranks, the first units of the invasion force to land. Their mission was to create a furore with Very pistols and gramophone created noises among the parachuting dummies, as part of the FORTITUDE deception plan. Johnson reported the containers were dropped ten seconds after the last man due to a technical hitch in the lighting. They were four minutes over the target. Johnson had now flown for four consecutive nights.

At this time Group Captain R Hockey was on the planning staff for OVERLORD and said that;

A CARPETBAGGER Liberator B-24H No. 259 at Harrington, 12 August 1944 – Pilot Melinet. Note the special nose and mid-upper turret. A Liberator of this type probably took Violette Szabo and her three companions to France on the 6/7 June 1944. (Carl Bartram via Harrington Carpetbagger Museum)

He was pleased to include his old Squadron 138 in the spoof raids over the Pas-de-Calais. They carried out this operation, whose timing was critical, in the manner to be expected, which certainly helped to delay the enemy armour and movements towards to the real battle.

Four further 161 Squadron operations were flown, three by Hudson to Holland. All were SIS targets, HARLECH, flown by F/Sgt Morris, ST EDMOND, by F/O Ferris and WESTMINSTER, by F/Lt Menzies. Morris, in very poor visibility, found his turning point at Roosendaal but then the intercom with his gunner went u/s. It was decided that this wasn't the place to hang about under such circumstances and abandoned the sortie. Ferris dropped his agent, at his own request, some 8km SW of his drop point where he made for Moergestel Wood (just east of Tilburg). During the drop, flying at 700 feet two rockets were fired from the ground which blossomed out into two reddish flares at 3,000 feet. Menzies made his DR run from Rossum (on the Waal north of S-Hertogenbosch) identifying a wood south of his pinpoint here dropping two agents blind in 'indifferent visibility' at 700 feet below 10/10th cloud with a base of 1,000 feet. Most of this flight seems to have been flown at 50 feet!

P/O Tattersall in the meantime flew a Halifax to France operation POLITICIAN. Making a DR run from Buzançais (Indre), to 30km SW of Châteauroux (it is said), he dropped, from 700 feet, five passengers, ten containers and three packages. Although picking up the reception on his first run he found great difficulty getting on to it as it was badly lit. This was the very first JEDBURGH drop consisting of Capt W R Crawshay, Capt L Legrand, 2nd Lt C C R Mersoil and coded HUGH, Capt J Tonkin and 2nd Lt R Crisp jumped with them. Future SAS JEDBURGH operations were serviced by aircraft of No.38 Group and the CARPETBAGGER force. On the way home Tattersall, flying at 6,000 feet in a position of 49° 05′N, 02° 48′W, reported seeing a submarine ten miles off on the port side. It submerged when they approached. (No.3 Group said they weren't interested!)

The following night the 6/7th, five agents were parachuted by F/Lt Caldwell (161 Sqn) from 800 feet onto CHARITE in the Preuilly-sur-Claise (Indre-et-Loire) area. He then delivered eleven containers and six packages onto a STATIONER target. S/Ldr Wilkinson also 161, dropped five agents onto an SIS target, GONDOLIER 9, in the Somme area and F/Sgt Lawrence of 138 Squadron, making a DR run from Clermont-Ferrand, dropped two agents and 12 containers onto DONALD 6, his second SIS target, ASPHODEL, lacked a reception.

A further nine 138 Squadron sorties flew to France. One of these was flown by F/Lt G Kidd, SIS target BEAUNE in the Montereau area, who watched the reception committee come out of a house and position the lights in a field as he circled in the moonlight!

The night of 7/8th was an appalling one for 138 Squadron, nine sorties were to take-off for France, however, S/Ldr M A Brogan failed to do so. His Halifax LL390 swung on take-off, ineffective brakes on wet grass, caused the aircraft to strike a concrete pill-box collapsing the undercarriage and writing off the aeroplane. There were no injuries. He was to have flown HISTORIAN 10 a *reseau* operating in the Blois/Orléans area. Another crew led by F/O F H Lyne, RCAF, flying Halifax LL416 was also to fly HISTORIAN 10 but was lost before reaching their target, flak setting the aircraft on fire. Sgt A M Hinds, RCAF, the only survivor, baled out and landed in a wood near Nouan-sur-Loire (Loire-et-Cher). The six crew killed are buried at la Ferté-St-Cyr some 26km NE Blois just south east of Nouan. Hinds was hidden in a house near St-Viâtre some 40km south of Orléans until liberated by the Americans on the 17th September.

F/Sgt A D MacKay, RCAF, flying Halifax LL466 outward bound for DONALD 26 crashed and burst in flames on impact 2km S of Doudeville (Seine-et-Maritime), 11km N Yvetot, some 45km east of le Havre) all seven crew were killed. They are buried in St-Sver cemetery in Rouen.

There was yet another loss this night within the same area when Halifax LL306, flown by F/Lt H C Jones, RAAF, flying two SIS sorties PERIWINKLE & WALT 3, crashed with none of the crew surviving. They are buried in the churchyard of Veauville-les-Baons (4km N Yvetot just 6km south of where F/Sgt A D Mackay and his crew fell). Jones joined 138 Squadron on the 25th January 1944, two days before I arrived.

F/O Strathern, flying a 'no reception' sortie to HISTORIAN 3 in the Châteauneuf area, reported a twin-engined aircraft, showing navigation lights, dropping four to six flares in a line over the target area. F/Lt Johnson returned early from HISTORIAN 8 with engine trouble and intercom problems with the rear gunner. The aeroplane would not climb with full 'revs' and boost.

This night 161 Squadron mounted seven Halifax and one Hudson sortie, they were all cargo drops. F/O Johnstone on his way home from DIPLOMAT 5 flying at 8,000 feet was attacked for twelve minutes by a Ju 88 some 20km NE Beauvais. The Ju 88 was first sighted some 300 yards on the starboard quarter and came straight in, the rear gunner opening fire with a ten second burst. The enemy replied to Johnstone's corkscrewing aircraft with cannon and machine gun fire giving off white and red tracer. Some eight to twelve attacks were made in quick succession, so quick, that the rear gunner believed there were two attacking aircraft. After the final attack the enemy disappeared in a dive to starboard the rear gunner confident that he had hit it. In the meantime flak now burst at the aircraft height hitting it behind the starboard inner nacelle making a hole about a foot square to accompany the holes already made by the nightfighter. Before the attack, red fighter flares had followed them and they saw a large dull red explosion on the ground. Johnstone, injured, brought back his aircraft and was awarded the DFC for his effort.

Flying low level by moonlight through defences now widely alerted was proving to be a very hazardous occupation. There had to be a change in tactics and it was now decided to fly at height over the battle fields, – where the night fighters waited for them!

The 7/8th was also the night that Violette Szabo was parachuted in for her second and fatal mission. I am told a USAAF B-24 from Harrington, piloted by Lt Fenster, was sent to Tempsford to pick her up together with three others who were to accompany her. These were named as P Liewer, her first mission partner, R Mortier and Lt Jean-Claude Guiet, an OSS radio operator. It is said that Vera Atkins was once again at hand to escort Violette to her aeroplane. A report to Harrington, dated the 18th June, for operation STATIONER 110B (Seamstress/Porter/Salesman/Guardian) says, a message from the field states that 50% of the packages didn't open but did not mention the arrival of the agents.

Violette Reine Elizabeth Szabo, née Bushell (Louise), George Cross, Croix de Guerre. Three days after arriving in France having damaged her ankle she held off an SS ambush with a machine gun allowing her companion Jacques to escape she was shot at Ravensbrück on 26/1/45 (Courtesy Special Forces Club)

Robert Mortier accompanied her on the second mission.

It was almost a week before the Tempsford Squadrons got themselves airborne again, 138 on the 13/14th got two cargo sorties airborne to start a lengthy nine night assault on 61 French targets 39 being successful. Each were delivered 15 arms containers plus a number a packages. On the 14/15th S/Ldr Rothwell making a DR run from the Loire delivered an additional two agents onto PETER 38, he was aided by 'Rebecca' and S-phone.

No.161 Squadron Halifaxes were also airborne again on the 14/15th. Like her sister Squadron their effort was mainly devoted to cargo drops in France although on the 16/17th June HARRY 21 had three sorties

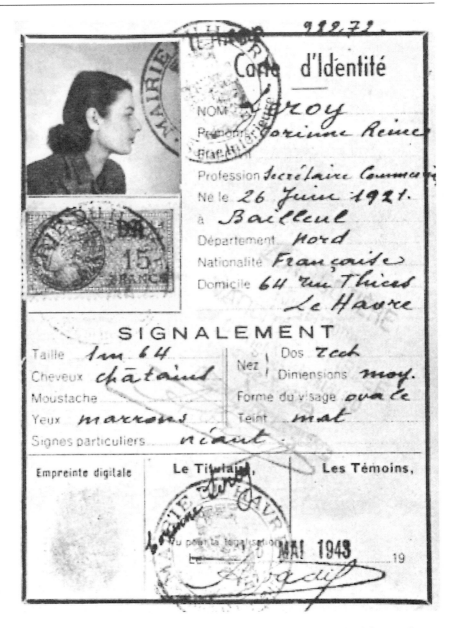

targeted. F/O Johnstone dropping 15 containers and eight packages onto it, P/O Green reporting 'no reception' and Capt Piltingsrud dropping two agents in addition to cargo. He reported it to be 'very dark'.

HISTORIAN was the only other target to receive agents in addition to war loads from 138 Squadron during the month of June. On the 17/18th HISTORIAN 2 appeared three times on the operations board. W/O MacFarlane, P/O Yardley and F/Lt Johnson making DR runs from Châteauneuf-sur-Loire, the latter refusing to drop since the wrong letter was flashing. The other two in spite of poor morse from the

dropping site each dropped four agents with a mixed load. Arriving back in the UK both MacFarlane, and Johnson reported seeing a line of stationary searchlights (Johnson said roughly from Rochester to Beachy Head) and what appeared to be six pilot-less aircraft flying north at a height of 10,000 feet. 'There was much flak, searchlights, could see reddish lights. One aircraft coned did not appear to be hit by flak'. The battle of the V1's had begun.

The last visit of the month to this reseau was on the 21/22nd when W/O MacFarlane dropped another six agents plus containers onto HISTORIAN 12, F/O Levy reporting 'no reception' on the same target. F/Sgt Lawrence made a cargo drop onto HISTORIAN 16.

The final 138 & 161 Squadron sorties for the month of June, the 29/30th, were centred upon two targets, HUBERT 12 and FREDERICK 2. Eight aircraft to the former and four to the latter. HUBERT 12 was situated to the north of Nantes and from the operational reports it appeared that utter chaos reigned not only on the ground, but also in the air. F/Lt Yardley gives us some idea where the target was located by making his DR run from a lake 47° 31′N, 01° 25′W (Grand Reservoir de Vioreau some 34km to the north of Nantes). 4/10th cloud with a base at 3,000 feet covered the area. All agreed that the reception was very poor. F/Lt Levy flew around for 30 minutes at 100 feet said it wasn't properly laid out, all he could see was an orange light on the apex of a barn roof and a number of parachutes laying on the ground. One pilot reported that he saw four aircraft milling around

Six Canadian members of W/O2 L L J McFarlane's (far right) crew. (L to R): F/O W F Tripp (Bomb Aimer), F/Sgt C S Buchan (Despatcher), F/O J A Galbraith, DFC, (Navigator), W/O H Knox WOp/AG), F/Sgt J H Walker (Air Gunner) – the RAF Flight Engineer, F/Sgt C S Burge, lived off base and was not available for this photograph.
(J A Galbraith)

at low level in the target area. To add to the confusion two Hudsons from 161 Squadron were also flying this target, F/O Ferris dropping six packages on a 'very poor reception' and F/O Ibbot failing to drop after circling for 20 minutes. To summarise, four 138 crews reported they found HUBERT 12 but no letter flashing and returned without dropping, three crews completed and one reported 'no reception'.

FREDERICK 2 fared a little better, two crews completing and two failing because of the weather. 10/10th cloud covered the target, F/O Wallace breaking through at 1,200 feet and pinpointing the lake to the north of the target. F/Sgt Paterson broke at 400 feet reporting it was a very good bonfire reception. F/O Carley passed over the reception but could not find it again as it was obscured by heavy rain. F/O Witham could not break through the cloud at 1,400 feet and came home. Two Hudsons of 161 Squadron were also on this target F/Lt Menzies under dark cloud cover of 450 feet found three bonfires in line, weather bad, and one package of his eight sticking making it necessary to make a third run. P/O Ragan also dropped eight packages.

Five of the aircraft engaged on this operation carried second pilots under training (F/O O'Bern, P/O Strathy, F/Sgt Hardie, F/O Sephton and Sgt Oullette – F/O Carley had had his 'baptism of fire' the previous night) all took their place on operational duty the following week, bringing 138 Squadron to full strength.

No.161 Squadron had a spate of engine problems causing P/O Tattersall to return early on the 22/23rd with a u/s port outer after 16 minutes in the air. The 27/28th saw F/Lt Caldwell returning early with an oil leak in his starboard outer and F/Lt Loos coming home on three engines after losing his starboard outer shortly after completing FIREMAN 11.

The month of June for Tempsford had been difficult. 138 Squadron bearing the brunt of the losses and of the 24 crews operating during the month, nine flew in excess of eight operations, three flying ten or more (W/O MacFarlane flew 11). Five crews were lost and a further two aeroplanes were lost on take-off making 138 Squadron's loss for the month seven aeroplanes. Their losses during the last two months now totalled twelve.

The Halifaxes and Hudsons of 161 Squadron were also worked hard but were without loss, although F/O Johnstone's encounter with the Ju 88 and flak took only nine days to get his 'X'- X-ray airborne again. Six 161 crews flew in excess of seven operations (one ten). Three Lysander pick up flights were made before 'D-Day'. With the invasion army spread out across Normandy it is not surprising they did not fly again until 2/3rd July exactly one month later. 1,115 pigeons were dropped.

* * *

The beginning of July now saw the American ground forces in complete command of Cherbourg and the entire Cotentin peninsula. The British and Canadians were held up in the ruins of western Caen.

July was going to be another busy month for both Squadrons. All of 138 Squadron's 173 sorties were bound for France. Likewise with the exception of one sortie, which went to Belgium, 161 Squadron Halifaxes flew 82 French sorties. The average load was 15 containers and seven to eight packages. A number of sorties flown by both Squadrons ended at Blida in North Africa, here to be rearmed for drops to be made on the return flight to the UK.

The majority of 138 Squadron targets in the opening days of July appear to be in the departments of Loire-et-Cher, Loiret, and Nièvre (i.e., HERMIT, HISTORIAN and GONDOLIER). Thus supplying an active SOE line not far from the battle front. It's not so much the delivery of the stores that is outstanding but the reception of them under what must have then been difficult and dangerous conditions.

The 5/6th July saw W/Cdr Burnett break the monotony of cargo flights by parachuting four passengers in addition to fifteen containers and seven packages, onto DONALD 19 a target in the Sancerre (Cher) area. The following night, the 7/8th F/Lt J Kidd dropped seven passengers in addition to the norm of 15 containers, eight packages, onto SCIENTIST 103 in the Corrèze area. This would appear to be the Inter-Allied Mission TILLEUL referred to by M R D Foot, which 'imposed important delays on enemy reinforcements for Normandy'. Another drop executed the same night by F/O Palmer onto DIPLOMAT 4 included three passengers and this could have been the completion of the EUCALYPTUS team, partly dropped by F/Lt Thomas on the 27/28th June.

In the meantime 161 Squadron opened their July Halifax sorties by successfully servicing six STATIONER targets in the Pyrénées. The next night, the 4/5th, saw the month's only deviation from France, P/O Bennett making a cargo drop to Belgium operation OSRIC 62. The same night F/Lt Loos dropped three agents on PLAYBILL, but was unable to complete his second target TOM 74.

The 5/6th saw four Hudson sorties to Holland. HARLECH flown by F/O Ferris failed because of the weather. F/O Ibbott dropped two agents onto ST MARK and P/O Morris dropped three onto RODEX 1. Regrettably the fourth, Hudson FK790 flown by F/Lt J W Menzies operation FIVES 1, was shot down by a nightfighter over the Waddenzee, Holland. Sadly none of the crew survived neither did the four Dutch agents on board, P J Quint (Fives), P Verhoef (Racquets), J A Walters (Bowls) and J Bockma (Halma).

A further disaster was avoided by the skilful piloting of P/O Tattersall whose Halifax struck some electric cables just prior to reaching target STATIONER 147. They made their DR run to the target from Isle-Jourdain (Vienne) a small town on the river Vienne some 40km SE of Poitiers. Ken Tattersall states that;

> . . . it was a beautiful moonlit night and they decided that they would fly as low as they could to avoid the night fighters. The rear gunner said that every time I pulled up he could see birds in their nests! We were

nearing the target when there was an almighty bang, the rear gunner said his turret was shaking and I said 'not as much as I was!' As all the engine temperature gauges were normal I did not give it another thought until I realised that the airspeed indicator was showing zero. I called down to the navigator to ask him what his ASI was reading and he, not at all pleased, said his was reading zero too. This confirmed that the pitot head had gone and that from now on the navigator was going to be the hardest worked member of the crew!

They dropped their load without any further problem and made their way home at 8,000 feet. It was daylight (0500) when they reached Tempsford and the Squadron Commander (W/Cdr Boxer) in the

F/O K R Tattersall, DFC. (Kenneth Tattersall)

control tower advised Ken to come in low over the two fields before the runway and made a smooth, almost perfect, landing. His crew, however, were not impressed and said he should lose his pitot head more often if it made for better landings! It appeared that the Squadron Commander was not impressed either calling Ken Tattersall 'a lucky b......!', not without reason since about a foot was missing from two of his propellers (they were made of laminated wood). Ken further says that had he been a few yards either side of where he struck the wire he would have thumped a pylon. The aeroplane, in spite of two new engines, was never used again on operations.

F/Lt Caldwell dropped five passengers who were 'jumping well and without hesitation' north of Paris in the Clermont area onto DONALD 6. He picked up Tempsford 'Rebecca' (now a permanent aid for returning aircraft) 90 miles out at 8,000 feet .

The 7/8th regrettably saw the loss of another 161 Squadron aeroplane this time a Lysander V9490 flown by Capt P Hysing-Dahl on operation PALAISE. He was unable to deliver his three passengers and, on his way home, miscalculated the corridor at the beach-head through which he should have flown. He was shot at by the Americans who hit his wing almost removing an aileron and puncturing his oil tank. Short of oil the engine seized and stopped. He ditched in the bright moonlight, the aircraft flipping over on to its back when the wheels made contact with the water. Unfortunately one passenger, Besnard was drowned. The remaining three survivors were picked up by an American motor torpedo boat but a second passenger, Leseur, did not survive his ordeal and died. The third, Baudry survived. Hysing-Dahl was wounded in the hand.

This was Per Hysing-Dahl's last Lysander sortie, post war he was to reach the highest political office in Norway, President of the Storling, the Norwegian parliament..

Sixteen 138 sorties went to France on the 7/8th. Most notable of these being seven passengers dropped from 700 feet by F/O J Kidd onto SCIENTIST 103 making his DR run from Lake Aron – this was, most likely, Etang-de-Beauloudray (Mayenne) east of Aron. F/O Carley flying SCIENTIST 104 was recalled after forty-five minutes in the air, his operation cancelled. P/O Palmer experiencing thunder in the target area made three runs to drop his three agents and parcels which were 'heavy and large'.

The night of the 9/10th saw four 'shuttle' sorties from 138 flown by F/Lt Walker and W/Cdr Burnett to DITCHER 47 and P/O Palmer and F/Lt Yardley to JOHN 60 and then landing at Blida in Algeria. W/Cdr Burnett reported low cloud and rain over the target and the reception being laid out in a little valley making the operation difficult in the prevailing conditions. In addition another 'Eureka' signal was being superimposed on that of his target. Walker could not find the target due to the weather and reported two 'Rebecca' signals were being picked up. Palmer dropped two agents and Yardley three, in addition to cargo both pinpointing on the Doubs, NE Chalon-sur-Saône, to make

The crew of Halifax LL251 NF-N, February 1944. (L to R): P/O Anason RCAF, (Bomb Aimer), F/Sgt Silverwood (Flight Engineer), F/Lt H A Walker, DFC, RCAF, (Pilot), P/O H Sauvaqueau, RCAF, (WOp/AG), P/O Johnson (Air Gunner). Kneeling: F/Sgt Hill (Despatcher), F/O Nichson (Navigator), Sgt Wall (u/t Flight Engineer). Walker successfully ditched LL251 in the Mediterranean in July 1944, only Johnson and Wall were flying with him at the time.
(H A Walker via K A Merrick)

their target DR run. It took them roughly seven hours to reach Blida.

Three Halifaxes departed the same night from 161 Squadron for Blida. Major Halle flew via STOCKBROKER 5, Capt Piltingsrud via JOHN 22 and P/O Tattersall via MASON 25, making his DR run in low cloud, from Verdun-sur-le-Doubs (Saône-et-Loire) some 15km NE Chalon dropping from 400 feet. The weather prevented Halle from completing his outgoing target. Piltingsrud describing weather conditions as abominable taking five runs to deliver, in addition to cargo, five passengers onto JOHN 22, a target in the Roanne (Loire) area,

F/O Sephton, (138) on the 10/11th made a DR run from the coast with the aid of 'Gee', dropping an agent onto SCIENTIST 107 a reseau in southern Normandy. This was Jack Hayes and his job was to supply tactical intelligence to the American army. Incredible as it may seem he recruited thirty local volunteers who infiltrated through the German line bearing his messages giving the position of enemy dispositions. His work finished in a month, the American army finding it of exceptional value.

The 11/12th saw the return operation from Blida. The three 161 Squadron crews and two 138 Squadron crews successfully completing PERCY 19 a target, from which 'Rebecca' signals were picked up some 40km away, as far as I can make out, in the area of Eymoutiers (Haut-Vienne). They all landed at Tempsford safely after approximately eight hours flight time. Of the seven aircraft that went out I can only account for six, Yardley appeared to have been delayed, not appearing on 138 Squadron operations again until early August.

This was P/O Tattersall's last operational flight of his tour having completed 39 trips for which he was awarded a well earned DFC. He came to Tempsford with me on the 27th January 1944. Of his home coming from Blida he says they brought with them a basket of fruit and some wine. Leaving the aircraft at Tempsford they opened a bottle of wine and shared it with their ground crew and the WAAF that drove them to de-briefing. What a wonderful moment that must have been for them.

F/Lt H A Walker, DFC, on the other hand took off Halifax LL251 from Blida at 20.50 hours eventually levelling out at 8,000 feet. At this height it was noticed that puffs of black smoke were coming from the port outer engine and the revs commenced to fluctuate between 2,500 and 2,900 rpm. Walker decided to return to Blida and radioed that he was returning. At 22.10 hours the engine spluttered and was feathered at the same time the bomb doors were opened and the containers jettisoned by the Air Bomber and the parcels by the Despatcher. It was found impossible to maintain height at 145–150 mph indicated with an air temperature of 28 degrees centigrade. Walker spotted a well lit ship some 10 miles away and having decided at 2,000 feet to ditch ordered the crew to ditching stations. The impact at 100 mph was 'no more than a good belly landing' (he had obviously had some practice!). The automatic dinghy release failed to work and those crew members that entered the fuselage to pull the manual release were overcome by the petrol fumes from the burst bomb bay overload tanks. Fortunately they were dragged through the rear escape hatch although it was discovered that the Navigator F/O M A Farr was missing and later presumed drowned. At 23.15 hours they were picked up by a lifeboat and after a search for the missing Navigator they were taken to the ship which was the British Hospital ship *Principasse Giovanni* bound for Oran. There were no other injuries to the crew. It was Walker's 70th operation and the last of his second tour.

On the 1st August S/Ldr R E Wilkinson took Hudson N7263 to Lyneham to pick up F/Lt Walker and his crew where from Rabat they had been flown in luxury by a BOAC Liberator. Landing at Tempsford the aircraft swung and struck a building writing it off. There were no injuries. Apart from the obviously shaken occupants, I don't think anyone could have cared, it was a very old aeroplane having been in service since August 1939.

The 17/18th saw S/Ldr Rothwell, P/O Palmer and F/Lt J Kidd each dropping three agents and fifteen containers from 600 feet onto GILES 2 a target in the Côtes-d'Armor some 60km NE Quimper. The agents were probably JEDBURGH teams. Rothwell flying home at 8,000 feet had his R/T and trailing aerials removed by lightning. Palmer complained he had difficulty over the target meeting one aircraft flying down wind at dropping height just after he had completed.

Author (second left) and P/O N St G Pleasance (far right) in Jack Dempsey's Bar, New York, May 1943. Nigel Pleasance was lost with his crew on the 18/19 July 1944 flying a 138 Squadron Halifax on Operation SHIPWRIGHT 9.
(Author)

Sources report the loss a 138 Squadron Halifax DT543 on the 17th July. There were no Allied aircraft lost at all on this date. In fact this 138 Squadron aeroplane was struck off their charge on the 20th July.

In the middle of a very successful period of operations there sadly occurred the loss of two 138 Squadron crews on the night of 18/19th. F/Lt J A Kidd flying Halifax LL364 was seen by the reception committee of DICK 89 to collide with an American B-24 Liberator piloted by Lt D A Michelson, USAAF, of the 801st Bomb Group, Harrington. Neither crew survived, there were eight in the American crew, Kidd and his crew are buried at Marigny l'Eglise which is 15km South of Avallon in the Yonne. His twin brother F/Lt G D Kidd, that night, was successfully flying SHIPWRIGHT 9. They were 20 years old.

The other loss was F/O N L St G Pleasance flying SHIPWRIGHT 9 who was shot down near St-Pair-sur-Mer (Manche). Sgt R H Lee

[8] The author had been with Nigel Pleasance at 22nd Air School in South Africa where they received their 'wings' and commissions at the same passing-out parade. Married and a sergeant in the TA before secondment to the RAFVR, Nigel was a great character and friend who will not be forgotten – he was on his eleventh operation when he was killed.

Short Stirling Mk IV LK119. This aircraft was originally in service with 138 Squadron as NF-R and was lost over Norway in March 1945 as MA-Y of 161 Squadron. (Mrs Madge Breeze via John Reid)

(WOp/AG) and Sgt J Allison (AG) are now buried in Bayeux (Calvados) having been moved from Avranches. Sgt W L Dalglish, RCAF (AG), on the other hand is buried at Beny-sur-Mer which is 4km south of 'Juno' Beach. It is said that he was taken prisoner and then thrown off a cliff by a German soldier. The remaining four names are on the Runnymead Memorial.[8]

The following night the 20/21st F/Lt G Kidd was out again flying a SIS target PARAPLUIE. Making a DR run from Châteauneuf he dropped eight passengers and fifteen containers from 650 feet. Leaving the target two fighter flares were dropped and he had to take evasive action. Electrical storms had been encountered both ways but on his way home at 11,000 feet both port outer and inner engines iced up (probably the carburettor heating had failed) losing 3,500 feet in height before they re-started.

F/Lt Palmer on the 30/31st July unloaded a further eight passengers together with nine containers on an SIS target MARTINI. The despatcher said one passenger was reluctant to jump. His second target PERMIT 7 lacked a reception. I have been unable to determine the purpose of these large personnel drops onto SIS targets. F/O Carley had the misfortune to have all fifteen of his containers hang up over his target FRANCIS 12. The bomb release panel lights indicated they had gone.

During the same period from 15/16th the 161 Squadron Halifaxes continued the good work, the Hudsons strangely quiet other than a few 'Ascension' sorties and a remarkable pick up flight by W/Cdr Boxer, the only one ever to be made without the aid of the moon. Moreover the

Short Stirling cockpit. The crew were all stationed behind the pilot, except for the bomb aimer who was in the nose when airborne (Short Brothers Ltd)

landing field (a small grass airfield east of le Blanc) had recently been ploughed up by the Germans. He said the take-off run was alarmingly prolonged! This was an SIS operation TENERIFE taking place on the 27/28th July.

P/O Ratcliffe appears on the list of operational crews for the last time on the 30/31st July. He was now 'tour expired' having arrived at Tempsford on the same day as Ken Tattersall and myself.

A number of crews had flown ten operations during July and those 138 Squadron crews who were nearly tour expired were to be posted to 161 Squadron to complete on Halifaxes. No.138 Squadron were now in the process of re-equipping with Stirlings. W/O MacFarlane was one the first to go and flew with both 138 and 161 during the month of July. F/Lt Yardley, F/Lt G Kidd, F/O Aitkin and F/O Strathy were to follow in August. The surviving twin, G E Kidd, never converted onto Stirlings and was to fly four more Halifax sorties for 161 Squadron before being posted. By strange coincidence a 32 year old F/Lt E P C Kidd (117499) joined 138 Squadron about the same time.

CHAPTER TWENTY-FIVE

August–September 1944

In August the Allied armies begin their thrust eastwards. A thrust that would seal the Falaise gap and liberate Paris. On the 15th August a landing was made in the Riviera by the Allies consisting mainly of US troops together with the Free French. In spite of this progress on the ground it was slow and pressure on the Tempsford crews continued.

No.161 Squadron made a bad start to their August operations when, on the 1st, S/Ldr R E Wilkinson, DFC, wrote-off Hudson N7263 when landing following a training flight. Six Halifax sorties were mounted on the 4/5th, three successes to France and two to Denmark. F/Lt Johnston dropping eight passengers onto MEXICO, a poorly lit target east of Paris, his DR run being made from Sézanne (Marne). He landed at Davidson Moor in Cornwall.

Regrettably F/Lt E A Loos, flying Halifax LL248 on operation BOB 166, crashed 5km SE of Vitry-le-François (Marne) which is SE of Reims. With the exception of the despatcher W/O G H Hall, who evaded, all were killed and are buried at Huiron. There is a small airfield on the map in the same position as they crashed and one wonders if this was where the attack came from.

Lysander V9748 was being flown by F/O J P Alcock to its target south of Vatan (Indre), operation PIROGUE, a double Lysander sortie. F/O Arkell, flying the second Lysander, reported that Alcock's aircraft had exploded when attacked with F/O Alcock and his passenger Lucien Germerau losing their lives. The remains of the aircraft came down near Messac (Ille-et-Vilaine) 32km SSW from Rennes. A crew from No.410 Squadron flying a Mosquito claimed to have shot down a Henschel Hs 126 that night and, as its silhouette would appear similar to that of a Lysander, there is little doubt that this is what it was.

Sixteen aircraft were launched by 138 Squadron the same night Four to Denmark and one a double target for F/Lt Palmer to France TOM 33 and Belgium PLAYBILL (SIS) on the latter he made his DR run from Avesnes to drop three agents. Lack of receptions in France were to fail three. A further fifteen sorties went to France the following night. Two were unsuccessful and F/O Ford, flying TOM 54 in the Péronne area, received hits in the tailplane but still managed to drop one agent and fifteen containers on target and was able, later, to land at Dunkeswell in Devon.

While 138 stayed on the ground on the 7/8th, 161 flew three

Hudson sorties two of which were to Holland, F/O Morris dropping S Postma (Sculling) and G H Reisiger onto operation SCULLING at Wieringermeer. Two Halifax sorties went to France. All five were successful.

Another sixteen 138 sorties were scheduled for the 8/9th but an SIS operation to have been flown to France by F/Lt Yardley was cancelled. Five of the remaining fifteen were to Belgium the remainder to France. Two of the Belgium sorties failed through lack of receptions. F/O Strathern coming home having dropped fifteen containers in a rising mist onto OSRIC 76 reported he was attacked by a Do 217 (a rare bird to encounter at this stage of the war and one questions its identification since this type ceased its role as a night fighter in October 1943). However, whatever the aircraft, Strathern's aeroplane was damaged by a burst of gun fire from it.

F/Sgt G W Paterson, RNZAF, flying Halifax LL308 to Belgium on operation OSRIC 45, was shot down. The only survivor, F/Sgt F E O Evans, RNZAF, the rear gunner, baled out and landed 2km south of Geraudot, 18km east of Troyes (Aube) (he must have meant SW as there is a large lake south of Geraudot). After burying his parachute, harness and Mae West he walked to a farm on the outskirts of Courteranges where he was given shelter. On the 12th August he attended the funeral of the five members of the crew who were killed in the crash and was told, by the FFI, that F/Sgt L P Searell, RNZAF, although wounded had been shot by the Luftwaffe. On the 26th August he contacted the Allied Forces and was flown home.

This night 161 despatched four Halifaxes to France. F/Lt Abecassis and F/Sgt Nicholls were both targeted onto TOM 53. Abecassis reported seeing an aircraft go down in flames just as he was running up for his drop. This must have been F/Sgt J W Nicholls, flying Halifax LL358, who crashed at Cugny (Aisne) some 22km SSW of St-Quentin. None of the crew survived and they are buried in Cugny

There were another thirteen successful sorties by 138 Squadron on the 9/10th each one dropping fifteen containers and seven packages onto targets in France – HARRY 31 receiving five sorties. The following night the final Halifax sorties of 138 Squadron flew to France. Lack of receptions failed three of them and one, flown by F/Lt Levy, returned early through engine failure. There followed seventeen days of Stirling conversion training, an aeroplane that could carry twenty four containers, the Halifax could only carry fifteen.

During the same period 161 Squadron were very active. On the 9/10th two Halifaxes went successfully to France and four Hudsons were dropping in Holland and Belgium. The only success here was F/O Helfer flying ROWING to Holland where he dropped two agents at Abbekerk. They were, F L J Hamilton (Rowing) and A M F Hamilton who had the unlikely code name of 'Tiddleywinks'.

A number of other successful 161 Halifax sorties were flown up to the 17/18th when F/Lt Green and F/Lt Abecassis dropped five agents between them onto BOB 256. They reported it was dark with low cloud and haze in the target area. On the 19th Major Halle and F/Lt Green parachuted three each onto BOB 172 in much improved conditions and these might well have been JEDBURGH flights. Eleven agents in all were dropped onto BOB targets. The moon waned on the 18th and, when it rose again for operations to begin on the 25/26th, Paris had been liberated.

No.138 Squadron mounted their first Stirling operations on the 28/29th putting eleven into the air. However, only four were successful, the remainder failed through lack of receptions. Two flew to Holland, F/Lt Levy flying RUMMY 1 and F/Lt Strathern flying GERRIT 1, but both lacked receptions.

This night 161 Squadron had the misfortune to lose a Halifax, LL388, flown by F/Lt P Green to Holland, on operation HENDRIK 1. Six containers and three packages were intended for this operation and three agents and one package were intended for operation STALKING. The aeroplane came down at Hedel approximately 4km north of S-Hertogenbosch. Green was wounded and taken PoW together with four others of the crew. W/O N F Slade, the navigator, died of wounds shortly afterwards and was buried at Engelen just south of Hedel. F/O A K M Dean, the Bomb Aimer, was the other death in the crew. The three Dutchmen on board were, J M Van der Meer (Stalking), K Buitendijk (Fishing) and G Kroon (Skating). The latter was believed killed by a 20mm canon shell but the other two managed to escape. It was the loss of a very experienced crew.

Six successful Stirling 138 maiden operational flights were made the following night, three Norwegian and three French. S/Ldr Rothwell parachuting the Squadron's first agents from a Stirling onto CRUPPER 7 in Norway, W/Cdr Burnett flying in a cargo drop to the same site.

Fifteen operations mounted for the last night of August, the 31/1st September, resulted in the loss of two Stirlings. F/Lt A J Wallace, RCAF, flying Stirling LK131 on his maiden flight, was sent to Holland in an attempt to complete GERRIT 1 which had been left uncompleted as there was no reception on the night of the 28/29th. Flak brought them down at Gilze-en-Rijen (halfway between Breda and Tilburg) killing seven of the eight crew members. The one survivor was made PoW. There was a German airfield at Gilze which claimed more than one Tempsford victim.

S/Ldr Brogan, returning on track for Roosendaal, in Holland, from a Belgium target KEES 1 in the vicinity of Maeseyck on the Maas, saw, ten miles (17km) to starboard, 'intense light flak lasting about four seconds'. This was followed by a large explosion and a ground fire which they assumed was from a shot down aircraft. From the position they gave it could hardly have been Wallace but, more likely, another incident near Eindhoven. At the time they were flying at 500 feet in clear weather and excellent visibility.

The other Stirling lost was LJ503 flown by F/O R B Hardie, RAAF, to BOB 325 in France. It came down at Lombard some 20km SW of Besançon (Doubs). None of the crew survived, six of the eight were

Australians, and are buried at Arc-et-Senans (Doubs). This was Hardie's second operation and it was said that he struck some trees. F/Lt Sephton flying the same target found himself in 10/10th cloud at safety height over the target area, wisely he abandoned his mission.

An operational loss is recorded this night of a 138 Squadron Halifax JD171. This was not so, no further Halifaxes were lost from Tempsford.

No.161 Squadron still flying Halifaxes flew five sorties this last day of August with a mixture of success. Two BOB targets were not completed due to 'cloud and poor visibility' on the other hand the same two targets were completed by other crews. F/Lt Kidd dropping three agents, fifteen containers and seven packages onto BOB 201 (probably a JEDBURGH operation). The remaining sortie was to Belgium, flown by F/Lt Abecassis on operation KARL, during which eleven containers went down with one 'hanging up'.

In spite of time spent converting to Stirlings, 138 Squadron in August flew 106 sorties. They also scattered, among a great deal of cargo, the amazing number of 927 pigeons. In doing so they lost one Halifax and two Stirlings. No.161 Squadron on the other hand flew 68 Halifax sorties and eleven Hudson dropping sorties (their pigeon count was 592!) Their losses were three Halifaxes and a Lysander. The eight Lysander pick-up operations for the month appear to have been the last, such was the progress made by the Allied armies. Likewise there were seven Hudson pick-up sorties which appear to be the tail end of this type of operation.

* * *

Tempsford's battle for the liberation of France continued into September with 138 Squadron making 40 sorties in all. On the 10th September F/Lt Witham flew an SIS operation, TITIAN, on which he dropped, in daylight from 400 feet, 15 containers onto three tricolours placed in a triangle. He made his DR run from the seaside town of le Crotoy, at the mouth of the Somme, some 20km NW of Abbeville.

Inter-mingled with these were six Danish sorties to the now familiar TABLEJAM targets where only cargo was dropped, together with four Dutch sorties between the 1/2nd and 8/9th.

S/Ldr G M Rothwell, DFC, flying, on the 8/9th, Stirling LK200 on his 71st operation DRAUGHTS & BACKGAMMON to Holland. 'Draughts' was T Biallosterski, on his second mission, and 'Backgammon', P de Vos. They met with a severe storm on the way out which they flew beneath, illuminating the waves with their landing light. They eventually flew into calm conditions and in brilliant moonlight made a pinpoint on the island of Vlieland.

After successfully parachuting their agents and cargo on the DZ at Spanbroek they turned for home setting course for Vlieland. They were flying at 400 feet as the island came into view when they struck what Rothwell thought was a balloon cable that had broken free. The starboard inner caught fire and shed its propeller. Only the port inner was showing fuel pressure, and his ASI was u/s. Unable to maintain height he crash- landed on the sand dunes at Cocksdorp on Texel. Rothwell was thrown clear through the roof and was made PoW along with three others of his crew, one of whom, F/Sgt R W Willmott, had a badly broken leg. Sadly three other crew members were killed.

During the same period 161 Squadron made their last Halifax flights on the 1/2nd September. F/Lt Kidd, flying operation DOWNEND 2, to Germany where, on the way to his DZ, he met with some light flak and green flares were dropped in front of his aircraft. He pinpointed a river north of Haren (some 28km east of Emmen in Holland) and set course for his target and in good visibility, he dropped blind from 800 feet above the ground the first US trained OSS agent, Jupp Kappius.

Major Halle completed AQUARIUS IV to Norway by dropping three agents, F/O Strathy attempting two Dutch targets, RUMMEY 2 and BOB II, without success on the former. These were 161's last Halifax sorties and these aircraft were probably among the ten aircraft ferried to Brindisi to replace those lost on operations over Warsaw.

Six Stirlings surplus to 138 Squadron requirements were transferred to 161 and their conversion training began.

A Hudson, flown by F/O Ferris to Germany on the 8/9th September, attempted an OSS operation, BIRCH, but had the rarity of having one of his agents refusing to jump. In the area of Germersheim (on the Rhine some 25km NNW Karlsruhe) one of the agents, who had been nervous

Stirling NF-H dropping in daylight over Belgium on Operation OSRIC. The pilots of this aircraft, on daylight OSRIC targets, were; F/Sgt L A Oullette (10 & 11 September 1944), F/Lt F J Ford (16 September 1944), F/Sgt H E C Shaw (17 September 1944). NF-H LK198 was lost over Norway on 8/9 November 1944 when W/O Oullette was the pilot. F/Lt Ford was lost on the same night. (F Bowman via K A Merrick)

F/O Spencer had the misfortune to swing LK208 MA-V on take-off, before a large gallery of spectators, and writing the aircraft off. He was about to embark on Operation OSRIC 900 on the 21 September 1944. (L Turner)

throughout, announced, on the fifth run over the pinpoint in clear weather, that he would 'no spring' The other agent, who was ready, decided that there was no purpose in him going alone, so Ferris brought them both back.

This night the first 161 Stirling operations, flown to France by F/Lt Levy and F/Lt Abecassis, were made to FREELANCE 15. From the isles in the Loire they made their way to St-Amand from where they made their way to their DZ. The location is believed to be St-Amand-Montrond on the river Cher (in the Code Postal there are 18 St-Amands!). Both, failing to see any reception on their first runs, made a second from Montluçon (Allier) but still without success. Abecassis remained 30 minutes over the target area forcing him to land at Ford because of petrol shortage.

Hudsons, other than those used for parachuting, were now day landing passengers, mail and urgent supplies. The Lysanders, to a lesser extent, were also engaged in similar activities.

With France almost liberated the attention of Tempsford was directed toward Belgium, although I imagine not quite in the manner they anticipated. On the 10th September sixteen Stirlings from 138 and two from 161 took-off in daylight for OSRIC 500 dropping in the fading light in excess of 200 containers (there were 22 hang ups!) onto bonfires of the Belgium White Army. A further 56 Stirling day sorties were carried out between the 11th and 21st without enemy opposition.

On the 21st F/O A J Spencer, of 161 Squadron, taking off Stirling LK208 in front of a large number of spectators, had the misfortune to swing, collapsing the undercarriage and breaking the aircraft's back. There were no injuries. The same day F/Lt Collis diverted to Tangmere, struck an obstruction on landing damaging the port wing of LK210.

What appears to be the last French operation took place on the 26/27th. Eight 138 Squadron Stirlings and, so the operations report would have us believe, one Halifax 'N', flown by a SAAF pilot Lt Nevin, taking off at 19.37 hours for Operation APPRENTICE in the le Blanc area. They dropped on lights and were home by 01.56 hours

The German Army were, at this time, engaged in crushing the shambles of operation MARKET GARDEN in the north. With the counter German Ardennes offensive to come, the Allies were not to move onwards into Germany until February 1945 leaving them, No.38 Group (who would have the additional responsibility of the Rhine crossing) and the Tempsford squadrons, a long hard winter. Targets in Norway, Denmark and Holland were now only those left for them.

It was not surprising that with the rising of the next moon, the 28/29th September, 138 sent four sorties to Norway and ten to Denmark. Only two of the Norwegian operations were successful. All were cargo drops, W/Cdr Burnett completing three SIS targets. The ten Danish sorties

Containers being recovered in daylight from Operation OSRIC. It would appear to be a 'C' type container which took four men to carry it, a piece of wood being passed through the handles provided.
(via K A Merrick)

The wreck of Stirling LJ932 NF-N, at Ludford Magna on 29 September 1944, following an attack from a Ju 88 over Denmark on Operation TABLEJAM 14 & 26. Both the pilot, F/Lt R W Read, and the flight engineer, F/O S Curtis, were awarded the DFC for this remarkable feat of airmanship. (Mrs W M Curtis)

consisted of 18 different sites, no mean task for the TABLEJAM reception committees from which only four were absent. 191 containers were dropped on the remaining 14 sites. F/Lt Strathern dropped two agents onto an SIS target POPLAR as well as servicing TABLEJAM 89.

F/Lt R W Read, flying Stirling LJ932, was returning from a successful two target operation in Denmark, TABLEJAM 14 & 26, having dropped, from 400 feet, twelve containers on each, when he met a Ju 88 over North Jutland. Now at a height of 500 feet it attacked, opening fire from below the port quarter. Read climbed into cloud but ten minutes later, at 3,500 feet, they were attacked again by the same aircraft who shot out the starboard outer engine and the starboard inner throttle box. They sustained heavy damage and for Read, with the assistance of his flight engineer F/O S Curtis, who was slightly wounded, to fly the aeroplane back to the UK in this condition was truly remarkable. They crash landed at Ludford Magna without further injuries other than to the two already injured. They had been in the air for six hours. A well earned DFC was awarded to both Read and Curtis.

The Squadron's September ended on the night of 30/31st with twelve sorties. Four to Denmark, seven TABLEJAM targets (all different sites from those of the 28/29th!) and eight to Norway, all were successful. F/Lt Witham dropping five agents into TABLEJAM 99 & 100 and F/Lt Ford dropping four agents into SADDLE 8 in Norway.

During the same period 161 flew two uncompleted operations to Denmark and two successes to Norway. On the 29/30th F/O J A Lamberton, flying Lysander V9749 on operation HAM, came down in the sea on a flight from le Bourget, Paris. He and his three passengers were lost. F/Lt Williams duplicated the same Lysander sortie taking out two passengers and three packages and bringing back the same number.

The introduction of the Stirling into Tempsford operations could

No. 138 Squadron Stirling, thought to be LK149, at end of runway. (H E C Shaw via K A Merrick)

hardly be called a success. The loss of five, four operationally, one pilot error and another disabled through a taxying accident during the month of September left much to be desired. Through the skill of F/Lt Read, aided by his flight engineer, F/O Curtis, the loss of a crew was averted. But there were the losses of a Hudson and a Lysander to be added to the months casualties. Tempsford was fortunate not to have been engaged during September in the supply drops of MARKET GARDEN where so many Stirlings of 38 Group met their demise.

Two SAAF pilots, Lt Nevin and Lt Haine, joined 138 Squadron this month to add their nationality to the nine that had already flown with the Squadron. British, Polish, Czech, Canadian, New Zealand, Australian, French, Norwegian, USA and now South African crew members made for an impressive cosmopolitan squadron. Later a Belgian gunner was to make it ten.

October–November–December 1944

The weather severely curtailed operations for October with No.138 Squadron flying only 40 sorties. Eleven of these went to Norway and twenty nine to Denmark. Their month started with twelve successful sorties on the 30/1st during which 72 containers and five agents were dropped onto Danish targets and 96 containers and four agents onto targets in Norway.

Of the remaining 28 sorties for the month eleven were unsuccessful. Nine agents were dropped into the seven Norwegian targets and four into the nineteen Danish. Two unrelated operations were aborted due to the navigator falling ill, a coincidence that had never happened before! Two unsuccessful operations (due to bad weather) to Denmark on the 15/16th required the assistance of Woodbridge to land them as Tempsford was fog bound. On the 22/23rd five sorties were despatched to TABLEJAM targets in Denmark all of which failed through the lack of receptions. A wasted, frustrating and dangerous night for those crews concerned, all landing at Kinloss. There were in all eleven failures for the month.

No.161 Squadron fared no better only ten operational sorties leaving the ground. It should be appreciated that many more operations were laid on for both Squadrons only to suffer last minute cancellations. On the 2/3rd S/Ldr Wilkinson flew an SIS sortie to Germany, operation BIRCH, where two agents were dropped blind. Thus completing this operation outstanding since the 8/9th September when one agent, in the Hudson of F/O Ferris, refused to jump.

The 4/5th saw three operations to Norway, WITHERS 1, flown by S/Ldr Abecassis, dropping three agents, eleven containers and seven packages returning to land at Kinloss. STIRRUP 2, flown by W/Cdr Boxer, was unsuccessful and SADDLE 7, whose pilot, F/O Prowse, dropped 24 containers onto it.

F/Lt Oliver, on the 6/7th, dropped two SIS agents from a Hudson into Holland on operation DOUG. S/Ldr G E Abecassis, from 161 Squadron, joined the four other successful 138 Squadron TABLEJAM operations to Denmark, flying Stirling LK238, but had the misfortune of being intercepted at an altitude between 500-1,000 feet by a night-fighter. The aircraft, on fire, crashed near Vemb with the death of W/O R F Philp, RAAF, a second bomb aimer – there was a crew of eight on board. He was initially buried alongside the wreck as was the

German practice at that time and re-interred at Gording in 15th June 1945.

Four evaded capture and their MI9 interrogation report makes interesting reading. P/O L N Flower, the fight engineer, 'sustained severe burns on the hands and face' but was separated from the rest off the crew some 15km east of the crash. Unable to continue he went to an isolated farmhouse were he was attended to by a doctor and spirited away to Sweden.

The other three evaders plodded eastwards for eleven days, nightly receiving food, shelter and, in one case, medical attention for their burns. They had walked approximately 110km traversing Denmark when 15km north of Arhus they found the assistance they were seeking. The remaining two members of the crew, which included the pilot, were made PoW. It is recorded that this was LK238's first operational flight.

No.161 Squadron was to suffer yet another loss on the 19th October, this time within sight of the airfield at Tempsford. F/Lt R V Levy, DFC, RNZAF, flying Stirling LK207 ten minutes into an air test, was seen to break up in the air, losing its tail section and crashing to the east at Potton narrowly missing the village school. Four other crew members were killed. Two regular members of the crew P/O Frost, despatcher, and F/Lt Hartley, navigator, not required, decided to remain on the ground. The aeroplane had flown four operations since its transfer from 138 Squadron on the 5th September and had flown a total of 84 hours 10 minutes. A heavy landing had been reported five days before its loss and the aircraft placed u/s. This crew had one more operation to complete to become 'tour expired'.

Numerous cargo flights were carried out during the month by the Squadron's Hudson aircraft as indeed were nine Ascension sorties. The latter coded WESTMINSTER were directing their radios onto Holland, only four were completely successful.

Bad weather had made it a disappointing October.

*   *   *

November started off optimistically enough for 138 Squadron who dispatched on the 1/2nd a maximum effort of eighteen aircraft, four to Norway and fourteen to Denmark. W/Cdr Burnett making his usual maximum contribution by parachuting five agents, twelve containers and six packages into SADDLE 10 in Norway. Seventeen of these Norwegian sorties were successful. No.161 Squadron also active this night dispatching four sorties to Norway and three to Denmark, six were successful. P/O Banbury was the last to land at Tempsford before fog closed it down leaving ten crews to divert to a chaotic circuit at Waterbeach. P/O Sleven returning from his first operation as captain found he could not retract his undercarriage when attempting an overshoot. He flew home to Tempsford in the morning with it down.

Six 138 sorties to Denmark of the 2/3rd gave some indication of the future weather, F/Lt Strathern struck by lightening, abandoned his sortie, and F/O Strathy not completing because of 'weather'. It was not until the 7/8th that 138 Squadron were airborne again when eight successful Norwegian sorties out of nine dropped three agents, 133 containers and 29 packages onto eight separate 'equine' targets. S/Ldr Watson was airborne for 10.52 hours before landing at Kinloss having dropped an agent, Yves Ogaard, seven containers and three packages into BRIDLE 7 a target some 45km east of Steinkjer. It would seem that he made his DR run from a lake just inside Sweden. F/Lt Sephton making three runs parachuted Erling Vestre and Tor Vinje into STIRRUP 4 together with 19 containers and nine packages, first having pinpointed Suldals Lake. F/Lt McGregor on the other hand found no reception at HOCK 1.

The night of the 8/9th saw seventeen 138 sorties and seven from 161 flying to Norway. Only one crew, that of 161's flight commander S/Ldr Read, completed. Twelve 138 Squadron sorties were decimated by the weather. S/Ldr Brogan's aircraft was struck by lightning which blinded him and rendered the instruments u/s but for the prompt recovery action of his bomb aimer F/O Wigley, sitting beside him, they would have undoubtedly dived into the sea. They jettisoned their load at base. Wigley was awarded the DFC. The aircraft of F/Sgt Witt of 161 was also struck by lightning. Two aircraft of 138, that of F/O Strathy and F/O Cornwallis had problems with their starboard inner engine and returned early.

There can be little doubt that night the appalling weather conditions, low cloud, icing at low level and thunderstorms, were responsible for the loss, on their outward journey, of two 138 Squadron aircraft and their crews. F/Lt F J Ford, flying Stirling LJ993, with two agents, Peter Deinbull and Arne Gjestland, twelve containers and eleven packages on board for CRUPPER 11, a target very roughly 100km north of Oslo, and W/O L A Oullette, RCAF, flying Stirling LK198 with twelve containers and six packages for PUFFIN 2, very roughly, 25km to the north of Oslo. It is assumed they came down into the sea the names of the two crews appearing on the Runnymead Memorial

It had been a terrible price to pay for the delivery of only 22 containers.

Five crews from 138 and four from 161 took off on the 21/22 for TABLEJAM targets in Denmark, six were successful, W/Cdr Boxer lacking a reception. On their return fog was beginning to blanket the country so most crews were diverted to Woodbridge. However, F/O Cornwallis' wireless operator failed to pick up the call and they flew north in search of a fog free airfield. They finally found one at Peterhead, a fighter airfield, whose main runway was considerably shorter than that of Tempsford. Having landed and taxying to dispersal the engines died through lack of fuel. The following day on their way home crossing the Humber the ever alert Royal Navy fired at them!

Both Squadrons on the 26/27th despatched another maximum effort. Fourteen aircraft from 138 flying to Denmark and four to Norway, 161 sending six Stirlings to Denmark and one to Norway, they also sent six Hudsons to Germany.

Only one 138 Squadron sortie failed when F/Lt Sephton, arriving at GROIN 3 in Norway, found there was no reception. F/Lt Carley, flying CRUPPER 30, made his DR run from Enderud (roughly 90km NW Oslo) and saw a bright reception on a frozen lake flashing the correct letter. Carley's crew took fifteen minutes to open, 'with great difficulty' the frozen doors covering the aperture in the fuselage floor. Making three runs, on the first from 700 feet, parachuting in Paul Strande, Alex Hagen, Peder Holst, Erling Malm, H Munthe-Kass. On the second and third, from 500 feet, dropping their twelve containers and six packages. All five agents were seen standing on the ground in the moonlight. The expected 'Rebecca' assistance, although restricted the range by the mountains in some areas, but now widely used in Norway, did not materialise. Carley landed at Lossiemouth. F/Lt McGregor also flying the same target took off twenty minutes after Carley and also made his DR run from Enderud. They too were unable to open the frozen hatch doors, three of the crew attacking it with a hammer. Eventually they were only able to drop eleven of their twelve containers one having hung up, bringing home to Lossiemouth the thirteen packages trapped inside the aircraft.

Two signals came from the field regarding this operation. One asking if the crew had any idea where they should search for the eleven

Crew of Stirling LK151 NF-E lost on Operation TABLEJAM 69, Denmark, on 26/27 November 1944. (L to R): F/Lt R R Witham, DFC, RAAF, (Pilot), F/O T P McHale, RCAF, (Navigator), Sgt R H Berrett (Flight Engineer), F/Sgt K Naylor (Air Gunner), F/Sgt A H Bedggood (Despatcher), F/O G H B Slinn, RAAF, (Bomb Aimer), P/O C Elleman (WOp/AG). (Mrs Iris Kingston via John Reid)

missing containers and two, suggesting the RAF use salt to prevent icing of the aperture so they could get the packages! My only comment is perhaps the Norwegians were taking too much for granted.

Of the Danish sorties that night Stirling LK151, flown by F/Lt R R Witham, DFC, RAAF, failed to return after dropping eighteen containers onto TABLEJAM 69 at Krengerup on the island of Fyn. It is thought they were shot down by a Ju 88 of 1/NJG3, crashing into the sea in Little Belt, near Assens. There were no survivors. Sadly a 19 year old, F/Sgt A H N Bedggood, an airgunner in the crew, was engaged to Iris Kingston, a WAAF who worked in the officers mess at Tempsford.

F/O Sleven also paid a visit to Fyn TABLEJAM 172/173 their success marred by flak from a mobile light flak battery damaging No.2 fuel tank and the bomb door control cables causing the bomb doors to drop open. The navigator and rear gunner were fortunate not be injured by shell splinters. They were diverted from a fog bound Tempsford to Lossiemouth. F/O Shaw was unable release his agent onto TABLEJAM 26/157, once more frozen hatch doors forced Shaw to bring him back home. Landing at Kinloss a military policeman wanted to know what a civilian without any identification was doing on the aeroplane! F/O Sicklemore was forced to return after his aircraft was hit by machine gun fire, his target was to have been TABLEJAM 150/87.

Of the 161 Squadron crews, F/Lt Gunton was caught by searchlights and flak, F/Lt Collis likewise and in addition was intercepted by a nightfighter after completing his drop of 23 containers. F/O Prowse was shot up by a Me 410 on his way to release 23 containers onto TABLEJAM 123, he was fortunate not to have any serious damage. F/O Woodward also met a night fighter and was in addition attacked by flak diverting him from his pinpoint. Low level, moonlit, winter operations to Denmark through a net of patrolling night fighters were not as easy as some historians and their Danish informants made them out to be.

Of the two Hudson SIS intended blind drops to Germany, ALDER,

F/Lt C Woodward and his 161 Squadron crew, late 1944. (L to R): F/Lt Woodward (Pilot), Sgt J Brooks (Air Gunner), unidentified (Flight Engineer), F/Sgt McCann (WOp/AG), Sgt L Dawson, RAAF, (Bomb Aimer), unidentified RNZAF, (Navigator), Sgt D Barsby (Despatcher). The last Special Duty operation flown by Woodward was VET 13 to Norway in April 1945, the first was the mysterious French Operation MARC 26 in November 1944. (D Barsby via K A Merrick)

The crew of LK149. (L to R): Sgt Clarkson, Sgt B Skinner, F/Sgt F Bowman, Sgt W Coulson, F/O H Shaw, F/Sgt R Buckingham, F/Sgt W Westwood. (H E C Shaw via K A Merrick)

flown by P/O Morris, and MULBERRY, by F/O Ragan, met ground fog over their dropping areas, (Ragan reaching Frieberg) which forced them both to return with their agents. Another SIS target, ASH, flown by F/O Ibbott, was a successful two-man blind drop. Of the remaining three sorties, VIVACIOUS II, flown by F/Lt Ferris, and FRILFORD, by F/Lt Webb, were both successful with Ferris, after identifying his dropping site, parachuting, blind, one agent and, likewise, Webb who dropped two. S/Ldr R E Wilkinson, flying Hudson T9463 to Germany on FLECKNEY 1 – a drop at Armstadt south of Erfurt, parachuted blind an OSS agent of Polish-German extraction. On the way home they were intercepted by a night fighter and the wreckage was found some 5km NE of Houfflalize near the south-east border of Belgium and Luxembourg. There were no survivors. The air gunner, F/Lt G H Ash, DFC, had flown twice with my crew in March. It is reported that the agent failed to complete his task. And it might be asked why the USAAF CARPETBAGGER force did not carry out this OSS mission?

It was the 29/30th that 138 Squadron flew fourteen sorties to Norway and 161 Squadron six. Only two got through, S/Ldr Watson dropping six containers onto an SIS target BEAVER 2 and F/Lt Sephton finding no reception at his target CRUPPER 23. The remainder failed because of the appalling weather, the worst of the century it was said. Pilots reporting 10/10th cloud at 2,000 feet and icing above it. A total of fifty sorties flown to Norway on the 8/9th and the 29/30th resulted in only 28 containers being dropped!

The month finished on the 30/1st with six successful Danish operations out of nine. P/O Shaw having suffered flak damage was forced to land at Carnaby, No.4 Group's 3,000 yards emergency runway on the Yorkshire coast. The Hudsons also flew seven Ascension WESTMINSTER sorties endeavouring to contact their informants in Holland, only three were successful.

In summing up November's operations one can only say that the appalling weather conditions were equally shared by those who flew them and by those manning the receptions on the ground.

*   *   *

December was to prove another miserable month. The 2/3rd saw three unsuccessful 161 Danish sorties. Four out of seven were completed by 138 Squadron. Weather forced F/O Strathy to return and F/Lt Strathern's aircraft was for the second time struck by lightning. F/O G F Nichols, flying Stirling LK143, failed to reach his TABLEJAM 169/177 target and crashed into the sea with, sadly, none of the crew surviving.

S/Ldr Watson, on the 5/6th, flew a solitary Stirling SIS sortie to Holland and dropped a mystery nine containers onto VAN-INGEN.

From the next day onwards fog curtailed much of the air activity in Southern England although Bomber Command, based in the north of England, continued its offensive. Ground mists and low cloud grounded the Allied Air Forces in Europe enabling the German counter offensive in the Ardennes on the 16th December to partially succeed. However five Hudson Ascension flights, homing onto Holland, took place during this difficult period, three important intelligence contacts being made. On the 23rd the fog cleared and the Allied air offensive in the Ardennes began.

Fourteen successful Stirling operations from Tempsford were mounted between the 23/24/25th for SHAEF reverting to their 'D-Day' role of dropping dummy paratroops in an effort to relieve the pressure from the Allies in the Ardennes salient. Coded TURMOIL 1 and 2 (the former load was seven containers, the latter four). 138's nine sorties went to the German side of the border, the five from 161 went through Belgium. Fog blacked out Tempsford on both return flights, the first time landings at Tangmere were made, the second on Christmas day, Lyneham in Wiltshire was used. The 27th saw all the diverted crews back at Tempsford making ready for operations to Norway.

On the 28/29th the weather over Norway was near perfect, clear skies, almost a full moon and in addition the Northern 'Gee' chain functioning well, resulting in ten agents, 120 containers and 74 packages being delivered. Several crews had difficulty in opening the fuselage hatch doors through icing, S/Ldr Read failing to do so brought his agent and packages home. F/Lt E Kidd's aircraft was struck by tracer but not before he had delivered his three agents, H Stridskelv, Gunnar Bjali, and Tore Fjeld, from 750 feet and his 16 containers and nine packages from 450 feet into REINS 7. The field report says two aircraft made a perfect drop, only one was sent from Tempsford to this target. Fog closing Tempsford on return most crews landed at North Creake in Norfolk which by all accounts was frozen solid!

The return to Tempsford at midday on 30/31st saw Norway again the centre of operations, most of the targets being duplicated. Twenty-one aircraft were dispatched in perfect weather, the full moon casting the shadow of the low flying aircraft on the water below. Only one of the seven 161 sorties failing when F/Lt Madders found 'no reception' at his CRUPPER 24 target, probably after F/O Prowse had delivered thirteen containers and five packets onto it. This was Madders second un-rewarded trip to Norway within 24 hours.

Fourteen sorties were dispatched by 138 Squadron with four failing. S/Ldr Brogan dropped five agents, eleven containers and eight packages onto PUFFIN 2 followed by F/O Sicklemore, with another thirteen containers and twelve packages – a lot of work for the reception committee, finding, collecting and hiding in the deep snow drifts. F/Lt Carley, further south, decided to abandon his sortie, HOCK 2, when he considered the weather conditions too dangerous for his four agents to jump. He was sent back the following night to complete, spending 26 minutes over the target area parachuting into the snow Th. O Lien, Ivar Tonseth, J P Bjelland and Alfred Floisand, together with twelve containers and fourteen packages. F/Lt R McGregor, RNZAF, was flying Stirling LK283 to operation CRUPPER 10 when F/O Shaw witnessed an engagement by flak from shipping, McGregor's aeroplane exploded with a 'terrific flash' and there were no survivors. East Moor, a Six Group bomber station, was the haven for those aircraft failing to beat the Tempsford fog.

The last night of the month the 31/1st saw seventeen Tempsford Stirling sorties celebrating New Year's eve on their way to Scandinavia, thirteen went to Denmark and four to Norway. Four TABLEJAM targets lacked receptions and two early returns of 161 Squadron were caused by the sickness of two crew members and a port inner failure causing F/Lt Collis to jettison his twenty containers. F/Lt Strathern returned early from Norway having been attacked by a Ju 88 which left his rear gunner, Sgt R E Austin, wounded.

Four Hudsons of 161 Squadron went to Germany on this night. Two returned because of the weather but F/Lt Helfer, flying ALDER, and P/O Morris, flying JUNIPER, successfully dropped blind two agents each.

Sometime during December G/Capt Fielden, having been hospitalised through an accident, relinquished command of Tempsford to G/Capt Palmer.

It has to be asked, just what justified the flurry of air activity to

Norway and Denmark, from November 1944 to April 1945 resulting in the loss of 28 aircraft (19 Stirlings, five Halifaxes and four Liberators) to Norway alone. At this time the Russians had cleared the Germans from the northern most territories of Norway and perhaps the possibility of their future influence in Scandinavia holds the answer.

Snow at Tempsford January 1945. At that time reputed to be the worst winter over Norway in living memory!
(H E C Shaw via K A Merrick)

January—February—March—April 1945

In the New Year the American Army Groups, aided by the British 21st Army Group, continued to mount their offensive in the Ardennes in an attempt to neutralise the German 'bulge'. Their advance was hampered by ice and snow and unimaginative leadership which allowed the bulk of the German army to escape eastwards and prolong the war until May.

Although Bomber Command continued their unrelenting offensive throughout the month of January, Europe's snow and ice brought the role of the Tempsford Squadrons to a virtual standstill. During four nights only three sorties took off for Norway and five to a French target, EXERCISE DOWNRIGHT 1, where, on the nights of 14/15 and 21/22, the opportunity was taken to baptise three new pilots onto operations. One failed because of the weather but the remaining four dropped a total of 69 containers and 24 packages. The 14/15th also saw the only 161 Stirling operation for January take place, weather preventing S/Ldr Read from completing EXERCISE DOWNRIGHT 1. There are no operational reports in the 138 Squadron files and this was the last French operation to be mounted by Tempsford.

Meanwhile snow had fallen over Bedfordshire obliterating Tempsford. In spite of attempts to clear the runways with shovels, training cross countries and sea searches for Bomber Command survivors in their dinghies were curtailed.

FETLOCK 2 was a Norwegian target to be flown on the 11th January by S/Ldr Watson and F/Lt Carley. Carley's trip was cancelled. Watson took off from Kinloss with the new 138 Squadron CO, W/Cdr Murray, as second pilot. Their task was to drop food to an isolated group at Naushorn 6km west of Torslake (I can find neither on my maps) in mountainous country peaking at 1,500 metres. When Watson arrived at the Norwegian coast at 08.12 it was daylight, so he aborted his mission. The following day they both got off the ground leaving Kinloss, Carley at 03.33 and Watson at 04.16. Carley reached the target area at 07.02 but was unable to see any reception lights. After circling for a short time he aborted. Watson was more fortunate, arriving over the target at 07.20, having pinpointed Sulen. Here he found a good reception laid out in a valley and flashing the correct letter. Owing to the mountainous terrain and it being quite dark he released his eight containers and five containers in one run from a height of 4,600 feet (a little in excess of 1,500 metres). It was now daylight and his run home really was low! He landed at Tempsford having been 11.44 hours in the air. A field report thanked them for the eight containers and five packages.

This was S/Ldr Watson's final operation with 138 Squadron. Promoted to Wing Commander he took command of 161 Squadron, succeeding W/Cdr A H C Boxer, DSO, DFC, who was posted to Staff College to continue his distinguished Royal Air Force career. Boxer's first Tempsford operation, as far as can ascertained, took place in May 1942 when, with the rank of Flight Lieutenant, he flew a 161 Squadron Whitley to France. Sadly W/Cdr Watson was to lose his life in less than a month.

The Hudsons attempted seven ASCENSION sorties, beaming into Holland for intelligence gathered behind the German lines but contact was made only twice. These were the last of the ASCENSION operations to be flown. On the 21/22nd, the commencement of the new moon period, two other Hudson sorties managed to take off for Germany, operations CARHAM 1 and COLBURN but both failed because of the weather. There had never been a month as bad as this since the arrival of the squadrons at Tempsford.

*   *   *

The 1st/2nd February saw 14 Stirling sorties (8 from 138) take-off from Tempsford for Norway, low cloud, rain, severe turbulence and icing at 600 feet were the order of the day.

Lt Haine and F/O Sleven aborting their sorties when meeting these conditions at 54 degrees North. However there were seven operations completed, four of them by 161 crews, landing on their return at Kinloss. Those who returned to Tempsford were allowed to drop their containers on the airfield. Jim Breeze says 'it was quite a sight to see next morning the multi-coloured parachutes scattered all over the airfield'. A procedure that should have been allowed long before this.

F/Lt Prowse reported he had 17 containers and four parcels hung up. F/Sgt Tucker of 138 Squadron had trouble with the retraction of his undercarriage on take-off. As his flight engineer, Sgt Haragan, was taken ill endeavouring to manually wind it in, it was decided to abort the sortie. I was astounded to read, in the Stirling Pilot's Notes, the complicated procedure for raising the undercarriage in an emergency. In addition, to raising the main wheels it took roughly 14 minutes winding a handle. To lower them it took 50 minutes! No wonder Haragan felt ill when he tried.

On the ground the Allies launched an offensive on the 7th March that would reach the Rhine.

A suggestion that the weather may be better over Denmark saw seven 138 Squadron aircraft take-off on the 9/10th for TABLEJAM targets,

F/Sgt Jim Breeze (Flight Engineer) seen here in the cockpit of Stirling LK119 NF-R. Jim was a member of F/O Sleven's crew and his diary was of great use to the author. (Jim Breeze via John Reid)

none completed. Worse, F/Sgt L S Tucker, flying Stirling LK279 on his second operation, TABLEJAM 190 to Denmark, was lost in a blizzard and, crashed into the little Belt, south of the Faeno Islands. There were no survivors. His 20 year old flight engineer, Sgt W M Haragan, was among them.

Before the next moon period 161 Squadron suffered another tragedy. On the 14th February F/O E Timperly, flying Stirling LK236, joined the Tempsford circuit from a local flight. In murky conditions a Mustang P-51, flown by F/O T W Kiley of 383 Fighter Squadron, USAAF, made an unauthorised low level pass at them striking the Stirling near the tail section. Both aircraft went out of control and crashed in a nearby field at Potton. There were no survivors.

The rising of the moon on the 20/21st February saw six 161 Squadron aircraft make for Denmark to service eleven TABLEJAM targets but four of these had no reception, including two that were flooded. No.38 Group sent 94 aircraft to Norway, half were successful.

During the next night the 21/22nd 23 Stirlings left Tempsford for Norway and Denmark. 138 Squadron handling all seven of the Norwegian sorties (completing six) and 161 completing seven to Denmark, in addition to flying off six Hudsons to Germany.

F/Lt Helfer, flying a Hudson on operation CARHAM, dropped a disenchanted captured German NCO plus four packs of leaflets into the Geissen area some 30km north of Frankfurt-am-Main. Records state that on his two other targets, PATHINO & POSTBOX, he dropped two and one package respectively – on what it is not said, but it is possible that someone parachuted blind with them. F/Os Morris (WALNUT, an SIS operation) and F/O Ragan (IMOLA/BOLINGBROKE) were beaten by the weather. F/Lt Ferris dropped three agents for operation COLAN and F/Lt Webb dropped two on an SIS operation coded MULBERRY. The remaining Hudson, T9405, was being flown on CROC, another SIS operation, by F/Lt D T Oliver and was shot down by flak at Meppen in Germany, some 15km east of the Dutch border. F/O J M Hartman, the airgunner, was very badly burnt in the crash and F/Lt F M Jarman, the WOp/AG, attempted to save him. The two crew who died were F/O J M Hartman and W/Cdr G Watson, DFM, the new OC 161 Squadron. Hartman was initially buried at Bekeloh, some 4km east of Meppen, and later at Reichwald. Watson, it was thought, died after having been taken PoW. The aircraft must have been shot down at low altitude otherwise they would have taken to their parachutes.

W/Cdr Watson was to be replaced by W/Cdr M A Brogan, DFC, a newly promoted Squadron Leader from 138 Squadron, a Command he was to hold for a little less than two weeks.

Of the 138 Stirling operations, that night, the weather prevented one Norwegian sortie from success. W/Cdr Murray, OC 138 Squadron and flying operation SNAFFLE 5, taking three runs to parachute four agents (Roger Backstom, Severre Arntzen, Aarge Larsen and Kjell Stordalen), eleven containers and nine packages. Both Flight Commanders, S/Ldr Brogan (to Norway) and S/Ldr Sephton (to Denmark) were out successfully this night.

The following night, the 22/23rd, fifteen 138 Squadron Norwegian sorties were despatched. S/Ldr Brogan, flying WITHERS 5, dropped seven containers but was unable to release his parcels as the aperture doors were iced up. Brogan reported it was a bad site, in a valley on the side of a hill making it impossible for him get lower than 2,000 feet above the ground to drop. He was away from base roughly nine hours. The field report, from WITHERS 5, complained that they had not found the containers and asked if and where he had dropped them!

F/O Shaw returned early with an electrical failure and F/O Sleven in sight of the Norwegian coast was attacked by a Ju 88 and an Me 110. The resulting corkscrew toppled the master gyro compass in the rear fuselage and the operation had to be aborted. They landed at Coningsby.

One 161 Stirling flown by S/Ldr Read to Norway was aborted because of the weather, but four Hudsons took-off for operations in Germany. F/Lt Helfer, flying CARSTAIRS, returned after 30 minutes with a 'technical problem', said to be his 'Gee' set and F/O Morris forced to return from COLBURN 1 because of the weather. However F/O Ragan completed IMOLA/BOLINGBROKE, dropping two agents not far from Miltenburg and F/L Ferris dropping three agents on his third DR run from Bingan on operation CLINT.

The next night 23/24 saw 161 Squadron making seven successful

Stirling LK149 NF-D lost in the North Sea off Denmark on Operation TABLEJAM 181, 23/24 February 1944 - F/Sgt E W Sinkinson was the pilot.
(H E C Shaw via K A Merrick)

sorties out of eight to Norway in spite of thick cloud and night fighters, one of which an Me 110, intercepted F/Lt Gunton before reaching his target GROIN 8 where later he dropped three agents, thirteen containers and five packages. Three other aircraft were successfully navigated to this target.

138 Squadron briefed seven crews of which three completed Norwegian targets and one Danish. One crew returning early with a sick bomb-aimer another, W/O Tomlin, swinging on take-off without damage, flew the same aeroplane the next night when sadly there was a loss. F/Sgt E W Sinkinson was flying his first operational flight in Stirling LK149 to Denmark on operation TABLEJAM 181. All were lost when they crashed into the sea off the west coast of Denmark. Two nights prior to this Sinkinson had flown his familiarisation flight to Norway with F/Lt Kidd. LK149 was the normal aeroplane of P/O Shaw and was one of the few Stirlings fitted with a radio altimeter

The 24/25th saw 161 Squadron mounting five successful sorties to Norway and Denmark. The three Hudson operations sent to Germany were not so fortunate. Two of them returning because of the weather and F/Lt Helfer managed to complete half of his two target sortie MONTFORD/EVERYBODYS and VASCO/TELEGRAPH. The pinpoints were about 15km apart. He was carrying four agents and managed to drop two of them on the former target which was near Nuremburg. Apparently they made wireless contact with London soon after landing. The weather made it impossible to complete the remaining operation and the agents were brought back.

Three Danish and nine for Norway were the task for 138 Squadron, three remained uncompleted. Capt Haine and F/Lt Wilkie were targeted onto WITHERS 5, last flown by S/Ldr Brogan on the 22/23rd. Wilkie complained about the difficult placing of the site, as had Brogan, but managed to get off his load from 800 feet. His packages drifted 500 yards off the line of lights due to the high wind. Haine spent 10 minutes over the target area having arrived 42 minutes before Wilkie, seeing no lights he went home. The field report said 'Load received OK perfect dropping. Have not yet found the first load (Haine's) thus still no food'.

Of the eleven Danish operations mounted by the Tempsford Squadrons on the 26/27th February the deteriorating weather washed out six, of the remaining six to Norway, the weather prevented the completion of two. F/O Shaw flying off the coast of Norway, looking for a pinpoint, had the misfortune to witness to port a burst of flak and an aircraft going down in flames into the sea. This was the demise of a very experienced crew led by F/Lt P B Cornwallis, flying Stirling LK272 on operation CRUPPER 27. His, and the names of his crew, are commemorated on the Runnymead Memorial. They first flew with the Squadron in September 1944.

The last day of February the 28/1st March saw Tempsford's 13 Stirling operations to Norway decimated by the weather. Winds up to 100 mph being plotted by one navigator and fuel being measured by the thimbleful upon landing, all for the delivery of a handful of containers. However, five Hudsons from 161 Squadron took off for Germany only one was abandoned because of the weather – F/O Morris flying an SIS target WALNUT, the second attempt. Another SIS operation, NERON, was completed by F/O Ibbott dropping two agents. The remaining three operations completed were those aborted by the weather on the 25/26th namely CARSTAIRS, COBURN and VASCO/TELEGRAPH. The latter flown by F/Lt Helfer who dropped his two agents near Nuremberg.

The appalling weather that continued into February seriously curtailed successful operations into both Norway and Denmark and undoubtedly contributed to No.138 Squadron's loss of three Stirlings. The tragic loss of a Stirling and its crew of 161 Squadron over the airfield at Tempsford due to a breach of discipline by a USAAF fighter pilot was unforgivable. The lack of information concerning the loss their of Hudson by flak over Meppen conceals, I believe, an undisclosed act of gallantry revealed only by a few comments on a Bomber Command loss card. It had been a difficult month for all concerned both in the air and on the ground be it at Tempsford or on the reception committees in Scandinavia.

*   *   *

Operations for March commenced on the 2/3rd when the weather improved over Norway allowing the completion of 15 sorties out of 16 attempted. The two Squadrons dropped between them six agents, 220 containers and 58 packages. In addition to four Stirlings, 161 Squadron despatched four Hudsons to Germany and one to Holland. Three failed

The crew of Stirling LJ999 NF-Q. (Back row L to R): F/Sgt W L Clarke (Despatcher), W/O M Maude, RAAF, (WOp/AG), F/Sgt J Breeze (Flight Engineer), Sgt J H Bloomer (Air Gunner). (Front row): F/Sgt T F Kyle (Bomb Aimer), F/O L G Sleven (Pilot), Sgt B Warsh (Navigator). F/O N E Tilly was the navigator when NF-Q was lost on the night of 4/5 March 1945. This was the last night of Special Duty operations flown by 138 Squadron and LJ999 was the last squadron Special Duty casualty. (Mrs J Breeze via John Reid)

because of the weather, WALNUT for the third time, ACACIA, and BENEDICT/EXPRESS/LEADER. F/O Ibbott completed an SIS operation, TARBES, by dropping two agents into Germany and the Dutch trip, BORSTAL, was completed by F/Lt Helfer dropping one agent over Barnewald.

A field report from a Norwegian site, STIRRUP 4, for this night, said 'Have opened one container which to our inexperienced eyes appears to be filled with old bricks. Send us instructions for the use of this revolutionary weapon in modern warfare!'.

The penultimate Special Duty sorties for No.138 Squadron took place on the 3/4th, nine to Norway and one to Denmark, flown by the Squadron Commander W/Cdr Murray. A further operation to Norway should have been flown by F/Lt O'Bern but his aircraft went 'u/s' at the last moment. 161 Squadron put four Stirlings into the air and two Hudsons. Of the Stirling sorties the weather failed four. Of the Hudsons BENEDICT/EXPRESS/LEADER again was a victim of the weather and the fourth attempt to complete WALNUT, this time flown by F/O Ragan who was intercepted by a Ju88 over Mildenhall when climbing out of Tempsford. Attacked from below, cannon fire from the Ju88, slightly wounded F/Sgt Stead, the air gunner, and severely damaged the control surfaces of the Hudson. Only the skilled piloting of Ragan got them back safely to Tempsford.

The wreckage of LJ999 at the southern end of Ringkøbing Fjord, Tippern Island, Denmark. The aircraft crashed after an on board explosion during Operation TABLEJAM 241. (Mrs J Breeze via John Reid)

The total effort for the night of the 4/5th March was directed at Denmark. Nine Stirling and one Hudson sortie were sent by 161 Squadron and the final six SD sorties to be flown by 138 squadron. The success of the nights' operations were marred by two losses. W/Cdr M A Brogan, DFC, the Commanding Officer of No.161 Squadron, flying Stirling LK312 to operation TABLEJAM 209, came down in the sea near Livo Island in Limfjorden, Denmark. There were no survivors, the sea slowly giving them up to be buried in three cemeteries in Denmark. Three of the crew had been awarded the DFC and one the DFM. W/Cdr L Ratcliff, DSO, DFC, AFC, took command of No.161 Squadron.

No.138 Squadron lost their final crew on the last of its SD operations when F/O L G Sleven, flying home from operation TABLEJAM 241 in Denmark, had an explosion inside the fuselage of Stirling LJ999 (they never knew what it was) causing them to hit the shallow water, at the southern end of Ringkøbing Fjord near Tippen Island at a speed of 240 mph. A lucky crew scrambled out of the aircraft with only a few cuts and bruises, to be made PoW.

Those 138 Squadron aircrew, who were nearly tour expired, were transferred to No.161 Squadron. The remainder after conversion to Lancasters at 1662 HCU Lindholme were posted to Tuddenham on the 9th March 1945. It would appear that Harris had at last gained the resources of the SD Squadron he had for so long strived and 138 Squadron at last gained a decent airfield from which to operate. Strangely the resident Squadron at Tuddenham, No.90, were reduced to two flights to make room for them.

The crew of Stan Tomlin (The Hon. Secretary of the Tempsford reunion) standing in front of their 138 Squadron Lancaster at Tuddenham after conversion from Stirlings. (L to R): F/Sgt L Pavin (Rear Gunner), F/O J Foster (Bomb Aimer), F/O R Millman (Navigator), W/O S Tomlin (Pilot), Sgt Thew ? (Flight Engineer), F/Sgt J Delcourt – a Belgian – (Mid-upper Gunner), F/Sgt K Welford (WOp/AG). Stan Tomlin was commissioned shortly after this photograph was taken and remained in the RAF to fly Canberras. (S Tomlin)

The Squadron's SD operational figures that I have are difficult to verify because of the very secrecy of their operations, but what figures I have are: 2,569 sorties, 70 aircraft lost (2.7 per cent). They flew 105 Lancaster sorties in their bomber role from March to May 1945 losing one crew. They were also to be the first Vickers Valiant Squadron formed in February 1955 and took part in the Suez Operation of October 1956. They were disbanded on the 1st April 1962.

In the meantime there was to be little respite for No.161 Squadron, now part of No.38 Group and the only SD Squadron at Tempsford. The 8/9th March seeing four out of five successful cargo sorties going to Denmark in the last of the moon phase. The following day the 10th March the Allied armies reached the Rhine.

With the rising of the moon on the 17/18th four sorties flew to Holland during which four agents and 72 containers were dropped. One sortie failed through lack of a reception, which was not surprising since these sites must have been just behind the German lines. The 20/21st March saw eight Stirlings make their way to Denmark, seven successfully. Five Hudsons en route for Germany were not so fortunate.

The two successful Hudson operations were COLEHILL, flown by F/Lt Webb who dropped an agent in the Steinhudermeer area 30km west of Hanover, and F/O Morris, who completed ACACIA, outstanding since the 2/3rd, he too dropped one agent.

F/O G S Ragan, RCAF, making the fifth attempt to complete the SIS operation WALNUT in Hudson AE595, were reported shot down near an aerodrome at Rheine, Germany some 40km east Enschede, Holland, 30km inside the German border. There were no survivors and they are buried in Reichwald Forest. It is not known whether his agent was dropped.

F/Lt R N Ferris, RCAF, with his all Canadian crew were flying Hudson T9445 on an SOE operation, NORVIC. They were shot down over France, there were no survivors and they are buried at Heverlee. They had parachuted their solitary agent over the Rhine at Remagen who unhappily lost his package containing his explosives when the cord, attaching it to his leg, broke as he dropped from the aircraft. Thus he was unable accomplish his mission.

The final Hudson operation this night was the third attempt to complete BENEDICT/EXPRESS/LEADER. The pilot of Hudson FK803 was F/Lt T Helfer and he aborted his operation over Erfurt because of bad weather. On entering Luxembourg airspace they received a burst of gun fire from a nightfighter which set them on fire. Helfer badly burned and with his parachute on fire was the only one to escape with his life, the aircraft crashing in flames on a hill above Maulesmuhle. Here three of the crew are buried together with the three Belgian agents, Lt G Corbisher, Lt L de Winter and Lt J Morel who died with them. It was thought that an American nightfighter shot them down.

The following night there were five Stirling Dutch sorties planned and two Norwegian. The latter were completed but two of the Dutch sorties failed to leave the ground. The rear turret of F/Lt Gunton becoming u/s and S/Ldr Read's target, RUMMY 31, having a last minute cancellation. F/Lt A H Aitken was flying Stirling LK209 on operation ROWING 3 to drop arms near Harlingen on the north east coast of Holland. They were hit by flak and crashed on the sand dunes near the island of Vieland. There was only one survivor, F/Sgt J T White managed to bale out at low altitude, some young fir trees cushioning him in his partly deployed parachute, he then evaded. F/Lt Aitken, found by some Dutchmen seriously injured, died on his way to hospital in Harlingen were he is buried.

From the night of the 23/24th to the 24/25th thirteen successful Norwegian sorties out of fifteen were flown. Most notable of these were three sorties that took off from Peterhead (of all places!) in Scotland on the 24/25th to a target BRIDLE 18, situated at 64° 58′N, 14° 06′E in northern Norway near the Swedish border. Here three Stirlings flown by F/O Witt, F/Lt Madders and F/Lt Kidd each dropped four agents eleven containers and nine packages. Witt landed at Sumburgh in the Shetlands, Madders and Kidd at Lossiemouth. F/O Ibbott flew a

Hudson on its first and only sortie to Norway, an SIS operation ROLLO, on which he parachuted one agent one container and two packages. He too landed at Lossiemouth.

On the 24th March, the crossing of the Rhine, operation VARSITY took place during which No.38 Group with their glider towing Halifaxes and Stirlings were fully committed.

The following night the 25/26th due to the deteriorating weather, F/Lt Gunton was the only aircraft to get off the ground. He flew from Lossiemouth two SIS targets SLOTT and ALFHILD in Norway dropping seven containers on the former and two agents eight containers and two packages on the latter. These targets were north of Narvik and they were airborne eight and half hours.

Seven 161 Stirling sorties to TABLEJAM targets in Denmark on the 30/31st were successful each site receiving, 24 containers and one package each. F/O Morris flying CHALGROVE 1 to Germany failed because of the weather. Two sorties went to Norway. F/Lt Kidd and F/Lt Madders flying BIT 14.

There were six aircraft lost in the bright moonlight over Norway this night: – from Tarrant Rushton: Halifax Mk VII PN243, flown by F/O Ireland on operation OSTLER 2, of No.298 Squadron.

From Shepherds Grove: Stirling PK225, flown by F/Lt Anderson on operation STIRRUP 8, and Stirling LK332, flown by F/Lt Trevor-Roper operation SNAFFLE 6, both of No.299 Squadron. Stirling LJ888, flown by F/Sgt Catterall on operation BIT 20, and Stirling LK197, flown by F/O Campbell on operation FLANK 10,

Stirling LK119 NF-R of 138 Squadron before transfer to 161 Squadron as MA-Y. The aircraft had flown twenty-nine operations with 138 and five with 161 before it was lost. (J Breeze via John Reid)

both of No.196 Squadron. (It is probable that all these crews participated in Operation VARSITY on the 24th, their Squadrons certainly did)

The sixth and final loss came from Tempsford, a 161 Squadron Stirling LK119 flown by F/Lt E P C Kidd, DFC, on operation BIT 14.

F/Lt Madders flying the same target as Kidd had the blood chilling experience of witnessing four of the above aircraft being shot down. The aircraft of F/Lt Kidd was engaged by a nightfighter who set it on fire and it exploded and crashed into the woods at Hegland. They are buried at Arendal some 60km NE Kristiansand. F/Lt Kidd was 32 years of age and this was to have been the final flight of his operational tour. F/Lt Madders reported 'no reception', was unable to deliver his two agents bringing them back to Tempsford.

There had been 63 aircraft from No.38 Group airborne over Holland, Denmark and Norway, in the moonlight that night, a 9.5% loss. April would not improve the Group's excessive loss rate. March had seen Tempsford lose four Stirlings and three Hudsons, more than enough by any standards.

The crew of LK119 MA-Y lost on the 30/31 March 1945 over Norway. Top: F/Sgt H Minshull (Air Gunner). Middle row (L to R): Sgt R A Burgess (Flight Engineer), F/Sgt G A Neath, DFM, (Navigator), F/O T S Macaulay (Bomb Aimer), F/Lt P C Kidd, DFC, (Pilot). Front row: F/Sgt A D Shopland (WOp/AG), W/O A M Taylor (Air Gunner). They are buried at Arendal, Norway. (Michael Kidd via John Reid)

*   *   *

The first six 161 Stirling sorties for April (2/3rd) ended in total failure caused by bad weather. Two SIS Hudson sorties were flown to Germany, NACHTIGAL by F/Lt Webb who reported it was too dark in the target area, north of Osnabruck, and brought back his two agents. F/O Ibbott flew NEGUS and had a successful drop after pinpointing a bend in the River Weser from where he made a DR run to his DZ.

F/O Morris was out for two consecutive nights, the 3/4th and 4/5th, flying a Hudson on an SIS operation BARNABUS to Holland where he dropped two agents. CURLAND was his German target on the 4/5th parachuting two OSS agents south of Munich. The next night saw three of four Stirling sorties for Holland completed. Two of them targeted on CUBBING 3 which received 48 containers and six packages delivered behind the German lines. A hazardous disposal operation for the reception committees in a fluid ground battle front.

Four completed Norwegian sorties on one target VET 12 and two to Holland frustrated by weather conditions, made up the Stirling effort for the 11/12th. A Hudson FK763 flying operation FLAP to Germany piloted by F/Lt D B Webb, returned to the UK with an engine failure and was compelled to bale out with his crew. The aircraft crashed at Dorking in Surrey. There were no injuries

The next night saw 24 containers each delivered successfully to four Danish TABLEJAM targets. F/Lt Collis flying TABLEJAM 192 being fortunate enough to beat off an attack from a Me 410 after servicing his target with 24 containers. Five Danish targets were flown (Collis among them!) on the 14/15th this time F/O Witt had his Stirling damaged in the starboard elevator by flak on his way in, aborted and skilfully returned to Tempsford. A return to Norway was inevitable on the 17/18 and of the three successful trips out of four W/O Potaka flying VET 3 parachuted in among his cargo three agents P Vexels, O Veras and R Christopherson. He reported the weather over his target as good.

The Hudsons were out to Germany the following night F/O Nicholson flying CATMORE to southern Germany, experienced a problem with the release of his agent who was caught up by the rope of his leg bag on the side of the slide. He was pulled back into the aircraft and then safely released. F/O Ibbott had two targets FLAP which had failed on the 11/12th reporting 'no reception'. This is the first Hudson target which suggested that they were dropping onto a reception in Germany, in this case three containers. On his second target PERISCOPE two agents and their package were dropped.

The following night the 19/20th F/O Wilson flying a Stirling to CRUPPER 23 in Norway had to use cloud cover to escape the attentions of a Me 410. While a double German target, NABEL and MYSTERE, was flown by F/O Morris in his Hudson parachuting two blind onto each. Bad weather prevented the success of F/O Ibbott's operation, NACHTIGAL, but four of the six Norwegian Stirling targets were a success.

Three more operations on the 21/22nd to Germany by the Hudson flight, two succeeding. F/O Ibbott parachuting two on operation NACHTIGAL, outstanding since 19/20th, and BANYAN, completed

by F/Lt Nicholson when he dropped a single agent. F/O Morris although finding his target ALDER II found that his two agents refused to jump so he returned them to Tempsford along with the two cycles that should have dropped with them.

The 22/23rd April saw Capt Hysing-Dahl back in the crew room to fly a Stirling at the start of his third operational tour which would only last four trips before the war would finish. During his absence from Tempsford he had flown, mainly in the Middle East, with No.1 Ferry Squadron, Pershore. During this time he collected a green endorsement for two hours flying in a Beaufighter on one engine. His last four operations were 22/23rd April to Norway operation RUMP 9 where in bright moonlight and unlimited visibility dropped 17 containers and seven packages. The next night 23/24th he flew to Holland operation CHECKERS 1 a target south of Amsterdam (52° 10'N, 04° 47'E) where on a reception of two reds and two whites, one flashing 'A' he delivered two agents and 24 containers from 650 feet. It was nearly a full moon and the light over the target was very bright, was recorded as 'an uneventful trip'. The 25/26th April saw him flying to Norway operation VET 15, at 58° 31'N, 07° 31'E, the lights of which he saw from 8km (5 miles). Here he dropped an agent, 21 containers and eight packages from 650 feet 'in a good short stick'. F/Lt Woodward also completed this target. The weather was clear with unlimited visibility.

During this period of time Tempsford parachuted nine agents into

A group of 161 Squadron aircrew taken at Tempsford in 1945. (L to R): T Thomas, John Bradbury, Harry Ibbot, unknown, McMillan (R W ?), unknown, K R Tattersall (just posted in for a second tour on Hudsons), remainder unknown. (K R Tattersall)

The officers of RAF Tempsford, 12 June 1945.
Front row (L to R): F/O Thomas, F/Lt Dixon, S/Ldr Simpson. S/Ldr Pearson, S/Ldr MacMillan,
S/Ldr Holdcroft, W/Cdr Ratcliff, G/Capt Palmer, S/Ldr Wagland, S/Ldr Stewart, F/Lt Powell,
F/O Speed, F/O King, F/O Foster, F/Lt Holloway, F/Lt Anderson.
Second row (sitting): Unknown, F/O Manger, F/Lt Johns, unknown, F/Lt Cairncross, F/Lt Wainwright.
Third row: F/O Barns, F/O Witt, F/O Tattersall, F/LT Helfer, F/O Stokes, F/Lt Bradbury,
unknown, F/Lt Short, F/O Drysdale, unknown, F/Lt Grange, F/O Cheeseman, F/Lt Dyer,
F/Lt Grimway, F/O Flowers, S/Ldr Read.
Back row: Unknown, unknown, F/Lt Oliver, F/O Smith, F/Lt Nicholson, unknown, Capt Hysing-Dahl,
F/O Cruickshank, F/O Potaka, F/O Dunmall, F/O Stanley, unknown, F/O Muir, unknown, unknown,
F/Lt Gibbs, P/O Bell, F/Lt Bradshaw. (J Nicholson via K A Merrick)

No.161 Squadron officers and aircrew, June 1945. The Squadron was officially disbanded on the 2 June
1945. (D Barsby via K A Merrick)

Germany by Hudson and five by Stirling to each of Holland and Norway.

Bad weather grounded 161 Squadron until 2/3rd May when six Stirlings took-off for Norway on which was to be the very last SD drop of the War. BLINKERS 5, flown by F/O Crequer, F/O Gray, F/Lt Caincross and F/Sgt Adams of which the latter three reported 'no reception', F/O Crequer completed. BLINKERS 2 (situated 60° 58'N, 05° 44'E) was completed by F/O Whiteley and Capt Hysing-Dahl by dropping 16 containers and ten packages. Hysing-Dahl reporting that he saw Whiteley making his drop as he arrived. It was appropriate that the last SD drops were made by No.161 Squadron crews and among them should be a Norwegian, Capt P Hysing-Dahl, DFC, RNoAF. It was also thought that he dropped the last agent on the 25/26th April.

On the 8th May Germany surrendered. Thereafter Tempsford was committed to transport duties, not the least of these was the repatriation of PoW's. Sadly not even this domestic duty could be conducted without loss. F/Lt R C Hawkins, DFM, flying Hudson AE505 first to Luneburg, when a full load could not be found for him he was diverted to Brussels. Here attempting to land he bounced the aircraft heavily, appearing to overshoot the aircraft stalled and nose dived into the ground killing the crew.

On the 2nd of June 1945 No.161 Squadron was disbanded. In spite of its distinctive and meritorious service it was not considered worthy of retention by the Royal Air Force.

It was never my intention to comment on what the pioneering Tempsford Squadrons achieved with their Whitleys, Halifaxes, Stirlings, Hudsons and Lysanders in terms of their contribution to Victory. I trust I have achieved what I set out to do that is to tell what they did and the price they paid for it. I have relived many moments in writing these pages, moments involving old friends, names and faces which I thought I had buried for ever, may they now rest in peace.

Aircraft and Crew Losses

Date	Pilot	Aircraft	Sqn Letter	Unit/Sqn

11 Oct 40   P/O Greenhill   Whitley P5025   (419 Flt)
DETAILS: Local flight, aircraft written off landing at Stradishall, No personal injuries.

21 Oct 40   F/Lt W R Farley   Lysander R9027   (419 Flt)
DETAILS: Returning from French pick-up operation. Bad weather, out of fuel, forced landed near Oban, aircraft written off.

17/18 Feb 41   S/Ldr F J B Keast   Whitley T4264   (419 Flt)
DETAILS: Shot down by flak, Namur, Belgium.
POW: S/Ldr F J B Keast, F/O K S McMurdie, F/O E N Baker, Sgt A J Cameron, Sgt D W Davies, Sgt D H Bernard.

10/11 Apr 41   F/O A J Oettle   Whitley T4165   (419 Flt)
DETAILS: Stalled overshooting at Tangmere.
KILLED: Sgt L G Morris, Sgt A J Cowan. Injured: F/O A J Oettle, F/O J Molesworth, P/O Wilson, Sgt Briscoe. Six Polish passengers were slightly injured.

25 Jul 41   F/Lt A D Jackson   Whitley Z6727   (419 Flt)
DETAILS: Test flight, crashed on take off, aircraft written off. Eight passengers injured.

30 Oct 41   F/Lt A J Oettle, DFC   Whitley Z9223   (138 Sqn)
DETAILS: Routine flight, stalled on approach to landing.
KILLED: F/Lt A J Oettle, DFC, F/Sgt H F Rochford, DFM, RNZAF, LAC W J Lee.

1/2 Nov 41   F/O T J Jasinski   Halifax L9612   (138 Sqn)
DETAILS: Returning from Poland short of fuel, crashed landed Tormelilla Sweden, No personal injuries, crew repatriated.

28 Nov 41   F/Lt A J de V Laurent   Lysander T1771   (138 Sqn)
DETAILS: In bad visibility flew into trees at Hungry Hill, Farnham, Surrey.
KILLED: F/Lt A J de V Laurent and LAC J A Harkness.

27/28 Dec 41   F/Sgt A W Reimer, RCAF   Whitley Z9385   (138 Sqn)
DETAILS: Returning from France in bad weather, crashed on airfield thought shot down by German night fighter.
KILLED: Sgt J R Petts, RCAF, Sgt G R S Gordon, Cpl H A Pickering, WOp/AG and RG baled out. F/Sgt Reimer died 2 weeks later.

3 Jan 42   None   Whitley Z9295   (138 Sqn)
3 Jan 42   None   Whitley Z9140   (138 Sqn)
DETAILS: Damaged in air raid on Luqa, Malta. Written off.
28/29 Jan 42   S/Ldr J Nesbitt-Dufort, DFC   Lysander T1508   (138 Sqn)
DETAILS: Forced landed in France returning in bad weather from pick-up operation BERYL. No
injuries to crew or passengers Maurice Duclos and Roger Mitchell.

28/29 Jan 42   Sgt E E Jones   Whitley Z6728   (138 Sqn)
DETAILS: Ditched 20 miles from English coast. Operation MUSJIDE etc., Belgium.
LOST: Sgt E E Jones Sgt D Gold, F/Sgt G E A Baxter, Sgt A Brittain P/O D O Weeks, Sgt F W
Smith, W/Cdr J E D Benham.

10/11 Mar 42   S/Ldr B Romanoff   Whitley Z9125   (138 Sqn)
DETAILS: Crashed taking off for French operation FRENSHAM
KILLED: S/Ldr B Romanoff, Sgt J Janec, Sgt M Politzer, Sgt L Fornusek F/O V Jelinek, INJURED: Sgt
B Vaverka.

27/28 Mar 42   F/Sgt J Thompson   Whitley T4166   NF-B   (138 Sqn)
DETAILS: Crashed in sea at Dan Helder. Operation WATERCRESS etc., Holland.
LOST: P/O S Widdup, P/O R W Franklin, F/Sgt J Thompson, Sgt K Hailstone, Sgt G R Wood, Sgt
W C Evans.

20/21 Apr 42   W/Cdr WR Farley, DFC   Halifax V9976   (138 Sqn)
DETAILS: Struck hill in fog at Kreuth, south of Munich. Operation WHISKEY, Austria.
KILLED: W/Cdr W R Farley, DFC, F/O R Zgmuntowicz, PAF, F/L A H Veollnagel, PAF, F/O J A
Pulton, F/Sgt B Karbowski, PAF, Sgt C Madracki, PAF, Sgt L Wilmanski, PAF, Sgt M Wojciechowski,
PAF. AGENTS: Vsevolod Troussevitch, NKVD, Peter Starisky, NKVD.

20/21 Apr 42   P/O I A Miller   Whitley Z9158   NF-V   (138 Sqn)
DETAILS: 'Nickling' over St-Etienne area, France. Diverted to Boscombe Down and struck high ground
at Porton, Wilts.
KILLED: P/O I A Miller, Sgt R F Shaddick, F/Sgt W E J Lines, RCAF, Sgt S W F Leigh. INJURED: Sgt
K Hubbard.

28/29 May 42   P/O A J Mott   Lysander V9595   (161 Sqn)
DETAILS: Bogged down in small airfield at le Fay, south of Issoudun. Aircraft lost but pilot evaded.

22 Jun 42   Sgt W Smith   Whitley Z9224   (161 Sqn)
DETAILS: Crashed on take-off, ASI u/s. No personal injuries but aircraft written off.

25/26 Jul 42   F/Sgt J Owen   Whitley Z9282   NF-M   (138 Sqn)
DETAILS: Crashed at Vire, (Bombing Cholet) France.
KILLED: F/Sgt J Owen, Sgt D Thornton, Sgt J Whalley, F/Sgt W G Rock. PoW: Sgt P H Avery.

29/30 Jul 42   S/Ldr W T Davies, DFC   Whitley Z9230   NF-N   (138 Sqn)
DETAILS: Operation LETTUCE 5, Holland. Shot down by night-fighter while running up to target.
KILLED: S/Ldr W T Davies, F/Sgt L S Franklin, F/Sgt T M Gray, Sgt E H Kerry, Sgt D F Staton, Sgt
P T Wright, Sgt G B Wood.

24/25 Aug 42   S/Ldr H A Outram   Whitley Z9232   NF-L   (138 Sqn)
DETAILS: Operation SYRINGA 7, France. Crashed-landed at St-Loup (Loire et Cher) No injuries.
EVADED: S/Ldr H A Outram, P/O L Wilson, P/O E R W Wood, DFM, F/Lt H L Holliday, Sgt G F
Foster.

31/1 Sept 42   S/Ldr W G Lockhart , DFC   Lysander V9597   (161 Sqn)
DETAILS: Taxyed into a ditch after landing in France at Arbigny (Ain), some 20km NNE of Mâcon. Aircraft deliberately burnt. No injuries. Operation BOREAS II.

19/20 Sept 42   F/Sgt J D Walls   Whitley Z6940   (161 Sqn)
DETAILS: Crashed near Boulogne. Operation TERRIER, Belgium.
KILLED: F/Sgt J D Walls, F/Sgt F McL Macdonald, RCAF, P/O M R Symonds, Sgt W E R Wright, Sgt A R Ashford, Sgt H Pateman.

24/25 Sept 42   P/O D C Boothby   Whitley Z9131   MA-Q   (161 Sqn)
DETAILS: Baled out, Operation MONGOOSE etc., Belgium. Aircraft crashed near Sevigny-Waleppe (Ardennes), France.
DIED OF WOUNDS: Sgt R E Franklin. EVADED: P/O D C Boothby, P/O L G A Reed, Sgt C A Blyth. PoW: W/O J Rayson, Sgt L C G Quirke, Sgt P G Clayton.

26/27 Sept 42   F/Sgt D H Freeland   Whitley Z9275   NF-G   (138 Sqn)
DETAILS: Aircraft crashed near Merville (Nord), France. Operation INCOMPARABLE 1, Belgium.
KILLED: F/Sgt D H Freeland, F/Sgt E G Hayhoe, F/Sgt F G Green. PoW: Sgt J H Cox, Sgt P G Moore.

1/2 Oct 42   F/Sgt S Klosowski, PAF   Halifax W7776   NF-B   (138 Sqn)
DETAILS: Shortage of fuel caused forced landing at Goldsborough, Yorkshire. Operation CHISEL, Poland. No injuries

2/3 Oct 42   P/O E Edge   Whitley Z6653   MA-O   (161 Sqn)
DETAILS: Engine trouble, aircraft ditched off Dutch coast. Operation LETTUCE 7.
LOST: Sgt J R S Scott, P/O J A C Kite, Sgt K T Harbridge, Sgt A Gander. PoW: P/O E Edge, Sgt D L Taafe.

21/22 Oct 42   P/O W W S Smith, DFC   Whitley BD228   MA-S   (161 Sqn)
DETAILS: Crashed base, Operation LUCKYSHOT 8, etc., Belgium,
KILLED: P/O W W S Smith, DFC. SEVERELY INJURED: Sgt Lamont, F/Sgt Ward. MINOR INJURIES: P/O Farley, Sgt Pope, Sgt Moxom.

21/22 Oct 42   P/O G F B Newport-Tinley   Whitley P5029   NF-E   (138 Sqn)
DETAILS: Engine failure ditched off Eastbourne Pier, Sussex. No injuries, crew rescued by Royal Navy. Ran out of fuel after completing Operation SPRUCE 2 in France.

29/30 Oct 42   W/O S Klosowski, PAF   Halifax W7774   NF-T   (138 Sqn)
DETAILS: Ditched off Sheringham, Norfolk, Operation WRENCH, Poland. No injuries, crew rescued by lifeboat.

29/30 Oct 42   W/O F Zaremba, PAF   Halifax W7773   NF-S   (138 Sqn)
DETAILS: Operation PLIERS, Poland, crashed in southern Norway.
KILLED: P/O F Pantkowski, PAF, W/O F Zaremba, PAF, F/O M Wodzicki, DFC, PAF, F/Sgt T Madejski, PAF, F/Sgt F Sobkowiak, PAF, F/Sgt W Zuk, PAF, Sgt C Kozlowski, PAF and three Polish agents.

31 Oct/1 Nov 42   P/O J E Turnham   Whitley Z9159   NF-D   (138 Sqn)
DETAILS: Operation PRODUCER 2, France. Crashed crew buried at Abbeville (Somme).
KILLED: P/O J E Turnham, F/Sgt J R O'Leary, RCAF, P/O L Wheatley, Sgt F Morrison, Sgt A Hallewell, Sgt S White.

18/19 Nov 42   P/O O A Cussen   Whitley Z9160   (161 Sqn)
DETAILS: Gibraltar to UK, forced landed at Armacao de Pera (Algarve) Portugal.
INTERNED: P/O O A Cussen, F/O J A Broadley, Sgt R A Sharpe, F/Sgt H Stephens.

22/23 Nov 42   F/Sgt J A Hey   Whitley Z6629   MA-N   (161 Sqn)
DETAILS: Operation PERIWIG 7 etc., Belgium, presumed lost at sea.
LOST: F/Sgt J A Hey, Sgt G L Harrison, RCAF, Sgt C R Kenzie, Sgt H Moxon, Sgt R W Andrews,
Sgt H Metcalf. SIS agent Lt Fernand de Bisschop was also lost.

10 Dec 42   F/O L M Anderle, DFC   Halifax L9618   NF-W   (138 Sqn)
DETAILS: Missing between Egypt and Malta.
LOST: F/O L M Anderle, DFC, W/O V Panek, P/O V Krcha, Sgt F Vanicek, P/O J Tesar, F/Sgt B
Hajek, P/O M Rozprym. PASSENGER: P/O W T C Chambers. GROUND CREW: Cpl R E Chandler, AC1
H H Hutchinson.

17 Dec 42   F/O K L Dobromirski, PAF   Halifax DT542   NF-Q   (138 Sqn)
DETAILS: Crashed taking off from Luqa, Malta, for Gibraltar.
KILLED: F/O K L Dobromirski, PAF, F/O S Pankiewicz, PAF, F/O Z A Idzikowski, PAF, Sgt R
Wysocki, PAF, F/Sgt A E Kleniewski, PAF, F/Sgt O F Zielinski, PAF, Sgt A C Watt. PASSENGERS: S/Ldr
J H Wedgewood, DFC, F/Lt P Earle, F/Lt L A Vaughan, DSO, DFC, Maj Lord A A B Apsley, DSO,
Maj A D C Millar. GROUND CREW: Sgt D Spibey, Cpl D S Hounslow, LAC C D Browne, LAC R Clegg,
AC1 S E Kelly.

17 Dec 42   F/Lt J C K Sutton   Halifax W1002   NF-Y   (138 Sqn)
DETAILS: Malta to Gibraltar. Engine failure, crash landed le Kreider 200 miles south of Oran, Algeria.
No injuries.

22/23 Dec 42   F/O G F B Newport-Tinley, DFC   Halifax W7775   NF-R   (138 Sqn)
DETAILS: Operation MARROW 12, Holland. Crashed near Meppel.
KILLED: F/O G F B Newport-Tinley, DFC, Sgt B M Pick, Sgt B S Nixon, W/O C A Howard, DFC,
F/Sgt H C Taylor, Sgt C C Hayes. PoW: Sgt W H Bloxham, Sgt F O Tierney, RCAF.

15/16 Jan 43   P/O H S Readhead   Halifax DG285   MA-X   (161 Sqn)
DETAILS: Crashed near Rennes (Ille-de-Vilaine) Northern France.
KILLED: P/O H S Readhead, P/O R Gray, Sgt S M Anderson, P/O W W Roy, RCAF, Sgt W Wilson,
Sgt L P Manning, Sgt H G Martins.

4th Feb 43   F/O R C Hogg   Halifax DG271   NF-C   (138 Sqn)
DETAILS: Returning to Tempsford from Tangmere swung on take-off. Undercarriage collapsed. No
injuries but aircraft written off.

19/20 Feb 43   P/O P Kingsford-Smith   Halifax W1012   NF-Z   (138 Sqn)
DETAILS: Operation BURGUNDY etc., France, crashed near Tours.
ALL PoW: P/O P Kingsford-Smith, RAAF, F/O R C Hogg, Sgt F R Jerome, F/Sgt A F A Dawkins,
RCAF, Sgt H J Long, Sgt E J Ramm, Sgt D Robinson, Sgt J Davison.

14/15 Mar 43   S/Ldr C F Gibson, DFC   Halifax BB281   NF-O   (138 Sqn)
DETAILS: Crashed near Munich. Operation BRONZE, Czechoslovakia. All buried in Durnbach War
Cemetery, Germany.
KILLED: S/Ldr C F Gibson, DFC, F/Sgt D C Lisson, RCAF, Sgt M J Hudson, F/Sgt J S Rigden, F/Sgt
A Stokes, DFM, Sgt L P Ward, Sgt H J Sharood, F/Sgt M P T Myers, RCAF.

14/15 Mar 43   F/Lt A E Prior, DFM   Halifax DG245   MA-W   (161 Sqn)
DETAILS: Operation IRIDIUM Czechoslovakia. All buried in Durnbach War Cemetery, Germany.
KILLED: F/Lt A E Prior, DFM, P/O A J Kingham, Sgt F J Mowles, F/O R W Taylor, DFC & Bar, RCAF, F/Sgt G McWilliam, Sgt J H Kempton, Sgt F D Bell.

14/15 Mar 43   F/Sgt L R Smith   Halifax DT620   NF-T   (138 Sqn)
DETAILS: Crashed in Denmark. Operation SLATE, Poland.
KILLED: F/Sgt L R Smith, Sgt H R Harrap, RNZAF, Sgt T Mairs, Sgt C F Chambers, F/Sgt E S Masson, RCAF, Sgt D R Ross, RCAF, Sgt A C Sixsmith.

14/15 Mar 43   F/O G A Osborne   Halifax DG283   MA-Y   (161 Sqn)
Details: Crashed Fawley, Bucks, outward. Operation DIRECTOR 34.
KILLED: Sgt H Shearer, Sgt B Crane. Injured: F/O G A Osborne, Sgt Stevens, F/O D Thornton, Sgt R Poltock.

19/20 Mar 43   F/O H L Wynne, DFM   Halifax DG244   MA-Y   (161 Sqn)
DETAILS: Lost without trace. Operation VEGA 3, Norway.
LOST: F/O H L Wynne, DFM, F/Sgt R R S Rolfe, Sgt T B Colwell, F/O W H Franklin, DFC, Sgt J C Insole, Sgt E W Foster, P/O T W Challoner, DFC.

24/25 Mar 43   F/O E Clow, RNZAF   Halifax HR665   NF-L   (138 Sqn)
DETAILS: Ditched Ijsselmeer, Holland. Operation ST JOHN, etc.
PoW: F/O E Clow, Sgt F Boyd, Sgt T W R Holmes, Sgt F Ross, F/Sgt R D Alexander, Sgt W A A Floyd, RCAF, Sgt S W Reynolds. Dutch Agents: DROWNED; A Bergman. ESCAPED; Mr Gerbrand.

12/13 Apr 43   W/O S Jensen, DFM, PAF   Halifax BB340   NF-D   (138 Sqn)
DETAILS: Operation DIRECTOR 22, etc., France, crashed Douvres-la-Délivrande (Calvados).
KILLED: Sgt J Lesniewicz, PAF. PoW: W/O S Jensen, DFM, F/Lt J Izycki, PAF, W/O L Zaborowski, PAF, W/O L Urbanski, PAF. EVADED: F/O B Korpowski, PAF, Sgt A N Dent, Sgt G Evans. Agents: SURVIVED CRASH; Claude Jumeau, Lee Graham.

13th Apr 43   F/O O A Cussen   Halifax DG409   MA-W   (161 Sqn)
DETAILS: Air test. Port inner engine failed during take-off. Aircraft crashed and written off. No injuries.

13/14 Apr 43   Sgt W A Cook, RNZAF   Halifax BB363   NF-T   (138 Sqn)
DETAILS: Came down in sea off Bournemouth. Operation PORCUPINE, Belgium.
LOST: Sgt W A Cook, RNZAF, Sgt J Doy, Sgt E G Hammett, W/O R W Ward, DFC, Sgt W Skelton, F/Sgt H E Davidson, DFM, F/Sgt A E King Sgt J R Callan, Sgt E J Kimberley.

17/18 Apr 43   F/O T Ginter, PAF   Halifax DT725   NF-J   (138 Sqn)
DETAILS: Crashed at Ussy (Calvados). Operation LIME 9. France.
KILLED: F/O T Ginter, PAF, Sgt J H Aspen, F/Lt B S Lawrenczuk, PAF, Sgt S Gadomski, PAF, F/Sgt J K Mironow, PAF, Sgt F Ulasiuk, PAF.

11/12 May 43   F/O J Polnik, PAF   Halifax DT627   NF-P   (138 Sqn)
DETAILS: Lost at sea. Operation LEEK 7, Holland.
LOST: F/O J Polnik, PAF, F/Sgt B Wojno, PAF, Sgt E Piatkowski, PAF, F/O J Polkowski, PAF, Sgt J Kurzak, PAF, Sgt K Germansinski, PAF, Sgt P Bednarski, PAF

12/13 May 43   S/Ldr C G S R Robinson, DFC   Halifax BB313   NF-M   (138 Sqn)
DETAILS: Crashed W of Troyes (Aube). Operation DONKEYMAN 1, etc., France.

PoW: S/Ldr C G S R Robinson, DFC, F/O F C Jeffery, P/O R G Johnson, F/O R R Piddington, F/Sgt L Martin, DFM. EVADED: Sgt J C Tweed, Sgt W H Marshall, DFM, P/O J T Hutchinson, DFC.

13/14 May 43   F/O T Noble   Halifax BB328   NF-U   (138 Sqn)
DETAILS: Crashed Pont-Audemer (Eure). Operation PHYSICIAN, etc., France.
KILLED: F/O T Noble, Sgt J Woods, Sgt D F West, Sgt K Hubbard, Sgt D A Ball, Sgt J P Keating, RCAF.

16 May 43   F/Lt J E Bartrum   Lysander R9106   MA-K   (161 Sqn)
DETAILS: Crashed and caught fire during training flight at Tempsford.
KILLED: F/Lt J E Bartrum.

18 May 43   F/Lt R W J Hooper   Halifax JB802   NF-S   (138 Sqn)
DETAILS: Aircraft, overshooting at Maison Blanche, struck Arab dwelling and crashed. Crew suffered minor injuries and aircraft written off.

21/22 May 43   F/Sgt P B Norris   Halifax BB329   NF-Z   (138 Sqn)
DETAILS: Crashed Polder Noordbeemster. Operation MARROW 35/36, Holland.
KILLED: Sgt S Boothroyd, Sgt W H Wilde. PoW: F/Sgt P B Norris, Sgt J H Dixon, Sgt L W Tomlinson, Sgt A W Mureph, Sgt F W Green.

11/12 Jun 43   F/Lt A F Foster, DFC   Halifax DG406   MA-V   (161 Sqn)
DETAILS: Reported 'lost without trace'. Operation PHYSICIAN 32, etc., France. Probably came down in the English Channel.
KILLED: F/Lt A F Foster, DFC, S/Ldr A de Q Walker, DFC, Sgt J S Riddell, P/O J T O'Brien, DFM, P/O L Roberts, DFM, Sgt A Moon, P/O F L Williams.

19 June 43   W/O S Klosowski, PAF   Halifax W1229   NF-A   (138 Sqn)
DETAILS: Training flight. Crashed landed in cross wind. No injuries but aircraft written off.
OTHER CREW: F/O J A Krzehlik, PAF, F/Sgt M Rzewuski, PAF.

22 June 43   W/O S Klosowski, PAF   Halifax DT727   NF-K   (138 Sqn)
DETAILS: Training flight. Crashed into a hangar at Tempsford when attempting a three engine landing. No injuries but aircraft written off.
OTHER CREW: F/O J A Krzehlik, PAF, F/L N Matylis, PAF.

22/23 Jun 43   P/O R G Higgins   Halifax DG405   MA-Y   (161 Sqn)
DETAILS: Crashed into Ijsselmeer, Holland. Operation LEMONTREE, etc.
KILLED: P/O R G Higgins, Sgt N Blanchard, Sgt M H Moore, RCAF, Sgt C W Hartin, Sgt G George, Sgt F Groom, Sgt R D Pryde-Martin, Sgt G N Cochrane.

23/24 Jun 43   F/Sgt T Z Zabicki, PAF   Halifax BB379   NF-J   (138 Sqn)
DETAILS: Operation TURNIP 2, Holland. Crashed at Oostzaan.
KILLED: F/Sgt T Z Zabicki, PAF, F/Sgt W Sicinski, PAF, F/O W S Kalkus, PAF, F/Sgt K Kidziak, PAF. PoW: F/Sgt S Roehr, PAF, F/Sgt J Rek, PAF, Sgt E P Kasperowicz, PAF.

12/13 Jul 43   F/Lt J Morawski, PAF   Halifax JD155   NF-M   (138 Sqn)
DETAILS: Crashed St-Paul-sur-Risle (Eure). Operation ROACH 94, etc., France.
KILLED: F/Lt J Morawski, PAF, F/Sgt E Jonski, PAF, Sgt T Tomaszewski, PAF, F/Lt N Lewicki, PAF, F/Sgt L S Bonk, PAF, F/Sgt E Rusinski, PAF, F/Sgt J Nawrot, PAF.

16/17 Jul 43   G/Capt E Fielden, CVO, AFC   Hudson T9465   MA-T   (161 Sqn)
DETAILS: Operation BUCKLER. Aircraft struck by Blenheim whilst parked at Blida, Algeria and written

off.

22/23 Jul 43   Sgt D A Crome   Halifax DK119   MA-U   (161 Sqn)
DETAILS: Crashed near St-Sauvier (Allier). Operation PRINCESS, etc., France.
KILLED: F/Sgt L M Lavallee, RCAF. PoW: Sgt S F Hathaway, Sgt E A Allen. EVADED: Sgt D A Crome, Sgt R O Hunter, Sgt D G Patterson, Sgt R W Paulin, Sgt T J Kanakos, RCAF.

12/13 Aug 43   W/O2 R A Scott, RCAF   Halifax BB334   NF-X   (138 Sqn)
DETAILS: Crashed Ecorcei (Orne). Operation SPRUCE 20, France.
KILLED: F/Sgt D A J Cameron, RCAF, F/Sgt A G Foster, RCAF. PoW: Sgt T S Harries, F/Sgt A Manson, Sgt D H Owen. Evaded: W/O2 R A Scott, RCAF, Sgt J G A Trusty.

14/15 Aug 43   S/Ldr F C Griffiths, AFC   Halifax JD180   NF-O   (138 Sqn)
DETAILS: Crashed at Meythet (Haute-Savoie). Operation PIMENTO 12, France.
KILLED: Sgt F R Davies, F/O S J Congdon, DFM, P/O R A Mackenzie, F/Sgt R W Peters, DFM, F/Sgt F Pollard, Sgt J Maden (Shot by the Italians). EVADED: S/Ldr F C Griffiths, AFC.

16/17 Aug 43   F/O J A Krzehlik, PAF   Halifax JD312   NF-J   (138 Sqn)
DETAILS: Crashed near Arx (Landes). Operation WHEELWRIGHT 17, etc., France.
EVADED: F/O J A Krzehlik, PAF, F/O J A Wroblewski, PAF, Sgt W Kieruczenko, PAF, F/O K Zankowski, PAF, F/Sgt M Pawlikowski, PAF, Sgt R Kozik, PAF, W/O W Kosinski, PAF.

17/18 Aug 43   F/Sgt N W Hayter, RAAF   Halifax JD179   NF-Z   (138 Sqn)
DETAILS: Crashed near l'Aigle (Orne), France. Operation BOB 43.
KILLED: F/Sgt N W Hayter, RAAF, Sgt W S Davies, Sgt F Boles, Sgt H G Ansell, Sgt J A Hutchinson, F/Sgt A B Robinson, RAAF, Sgt G W F Duckett.

18/19 Aug 43   P/O K H C Brown   Halifax DG253   NF-F   (138 Sqn)
DETAILS: Returned early and ran off end of runway. Aircraft was written off. No injuries.

14/15 Sep 43   P/O W H James   Halifax HR666   NF-E   (138 Sqn)
DETAILS: Crashed in sea off Korsor, Denmark. Operation FLAT 12A, Poland.
KILLED: P/O W H James, F/O D B Ireland, Sgt J E Irwin, Sgt B A C Hunt, Sgt R H D Bouttell. PoW: Sgt D H White, RCAF, Sgt T A Payne, RCAF.

14/15 Sep 43   F/Lt F J Jakusz-Gostomski, DFC, PAF   Halifax JD154   NF-V (138 Sqn)
DETAILS: Crashed into a block of flats at Skalmierzyce Nowe, Poland. Operation FLAT 22.
KILLED: F/Lt F J Jakusz-Gostomski , DFC, PAF, F/Sgt L Misiak, PAF, Sgt Z Kuczkowski, PAF, F/Lt K P Gebik, DFC, PAF, F/Sgt V Jablonski, PAF, Sgt H Fojer, PAF, W/O K Pacut, PAF.

14/15 Sep 43   F/Lt A J Milne, DFC   Halifax JD269   NF-Q   (138 Sqn)
DETAILS: Crashed near Esberg, Denmark. Operation NEON 9, Poland.
KILLED: F/Lt A J Milne, DFC, F/Sgt F Shuttleworth, P/O T R Wilson, F/O I Maclean, DFC, P/O P E Rollins, P/O J R Scarles, Sgt E J Smyth. Agents: Lt W Siakiewcz, PLA, Lt K Lewko, PLA, Lt R Skowronski, PLA.

14/15 Sep 43   F/O E C Hart   Halifax JN910   NF-K   (138 Sqn)
DETAILS: Crashed in Baltic near Rugenwalde. Operation FLAT 12, Poland.
KILLED: F/O E C Hart, Sgt K C Windsor, RCAF, F/O J D L Cloutier, RCAF, Sgt L C Gay, Sgt S J Smith, Sgt W H Mudge, Sgt K R Norrie. PoW: Sgt A S Dove.

16/17 Sep 43   F/Sgt T Miecznik, PAF   Halifax BB309   NF-T   (138 Sqn)
DETAILS: Crashed Slaglille, Denmark. Operation NEON 3, Poland.

KILLED: Sgt E Kasprzak, PAF, F/Lt W Wasilewski, PAF, F/Sgt W Michalski, PAF, Sgt W Patlewicz, PAF, F/Sgt W Barzdo, PAF. EVADED: F/Sgt T Miecznik, PAF. POW: Sgt R Puchala, PAF.

16/17 Sep 43   F/Sgt L A Trotter, RAAF   Halifax JD156   NF-W   (138 Sqn)
DETAILS: Crashed in sea off Jutland peninsula. Operation FLAT 5, Poland.
KILLED: F/O J R Bradley, RCAF, Sgt H Johnson, F/Sgt G E Snook, RAAF. POW: F/Sgt L A Trotter, RAAF, Sgt S Francis, F/Sgt G T Jones, F/Sgt D R Quinlivan, RAAF.

19/20 Sep 43   F/Sgt N L Sherwood   Halifax BB317   NF-N   (138 Sqn)
DETAILS: Ditched in North Sea. Operation PARSNIP 7, etc., Holland.
KILLED: F/Sgt N L Sherwood, Sgt B S Burch, Sgt R T Chinn. PoW: Sgt L A Wilson, RCAF, P/O J Loughran, Sgt O J Davies, Sgt R W Scales.

19/20 Sep 43   S/Ldr R P Wilkin, DFC, RCAF   Halifax DG252   NF-B   (138 Sqn)
DETAILS: Crashed in sea. Operation CATARRH 14, etc., Holland.
LOST: S/Ldr R P Wilkin, DFC, P/O G A Berwick, DFM, F/O J W H Brown, DFM, F/O H Burke, DFM, F/Sgt A Hughes (five man crew).

9/10 Oct 43   W/O B Hulas, DFC, PAF   Liberator BZ858 NF-F   (138 Sqn)
DETAILS: Aircraft abandoned over Sweden. Operation COTTAGE 7, Poland.
INTERNED: W/O B Hulas, DFC, PAF, F/L C Nowacki, PAF, Sgt W Rucinski, PAF, F/Lt M Malinowski, PAF, F/Sgt B Wozniak, PAF, F/Sgt S Miniakowski, PAF, W/O J Dubiel, PAF.

18/19 Oct 43   S/Ldr C W Passey, DFC   Halifax LW281   NF-W   (138 Sqn)
DETAILS: Crashed near Antwerp, Belgium. Operation BADMINGTON, etc., Holland /Belgium.
POW: Sgt J Bruce. Evaded: S/Ldr C W Passey, DFC, F/O G E A Madgett, F/O G H Ward, DFM, F/Sgt J E Grout, F/Sgt K L Rabson, DFM, P/O R P Mantle, Sgt J P Healey, RCAF , J B van Schelle (Dutch agent).

20/21 Oct 43   F/Sgt T W Lewis   Halifax EB239   MA-Y   (161 Sqn)
DETAILS: Crashed Valenciennes (Nord), France. Operation PLAYBILL, etc., Belgium.
KILLED: F/Sgt T W Lewis, Sgt C E Young, Sgt H J Crawford, Sgt J Ramsden, Sgt T B Young, Sgt W Crouch, Sgt D R Feely.

3/4 Nov 43   P/O H F Hodges   Halifax DT726   NF-H   (138 Sqn)
DETAILS: Crashed into mountain at Marcols-les-Eaux, (Ardèche). Operation JOHN 13, France.
KILLED: P/O H F Hodges, Capt J A Estes, USAAF, Sgt H T Penfold, RCAF, F/Sgt H Smith, P/O R K Pulling, Sgt J Barthelemy, F/Sgt R L Nott, RAAF. EVADED: Sgt J F Brough.

5/6 Nov 43   F/Lt S N Gray   Halifax DK232   MA-T   (161 Sqn)
DETAILS: Swung on take-off, undercarriage collapsed and aircraft written off. Prior to Operation SACRISTAN 5, France.
CREW: F/Lt S N Gray, F/Sgt P A Fry, F/O L H Thomas, Sgt D G Patterson, P/O Shine, Sgt Betts.
INJURED: P/O Pearse.

6/7 Nov 43   F/Sgt K R Copas   Halifax JN921   NF-B   (138 Sqn)
DETAILS: Crashed near Liesse, (Aisne). Operation TOM 6, France.
KILLED: F/Sgt K R Copas, Sgt R T Brown, F/O R Morrish, Sgt C W Charro, Sgt W Aitkenhead, Sgt F Lawrenson, Sgt J R G Day, Sgt A R Flatters.

8/9 Nov 43   F/O J M McBride   Lysander V9723   MA-H   (161 Sqn)
DETAILS: Tyre burst on landing at Tangmere. Aircraft swung and was written off. No injuries. Operation

CANADA, France.

10/11 Nov 43   P/O M A Line, RAAF   Halifax EB129   MA-W   (161 Sqn)
DETAILS: Crashed at Brunelles 45 km west of Chartres, France. Operation PENNYFARTHING.
KILLED: P/O M A Line, RAAF, Lt B W Gross, USAAF, Sgt R Cotterill, Sgt E R Watts, Sgt H R Batten, F/Sgt E Harrison, RAAF, F/Sgt W R R Shore, RCAF. POW: F/O J G Pilkington.

16/17 Nov 43   F/Lt R W J Hooper   Lysander V9548 MA-D (161 Sqn)
DETAILS: Bogged on ground near Niort, France. Operation SCENERY. Aircraft set on fire. Pilot evaded.

10/11 Dec 43   F/Lt A C Bartter   Halifax BB378   NF-D   (138 Sqn)
DETAILS: Crashed Tostrup, Denmark. Operation TABLEJAM 18/17.
POW: W/O F Turvil, Sgt N Anderson, F/Sgt B H Atkins, Sgt S G Smith, Sgt W R Riggs. EVADED: F/Lt A C Bartter, F/O C W Fry, RCAF, F/O E Howell. SAFE: Dr Flemming Muus (SOE agent).

10/11 Dec 43   F/O G H Weeden, RCAF   Lancaster ED825 AJ-E   (617 Sqn)
DETAILS: Hit by flak crashed near Meharicourt (Somme), France.
KILLED: F/O G H Weeden, RCAF, Sgt A W Richardson, P/O R N Jones, F/Sgt E J Walters, RCAF, F/Sgt R G Howell, Sgt B Robinson, WO2 R Cummings, RCAF.

10/11 Dec 43   W/O G F Bull   Lancaster ED886 AJ-D   (617 Sqn)
DETAILS: Crashed Terramesnil (Somme), France.
KILLED: Sgt J McL Stewart, F/Sgt D M Thorpe, RCAF. POW: W/O G F Bull, Sgt C C Wiltshire, Sgt C M Chamberlain, F/Sgt N Batey. EVADED: F/Sgt J H Williams.

10/11 Dec 43   F/O J R G Bathgate, DFC, RNZF Lysander V9673 MA-J   (161 Sqn)
DETAILS: Shot down crashing at la Ville-aux-bois-lès-Pontavert (Aisne), France. Operation STEN.
KILLED: F/O J R G Bathgate, DFC, Capt Claudius Four (passenger).

16/17 Dec 43   F/Sgt T M Thomas   Halifax LW280   NF-K   (138 Sqn)
DETAILS: Crew baled out, aircraft crashed into sea off Harwich. Operation MARC 1, France.
KILLED: Sgt T B Hawkes, Sgt J Lynch, Sgt R Marshall, Sgt J J Hannah. RESCUED: F/Sgt T M Thomas, Sgt J A Vick, Sgt J K K Vincent.

16/17 Dec 43   F/Sgt J G A Watson   Halifax LL115   NF-A   (138 Sqn)
DETAILS: Crashed at Capel Green near Woodbridge. Operation DETECTIVE 3, France.
KILLED: F/Sgt J G A Watson, Sgt N M Gillis, RCAF, Sgt J R Hoddinott, Sgt H D King, Sgt G Osborne. INJURED: P/O J Pearcey, RAAF, Sgt I Scaellenberg, Sgt W F Sutherland.

16/17 Dec 43   F/O R W Johnson   Halifax LL119   NF-L   (138 Sqn)
DETAILS: Aircraft abandoned crashing into sea off Felixstowe. Crew safe. Operation WHEELWRIGHT 36, France.
CREW: F/O R W Johnson, Sgt E Gibbons, P/O H G Vincent, Sgt L S Manson, RCAF, Sgt D Stuart, P/O K N James, Sgt W A Bellmann.

16/17 Dec 43   F/O D R Harborow, DFC   Halifax LK899   MA-T   (161 Sqn)
DETAILS: Crashed in river at Debden. Operation WHEELWRIGHT 37.
LOST: F/O W F McMaster, DFM. CREW SAFE: F/O Harborow, DFC, Sgt M Gaskin, Sgt H C Walton, P/O Charlton, Sgt Whyte Sgt Tweedle.
16/17 Dec 43   W/O W A Caldwell   Halifax LL120   MA-W   (161 Sqn)
DETAILS: Aircraft abandoned near Spilsby and crashed in sea off Skegness. Crew safe. Operation WHEELWRIGHT 47, France.
CREW: W/O W A Caldwell, Sgt Mottison, F/Sgt Morris, Sgt R F Philp, F/Sgt Wilson, Sgt Grant, Sgt

Matthews, Sgt Snell.

16/17 Dec 43   F/Lt S N Gray   Halifax DK206   MA-V   (161 Sqn)
DETAILS: Crashed near Capel St Andrews. Operation WHEELWRIGHT 50, France.
KILLED: F/Lt S N Gray, F/Sgt P A Fry, F/O L H Thomas. INJURED: P/O Shine, F/O Craven, Sgt Betts.

16/17 Dec 43   F/O J M McBride   Lysander V9367   MA-B   (161 Sqn)
DETAILS: Crashed in fog at Tangmere. Operation DIABLE, France.
KILLED: F/O J M McBride. Two agents uninjured: Marcel Sandeyron and one other.

16/17 Dec 43   F/Lt S A Hankey   Lysander V9674   MA-K   (161 Sqn)
DETAILS: Crashed in fog near Ford. Operation DIABLE, France.
KILLED: F/Lt S A Hankey and two passengers: Albert Kohan, Jacques Tayar.

19 Dec 43   Sgt H D Williams   Halifax BB364   NF-R   (138 Sqn)
DETAILS: Training flight, collided with chimney near Henlow.
KILLED: Sgt H D Williams, Sgt S Higham, Sgt H M Houghton, Sgt J N Polland, Sgt F H Adams, Sgt C A Kidd, Sgt J E Mooney, P/O C A Woolldridge, Sgt A J McIntyre.

8 Jan 44   P/O H M Kennedy   Halifax LK743   NF-J   (138 Sqn)
DETAILS: Crashed Tetworth Hill, Bedford. Operation TYBALT 3, etc., Belgium.
KILLED: P/O H M Kennedy, Sgt V A E Theedom, Sgt S Whiteley, Sgt E Thripp, F/Sgt D F Davies, DFM, Sgt P S Barlow, Sgt T S Howlett. Passengers: Capt H P Verhaegen, Sgt H Goffin, Sgt Michaux.

23 Jan 44   F/Sgt J W Robertson   Halifax LL182   MA-V   (161 Sqn)
DETAILS: Missing on air/sea rescue search.
LOST: F/Sgt J W Robinson, F/O J M Keay, Sgt E Heaton, Sgt E R Richardson, Sgt H C Walton, Sgt W Meikle, Sgt L Harvey.

23 Jan 44   F/O K F Smith   Halifax DG272   MA-U   (161 Sqn)
DETAILS: Missing on air/sea rescue search.
LOST: F/O K F Smith, F/Sgt K J Roberts, F/O W Preston, DFC, Sgt K Cushing, Sgt J R Bradshaw, F/Sgt J A Whyte, F/Sgt M Livingston, DFM.

7/8 Feb 44   S/Ldr T C S Cooke,   Halifax LW275   NF-O   (138 Sqn)
                    DFC, AFC, DFM
DETAILS: Aircraft abandoned near Hauterives (Drôme). Operation JOCKEY 5, France.
EVADED: S/Ldr T C S Cooke, F/O R W Lewis, DFC, F/O J S Reed, F/O L J Gornall, P/O E Bell, F/O A B Withecombe F/O R L Beattie, RCAF.

7/8 Feb 44   F/O G D Carroll   Halifax LL114   NF-P   (138 Sqn)
DETAILS: Crashed Autrans (Isere). Operation JOHN 35, France.
KILLED: F/O G D Carroll, P/O A E Reid, RCAF, Sgt R D Clement, Sgt P T Thompson, F/Sgt J A Taylor, RCAF, Sgt G S Woodrow, Sgt K W Radford.

10/11 Feb 44   F/O J W McDonald, RAAF   Lysander V9822   MA-E   (161 Sqn)
DETAILS: Crashed 5km N of Dun-sur-Auron (Cher) on landing. Operation SERBIE.
KILLED: F/O J W McDonald, RAAF, passengers Jean Lacroix was badly burnt and W Josset injured.
25 Feb 44   Halifax BB330
DETAILS: Damaged in minor accident and declared 'damaged beyond repair' (AM form 78).

3/4 Mar 44   F/O D S Bell, DFC   Lysander V9605   MA-B   (161 Sqn)
DETAILS: Forced landed near Plumetot (Calvados). Operation FRAMBOISE, France.

EVADED: F/O D S Bell, DFC and passengers Count Elie de Dampierre and Commandant R Lorilleaux.

3/4 Mar 44   F/O W C Kingsley, RCAF   Halifax LL279   NF-R   (138 Sqn)
DETAILS: Believed crashed in Bernay area, (Eure). Operation JOHN 23, France.
KILLED: F/O W C Kingsley, RCAF, F/O G A Roberts, RCAF, F/Sgt K F H Hart, Sgt J R Dutton, RCAF, F/O J E Wright, RCAF. PoW: Sgt H W Bradbury, Sgt E F Gillcash, RCAF.

4/5 Mar 44   P/O E H Edwards   Stirling EE944   HA-H   (218 Sqn)
DETAILS: Crashed at Tempsford, attempting three engine over-shoot.
KILLED: P/O E H Edwards, F/O B Denness, Sgt D G Davies, Sgt E Vamplough, F/Sgt P H Kilsby.
SAFE: Sgt H Porter, Sgt D Meredith.

28 Mar 44   F/O R L Baugham   Hudson FK767   (161 Sqn)
DETAILS: Training flight, dived into ground near Arsley, Beds.
KILLED: F/O R L Baughan, F/O N Brocklehurst, F/Sgt E C Brewer ,RNZAF, W/O2 D S Gillander, RCAF.

30/31 Mar 44   F/Lt B B Mill   Halifax LL287   NF-S   (138 Sqn)
DETAILS: Crashed near Hansweert, Holland. Operation OSRIC 27, Belgium.
KILLED: F/O E Francis, DFC, F/Sgt E Bates, W/O2 F Anderson, RCAF. Evaded: F/Lt B B Mill. PoW: F/Lt D R Beale, W/O J Weir, RAAF, W/O2 S E Godfrey, RCAF, F/Sgt G W Kimpton. Two Belgian agents, Lt R Deprez (Troilus) and Lt A Giroulle (Lucullus), were drowned.

31/1 Apr 44   F/O F B Clark   Halifax LL252   NF-K   (138 Sqn)
DETAILS: Crashed Vallee-de-Cousse, (Indre-et-Loire). Operation ORAGE, etc., France.
KILLED: Sgt E M Keep, Sgt R G Thompson. PoW: F/O F B Clark, F/O R J Carson, RCAF, Sgt W R McBurney, RCAF, Sgt E Wilkinson, Sgt D W L Brown, RCAF.

10/11 Apr 44   F/Sgt J E McGibbon, RCAF   Halifax LK738   MA-T   (161 Sqn)
DETAILS: Crashed near St-Hilaire-sur-Risle (Orne). Operation JOHN 98, etc., France.
KILLED: F/Sgt J E McGibbon, RCAF, Sgt E J Firth, RCAF, Sgt E Merser, Sgt D A Johnson, F/O J R H Willson, Sgt G O Parker, Sgt G T Doyle, RCAF, F/O P W Booth-Smith (2nd Pilot).

19 Apr 44   Sgt K E Vear, RCAF   Hudson T9439   MA-R   (161 Sqn)
DETAILS: Training flight, landed in Sweden.
INTERNED: Sgt K E Vear, RCAF, WO2 P F Boudreau, RCAF, F/Sgt J S O'Bryne, F/O D J Thornton, AC2 D A Barker (aircrew cadet, passenger).

27/28 Apr 44   F/Sgt G H Williamson, RAAF   Halifax LL356   NF-U   (138 Sqn)
DETAILS: Assumed lost off Dutch coast. Operation OSRIC 59, Belgium.
LOST: F/Sgt G H Williamson, RAAF, Sgt H Dootson, Sgt H F Benbow, Sgt G P Croad, F/Sgt A J G Barnes, RCAF, Sgt E R Clayworth, RAAF, Sgt J E Smyth, RCAF.

3/4 May 44   F/Lt L L Whittaker, DFC   Lysander V9664   (161 Sqn)
DETAILS: Shot down over Modésir airfield. Operation FORSYTHIA, France.
KILLED: F/Lt L L Whittaker, DFC.

7/8 May 44   W/Cdr W McF Russell, DFC & Bar Halifax LL280 NF-O   (138 Sqn)
DETAILS: Crashed St-Denis-de-Orques (Sarthe). Operation CITRONELL 1, France.
KILLED: W/Cdr W McF Russell, DFC & bar, F/O D Brown, DFC, F/O J A Armour, DFC, DFM, F/Sgt G Cable, DFM, F/O B P McGonagle, DFC, F/O A F Bryce, F/O N Simister, DFM.

7/8 May 44   F/Lt H H McMullan, RAAF   Halifax LL192   NF-A   (138 Sqn)

DETAILS: Crashed into Kattegat. Operation TABLEJAM 46, Denmark.
LOST: F/Lt H H McMullan, RAAF, F/O L F Stannard, Sgt B Stynes, Sgt R Boffey, F/O K J Murphy, RCAF, Sgt A A McPherson, Sgt L J Smith.
9/10 May 44   F/O A S Coldridge, RCAF   Halifax LL183   MA-W   (138 Sqn*)
*Borrowed from 161 Squadron.
DETAILS: Baled out near Rochechouart (Haute-Vienne). Operation PERCY 3, France.
EVADED: F/O A S Coldridge, RCAF, F/O D A Lennie, RCAF, F/O H D Medland, RCAF, Sgt E Jones, F/O R C Evans, RCAF, Sgt H Blackett. PoW: Sgt R Clark.

17 May 44   F/Sgt W M Strathern   Halifax LK736   (138 Sqn)
DETAILS: Engine on fire and crash landed at Great Barford, Beds.
KILLED: F/O V C Carter. Injured: F/Sgt W M Strathern, F/Sgt D W Robertson. Uninjured: Sgt Harper, Sgt Dunning.

23 May 44   F/L J V Perrins   Halifax DG286   138 Sqn)
DETAILS: Aircraft written off when a tyre burst on take-off, aircraft swung and under-carriage collapsed. No injuries to the six crew members or F/O N L St G Pleasance (pilot under instruction).

30 May 44   Halifax LL300   MA-Z   (161 Sqn)
DETAILS: Aircraft under maintenance in hangar, caught fire and written off.

31/1 Jun 44   F/O J P Gallagher, RCAF   Halifax LL419   NF-V   (138 Sqn)
DETAILS: Shot down over Holland. Operation OSRIC 78, Belgium.
KILLED: F/O J P Gallagher, RCAF, F/O T Carnegie, RCAF, Sgt W J Jeffrey, RCAF, Sgt C Jones, F/O J Zywina, RCAF, F/O H J P Brennan, RCAF, P/O H Barker, RCAF, F/O G W Hemsley.

31/1 Jun 44   W/O H F G Murray   Halifax LL276   NF-F   (138 Sqn)
DETAILS: Crashed at Halsteren, Holland. Operation OSRIC 74, Belgium.
KILLED: W/O H F G Murray, Sgt T McClusky, Sgt A P Cliff-McCullock, Sgt R Robinson, F/O J L Solomon. PoW: F/O J Pearcey, RCAF, F/Sgt F Stead, F/Sgt L P Notten.

31/1 Jun 44   F/Lt W M Hale, RCAF   Hudson V9155   MA-Q   (161 Sqn)
DETAILS: Crashed near Gilze-Rijen, Holland. Operation BEZIQUEZ, etc., Holland.
KILLED: F/Lt W M Hale, RCAF, F/O J Gall, DFC, RNZAF, F/O A G Maskall, DFM, F/O M H Hughes. Dutch agents killed: C M Dekkers (Poker), J Kuenen (Football).

1/2 Jun 44   P/O D A Hayman, RAAF   Halifax LL289   NF-P   (138 Sqn)
DETAILS: Crashed at Longué-Jumelles (Maine-et-Loire). Operation PERCY 7, France.
KILLED: P/O D A Hayman, RAAF, F/O D Hargreaves, F/Sgt A H O Dickel, Sgt D A Page, P/O J C Fardon, RAAF. PoW: P/O G G Houston, Sgt A Lyall (repatriated).

2 Jun 44   F/Lt H Stiles, DFC   Halifax LL284   NF-E   (138 Sqn)
Details: Crashed near Sandy, Beds. on take off. Operation TYBOLT 29, Belgium.
UNINJURED: F/Lt H Stiles, P/O Bryant. SLIGHTLY INJURED: P/O W P Casey, . SUFFERED FRACTURES: P/O W H Marshall, F/O L Ashton, Sgt C E Terrall. DISLOCATED SHOULDER: P/O G Sutherland.

2/3 Jun 44   F/Lt T M Thomas   Halifax LL307   NF-J   138 Sqn)
DETAILS: Crashed at Tholen, Holland. Operation RODERIGO 1, etc., Belgium.
KILLED: F/Lt T M Thomas, F/O D A J Smith, F/Sgt E Nelson, Sgt E Parry, F/O L V Warboys, F/Sgt J K R Vincent, Sgt J A Vick. Two of the three agents in the aircraft were killed, Sgt H Filot and Sgt L Stroobants. The third, G Masereel, was captured.

7 Jun 44   S/Ldr M A Brogan   Halifax LL390   NF-S   (138 Sqn)
DETAILS: Aircraft written off when it swung on take-off. Operation HISTORIAN 10, France. No injuries to crew.

7/8 Jun 44   P/O F H Lyne, RCAF   Halifax LL416   NF-O   (138 Sqn)
DETAILS: Crashed near la Fert-St-Cyr, (Loire-et-Cher). Operation HISTORIAN 10.
KILLED: P/O F H Lyne, RCAF, Sgt J Hamilton, RCAF, F/Sgt R W Westergard, RCAF, Sgt W B Bishop, F/Sgt A R Smith, RCAF, Sgt W H Moffat, RCAF. EVADED: Sgt A McC Hinds, RCAF.

7/8 Jun 44   F/Lt H C Jones, RAAF   Halifax LL306   NF-R   (138 Sqn)
DETAILS: Crashed at Veauville-les-Baons (Seine-Maritime). Operation PERIWINKLE, etc., France.
KILLED: F/Lt H C Jones, RAAF, F/Sgt H A Monsen-Elvik, F/Sgt J G Chadwick, Sgt D J A Kemp, F/O D S Johnstone, RNZAF, Sgt G B C Moore, Sgt F W Herbert.

7/8 Jun 44   F/Sgt A D McKay, RCAF   Halifax LL466   NF-T   (138 Sqn)
DETAILS: Crashed near Doudeville (Seine-Maritime). Operation DONALD 26, France.
KILLED: F/Sgt A D McKay, RCAF, Sgt W T Cheshire, F/O K Bateman, Sgt J R Ireland, F/O C J Ennis, DFC, Sgt D W Drummond, Sgt E W Carlson, RCAF.

5/6 Jul 44   F/Lt J W Menzies, DFC   Hudson FK790   MA-R   (161 Sqn)
DETAILS: Shot down over the Waddenzee, Holland. Operation FIVES 1, Holland.
KILLED: F/Lt J W Menzies, DFC, F/O K R Bunney, Sgt D J Withers, Sgt E R Eliot. Dutch agents killed: P J Quint (Fives), P Verhoef (Racquets), J A Walters (Bowls), J Bockma (Halma).

7/8 Jul 44   Capt P Hysing-Dahl, DFC, RNoAF   Lysander V9490   MA-H   (161 Sqn)
DETAILS: Ditched in English Channel. Operation PALAIS.
RESCUED: Baudry, Capt P Hysing-Dahl, DFC, RNoAF. Drowned: J M L Besnard. DIED: Leseur.

11/12 Jul 44   F/Lt H A Walker, DFC   Halifax LL251   NF-N   (138 Sqn)
DETAILS: Ditched in Mediterranean. Operation PERCY 19, France.
LOST: F/O M A Farr. Remainder of crew, F/Lt H A Walker, DFC, F/O J Cacchioni, RCAF, P/O C D Johnson, Sgt W Wall, Sgt W J Stoneham. RESCUED: F/Sgt Coulson.

18/19 Jul 44   F/O N L St G Pleasance   Halifax LL387   NF-P   (138 Sqn)
DETAILS: Crashed in sea near St-Pair-sur-Mer (Manche). Operation SHIPWRIGHT 9, France.
LOST: F/O N L St G Pleasance, Sgt T Fergus, Sgt R L Lee, Sgt E R Hearn, F/Lt H E Binns, Sgt W L Dalglish, RCAF, Sgt J Allison.

18/19 Jul 44   F/Lt J A Kidd   Halifax LL364   NF-B   (138 Sqn)
DETAILS: Collided over DZ with B-24 of 801st BG Crew buried at Marigny-l'Eglise (Nievre) near to where they crashed. Operation DICK 89, France.
KILLED: F/Lt J A Kidd, F/O K R Urquart, RCAF, Sgt C Taylor, Sgt C F T Miles, F/Sgt B Stroud, Sgt G B Byrne, Sgt J R Moody.

1 Aug 44   S/Ldr R E Wilkinson   Hudson N7263   (161 Sqn)
DETAILS: Swung on landing and struck airfield buildings. No casualties aircraft written off.

4/5 Aug 44   F/Lt E A Loos   Halifax LL248   MA-U   (161 Sqn)
DETAILS: Crashed near Huiron (Marne). Operation BOB 166, France.
KILLED: F/Lt E A Loos, F/O I A Blaikie, RNZAF, P/O K F Morgan, RNZAF, Sgt B F Holland, F/Sgt D G Patterson, F/O R B Hall. EVADED: W/O J H Hill.

4/5 Aug 44   F/O J P Alcock   Lysander V9748   MA-D   (161 Sqn)

DETAILS: Shot down by night fighter, probably an RAF Mosquito, crashed near Messac (Ille-et-Vilaine). Operation PIROUGE, France.
KILLED: F/O J P Alcock, Lucien Germerau (passenger).

8/9 Aug 44   F/Sgt J W Nicholls   Halifax LL358   MA-Y   (161 Sqn)
DETAILS: Crashed near Cugny (Aisne). Operation TOM 53, France.
KILLED: F/Sgt J W Nicholls, W/O1 J B Grady, RCAF, Sgt A A Rivers, Sgt B C F Dean, P/O G E Rhead, Sgt C G Bragg, Sgt E Markson.

8/9 Aug 44   P/O G W Paterson, RNZAF   Halifax LL308   NF-Q   (138 Sqn)
DETAILS: Crashed in the area of Géraudot (Aube). Operation OSRIC 45, Belgium.
KILLED: P/O G W Paterson, RNZAF, P/O A W Atterton, Sgt H Bedford, Sgt S R Curtis, Sgt C C Dowse, F/Sgt L P Searell, RNZAF. EVADED: F/Sgt F E O Evans, RNZAF.

28/29 Aug 44   F/Lt P Green   Halifax LL388   MA-W   (161 Sqn)
DETAILS: Crashed at Hedel, Holland. Operation HENDRIK, Holland.
KILLED: F/O A K M Dean. Died from wounds: W/O N F Slade. PoW: F/L P Green (wounded), W/O G Dugdale, Sgt N Huntley, F/O C Carter, Sgt N Hayward. Three Dutch agents on board escaped: J M Van der Meer, K Buitendijk. Believed killed: G Kroon.

31/1 Sep 44   F/Lt A J Wallace, RCAF   Stirling LK131   NF-T   (138 Sqn)
DETAILS: Crashed near Gilze-en-Rijen. Operation GERRIT 1, Holland.
KILLED: F/Lt A J Wallace, RCAF, F/O P E McNamara, RCAF, Sgt R W Bullen, Sgt R F G Bailey, Sgt G C Hanson, Sgt W A Baxter, F/O C B Thompson, RCAF. PoW: Sgt C Bowker.

31/1 Sep 44   F/O R B Hardie, RAAF   Stirling LJ503   NF-P   (138 Sqn)
DETAILS: Crashed at Lombard (Doubs). Operation BOB 325, France.
KILLED: F/O R B Hardie, RAAF, F/Sgt M Stanley, RAAF, Sgt J C Alexander, F/Sgt G W McLeod, RAAF, F/Sgt N E Barnes, RAAF, F/Sgt S J Hayes, RAAF, F/Sgt R A Ashton, RAAF, Sgt G M Jack.

8/9 Sep 44   S/Ldr G M Rothwell, DFC   Stirling LK200   NF-J   (138 Sqn)
DETAILS: Crashed at Cocksdorp, Texel. Operation DRAUGHTS, etc., Holland.
KILLED: F/O J Hulme, F/O T R Court, DFC, F/O G W Walton, DFC, BEM. PoW: S/Ldr G M Rothwell, DFC, F/O R A McKitrick, DFC, P/O C D Shaw, DFM, F/Sgt R W Willmot.

21 Sep 44   F/O A J Spencer   Stirling LK208   MA-X   (161 Sqn)
DETAILS: Swung on take-off, aircraft written-off, no casualties.

28/29 Sept 44   F/Lt R W Read   Stirling LJ932   NF-N   (138 Sqn)
DETAILS: Crashed at Ludford Magna, Lincs. Operation TABLEJAM 14, etc., Denmark.
INJURED: F/Lt R W Read, F/O S Curtis. UNINJURED: F/O R C Bryant, DFC, F/O P Casey, RCAF, F/Lt M A D Riddel, DFM, F/Sgt W Waddington, W/O N R Hutchins, RAAF.

29/30 Sep 44   F/O J A Lamberton   Lysander V9749   MA-M   (161 Sqn)
DETAILS: Missing en route from le Bourget, Paris to Tempsford.
MISSING: F/O J A Lamberton. Passengers: F/Lt C P Clark, S/Ldr A W A Compton. Major J W Saunders, MBE.

6/7 Oct 44   S/Ldr G E Abecassis   Stirling LK238   MA-X   (161 Sqn)
DETAILS: Crashed in flames Vemb, Denmark. Operation TABLEJAM 26, etc., Denmark.
Killed: W/O R F Philp, RAAF. PoW: S/Ldr G E Abecassis, F/O K H Walker. EVADED: F/Lt R R Gee, P/O L N Flower, P/O P J Moloney, F/O S C Woodham.

19 Oct 44   F/Lt R V Levy   Stirling LK207   MA-W   (161 Sqn)

DETAILS: Aircraft broke up during air test.
KILLED: F/Lt R V Levy, P/O J W Stigger, Sgt A J Coveney, Sgt W G Atkinson, Sgt P Kelly.

8/9 Nov 44   F/Lt F J Ford   Stirling LJ993   NF-M   (138 Sqn)
DETAILS: Lost at sea through bad weather. Operation CRUPPER 11, Norway.
LOST: F/Lt F J Ford, P/O J R Tanner, F/Lt E Howell, DFC, P/O D I B Fisher, F/O M W Oliver,
F/Sgt B F F Grimes, F/Sgt D J Cornish. Norwegian agents: Peter Deinboll, Arne Gjestland,

8/9 Nov 44   W/O L A Oullette, RCAF   Stirling LK198   NF-H   (138 Sqn)
DETAILS: Lost at sea through bad weather. Operation PUFFIN 2, Norway.
LOST: W/O L A Oullette, RCAF, P/O L W Nelson, RCAF, F/O S H Sharpe, F/Sgt A F Birdseye,
F/Sgt R A Best, RCAF, P/O P Barnicke, RCAF, Sgt A J Jeffrey.

26/27 Nov 44   F/Lt R R Witham, DFC, RAAF   Stirling LK151   NF-E   (138 Sqn)
DETAILS: Crashed in sea near Assens, Denmark. Operation TABLEJAM 69, Denmark..
LOST: F/Lt R R Witham, DFC, RAAF, F/O G H B Slinn, RAAF, F/O T P McHale, RCAF, Sgt R H
Berrett, F/Sgt K Naylor, F/Sgt A H Bedggood, P/O C Elleman.

26/27 Nov 44   S/Ldr R E Wilkinson, DFC   Hudson T9463   MA-L   (161 Sqn)
DETAILS: Crashed SE border of Belgium and Luxembourg. Operation FLECKNEY 1, Germany.
KILLED: S/Ldr R E Wilkinson, DFC, F/O J Weddell, F/Lt F J J Champion, DFM, F/Lt G H Ash, DFC.

2/3 Dec 44   F/O G F Nichols   Stirling LK143   NF-B   (138 Sqn)
DETAILS: Lost at sea. Operation TABLEJAM 169, etc., Denmark.
LOST: F/O G F Nichols, P/O C E Terrell, F/Sgt J G Harris, Sgt A C Butler, F/Sgt J A Golding, Sgt
F A W Filer, F/Sgt L W Poulson, RAAF.

30/31 Dec 44   F/Lt R McGregor, RNZAF   Stirling LK283   NF-S   (138 Sqn)
DETAILS: Lost at sea from ship-borne flak. Operation CRUPPER 10.
LOST: F/Lt R McGregor, RNZAF, F/O G A Comer, RAAF, W/O G Harris, F/Sgt D A Kenningham,
Sgt D J Perkins, Sgt R E Ward, Sgt G Harrison.

9/10 Feb 45   F/Sgt L S Tucker, RAAF   Stirling LK279   NF-L   (138 Sqn)
DETAILS: Crashed into Little Belt, Denmark Operation TABLEJAM 190, Denmark.
LOST: F/Sgt L S Tucker, RAAF, Sgt W M Haragan, F/Sgt G C Toes, W/O R J Ball, F/O G E Mercer,
F/Sgt R Y French, F/Sgt W J Carthew.

14 Feb 45   F/O E Timperley   Stirling LK236   MA-Y   (161 Sqn)
DETAILS: Local flight struck by USAAF Mustang P51 making unauthorised pass.
KILLED: F/O E Timperley, Sgt D H Mayers, Sgt W G Cornish, F/O G C Wiggins, F/Sgt C W Saunders,
F/Sgt P N Carr, Sgt P N Ellis. P51 PILOT KILLED: F/O T W Riley USAAF, 364 FG, 363 F-Sqn.

21/22 Feb 45   F/Lt D T Oliver   Hudson T9405   MA-K   (161 Sqn)
DETAILS: Crashed near Meppen. Operation CROC, Germany.
KILLED: W/Cdr G Watson, DFM, F/O J M Hartman, Safe: F/Lt D T Oliver, F/Lt F M Jarman, RAAF,
F/L O H Morgan, RCAF.

23/24 Feb 45   F/Sgt E W Sinkinson   Stirling LK149   NF-D   138 Sqn)
DETAILS: Lost at sea. Operation TABLEJAM 181, Denmark.
LOST: F/Sgt E W Sinkinson, F/Sgt G Cole, F/Sgt B R Hasler, F/Sgt H T Batten, Sgt W Webster, Sgt
G A Letts, P/O A Sharman.
26/27 Feb 45   F/Lt P B Cornwallis   Stirling LK272   NF-P   (138 Sqn)

DETAILS: Damaged by flak, crashed into North Sea. Operation CRUPPER 37, Norway.
LOST: F/Lt P B Cornwallis, F/O L J Gornell, DFC, P/O S A Pepworth, DFM, Sgt J E Cory, F/Sgt S S Hagerty, RCAF, F/O J E Stanton, RAAF, W/O B D Tovey, RAAF.

4/5 Mar 45   W/Cdr M A Brogan, DFC   Stirling LK312   MA-W   (161 Sqn)
DETAILS: Lost at sea near Livo Island, Denmark. Operation TABLEJAM 209, Denmark
LOST: W/Cdr M A Brogan, DFC, F/O N Clarke, W/O E E Gray, W/O F Mahoney, F/Lt H O Sharman, DFC, F/O F J Watson, DFM, F/O H T Wigley, DFC.

4/5 Mar 45   F/O L G Sleven   Stirling LJ999   NF-Q   (138 Sqn)
DETAILS: Crashed at Tipperpold, Denmark. Operation TABLEJAM 241, Denmark.
PoW: F/O L G Sleven, P/O N E Tilly, F/Sgt J F Kyle, F/Sgt G M Maude, Sgt J T Breeze, Sgt W L Clarke, Sgt J F Bloomer.

20/21 Mar 45   F/Lt T Helfer   Hudson FK803   MA-N   (161 Sqn)
DETAILS: Shot down by night fighter – possibly USAAF. Operation BENEDICT, etc., Germany.
KILLED: F/O F H Thompson, DFM, F/Lt R F Escreet, DFM, F/O H S Johnson. Belgian agents: Lt G Corbisher, Lt L de Winton, Lt J Morel. SURVIVED: F/Lt T Helfer.

20/21 Mar 45   F/O G S Ragan, RCAF   Hudson AE595   MA-L   (161 Sqn)
DETAILS: Shot down near airfield at Rheine, Germany. Operation WALNUT, Germany.
KILLED: F/O G S Ragan, RCAF, W/O1 F E Grey, RCAF, F/Sgt P Bradley, F/Sgt C A Thomas, RNZAF.

20/21 Mar 45   F/Lt R N Ferris, RCAF   Hudson T9445   MA-O   (161 Sqn)
DETAILS: Shot down by night fighter. Operation NORVIC, Germany.
KILLED: F/Lt R N Ferris, RCAF, F/O J E Traill, RCAF, F/Lt A F Penhale, RCAF, W/O1 R G Hutton, RCAF.

22/23 Mar 45   F/Lt A H Aitken   Stirling LK209   MA-T   (161 Sqn)
DETAILS: Crashed in sea near island of Vlieland. Operation ROWING 3, Holland.
Killed: F/Lt A H Aitken, P/O R A Caston, Sgt W Horrocks, F/Sgt A R Paton, P/O W L Shaw, P/O R A Swift. PoW: F/Sgt J T White.

30/31 Mar 45   F/Lt E P C Kidd, DFC   Stirling LK119   MA-Y   (161 Sqn)
DETAILS: Crashed at Hegland in Holt, Norway. Operation BIT 14, Norway.
KILLED: F/Lt E P C Kidd, DFC, F/Sgt A D Shopland, F/Sgt G A Heath, DFM, F/O T S Macaulay, F/Sgt H Minshull, W/O A M Taylor, RAAF, Sgt R A Burgess.

11/12 Apr 45   F/Lt D B Webb   Hudson FK763   MA-P   (161 Sqn)
DETAILS: Engine failure returning to UK, crew baled out, aircraft crashed at Dorking. No injuries. Operation FLAP, Germany.

18 May 45   F/Lt R C Hawkins, DFM   Hudson AE505   MA-L   (161 Sqn)
DETAILS: Crashed at Brussels following a heavy landing
KILLED: F/Lt R C Hawkins, DFM, F/O E F Clemens, P/O E Hadley, F/O M Watson, DFM, Sgt E A Cox, LAC A Appelyard.

References, Files and Publications

PARACHUTE AIR OPERATIONS ONLY. PUBLIC RECORD OFFICE FILES:-

No.138 Squadron Pilot's Operation reports:-
AIR20/8334 1941–42, 1419 Flight/138 Squadron.
AIR20/8452 1942
AIR20/8476 1943
AIR20/8477 1943
AIR20/8478 1944
AIR20/8479 1944
AIR20/8480 1944
AIR20/8481 1944
AIR20/8482 1944
AIR20/8365 1944/45

No.161 Squadron Pilot's Operation reports:-
AIR20/8456 1942/43.
AIR20/8498 1943
AIR20/8500 1943
AIR20/8293 1943–44
AIR20/8501 1944–45
AIR20/8499 1945

Rough diary of operations:-
AIR20/8459 No.138 Squadron.
AIR20/8460 1942–44 No.161 Squadron.
AIR20/8461 1944–45 No.161 Squadron.

Operational Record Books:-
AIR27/956 No.138 Squadron 1941–44.
AIR27/957 No.138 Squadron 1945.
AIR27/1056 No.161 Squadron 1942–45.
AIR28/820 RAF Tempsford 1941–45.

Bomber Command Loss Cards for 138 & 161 Squadrons for 1944/45 – courtesy of the RAF Museum.

PUBLICATIONS:-

Atherton, Louise, *SOE in Eastern Europe*, Public Record Office, 1995
Abbreviation in chapter notes – SOEEE.
Atherton, Louise, *SOE Operations in Scandinavia*, Public Record Office, 1944

Abbreviation – SOEOS.

Chorley, W R, *Bomber Command Losses 1939/1940/1941/1942/1943/1944*, Midland

Counties Publications, 1992/93/94/96/97.

Abbreviation – BCL.

Cookridge , E H, *Inside SOE*, Arthur Barker, 1966

Abbreviation – ISOE.

Foot, M R D, *SOE in France*, HMSO, 1966.

Abbreviation – SOEF.

Jones, Lianne, *A Quiet Courage*, Bantam Press, 1990.

Abbreviation – AQC.

Merrick, K A, *Flights of the Forgotten*, Arms and Amour Press, 1989.

Abbreviation – FOTF.

Middlebrook, Martin, & Everitt, Chris, *The Bomber Command War Diaries*,

Viking Press, 1985.

Abbreviation – BCWD.

Public Record Office.

Abbreviation – PRO.

Verity, Hugh, *We landed by Moonlight*, AirData/Crécy, 1995.

Abbreviation – WLBM.

West, Nigel, *Secret War*, Coronet Books, 1993.

Abbreviation – SW.

Notes to Chapters

CHAPTER ONE – 1940
19/20 Oct Operation FELIX 1 – FOTF, p.20, WLBM p.35. R C Hockey
flights and passengers (RCH flying log book).

CHAPTER TWO – JANUARY–AUGUST 1941
17/18 Feb Loss of S/Ldr Keast – FOTF, p.24.
14/15 Mar Operation SAVANNA – SOEF, p.153.
    Maryland test flights (Gp/Capt R C Hockey private papers).
5/6 May BOMBPROOF – SOEF, p162.
10/11 May AUTOGYRO, etc. – SOEF, p163.
11/12 May JOSEPHINE – SOEF, p158.
5/6 Jul TORTURE – SOEF, p166.
9/10 Jul ADJUDICATE – SOEEE, p.27.
9/10 Jul AUTOGYRO C – SOEF, p169.
6/7 Aug THEORUM, etc. – SOEF, p169.
7/8 Aug FAUX, etc. – SOEF, p168.
7/8 Aug GLASSHOUSE – ISOE, p408.
29/30 Aug TROMBONE – SOEF, p167.

CHAPTER THREE – SEPTEMBER–OCTOBER 1941
2/3 Sep Operation ADJUDICATE – SOEF, p176.
4/5 Sep LEVEE, etc. – WLBM, p39.
9/10 Sep ESMOND/COLUMBUS – ISOE, p562/563.
10/11 Sep BARTER – SOEF, p167.
3/4 Oct PERCENTAGE – G/Capt Hockey private papers.

CHAPTER FOUR – NOVEMBER–DECEMBER 1941
6/7 Nov Operation CUTLASS – SOEF, p168.
7/8 Nov CATTARH – ISOE, p423.
26/27 Nov PLAICE – SOEF, p189.
28 Nov F/Lt Laurent – Letter from *Armée De L'Air Service Historique* dated
29/9/97 to J B Chamberlain giving service CV.
8/9 Dec STOAT – WLBM, p44.
8/9 Dec COOL – SOEF, p168.
28/29 Dec ATHROPOID – G/Capt Hockey private papers, SOEEE, p27
    and AIR20/8306, 138 Squadron Air Transport Operations.

CHAPTER FIVE – JANUARY–FEBRUARY–13 MARCH 1942
1/2 Jan Operation MAINMAST – SOEF, p182.
6/7 Jan Operation flown by Hockey/Wilde (Hockey Log book).

6/7 Jan SHIRT, etc. – agents fate, translated from letter dated 18/3/42 – Polish GHQ VI Bureau.
27/28 Feb CARROT, etc. – SW p121 and ISOE, p426 (Date wrong).
1/2 Mar BERYL II, etc. – WLBM, p192, 216.
3/4 Mar RUM – PRO H54/342
10/11 Mar FRENSHAM 1 – Hockey private papers.

CHAPTER SIX – TEMPSFORD 14th MARCH–8th APRIL 1942
25/26 Mar Operation WHISKEY – PRO H54/342.
27/28 Mar STEEL/ZINC, etc. – SOEEE, p31,33,34. Names – SW, p116.
27/28 Mar WATERCRESS, etc. – ISOE, p422.
28/29 Mar GROUSE – ISOE, p514/5.
28/29 Mar TURNIP, etc. – ISOE, p422.
28/29 Mar LETTUCE, etc. – ISOE, p423.
1/2 Apr SYCAMORE, etc. – SOEF, p192.
5/6 Apr LEEK, etc. – ISOE, p423. Rabinowitch personal message – ISOE, p181.

CHAPTER SEVEN – 9th APRIL–31tst MAY 1942
16/17 Apr TABLETOP – ISOE, p564/5.
24/25 Apr CATTARH III – FOTF, p56.
27/28 Apr BIVOUAC, etc. – SOEEE, p27/28, SW, p116.
29/30 Apr STEEL/INTRANSITIVE, etc. – SOEEE, p30, SW, p116.
28/29 May TENATURE – WLBM, p49.
29/30 May CATTARH, etc. – ISOE, p427. Packing of Eureka FOTF, p58.
30/31 May PRIVET, etc. – SOEF, p194/5.

CHAPTER EIGHT – JUNE–31st AUGUST 1942
21/22 Jun BARSAC – SOEEE, p27, Cargo manifest, AIR20/8451.
22/23 Jun LETTUCE 3, etc. – ISOE, p428, Cargo manifest, AIR20/8451
23/24 Jun Lysander Bombing FOTF, p59, AIR20/8460
24/25 Jun BURGUNDY – SOEEE, p28, Cargo manifest, AIR20/8451.
26/27 Jun CATTARH/MARROW – ISOE, p431, Cargo manifest, AIR20/8451.
27/28 Jun MONKEYPUZZLE – SOEF, p196.
1/2 Jul PIMENTO – Brooks – Special Forces Club Newsletter, Autumn 1988, via Mark Seaman. SOEF, p218.
3 Jul Bomb Target Committee letter – AIR20/8170
7/8 Jul 138 Squadron Nickels – AIR20/8454.
23/24 Jul LETTUCE 4, etc. – ISOE, p428.
26/27 Jul Bombing sorties – AIR28/820 Tempsford ORB.
27 Jul Bombing Gien – FOTF, p61. Photos – AIR20/8170
29/30 Jul LETTUCE 5 – BCL, p42.
29/30 Jul SCIENTIST, etc. – SOEF, p199.
31/1 Jul TABLETALK, etc. – ISOE p566.
24/25 Aug SYRINGA 7 – PRO WO208/3310.
31/1 Aug/Sep AMETHYST/DIRECTOR 2 – SOEF, p146.

CHAPTER NINE – 138 SQN OPS END OF AUGUST–SEPTEMBER 1942
24/25 Sep MANGOLD, etc. KALE, etc. – SW, p122.

24/25 Sep MONKEYPUZZLE – SOEF, p465, AQC, p53.
25/26 Sep DETECTIVE, etc. – SOEF, p22.

CHAPTER TEN – OCTOBER 1942
1/2 Oct CABBAGE, etc. – ISOE, p456.
1/2 Oct CRAB 3/PHYSICIAN, etc. – SOEF, p457
3/4 Oct BITTERN – SOEOS, p28
18/19 Oct TABLETOP A – ISOE, p569.
18/19 Oct GOUSE 2 – ISOE, p516.
21/22 Oct CELERY A, etc. – ISOE, p457.
24/25 Oct ANTIMONY – SW, p116, SOEEE, p27.
24/25 Oct BLUNDERHEAD – R Seth, *Encyclopaedia of Espionage*, Book Club
    Associates, 1974, p568.
27/28 Oct MARROW 10, etc. – ISOE p457.

CHAPTER ELEVEN – NOVEMBER–DECEMBER 1942
9 Nov Albermarle escort – AIR20/8317.
11 Nov Air transport for TORCH – AIR20/8309.
18/19 Nov P/O Cussen crash landing Portugal – WO208/3312.
18/19 Nov SCIENTIST 2, etc. – SOEF, p223.
25/26 Nov STEWARD – AIR20/8460
17/18 Dec Loss of F/Lt Sutton's Halifax W1002 (Conversation with W/Cdr
    J C K Sutton, MBE, August 1996).
20/21 Dec COCKLE – SOEF, p220
28/29 Dec TURNIPS, etc., LETTUCE 4, etc. – ISOE, p458.
29/30 Dec BOOKMAKER, etc. – SOEF, p189.

CHAPTER TWELVE – JANUARY 1943
18/19 Jan MERCURY IRIDIUM – SOEEE, p30.
22/23 Jan CRAB 11, etc. – SOEF, p291.
23/24 Jan MINER – WLBM, p194.
23/24 Jan GUNNERSIDE – SOEOS, p30, ISOE, p519.
23/24 Jan CHEESE 3 – SOEOS, p29.
25/26 Jan DESIGNER, etc. – SOEF, p283, AQC, p166.
26/27 Jan ATALA – WLBM, p194
26/27 Jan GAUGE – FOTF, p71.

CHAPTER THIRTEEN – FEBRUARY 1943
13 Feb PULLOVER – FOTF, p73.
13/14 Feb SIRENE, etc. – WLBM, p81.
13/14 Feb MARROW 16, etc. – ISOE, p466/467.
16/17 Feb CARHAMPTON – SOEOS, p29.
16/17 Feb TURNIP, etc. – Names ISOE, p 457.
16/17 Feb TABLETOP, etc. – Names ISOE, p572
18/19 Feb MARROW 18/GOLF, etc. – Names ISOE, p467.
24/25 Feb ECLIPSE – WLBM, p195.
25 Feb RODNEY – FOTF, p73.
26/27 Feb PAULINE, etc.- Marcel Ruby, *F Section SOE*, Grafton Books,
    1990, p179.

CHAPTER FOURTEEN – MARCH 1943
9/10 Mar SEAKALE, etc. – Names ISOE, p467.

11/12 Mar TABLETOP 1 – ISOE, p573.
12/13 Mar PHEASANT Putt/Pickard – WLBM, p82.
12/13 Mar MARDONIUS – SOEOS, p316.
19/20 Mar SIRENE 2 – SOEF, p240.
23/24 Mar JOCKEY, etc. – WLBM, p195.
23/24 Mar BUTLER, etc. – SOEF, p258

CHAPTER FIFTEEN – APRIL 1943
12/13 Apr DIRECTOR 22 – FOTF, p78, WO208/3313.
12/13 Apr PRUNUS – SOEF, p275/6.
14/15 Apr STOCKBROKER, etc. – SOEF, p286, AQC, p172.
14/15 Apr SCIENTIST, etc. – SOEF, p252, Jerrard Tickell, *Odette*, Pan
    Books Ltd, 1955, p233-235
16/17 Apr PETUNIA – WLBM, p196
18/19 Apr SCULLION, etc. – SOEF, p250.
21/22 Apr TABLETOP 2, etc. – ISOE, p580
21/22 Apr NETBALL and LACROSSE – ISOE, p470.
22/23 Apr TOMY – WLBM, p196.

CHAPTER SIXTEEN – MAY–JUNE 1943
12/13 May DONKEYMAN 1 – WO208/3313.
14/15 May SHAWL, etc. – SOEF, p286.
21/22 May POLO, etc. – SW, p133, ISOE, p470.
13/16 Jun SACRISTAN, etc. – SOEF, p259.

CHAPTER SEVENTEEN – JULY–AUGUST 1943
15/16 Jun ARCHDEACON, etc. – SOEF, p314.
17/18 Jun PARSON, etc. – SOEF, p261.
15/16 Jul HERD, etc. – AIR20/8258.
22/23 Jul PRINCESS – WO208/3314.
22/23 Jul GAMEKEEPER – SOEF, p323, WLBM, p198.
24/25 Jul SCIENTIST 50, etc. – SOEF, p261.
12/13 Aug SCULLION A – SW, p283.
12/13 Aug SPRUCE 20, etc. – WO208/3316, FOTF, p88.
13/14 Aug MESSENGER, etc. – SOEF, p256, AQC, p197/198.
14/15 Aug SCIENTIST – Norwegian crew members (private letter Edvard
    E Rieber-Mohn).
14/15 Aug PIMENTO 12 – WO208/3314.
16/17 Aug WHEELWRIGHT 17 – WO208/3314.
17/18 Aug DRESSMAKER A, etc. – SOEF, p250.
20/21 Aug SACRISTAN, etc. – SOEF, p260.
22/23 Aug WHEELWRIGHT 19 – SOEF, p285, p466, AQC p180.

CHAPTER EIGHTEEN – SEPTEMBER–OCTOBER 1943
18/19 Sep BOMB – WLBM, p201.
22/23 Sep WRESTLER, etc. – SOEF, p381.
10/11 Oct FEATHER – ISOE, p545,
11/12 Oct BUNDLE – SOEOS, p28.
18/19 Oct BADMINGTON – SOEF, p326, WO208/3317, WO208/3323.

CHAPTER NINETEEN – NOVEMBER–DECEMBER 1943
3/4 Nov JOHN 13 – WO208/3316.

9 Nov – Royal Visit to Tempsford (The programme, related to in the text, is reproduced by gracious permission of Her Majesty the Queen.)

15/16 Nov CONJURER- WLBM, p203.

10/11 Dec TABLEJAM 18/19 – AIR20/8249, WO205/3316, ISOE, p585.

10/11 Dec Lancaster casualties courtesy of Robert M Owen.

10/11 Dec STEN – WLBM, p204.

CHAPTER TWENTY – JANUARY–FEBRUARY 1944

4/5 Jan EIGER – SOEEE, p29.

4/5 Jan ARQUEBUS 1 – SOEPS, p16.

4/5 Jan WHEELWRIGHT 50 – SOEF, P378, AQC, p190.

6/7 Jan EVEREST 1 – SOEEE, p30.

6/7 Jan JOHN 38 – SOEF, p357.

3/4 Feb BUTLER 14 and PHONO 8 – SOEF, p328.

5/6 Feb SPIRTUALIST 1 – SOEF, p368.

7/8 Feb JOCKEY 5 – WO208/3319.

8/9 Feb CALANGUE – SW, p298.

8/9 Feb PHONO 5 – SOEF, p341/2.

10/11 Feb SERBIE – WLBM, p205.

29/1 Feb BUTLER 12 – SOEF, p335.

29/1 Feb PETER 16 – Bruce Marshall, *The White Rabbit*, Evans Brothers Ltd, 1952, p94, SOEF p363, p403.

29/1 Feb PHONO 4 – SOEF, p342, AQC, p216.

CHAPTER TWENTY-ONE – MARCH 1944

2/3 Mar MUSICIAN 12 – BCWD, p478.

2/3 Mar MUSICIAN 7 – SOEF, p332.
    ARCHDEACON – (Monies parachuted) SOEF, p345.

2/3 Mar STATIONER 31 – SOEF, p378.

3/4 Mar F/O Bell – WO28/3319

7/8 Mar PAUL 54 – SOEF, p380.

18/19 Mar WHEELWRIGHT 64 – SOEF, p466, AQC, p224.

31/1 Mar FARO – BBO records via Guido Zembsch-Schreve.

CHAPTER TWENTY-TWO – APRIL 1944

5/6 Apr STATIONER targets – SOEF, p380.

5/6 Apr STATIONER 59 – SOEF, p381.

5/6 Apr UMPIRE and LILAC – WLBM, p206, AIR20/8260.

5/6 Apr R J Minney, *Carve Her Name With Pride*, Newnes 1956, p140.

19 Apr Sgt K E Vear – FOTF, p112, Bomber Command Loss Card.

28/29 Apr MAKIR – see 6/7 May.

CHAPTER TWENTY-THREE – MAY 1944

3/4 May Mailly-le-Camp, etc. – BCWD, p505.

3/4 May FORSYTHIA – WLBM, p207.

3/4 May PIMENTO – SOEF, p374.

6/7 May, 28/29 Apr MAKIR – Oluf Reed Olsen, *Two Eggs On My Plate*, The Companion Book Club, 1954, p210. BCWD p502.

8/9 May PERCY 3 – WO208/3323.

31/1 May BEZIQUEZ – BBO records via Guido Zembsch-Schreve.

CHAPTER TWENTY-FOUR – JUNE–JULY 1944

5/6 Jun OVERLORD – G/Capt R C Hockey remarks – *RAF Historical Society*, issue No.5, Feb 1989, p20.

5/6 Jun POLITICION – Paul McCue, *Operation Bulbasket*, Pen & Sword, 1996, p19.

7/8 Jun HISTORIAN 10 – WO208/3324.

7/8 Jul PALAISE – WLBM, p208.

10/11 Jul SCIENTIST 107 – SOEF, p408.

11/12 Jul F/Lt H A Walker – Ditching AIR20/8249.

27/28 Jul TENERIFE – WLBM, p208.

CHAPTER TWENTY-FIVE – AUGUST–SEPTEMBER 1944

4/5 Aug PIROQUE – WLBM, p208, FOTF, p124.

8/9 Aug OSRIC 45 – WO208/3325.

9/10 Aug ROWING – BBO records via Guido Zembsch-Schreve.

28/29 Aug HENDRICK 1 – BBO records via Guido Zembsch-Schreve.

8/9 Sep DRAUGHTS, etc. – Jim Breeze/John Reid. BBO records via Guido Zembsch-Schreve.

29/30 Sep HAM – AHB5.

CHAPTER TWENTY-SIX – OCTOBER–NOVEMBER–DECEMBER 1944

6/7 Oct TABLEJAM – WO208/3324, John Reid.

19 Oct F/Lt A Levy, DFC, RNZAF – Jim Breeze/John Reid.

26/27 Nov FLECKNEY 1 – AIR20/8461, FOTF, p133.

26/27 Nov CRUPPER 30 – Names via John Reid Norwegian sources.

28/29 Dec REINS 7 – Names via John Reid Norwegian sources.

31/1 Dec HOCK 2 – Names via John Reid Norwegian sources.

CHAPTER TWENTY-SEVEN – JANUARY–FEBRUARY–MARCH– APRIL 1945

21/22 Feb CROC – Bomber Command Loss Card P428838/45.

21/22 Feb CARMAN – Gibb McCall, *Flight Most Secret*, William Kimber, 1981, p232.

21/22 Feb SNAFFLE 5 – Names via John Reid Norwegian sources.

24/25 Feb MONTFORD, etc. – Gibb McCall, p233.

Index–Personnel

Index–Agents/Parachutists

This index is of the Agents/Parchutists mentioned by name in the text. There were many more, regrettably unidentified and in addition dropped by No.38 Group or the B24's of "Carpetbagger" Force. In all there are recorded in the text operations from which upward of 1400 agents/parachuists were dropped.

The country involved is indicated by the following symbols:-
(Aus) Austria, (B) Belgium, (Cor) Corsica, (Cz) Czechoslovakia, (D) Denmark, (Est) Estonia, (F) France, (G) Germany, (H) Holland, (N) Norway, (P) Poland

Operation Codes

The following code names appearing in the text of this book were given mainly to parachute operations conducted by the Tempsford Squadrons. There must have been many more. Some of these operations were conducted collectively e.g. 'BALACLAVA/WALLABY/SPRINGBOK' but are shown individually in this listing. Other codes show only the basic circuit name e.g. 'STATIONER' a large circuit in France with many individually numbered DZs e.g. 'STATIONER 17' 'STATIONER 35'. Apart from blind drops and sites operated by the enemy, each code name represents a line or a triangle of lights in a field or a mountain valley attended by a few men during the moon period, regardless of the weather, awaiting the arrival of their aeroplane. In all, these code names represent the prodigious effort of European resistance against a common enemy. The names and dates of these operations were taken from the following PRO files, AIR20/8459/8460/8461.

AUSTRIA
Everest; Sodawater; Whiskey.

BELGIUM
Albion; Balaclava, Balthasar, Binder, Buckler, Bullfrog, Burgundy; Canticle, Caracal, Cawder, Cezarewich, Chicken, Claudius, Conjugal; Dingo, Duncan; Elkhound; Floats; Gags, Gibbon, Golfer, Grantham, Gratiano; Hillcat, Hireling; Iago, Incomparable, Intersection; Joiner; Karl, Koala, Kees; Labrador, Lamb, Lemur, Luckyshot; Madumus, Major Domo, Mandrill, Manfriday, Manningtree, Marbles, Marine, Marmoset, Mastiff, Mill, Mink, Mistletoe, Mongoose, Montand, Mouflon, Mule, Muskrat, Mustide, Mustick; Ocelet, Osric, Outcaste, Othello; Periwig, Playbill, Pointer, Porcupine, Porter, Primo, Props; Quintro; Retriever, Rhumbold, Roderigo, Rowntree; Sable, Secundo, She, Shrew, Springbok, Stoat; Thersites, Toad, Turmoil, Tybalt; Vampire; Wallaby, Weasel.

CORSICA
Sea Urchin.

CZECHOSLOVAKIA
Anthropoid, Antimony; Bioscope, Bivouac, Bronze; Intransitive, Iridium, Iron; Mercury; Outdistance; Percentage; Silver, Steel; Zinc.

DENMARK
Chilblain, Columbus; Spaghetti; Tablehabit, Tablejam, Tablejelly, Tablegossip, Tablelamp, Tableleg, Tablemanners, Tablemat, Tablemustard, Tablesandwich, Tabletalk, Tabletop.

ESTONIA
Blunderhead.

FRANCE
Achilles, Acrobat, Actor, Adjudicate, Ajax, Almond, Amethyst, Ampere, Apollo, Apostle, Apprentice, Ararat, Arboretum, Archdeacon, Artist, Aspen, Asymptote, Atala, Author, Autogyro; Baboon, Baccarat, Baker, Baldric, Baracuda, Barber, Bargee, Bark, Barrat, Barter, Bass, Baton, Battern, Beagle, Beau Geste, Beaune, Berenice, Beret, Beryl, Bevy, Bijou, Blackthorn, Bludgeon, Bluefish, Blunderbus, Bob, Bookmaker, Boon, Bombproof, Boquet, Boreas, Boris, Botte, Bougle, Brace, Brandy, Bravery, Breach, Breadroll, Breugel, Briar, Brice, Bridge, Brill, Brimstone, Brock, Brops, Bruce, Bruin, Bruxelles, Buckhound, Burr, Busker, Butcher, Butler, Buttercup; Calangue, Camelia, Canada, Cardinal, Canna, Carman, Cart, Catalpha, Catfish, Chardin, Charlotte, Charite, Chemist, Chestnut, Christs, Chrome, Chub, Circle, Citronelle, Clam, Cockle, Collie, Cool, Corinne, Corpus, Cotre, Cottonwood, Crab, Crayfish, Creme, Cutlass, Cuttlefish, Cyprus; Dace, Daffodil, Darenth, Dastard, Datchworth, Deacon, Dean, Delegate, Designer, Detective, Diable, Dick, Dido, Digger, Diplomat, Director, Ditcher, Donald, Donkeyman, Downstairs, Downright, Draughtsman, Dressmaker, Driver, Dyer; Easter, Eclipse, Eel, Elder, Electrician, Elm, Emile, Eucalyptus; Fabulous, Facade, Farmer, Farrier, Farthing, Faux, Felix, Fengler, Firefly, Fireman, Fitzroy, Flaman, Forsyth, Fortitude, Framboise, Francis, Francoise, Frederick, Freelance, Frensham, Fresia, Fuerty; Galler, Gamekeeper, Gardenia, Garterfish, Gazelle, Gean, Gibel, Giles, Gipsy, Glazier, Goat, Goldfish, Gorilla, Gondolier, Gorse, Greenheart, Gudgeon; Haddock, Hagfish, Halifax, Hals, Harry, Hector, Helm, Hermit, Heron, Historian, Honeysuckle, Hornbeam, Hubert, Hugh, Hypatica; Ilex, Inkfish, Interallee, Iris, Iroquois, Irradicate; Jacques, Jaguar, Jalouise, Jedburgh, Jellyfish, Jockey, John, Joker, Josephine, Joully, Judge, Juggler; Ker, Knuckleduster; Lalaie, Lear, Levee, Lilac, Lime, Ling, Linkman, Lobster, Lougre, Louise, Lucerne, Lupin, Lumond; Mackerel, Mainmast,

Malphomeme, Mariote, Marksman, Marc, Marlborough, Marree, Martini, Mason, Mercury, Messenger, Mexico, Mignone, Miner, Minister, Minnow, Minster, Mirage, Mistral, Monkeypuzzle, Mouse, Moustache, Musician, Mussel Minor, Muster, Narcisus, Nelson, Neptune, Normandy, Nutmeg; Oaktree, Opal, Orage, Orange, Oriel, Ouragon, Outclass, Outhalle, Overcloud, Overture; Palaise, Palm, Pampas, Parapluie, Parson, Paul, Pauline, Pear, Penny, Pennyfarthing, Perch, Percy, Periwinkle, Permit, Perry, Peter, Petunia, Phono, Physician, Pierre, Pike, Pilchard, Pimento, Piquier, Piroque, Pitinette, Plaice, Platypus, Playwright, Plumber, Ponton, Politician, Princess, Privet, Producer, Prosper, Prunus, Publican; Rageur, Rat, Rebecca, Redcross, Reporter, Roach, Rum; Sabot, Sacristan, Sadler, Samoyede, Sardine, Salesman, Savanna, Scenery, Scientist, Scullion, Serbie, Sexto, Shakespeare, Shipwright, Shrimp, Sirene, Skate, Sling, Snake, Soldat, Spaniel, Speed, Spindle, Spiritualist, Spruce, Squid, St James, Stationer, Steward, Stockbroker, Stonemason, Student, Supply, Surgeon, Suzanne, Swordfish, Sycamore, Sylvester, Syringa; Task, Tempete, Tenature, Teneriffe, Tennis, Tenterhook, Terrier, Tertio, Theorim, Tiger, Tilleul, Tinker, Tiptree, Titanic, Titian, Tobacconist, Tom, Tomcod, Tomy, Torch, Torture, Trainer, Trirem, Tripod, Trombone, Tropical, Turquoise, Tuxedo; Ukelele, Umpire, Union; Valient, Ventriloquist, Verger, Vermilion, Vesta, Vestige, Vygelia; Wallflower, Walt, Weaver, Wheelwright, Whirlwind, Whitebeam, Whitsun, Winkle, Wisteria, Wrestler; Yannick, Yolande; Zebra.

GERMANY
Acacia, Ash, Alder; Banyan, Benedict, Birch, Bolingbroke; Calvados, Carham, Carstairs, Catmore, Chalgrove, Clint, Colan, Colburn, Colehill, Croc, Curland; Denver, Downend; Eiger, Elm, Everybodys, Express; Flap, Fleckney, Frilford; Herd; Imola; Juniper, Jungfrau; Leader; Montford, Mulber, Mystere; Nabel, Nachtigal, Negus, Neron, Norvic; Pathino, Periscope, Postbox; Rigi; Squad; Tarbes, Telegraph, Tonic, Turmoil; Varsity, Vasco, Vivacious; Walnut.

HOLLAND
Admiral, Aramis; Backgammon, Badminton, Barnabus, Barsac, Beetroot, Beziquez, Borstal, Blundells, Bradfield, Broadbean, Broccoli; Cabbage, Carrot, Catarrh, Cauliflower, Celery, Checkers, Chicory, Chive, Cress, Croquet, Cubbing, Cucumber; Doug, Draughts; Endive; Faro, Fencing, Fives; Gasper, Gerrit, General, Gherkin, Glasshouse, Golf; Harlech, Hendrick, Harrow, Hockey; Irene; Kale, Kohlrabi; Lacrosse, Lancing, Leatherhead, Leek, Lemontree, Lettuce; Mangold, Marrow, Meneorates, Mustard; Nash, Netball; Parsley, Parsnip, Pembroke, Polo, Pumpkin; Radish, Rowing, Rugger, Rummy; Sauternes, Sculling, Seakale, Sedburgh, Spinach, Sprout, Squash, St Edmond, St Henry, St Mark, St Martin, St Paul, St Peter, St Valentine, Stalking; Teaman, Tennis, Tomato, Turnip; Van-Ingan; Watercress, Westminster.

ITALY
Loganberry.

NORWAY
Alfhild, Algol, Anvil, Aquarius, Arquebus; Beta, Beaver, Bit, Bittern, Blinkers, Bridle, Brunhild, Bundle; Carhampton, Castor, Centaur, Chaffinch, Cheese, Clairvoyant, Cockerel, Corona, Crane, Crupper; Dag; Fasting, Feather, Fetlock, Fieldfare, Flank; Gannet, Girth, Goldfinch, Goshawk, Grebered, Groin, Grouse, Gunnerside; Hammond, Hoch, Humnah; Lapwing, Lark, Leo; Makir, Manir, Mardonius, Menton; Njord; Octans, Orion, Osprey, Ostler, Otto; Pheasant, Puffin, Pullover; Raven, Redwing, Reins, Rollo, Rump; Sandpiper, Saddle, Slott, Snaffle, Stirrup, Swallow; Thrush, Thrushred; Veg, Vet, Virgo; Withers, Woodcock.

POLAND
Area, Astor, Attic; Basin, Beam, Belt, Boot, Brick; Cellar, Chickenpox, Chisel, Collar, Cottage, Cravat; Daisy, Door, Doric; Filc, Flat, Flax, Floor, Furze; Gauge, Gimlet, Glass; Hammer; Jacket; Key, Knob; Lathe, Legging, Lily, Lock; Measles; Neon, Nettle; Pipe, Pliers; Rasp, Rheumatism, Rivet, Rose; Saw, Screwdriver, Shirt, Slate, Smallpox, Spanner, Spokeshave, Step, Stock, Stone; Tile, Tulip, Vice; Wall, Window, Wrench; Yard.

RADIO INTELLIGENCE SORTIES
Ascension; Escort; Fioble; Rodney; Westminster.

SWEDEN
Bladur.

TUNISIA
Kipling.

YUGOSLAVIA
Bullseye

HOLLAND
An area of disaster for the SOE with the Germans in complete control

Terschelling

NOORD SEE

Vlieland

WADDENSEE

Harlingen

•Groningen

•Leeuwarden

Texel

•Assen

•Sneek

Den Helder •

•Heerenveen

Emmen •

Calantsoog •

Medemblik •

Meppel •

Enkhuizen •

•Hoorn

Alkmaar •

ZUIDER SEE

•Zwolle

Ijmuiden •
Zandvoort •

AMSTERDAM

•Almelo

Apeldoorn •

•Enschede

•Deventer

S–Gravenhage
(The Hague) •

•Utrecht

Arnhem •

Rotterdam

Dordrecht •

Nijmegen •

•S–Hertogenbosch

Tholen

Roosendaal

Breda

•Tilburg

•Eindhoven

Gilze–Rijen

•Antwerp